Arnold Palmer

Chuck Noll

Johnny Lujack

Jim Covert

74

Mario Lemieux

Suzie McConnell-Serio

Dan Marino

13

[illegible]

Dick Groat

Regards

Billy Conn

HOMETOWN HEROES

Profiles in Sports and Spirit

By Jim O'Brien

> *"I consider myself a Pittsburgher.*
> *This is my town."*
> — Mario Lemieux
> Summer of '99

From the Rogel Family collection

Fran Rogel was a star at Penn State (1948-49) and with the Pittsburgh Steelers (1950-57), but nowhere was he more revered than in his hometown of North Braddock for his achievements as a star at Scott High School. He's recalled in chapter on Chuck Klausing.

This book is dedicated to my family, friends, teachers, mentors, and all my heroes.

Copyright © 1999 by Jim O'Brien

James P. O'Brien — Publishing
P.O. Box 12580
Pittsburgh PA 15241
Phone: (412) 221-3580
E-mail: jpobrien@stargate.net

First printing: September, 1999

Manufactured in the United States of America

Printed by Geyer Printing Company, Inc.
3700 Bigelow Boulevard
Pittsburgh PA 15213

Typography by Cold-Comp
810 Penn Avenue
Pittsburgh PA 15222

ISBN 1-886348-04-9

**Johnny Lujack
Quarterback
University of Notre Dame
1947 Heisman Trophy Winner**

Books By Jim O'Brien

COMPLETE HANDBOOK OF PRO BASKETBALL 1970-1971

COMPLETE HANDBOOK OF PRO BASKETBALL 1971-1972

ABA ALL-STARS

PITTSBURGH: THE STORY OF THE CITY OF CHAMPIONS

HAIL TO PITT: A SPORTS HISTORY OF
THE UNIVERSITY OF PITTSBURGH

DOING IT RIGHT

WHATEVER IT TAKES

MAZ AND THE '60 BUCS

REMEMBER ROBERTO

PENGUIN PROFILES

DARE TO DREAM

KEEP THE FAITH

WE HAD 'EM ALL THE WAY

HOMETOWN HEROES

To order copies directly from the publisher, send $26.95 for hardcover edition. Please send $3.50 to cover shipping and handling costs per book. Pennsylvania residents add 6% sales tax to price of book only. Allegheny County residents add an additional 1% sales tax for a total of 7% sales tax. Copies will be signed by author at your request. Discounts available for large orders. Contact publisher regarding availability and prices of all books in *Pittsburgh Proud* series, or to request an order form. Several of them are sold out or are available only in hardcover editions. E-mail address: jpobrien@stargate.net.

Contents

Acknowledgments

Everyone has heroes. Arnold Palmer is some people's hero, but even Arnold Palmer had heroes while he was growing up in Latrobe. He loved Bobby Jones and Byron Nelson. He wanted to grow up to be a champion golfer like them.

I've always had heroes, and I keep adding to the list. The people I've written about in this book are all heroes of mine, and I'm grateful for their time and cooperation.

My heroes include the people who believe in my books and what they represent and have enabled me to write and publish books that boast about what's been accomplished in the tri-state area. My "Pittsburgh Proud" sports book series would not have been possible without the encouragement and financial support of some wonderful people in the business and corporate community.

Special thanks are offered for loyal and strong support from Alex Pociask of AP Construction Services Group, Bob Czerniewski of Stevens Painton Corporation and Tom Snyder of Continental Design & Management Group. They have been my biggest boosters.

Other loyal patrons include Anthony W. Accamando, Jr. of Adelphia Cable Communications; Dennis Astorino of LD Astorino Associates, Ltd.; Pat McDonnell and Allison Hoffman of Atria's Restaurant; Ronald B. Livingston Sr. of Babb, Inc.; Bill Baierl of Baierl Automotive Group; Rich Barcelona of Bailey Engineers, Inc.; Paul Lang of Bayer Corp.; Andrew F. Komer of Bowne of Pittsburgh; Miles R. Bryan of Bryan Mechanical Inc.; Charles L. Cost of Cost Company.

Don Carlucci of Carlucci Construction Co.; Tom Sweeney of Compucom, Inc.; Armand Dellovade of A.C. Dellovade, Inc.; Walter Sapp of Daniel-Sapp-Boorn Associates, Inc.; Don DeBlasio of DeBlasio's Restaurant; Jim Broadhurst of Eat'n Park Restaurants; Everett Burns of E-Z Overhead Door & Window Co.; Ron Parkinson of J. Messner, Inc. and the Greater Pittsburgh Chevrolet Dealers Assn.

John R. McGinley Jr. of Grogan, Graffan, McGinley & Luccino, P.C.; Frank B. Fuhrer of Fuhrer Wholesale Co.; Joe Faccenda of Giant Eagle, Inc.; Frank Gustine Jr. of The Gustine Company; Ed Harmon of F.E. Harmon Construction, Inc.; Jeffrey Berger and John Hans of Heinz, U.S.A., H.J. Heinz Co.; Mike Hagan of Iron & Glass Bank; William V. Campbell of Intuit, Larry Werner of Ketchum Public Relations; Jack Mascaro of Mascaro Construction Company; Joseph A. Massaro, Jr. of The Massaro Company.

F. James McCarl and Robert B. Santillo of McCarl's, Inc.; Clem Gigliotti of Merit Contracting, Inc.; David S. Jancisin of Merril Lynch; Jack B. Piatt of Millcraft Industries, Inc.; John C. Williams Jr. of National City Bank of Pennsylvania; Jack Perkins of Mr. P's in Greensburg; A. Robert Scott of *Point*; Joe Browne Sr. of National Football League.

6

Lloyd Gibson and John Schultz of NorthSide Bank; Pat Rooney of Palm Beach Kennel Club; Patrick J. Santelli of Pfizer Labs; Thomas H. O'Brien, James E. Rohr and Sy Holzer of PNC Bank Corp.; Joseph Costanzo, Jr. of The Primadonna Restaurant, Dennis S. Meteny of Respironics, Inc.; Fred B. Sargent and Ed Prebor of Sargent Electric Co.; Sam Sciullo of *Inside Panther Sports.*

Jim Roddey and Michael J. Fetchko of SportsWave, Inc. (International Sports Marketing); Daniel A. Goetz of Stylette, Inc.; Dick Swanson of Swanson Group Ltd.; Barbara and Ted Frantz of Tedco Construction Corp.; W. Harrison Vail of Three Rivers Bank.

John Paul of University of Pittsburgh Medical Center; Thomas J. Usher of USX Corporation; Clark Nicklas of Vista Resources, Inc.; Charles and Stephen Previs of Waddell & Reed Financial Services; Ray Conaway of Zimmer Kunz; John Williamson of J.C. Williamson Company.

Friends who have been boosters include John Bruno, Beano Cook, Art Cipriani, Bob Friend of Babb, Inc., Darrell Hess of DJ Hess Advertising, Harvey Hess, Mrs. Elsie Hillman, Tommy Kehoe, Jim Kozak, Jim Meston, George Morris, Andy Ondrey, Mrs. Janis O'Brien, Tom O'Malley, Arthur J. Rooney Jr.; George Schoeppner. Friends who have offered special encouragement and prayer and those who have opened up doors for our endeavors include Bill Priatko, Rudy Celigoi, Ron Temple, Bob Shearer, Jim Kriek, Foge Fazio, Pete Mervosh, Mike Ference of Ference Marketing & Communications; Bob Wissman; Kenneth E. Ball; Terry Mangan of Thomas E. Starzl Transplantation Institute; Bob Lovett and Art Stroyd of Reed Smith Shaw & McClay; Bob Harper and Art Rooney II of Klett Lieber Rooney & Schorling; Herb Douglas of Schiefferlin & Somerset, Rev. Bob Norris of Westminster Presbyterian Church, Sandy and Marshall Goldstein; Sally O'Leary of the Pirates' Black & Gold Alumni Newsletter; Kenneth J. Wenger and Don Schwall of Bob Prince Charities; Chuck Klausing; Nellie Briles of the Pittsburgh Pirates; John Longo of WCNS Radio in Latrobe, Rob Pratte of KDKA Radio and Jack Bogut of WJAS Radio. My heartfelt thanks to Mavis Trasp, my "Christmas angel" and her daughter, Sherry Kisic, and their friends at Century III Mall for all their kindnesses.

There is a strong belief on our part that these books should be produced entirely in Pittsburgh. Bruce McGough and Tom Samuels and their staff (especially Charlie Stage who coordinates the production), at Geyer Printing have produced all of the books in this series. Denise and Keith Maiden and Cathy Pawlowski of Cold-Comp Typographers did their usual first-rate effort. The cover design was done by Giuseppe Francioni and Christopher Longo of Prisma, Inc. This team has worked on all of my All-Pittsburgh books. Two retired gentlemen, Stan Goldmann and Ed Lutz, who helped me get started, are cherished friends. *The Almanac* newspaper in the South Hills, for which I have been writing a man-about-town column for the past decade, has promoted my book signing appearances through the years, as has *The Valley Mirror* in Homestead-Munhall.

Pittsburgh photographers David Arrigo, Michael F. Fabus, George Gojkovich, Hans Jonas of Jonas Photography, Jack A. Wolf and Bill Kovach provided so many wonderful photos. Artist and graphics designer Marty Wolfson, who worked with me to publish several of my earlier books, provided a drawing of Billy Conn.

Connellsville historian Bart Mallory, Walt Bielich of the University of Pittsburgh Varsity Letter Club and Tim Conn, the son of Billy Conn, Dan Marino Sr., Mike White of the *Post-Gazette*, were most helpful to me in digging up stuff for this book.

Special thanks for his cooperation and efforts to Donald "Doc" Giffin of Arnold Palmer Enterprises.

Sports publicists who merit thanks are Ron Wahl of the Steelers, Jim Trdinich, Ben Bouma and Mike Kennedy of the Pirates, Tom McMillan and Cindi Himes of the Penguins, Doug Miller of the New York Jets, Harvey Greene of the Miami Dolphins; Pat Hanlon of the New York Giants, Mike McCall of the Washington Redskins, Bryan Harlan of the Chicago Bears, L. Budd Thalman of Penn State University, E.J. Borghetti and Patti Shirk of the University of Pittsburgh, Shelly Poe and Kevin Keys of West Virginia University, Dave Saba of Duquesne University; John Heisler of the University of Notre Dame, Todd V. Jay of Edinboro University, Joe Horrigan of the National Football Hall of Fame, Robin Deutsch of the Basketball Hall of Fame, Baseball Hall of Fame and Museum, David Cooper of the Phoenix Suns, Bill King II of the Milwaukee Bucks, Lori Montgomery of the Detroit Shock and the publicity staff of the Cleveland Rockers.

The foundation for my heroes listings these days are my wife, Kathleen, my daughters, Sarah and Rebecca, and my mother, Mary O'Brien, who have always offered their love and support. Sarah O'Brien is a splendid editor. Thank you all.

— Jim O'Brien

Coverboys Connellsville High School football team of the early '40s takes halftime pause on sideline.

Introduction
Keeping good company

"Nothing compares with being honored in your hometown."
— Johnny Lujack

Meeting Johnny Lujack was special. Lujack was one of the most celebrated college football players of his time. His career at the University of Notre Dame was interrupted by a nearly three-year stint in the U.S. Navy during World War II. He returned to gain All-America honors as a quarterback in his junior and senior seasons. The Fighting Irish did not lose a game during that span, and he was the Heisman Trophy winner in 1947. In all, Lujack led Notre Dame to three national championships.

His name will forever be linked with the Fayette County community of Connellsville and Notre Dame's rich sports tradition. He came home to Connellsville for a reunion of the undefeated 1941 Cokers on September 16-17, 1994. He wouldn't come back to be honored, at first, unless his entire high school team was invited to participate, which pointed up his specialness and unselfish manner.

It was an honor to meet him and talk to him. At 69, he still looked like an athlete. There was an aura about him, a sparkle in his bespectacled eyes. He still looked like a winner, the way he walked, the way he talked. He had a way with everyone, connecting with teammates, friends and fans, some whom he had not seen in over 50 years.

When he joined in singing the Notre Dame Victory Song with the choir at Connellsville High School it brought a warm glow to all in attendance. Johnny Lujack was a class act.

He was a sports hero from my childhood, the best kind of all. He looked proud as he posed for photographs with his Heisman Trophy and with teammates. He spoke softly, but firmly, with conviction. Johnny Lujack is one of those names you like to say aloud, over and over. Johnny Lujack. Johnny Lujack. He epitomized what a hometown hero is all about. In his playing days, he was six feet, 180 pounds but, as sports stars go, there were few bigger in this neck of the woods.

I have had this book in mind for many years, and have been actively seeking out and interviewing stars from the past and present over a six-year period. I wanted to write about men and women who had made their mark and brought positive attention to their hometowns or to Pittsburgh and the surrounding tri-state area. They're all not here in this one book, of course. Two of my boyhood favorites, Johnny Unitas and Stan Musial, come quickly to mind.

9

There are too many of them to cover in one book. And I promise to get to the others in future efforts. *Sports Illustrated* published a Top 20 "Favorite Athletes" list in July, 1999 that included Unitas, Palmer and Roberto Clemente, which points up the popularity of Pittsburgh sports figures.

There are some special moments that stand out from assembling the materials and information to write and publish this book.

A scene that comes to mind was the naming of a street in Oakland in honor of world champion boxer Billy Conn. That occurred on June 18, 1998 in front of St. Paul's Cathedral, the Catholic church that is home to the city's bishop.

It was the 57th anniversary of the still-debated heavyweight championship fight between Conn and Joe Louis at the Polo Grounds in New York. Back on June 18, 1941, Conn could have claimed the heavyweight title from Louis if he had been careful in the late rounds, but he wanted to knock out the champ and ended up getting counted out with two seconds left in the 13th round. Conn was ahead on two of the three scorecards, even on the other, when Louis rallied to finish him off. Only Louis knocked out Conn in his 75 pro bout career.

City fathers were putting up a sign — Billy Conn Blvd — at the corner of Craig and Fifth, just across Craig from where Duquesne Gardens once stood. This is an honorary deal, as the streets will retain their names. Conn came out of the East Liberty section of Pittsburgh to box often at the Gardens, the city's main sports arena at the time. It seated just over 5,000 in what was originally a street car barn. It's where the Pittsburgh Hornets of the American Hockey League played, where Donna Atwood and the Ice Capades began as a between-periods ice skating show, where some outstanding Duquesne University basketball teams once competed.

It was there in 1936 that Conn claimed a 10-round decision over another Pittsburgh boxing legend, Fritzie Zivic, to gain national attention. He boxed at least ten fighters who once held titles in main events at the Gardens. The Gardens were razed in 1956 — Pittsburgh was without its Hornets for the next five years — and an apartment building now stands on the site. Most of the residents are seniors, the sort of Pittsburghers who best remember Conn.

Conn was known as "The Pittsburgh Kid" and the city never had a bigger sports hero. Mayor Tom Murphy said so — calling him "Pittsburgh's greatest sports legend" — when undraping the street sign while standing on a stepladder. Mayor Murphy mentioned Mario Lemieux, Billy Mazeroski, Honus Wagner, Roberto Clemente and some of the Steelers as among the city's favorite sports heroes, but said Conn had a bigger following than any of them in his heyday.

Pittsburgh is a city often distorted by its own self-worship, but Conn was a legitimate sports hero who deserved to be memorialized in his hometown.

"The greatest strength of Pittsburgh is our history, and our sense of ourselves as a community," said Mayor Murphy. "We're really a small town. We remember our heroes; we don't forget our heroes.

Mayor Tom Murphy pulls the ripcord to unveil "Billy Conn Blvd" street sign at corner of Craig St and Fifth Ave in Oakland on June 18, 1998 — the 57th anniversary of Conn's celebrated heavyweight championship fight with Joe Louis in New York.

Two of Billy Conn's biggest fans were his wife, Mary Louise, at left, and their dear friend, Elsie Hillman, one of the city's political and philanthropic leaders. They were among those present for the honorary street re-naming ceremonies.

This tribute has been a long time coming. Billy Conn made history and put Pittsburgh on the map all over the world."

Billy's wife, Mary Louise, and three sons, Michael, Billy Jr. and Tim, were there for the ceremonies, along with some oldtimers who followed the fight game. Elsie Hillman, wife of industrialist Henry Hillman and one of Mary Louise Conn's closest friends, was there.

"I saw a lot of his fights," said Elsie Hillman, a mover and shaker in the city's political and business circles. "He was a true Pittsburgh sports hero. Mary Louise has been a dear friend for years."

"No matter where Billy went he always said Pittsburgh was the greatest," said Mary Louise when it was her turn to speak at the event. "Here's to Billy and the city of Pittsburgh!"

Conn had died five years earlier, at age 75, not far from the site at the Veterans Affairs Medical Center, once called the VA Hospital, above Pitt Stadium.

I had an opportunity that day following the honorary street-naming ceremony to join Conn's family and friends at a reception at a relative's home in Regent Square. None was happier than John Gamble of Coraopolis, a boxing buff and Conn fan who had prodded Pittsburgh officials into doing something to memorialize one of its greatest sports figures.

Gamble was present when Conn was enshrined in the charter class when the Boxing Hall of Fame in Canastota, New York was opened June 10, 1990. Gamble said that many of the great fighters present said Conn "was the epitome of the sweet science of boxing."

He also said that when Fritzie Zivic, an early rival, was dying at the VA Hospital that Conn came to visit him almost every day.

Bob O'Connor, the president of City Council, had promoted the street re-naming as well and was present for the dedication. "I grew up with their family," said O'Connor. "Billy Conn's father-in-law, 'Greenfield Jimmy' Smith, used to hit balls to us when we were kids learning how to play baseball."

A few months later, I visited with Conn's wife, and two of her three sons, Billy Jr. and Tim, at her apartment in Squirrel Hill. It was a treat to hear them reflect on Billy Conn, as husband and father and fighter and character, and see all the photographs of Conn and so many other celebrities that decorated the walls of a room that honors his memory.

In the summer of 1997, I traveled to Indianapolis with my good friend, George Von Benko, a sports broadcaster and sports consultant for RealPittsburgh — an Internet newspaper — for the 30th annual reunion of the American Basketball Association. We spent a weekend with many of the ABA stars, and were especially pleased to see and speak with Connie Hawkins, Billy Knight and Maurice Lucas, three of the finest basketball players to ever represent Pittsburgh.

The ABA, the Pittsburgh Pipers and the Pittsburgh Penguins all came into being, as did the Pittsburgh Phantoms, in 1967. Major league basketball, hockey and soccer all came to the city in the same year, imagine that.

In the summer of 1998, I spent a day at the St. Clair Country Club where I had an opportunity to talk to Mario Lemieux, Matt and Chris Bahr, Todd Blackledge and Bill Fralic. What I'll remember best, though, is something PGA golfer Bob Friend, Jr. said about his father, the former Pirates pitcher whom I know from interviewing him for several books.

"My father is the best man I have ever met," said young Friend. "I also have a great mother and a great wife." I was struck by what he said, and have been rooting for him ever since as he seeks to make a name for himself on the pro golf tour.

In February of 1998, my wife Kathie and I traveled to Orlando, Florida to attend a wedding, along with an NBA game between the Magic and the Los Angeles Lakers. While we were there we visited Disney World. We were walking down Main Street in Disney World when we spotted an inviting sports memorabilia store. I had to check it out.

The first pictures I saw once I entered the store were on plaques bearing the likenesses and signatures of Mario Lemieux and Jaromir Jagr of the Pittsburgh Penguins.

To the right were Steelers helmets signed by Terry Bradshaw and Franco Harris. One glass case was devoted to plaques, helmets and photos signed by Joe Namath, another with Danny Marino memorabilia, another with Joe Montana memorabilia.

Sure, there was signed stuff and likenesses of Babe Ruth, Ted Williams, Henry Aaron, Steve Young, Joe DiMaggio, Emmitt Smith, Troy Aikman, et al, but Pittsburgh-area athletes dominated the displays.

I saw some devoted to Tony Dorsett, Roberto Clemente, Arnold Palmer, Stan Musial and Lou Groza. Here I was in far-off Florida and I thought I was in downtown Pittsburgh or one of the suburban shopping malls.

It pointed up the rich sports tradition we have enjoyed back home in Western Pennsylvania. In this book, I decided to include profiles of some of my personal favorites from border states West Virginia and Ohio, namely Sam Huff, Jerry West and John Havlicek.

There are only good guys and good gals profiled here. There's no room for jerks.

When I was interviewing Suzie McConnell, the only woman who grew up and lived in Pittsburgh to win Olympic medals — a gold in 1988 and a bronze in 1992 in basketball — I asked her what she was proudest of, and she responded immediately, "My four children." We can learn a lot about proper perspective from these people.

Tony Dorsett spoke of family and friends and positive influences in his life when he was inducted, at age 40, into the Pro Football Hall of Fame in ceremonies at the Canton, Ohio shrine on July 30, 1994. I attend the annual Hall of Fame ceremonies as a rite of summer, but this was special because a Pitt guy was getting honored.

"It's been a long journey for me to get back here," said Dorsett. "From Aliquippa to Pittsburgh to Dallas and now to Canton. It's been a journey that's been filled with hope and been filled with heart."

Having luncheon interviews with Olympic gold medalists such as Roger Kingdom and Kurt Angle, and certainly with Arnold Palmer at the men's grill of the Latrobe Country Club were cherished experiences I enjoy sharing with you.

One of the special moments came on April 11, 1999 when I was seated at a sports banquet dais between Hall of Fame football coach Chuck Klausing and Dan Marino Sr., father of the Miami Dolphins quarterback. This was at an awards banquet sponsored by the Pittsburgh Chapter of the National Italian-American Sports Hall of Fame.

I asked Mr. Marino what was the greatest source of his pride in son, Danny Marino, the future Hall of Famer, and he replied, "Just because he's a good person."

Dr. Thomas E. Starzl, the internationally-known transplant surgeon at the University of Pittsburgh Medical Center, is a big fan of Dan Marino. Dr. Starzl is profiled here, along with Dr. John Gaisford, a plastic surgeon and burn research specialist at West Penn Hospital, long one of the area's top amateur golfers. Both are pioneers in their professions, and heroes on a different level.

When I was interviewing Sam Huff, the former star football player at West Virginia University and the New York Giants and Washington Redskins, I mentioned some of the people I would also be profiling in this book.

"I'm honored," said Huff. "I'm in good company."

Throughout the process of researching and writing this book, I felt the same way. My mother often told me that you are judged by the company you keep.

Jim O'Brien

Young fans pause in hallway at Allegheny Club in Three Rivers Stadium to check out Wall of Fame, where photos include those of Hall of Famers Chuck Noll and Walt Kiesling of the Pittsburgh Steelers, Lloyd and Paul Waner of Pittsburgh Pirates and Babe Ruth and Lou Gehrig of New York Yankees.

Johnny Lujack
The Kid From Connellsville

*"Always give 100 percent.
Then give another 10 percent."*
— Johnny Lujack

They came to Connellsville for a football game. The Upper St. Clair kids — the football players, cheerleaders, pom-pom girls, and band members — should have brought their notebooks. They could have come away with a history lesson as well. They were going to learn something about Johnny Lujack and where he came from.

It was more than a football game, as far as the citizens of Connellsville were concerned. They were paying tribute to Lujack and his teammates on the high school's undefeated 1941 football team, and that revived memories, good and bad, of those times and how The Great Depression and World War II impacted the community.

These are the people TV newsman Tom Brokaw wrote about in his 1998 best-selling book, *The Greatest Generation*.

The '41 team was tied by Brownsville in the final game of the season. The following year, the Cokers won all their games. Most of the players from those teams were now in their 70s, but on this special weekend they were young again.

One of the magic names in football history, Lujack led Notre Dame to three national championships (1943, 1946, 1947), was an All-American, won the Heisman Trophy as a senior and went on to a successful career with the NFL's Chicago Bears. Just saying the name Johnny Lujack gives one a good feeling.

"At our high school graduation exercise, a Pennsylvania congressman presented me with an appointment to West Point," said Lujack. "It was the first one ever presented to a kid in Connellsville, and I considered it a great honor. However, Notre Dame was my first choice, even though I didn't know if I could go there. My love affair with Notre Dame began as a kid, listening to all the Notre Dame games on the radio. I would take a piece of paper, draw the lines of a football field and chart the progress of the game. A 'subway alumnus' took me to South Bend, Indiana at his expense, and when Coach Frank Leahy accepted me, that was all I needed. Like dozens of fellows before and after me, a boyhood dream was about to come true. I would be a part of the great Notre Dame tradition.

"Without any attempt at false modesty, however, I never dared hope that I would be anything more than a very tiny part of that tradition. I knew I was in such fast company that my only ambition then was to make Notre Dame's traveling squad my junior or senior year."

Lujack was a little better than that. Upon graduation, he was heralded as the greatest athlete in Notre Dame history. He was the most publicized college football player since Red Grange.

Lujack, age 74 in 1999, has always been a class act. So he was a big hit at a banquet on the eve of the Connellsville-Upper St. Clair contest. The Coker Reunion was held September 16-17, 1994, and I was fortunate enough to be there both nights.

The NFL would be marking its "Throwback Day" the next day, and the Steelers would suit up in their godawful 1933 uniforms for their contest with the Indianapolis Colts, but Connellsville was satisfied to pay tribute to its own.

It was a perfect setting for a scholastic sports contest in this Fayette County community 55 miles south of Pittsburgh. There was nearly a full moon sitting above the Laurel Mountains, the temperature was in the mid-'60s, there was a full house of over 5,000 fans in a stadium surrounded by trees. One of those trees, a huge oak tree, was brought back as a seedling from Germany by Connellsville's John Woodruff.

As a 21-year-old freshman at Pitt, Woodruff won the 800 meters in the 1936 Olympic Games at Berlin Stadium — best known for Jesse Owens winning four gold medals — and Adolph Hitler gave all the winners an oak tree seedling to take home. Hitler couldn't have been thrilled about this as Woodruff and Owens dashed his Aryan supremacy propaganda.

It's believed that no other community in the country can claim a Heisman Trophy and Olympic gold medal winner as Connellsville can. Connellsville can also claim the first black football player at the University of Pittsburgh, Jimmy Joe Robinson. He lettered in 1945 under Coach Clark Shaughnessy and again in 1947 and 1948. He became a minister, the pastor of the Bidwell Presbyterian Church on Pittsburgh's North Side, and served the Pitt football team as chaplain during Foge Fazio's tenure as coach in the early '80s.

Lujack, Woodruff and Robinson performed at Connellsville High when the school's nickname was the Cokers, because Connellsville contributed coke to the area's all-important steel industry. Connellsville used to be Coker country, when coke foundries for U.S. Steel and glass factories were major industries there, when five different railroads ran through the southwestern Pennsylvania community. Those were the best of times and the worst of times in Connellsville. More recently, the Connellsville community was being challenged economically, ranking second in the state only to the Philadelphia area for unemployment.

The school colors for Connellsville in Lujack's days were black and orange. Now they were blue and white and the nickname was the Falcons.

The stadium was spilling over with fans this Saturday night in September of 1994 for the contest with Upper St. Clair, the region's most successful high school football program over the previous ten-

Johnny Lujack was the featured member of the 1941 Connellsville High School championship football team at its reunion in September, 1994. He brought along the Heisman Trophy he won in 1947 as the quarterback at the University of Notre Dame.

Three backfield performers for the '41 Cokers were, left to right, Dave Hart, Johnny Lujack and Wally Schroyer. All of them saw duty in the military service in World War II, as did the majority of their teammates.

Photos by Jim O'Brien

year period. Connellsville wanted a class opponent for this well-planned and much-anticipated community event. It was a sylvan setting, with trees framing the field wherever one looked.

Upper St. Clair, a Pittsburgh suburban community, was going up against more than a football team this starry night; the Panthers were going up against a legacy.

"I knew it would be difficult," related Jim Render, the head football coach at Upper St. Clair whose team was defeated by Connellsville in the 1991 WPIAL championship game at Three Rivers Stadium when Connellsville's football team and fans proved superior to Upper St. Clair's.

"It's always difficult," added Render. "Their coach, Dan Spanish, asked the WPIAL to book us for this game because they wanted it to be a big game. We knew what we were in for. I'd been telling our kids about Johnny Lujack and all that stuff.

"They've got that great community, a great stadium they've kept up pretty good. Their team is always tough and well-coached. It's a tough place. Then you lump in Johnny Lujack and the Class of '41, and it was a great night for them, and a demanding assignment for us."

USC nearly spoiled the fun, taking a 14-7 halftime lead. But Connellsville's offensive line averaged 6 feet 3, 234 pounds, and they beat down a USC defensive line averaging 5 feet 11, 196 pounds. Connellsville came away with a 22-14 victory. "We faced a bigger, stronger team," said Render. "It was a case of the strong beating the weak."

Lujack, 69 at the time of the reunion, gave the team a pep talk at a school assembly on Friday. "Always give 100 percent, and then give another 10 percent and you will be successful," said Lujack. When the school choir sang the Notre Dame Victory Song, Lujack joined in and the students went wild. They unfurled a banner that read: WELCOME BACK, MR. LUJACK.

"I still feel a pride and thrill when I hear the Notre Dame Victory March," he said when I spoke to him at the reunion dinner that night. "It's something hard to describe. I don't think I've ever heard it when goose bumps don't fly up and down my spine.

"In this age we're living in, perhaps we're supposed to be above emotion and sentiment, let alone admit to it. But I couldn't be prouder of admitting exactly how I feel about Notre Dame. I owe her more than I'll ever be able to repay. It's great to be a Notre Damer.

"There are so many things I think about when I step on the campus. There is the tradition, not only of Rockne and Gipp, but of Father Sorin, who is supposed to have built Notre Dame, and who saw it burn down, and who, while the bricks were still hot, was trying to put the thing together again.

"I still marvel at the beauty of the campus, which has never been exceeded by any campus I've ever seen. And I think back to the friendships I've made at Notre Dame that have gone on and on."

He regularly made the trip from Davenport, Iowa — an eight-hour round trip drive — to see Notre Dame football games. I mentioned to Lujack that I had come across him delivering a pep talk at a campus gathering at Notre Dame on the eve of a game with Pitt back in 1983 and thought that was a bit unfair. "Yeah, but we lost that game," allowed Lujack, recalling a 21-16 defeat of the Irish by Foge Fazio's team. "They haven't asked me back to do that again."

It seemed unfair for Render and his young, inexperienced team, one that did not appear at the time to be up to the school's usually strong standards. They would go on to reach the WPIAL's Quad A finals before losing to McKeesport. They were assembled in the end zone before the game at Connellsville because Render said it was about a hundred degrees in the visitors' dressing room under the stadium.

The players were unaware of what kind of sports-crazy community they were in. They did not see the signs when they were riding the buses down Rt. 119. There was a banner just before the city limits that read: YOU ARE IN FALCON COUNTRY.

They did not have their pre-game meal at Bud Murphy's Bar and Restaurant in Connellsville. The waitresses were wearing the school's blue and white football jerseys with their own first names — LISA and JANET — across their backs.

They did not see how the color photographs of the seniors on the Connellsville team were displayed there. I went to the dinner honoring the '41 team and the game the next night in the company of Bill Priatko, the athletic director of Yough High School at the time, who grew up as a fan of players from the '40s, like Lujack, and was a close friend of the former Connellsville athletic director, Stan McLaughlin.

(I had a reunion with McLaughlin when I spoke at a banquet in Connellsville in July of 1998. McLaughlin looked terrific, like he could still block and tackle. Three days later, at age 69, he had a heart attack and died.)

When Lujack was a nationally-acclaimed college quarterback, he was often referred to as "The Kid From Connellsville." His teammates included Dick Pitzer, who became an All-American end at Army, and played with two other Heisman Trophy winners at West Point, Doc Blanchard and Glenn Davis. Pitzer still took pride in telling people he played on the same team during his career with three Heisman Trophy winners.

"John threw me the ball enough to make me the top scorer," said Pitzer, who came to the reunion from Sun City Center, about 20 miles south of Tampa in west central Florida. "He had that stature about him. The way he called plays instilled belief in what we were going to do next. He was president of the class and all the students respected him. It's a shame he didn't throw the ball more; we might have really beaten some people.

"Connellsville was a community that was pretty well together," pointed out Pitzer. "Everyone had jobs. We had five different railroads in town. The B&O employed about 800 people. The Anchor Hocking Glass Company employed even more people. We had the coal mines and a spaghetti factory, LaPrimiata. There were jobs for everyone. Everybody had something.

"I came up here from Langley High School in Pittsburgh in 1941. I don't think I would have accomplished what I did if I hadn't come to Connellsville. I wouldn't have had the opportunity I had here, where the whole town was behind you. My dad was transferred here by West Penn Power. There was great spirit in the community and they really cared about you. I never got that feeling in a city school. We played on Friday afternoons in the City League and no one came to the games. No one was there.

"When I graduated from Army in 1946, they held a testimonial dinner for me in Connellsville. Chet Smith, who was the sports editor of *The Pittsburgh Press*, served as the emcee for the dinner. Stu Holcolmb, who was the end coach at West Point, was the main speaker. He later became the general manager of the Chicago White Sox.

"Johnny Lujack was one of the best all-around athletes I ever saw. I think John could have played professional baseball. He was smart, he made good grades, and he was very likable. Some people just have that natural talent. He was quite the javelin thrower in high school. I was just always impressed with the way he handled himself when I saw him in later years. There are some guys here I recognize. Some have changed a great deal. I haven't seen them in 53 years. I've seen John a few times through the years.

"When I was at Army, they let me play as a freshman, and I played against John at Yankee Stadium in 1943."

Lujack looked good at the reunion reception. He wore a white golf shirt, a green blazer, dark blue slacks and well-shined black shoes. And a constant smile. His eyes twinkled behind his eyeglasses.

Lujack loved seeing old friends, and people from his hometown who had rooted for him through his career. He did his best to suffer some who did what people always do at such reunions.

"I had a guy come up to me who said, 'You probably don't remember me...'

"And I had to say, 'I have to admit I don't remember you. When was the last time I saw you...in 1941? No, I don't remember you. I'm sorry.'"

Jim Kriek, the former sports editor of the *Connellsville Courier*, was among those who attended the reunion. He was supposed to be retired, but he was still covering prep sports as a correspondent and occasional columnist on Mike Ciarochi's staff at the *Uniontown Herald-Standard*.

"I've always thought very highly of Johnny Lujack," said Kriek, a dear friend from our days on the Steelers' beat in the early '80s. "He's three years older than I am. I first heard of him when he was at Notre Dame.

DICK PITZER
Coker End

JOHNNY LUJACK
Coker Captain

1941 Cokers lineup included backfield, left to right, Lujack, Schroyer, Bieshada, Hart, and line, Dixon, Blannon, Scacchi, H. Stefl, Feniello, Smyth, Olsweski.

"I was at my first sports-writing job in Chatham, New York, when I called the *Courier,* where I had applied for a job as sports editor of the paper. One of the executives at the *Courier* asked me, 'What do you know about Connellsville?' I mentioned John Lujack to him. He told me the town had also turned out John Woodruff, an Olympic gold medalist, and a major league baseball player named Gene Hasson, who had come up for a cup of coffee."

A check of the *Baseball Encyclopedia* revealed that Hasson, who was born in Connellsville, played two seasons (1937-38) for the Philadelphia Phillies. He batted .293, with 21 of his 49 hits going for extra bases, which makes one wonder why he played in only 47 games. More recently, Connellsville could claim Bob Bailor, who played 11 years in the major leagues (1975-1985) and was a coach with the Toronto Blue Jays when they won the World Series in 1993. So Connellsville could claim a World Series winner, to go with its Heisman Trophy and Olympic Gold winners. Not bad.

"It's a proud town," claimed Kriek, who still lives there with his wife, Joanne. "Some people boast about John, and some complain that he hasn't come back home much, or done much for the town. Personally, I don't think he owed the town any more than representing it in the classy manner that he always has. You hear the same complaints about Joe Montana in Monongahela, I'm told.

"I went to Philadelphia when John was inducted into the Pennsylvania Sports Hall of Fame, and I asked him about all the honors that had come his way.

"He said all his honors were great ones, as far as he was concerned, and he didn't take any of them lightly. He said, 'The greatest honor I ever had was when I got called up on the stage at Connellsville High School to get my sweater and letter. Don't misunderstand me, but those other awards were given to me by people who didn't know me, except athletically. Nothing compares with being honored in your hometown, where they really know all about you, warts and all.'

"When he came here to be honored with the '41 Cokers, I came over to the school on Friday afternoon when they were holding an assembly for the students. They had a banner welcoming him. The choir started to sing Notre Dame's fight song, and John came down off the stage and sang along with them. I thought that was great. He's always known how to mix with people. He signed autographs, and he had a few extra words for everyone. I liked that about him. He's a good man. And I know a good man when I see one."

> *"When you're from this area, it's not just where you're from. It defines who you are."*
> — Arnold Palmer

"We were all hungry Depression kids."
— Wally Schroyer,
Lujack's teammate

It was a different time. Johnny Lujack and nearly all his teammates on that Connellsville football team grew up during this country's two greatest crises, The Great Depression and World War II. They enlisted in the military service soon after coming out of high school, or following their first years at college. Many saw action in World War II. Many came home with medals and honors and scars and limps. Some didn't come home. Lujack served in the U.S. Navy nearly three years midway through his career at Notre Dame.

"There is much to remember," wrote New York author Pete Hamill, who was ten years old when The War ended, in August, 1945, in a 50th anniversary essay for *Travel Holiday*, "about how it was and how it ended. People my age and older still measure their lives by The War, which began for us at Pearl Harbor and ended on V-J Day. We remember separate periods called Before The War and After The War, one grim and spiky with economic depression, the other golden with triumph. But The War itself remains the centerpiece of memory."

There is a paragraph in a novel by John Knowles called *Peace Breaks Out* that is appropriate here: " 'Oh, Christ,' Pete (Hallam) groaned to himself. 'That monster war — sending last thin death waves over here to this little rural corner.' "

One of the school's all-around sports stars, John Wally Schroyer, started as a freshman at running back for Penn State University and then entered the Army. He lost a leg to machine-gun fire by the Germans at Anzio, and was a prisoner of war in five different concentration camps for 13 months.

"I got hit in a battle just above Naples and then again at Anzio," said Schroyer. "I was hit by a burp gun on February 18, 1944, and taken prisoner. I went to Rome and then north. I had three slugs in my leg and one went through my rib cage. It tore my calf real bad. I went to a hospital and they had to take my leg off beneath the knee. I went to five different POW camps, one in Poland, one in Austria, and three below Berlin. They had an exchange of prisoners and I got out in March of 1945.

"I grew up with a great group of guys. We were all hungry Depression kids. Everyone was poor, but no one knew you were poor. You just were."

Schroyer would become a popular figure in his hometown, serving for 28 years as the Register of Wills for Fayette County. A three-sport star at Connellsville, he was regarded by some local citizens as an even better athlete than Lujack. Schroyer simply smiles at such talk. He was one of those who organized the get-together in Connellsville, working on a committee headed by the school's athletic director, Jim Lembo.

Most of Lujack's teammates entered the military service. Dwayne Mortimer participated in the Invasion of Normandy on D-Day — its 50th anniversary was celebrated amid much international hoopla in the summer of 1994 — and Roy Doppelheuer remembers being one of seven players from that team who volunteered for the Army and were sent overseas six weeks later. Bernie Shafsky, a hard-hitting end for the Cokers, was killed in the invasion of France. Bernie Olsweski, a starting end, also lost his life in World War II.

The team's coach, Arthur Ruff, was an armed guard commander in the U.S. Navy, 1942-45, and saw military action.

Connellsville sports enthusiast and historian Robert "Bart" Mallory related a story about how Ruff once came home on a two-week leave and coached the Cokers in two games against Redstone and Uniontown. Ruff would teach for 41 years in the Connellsville school system and serve the WPIAL as a football and basketball official for the same span.

Mallory remained a big fan of Lujack. Mallory remembered staying after school when he was in seventh and eighth grade so he could see Lujack play basketball on the jayvee team. "He was everything you'd want to be in life," he said of his boyhood hero. "He was the most liked guy on the team; I never heard anything bad about him. School would let out at 3 o'clock, and the jayvee game started at 6:30, but you had to be there early to get a good seat. The Steelers weren't a big deal then. There was no Terry Bradshaw. The Cokers were our heroes. I loved Johnny Lujack early on."

Dick Pitzer went to West Point and was a starting end for two seasons (1944-45) when Army went undefeated and won back-to-back national championships. He was commissioned a second lieutenant in 1946 and was stationed in Japan with the Army of Occupation. He played service ball and was an assistant coach to Red Blaik in 1950. He worked for 32 years in the nuclear program at Westinghouse Electric before retiring in 1987.

Raymond C. Goron was a U.S. Navy medical corpsman on Iwo Jima. Carl Dennis underwent 27 months of pilot's training in the Air Force, stationed in Kentucky. Jim Daberko served in the Navy from 1943 to 1946.

Richard "Cheezy" Dixon, a starting end for the '41 Cokers, served in the Navy and then moved to Los Angeles and became a mailman. His wife's best friend married Hall of Fame baseball player Duke Snider. Cheezy and Duke became close friends and golfing partners.

Tackle Jim Smyth started a distinguished military career as a Marine officer. He would serve in Okinawa and China, Korea and Japan, and later in Vietnam, where he won a Navy Commendation Medal. He retired in 1970 with a Navy Achievement Medal, and became a teacher, then an assistant principal in Beaufort, S.C., where he became a friend of Pat Conroy, the highly-acclaimed author of *Prince of Tides, Lords of Discipline, The Great Santini* and *Beach Music*.

Talking about Lujack at the dinner, Smyth told us, "He was very smart, and he was a great athlete, always in shape. He had three brothers who should be given an awful lot of credit for him being such a good athlete.

"He was just a natural basketball player. He was just as good in track and field. The school didn't have a baseball team, or he'd have been a star in that. He was absolutely in magnificent shape all the time. There was no fooling around with John. He was fond of everyone on the team, and he could get the extra out of you. I went to Colgate University and played football there for Andy Kerr, who was a real famous coach of that era. I went into the Marine Corps for a few years. Andy lined up the whole team for a V-12 officer training program."

Guard Gary Feniello went to Pitt for a year, then served in special forces in the Army from 1943 to 1946. When he came out, he went to Wake Forest, and later played two seasons with both the Pittsburgh Steelers and then the Cleveland Browns. He was a mailman for 30 years.

Donald Graves came from New York City to see his old team-mates. He played tackle and guard as a junior on the 1941 team. In later years, he took pride in telling people he came from Connellsville, and that he had blocked for John Lujack, and remembered that as a 12-year-old growing up on Davison Hill in South Connellsville he thrilled to the news that Johnny Woodruff had won a gold medal in the 800 meter run at the 1936 Olympic Games.

Center Harold Stefl served in the Navy in 1944-45, then went to Bucknell where he co-captained the football team. He was later the head football coach at high schools in Minersville and Mohlenberg.

Roy Doppelheuer served in the Army's 34th Infantry Divsion, in the North Africa and Italy Campaigns, and was wounded twice in combat. He went on to a successful career in the construction industry.

Charlie Sapanara served in the infantry in World War II, and received a medical discharge. He became a funeral director.

Jack Conway enlisted in the U.S. Navy in 1943 and served in the Atlantic and Pacific until 1946. He worked at Republic Steel in Niles, Ohio, for 36 years.

John Richards served in the U.S. Navy in the South Pacific from 1943 to 1946. Richards obtained a B.A. degree from Geneva College in 1950, and a master's in education two years later at Pitt. He had a successful business career and was a PIAA official in three sports for 18 years, and officiated in the WPIAL basketball tournament.

Donald J. Stefl served in the U.S. Army's 10th Armored Division in the European Theatre. He won a purple heart and a bronze star with an oak leaf cluster for combat duty. He obtained a B.S. degree in ceramic engineering at Rutgers University, and later became a ceramic engineer at the Freeport (Pa.) Brick Co.

Running back Alfred "Bizz" Bieshada served in the Marine Corps on Guadalcanal with the Carlson Raiders and was wounded in action. Bizz later played football for two years at John Carroll University.

One of his teammates was Don Shula, who went on to play in the National Football League and coach the Baltimore Colts and Miami Dolphins.

Emmett Delligatti came from Cleveland for the reunion. He was a senior left halfback on the '41 Cokers club. When he came out of the Army, he returned to Connellsville and cut slacks at a Connellsville sportswear factory. Talking about Lujack, Delligatti said, "There weren't too many people in Connellsville who went as far as John did."

Dave Hart, the former Johnstown High and Navy football coach who later became the head football coach at Pitt, special assistant to the president at Robert Morris College, the athletic director at Louisville and Missouri, and the commissioner of the Southern Conference, was a junior halfback on that '41 team. "It was a special group, no doubt about it, and it still is," said Hart, the keynote speaker at a banquet the following night.

That was the weekend when President Clinton was threatening to send troops into Haiti. It's unlikely any of the football players at Connellsville or Upper St. Clair were considering enlisting in the military to serve their country.

Yes, the '41 kids from Connellsville were special.

"His only concern was his teammates."
— Jim Lembo,
Athletic Director,
Connellsville H.S.

John Lujack was the handsomest of sports heroes. He was born in Connellsville on January 4, 1925. He starred in several sports in high school, and was a 6-foot, 187-pound quarterback for the Cokers.

Lujack was reluctant to return home for the reunion, at first, when Jim Lembo, the athletic director at Connellsville High School, called Lujack and told him of his plans to honor him at a special dinner and football weekend. Lujack said he was grateful, but would return for such a weekend only if the entire team was brought back and similarly honored.

Lujack was always the quintessential team man. "His only concern, after 53 years, was his teammates," allowed Lembo, who coordinated all the activities and put on quite a show. "His objective was to provide our community with an opportunity to recognize their accomplishments and to establish an everlasting memory."

Lujack made Lembo comfortable in his company right away at the reunion when he corrected his host who had initially addressed him as "Mr. Lujack" by saying, "Just call me John."

Lujack took over at quarterback for Notre Dame as a sophomore in 1943 when Heisman Trophy winner Angelo Bertelli joined the

26

Johnny Lujack was also a star on the Connellsville High School basketball team. He could truly do it all.

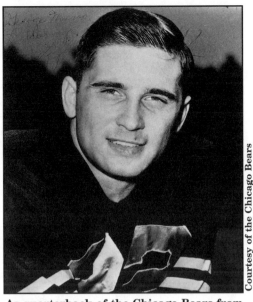

As quarterback of the Chicago Bears from 1948 to 1951.

Johnny Lujack

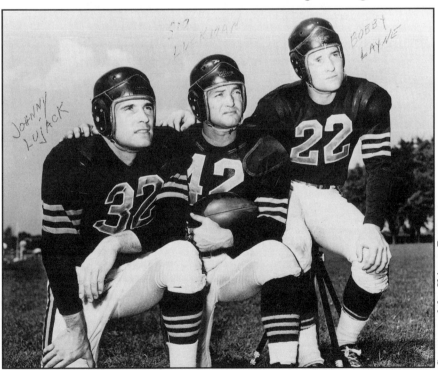

Lujack, at left, joined some fast company when he came to Chicago Bears. There were two outstanding quarterbacks whose draft rights were originally given away by the Pittsburgh Steelers, namely Sid Luckman (42) and Bobby Layne (22). Layne later came with Buddy Parker from the Detroit Lions to put some sizzle in the Steelers' lineup from 1958 to 1962.

Marines, and Lujack ended up helping the Irish to three national titles and established a reputation as one of the great T-formation quarterbacks in college football history.

In his first starting assignment at Notre Dame, Lujack led the Irish to a 26-0 victory over Army. He threw passes for two touchdowns, ran for another and intercepted a pass.

He spent nearly three years in the Navy and returned in time to earn consensus All-America honors as a junior and senior.

Lujack was quite the athlete. He also played halfback as a sophomore, played defensive back, kicked extra points and punted. He probably made his biggest play on defense. He preserved a scoreless tie in 1946 between the second-ranked Irish and top-ranked Army by making a touchdown-saving tackle of Cadet fullback Doc Blanchard.

As a junior, Lujack finished third in the Heisman Trophy balloting. Army's Glenn Davis won the award.

As a senior, Lujack was named the Athlete of the Year by the Associated Press, which was quite an honor considering that the Yankees' Joe DiMaggio finished runner-up in the balloting. His name remains a magic one in sports lore. The Irish didn't lose a game in his last two seasons, a tie with Army in 1946 the only non-win.

He won the Heisman Trophy in 1947, beating out Bob Chappuis of Michigan, Doak Walker of SMU, Charley Conerly of Mississippi, Harry Gilmer of Alabama, Bobby Layne of Texas, Chuck Bednarik of Penn, and Bill Swiacki of Columbia. What a great class!

Lujack was the Most Valuable Player in the East-West Game in 1948.

He was eligible for the NFL draft in 1946 and was one of four Notre Dame players picked in the first round that year, including George Connor, Frank Dancewicz and Emil Sitko. A total of 16 Notre Damers were drafted that year.

To show you the kind of talent Notre Dame had in those days, consider some of the guys who played quarterback for the Irish when Lujack was in the U.S. Navy in 1944 and 1945. They included Dancewicz, Joe Gasparella (later a player with the Steelers and a coach at Carnegie Mellon), Johnny Dee (later the varsity basketball coach at Notre Dame), George Ratterman and Frank Tripucka.

Lujack played four years with the Chicago Bears, leading the team in scoring each year, tying a record with eight interceptions as a rookie, throwing for a record 468 yards in one game in 1949, and playing in the NFL's Pro Bowl his last two seasons.

He was a backfield coach for two seasons following his retirement from football in 1952. He became a highly-successful businessman, operating an automobile dealership in Davenport, Iowa. He was elected to the National Football Foundation Hall of Fame in 1960.

"The quarterback is a freak of football. He is granted the privilege of being fragile in a vicious sport. His skills are delicate in a game that demands ruggedness from its other practitioners."
— Jimmy Cannon

Connellsville historian Bart Mallory shared some stories about the '41 Cokers. When Gary Feniello was playing service ball at Fort Warren, Texas, he displeased a player on the other side of the line with his questionable tactics. The college player from Mississippi gave Gary some advice: "Boy, I'm going to teach you a lesson today." And then he proceeded to give Gary the beating of his life. That player ended up in the Pro Football Hall of Fame. His name, fittingly enough, was Frank "Bruiser" Kinard. Dick Pitzer, Johnny Richards and Dave Hart did not start or play in the first quarter of the 1942 opening game because of an infraction of training rules. What disgraceful misdeed had Coach Ruff caught them doing just five hours before the game? He saw them outside of Fred Funari's Place eating ice cream, a no-no in his pre-game meal plan.

Mallory points out that every branch of the military service was represented by the backfield and an assistant coach from that '41 Connellsville squad: Alfred Bieshada (Marines), Lujack (Navy), Wally Schroyer (Army), Dave Hart (Air Force) and coach Edward Spotts (Coast Guard). Pitzer played on two national championship teams at Army (1944 and 1945), and Lujack played on national championship teams at Notre Dame in 1943, 1946 and 1947. That means that a Connellsville alumnus started for a national championship team five years running. In the 1946 game between Army and Notre Dame, the Irish players voted Pitzer the game's outstanding player.

Connellsville Coker teammates Dave Hart and Bill Sohonage served in the Air Force together and both saw combat action in the European Theater of operations, including the famous bomb runs to Hitler's number one concern, the heavily-fortified Polesti oil fields of Romania. They were waist-gunners on a B-17. One time their airplane was forced to land in Russia. On another bomb run, Hart lost his oxygen due to a flak burst, and Sohonage shared his oxygen with Hart until the plane landed safely at their home base in England.

When the Connellsville High football players have a reunion they have real "war stories" to share with one another.

"I could never write anything bad about a kid who was giving his all, whether it was Little League baseball or a high school sport. It offers a great deal of satisfaction that many athletes kept what I wrote about them and have a special regard for me and my writings. Kids in sports I always regarded as my heroes."
— Joe Tronzo, legendary sportswriter,
Beaver County Times and World War II vet,
who died at age 75 on April 29, 1999

Harvey Haddix
He is still her hero

"Harvey Haddix saved my life."
— Mary Dennis

The Pittsburgh Pirates marked a memorable day in team history on May 26, 1999 — the 40th anniversary of Harvey Haddix's 12 perfect innings against the Milwaukee Braves. It's a feat that's still regarded as one of the greatest pitching performances in baseball history.

Haddix wasn't feeling too well that night, but he pitched the longest "perfect game," only to lose in the 13th on an error, an intentional walk and a home run by Joe Adcock that was later ruled a double because he passed Henry Aaron on the basepaths.

Haddix has always been one of the most popular pitchers in Pirates' history. When the team celebrated its 100th anniversary in 1987, Haddix was named the Pirates' all-time best left-handed thrower, while Vernon Law was voted the best right-handed pitcher, and ElRoy Face the best relief pitcher.

I was signing copies of my "Pittsburgh Proud" sports book series at Waldenbooks at South Hills Village during the Christmas season in 1998 when two women walked up and started checking out the books.

One of them, Mary Dennis from Seminole, Florida, was flipping through the pages of *MAZ And The '60 Bucs,* and stopped when she saw the chapter on Harvey Haddix. She caught me off guard with a startling remark:

"Harvey Haddix saved my life," she said. "So he's my hero."

I asked her to explain her observation, and she told me the sort of story that makes my hair stand up on end on the nape of my neck. She said she was originally from Washington, Pa., and had grown up a Pirates fan, and often attended games at Forbes Field.

"I was in the Women's Air Corps, and I was stationed at an air defense unit outside of Syracuse, N.Y. in 1959," she related. "I used to be able to pick up the KDKA signal on some nights — when the stars were aligned a certain way or something — and I'd listen to the Bucs' games as often as I could. Some nights you just couldn't get it.

"This one night the Pirates were playing the Braves in Milwaukee. Some of my girlfriends at the base wanted me to go out with them and go to a party that night. I was listening to the baseball game when they wanted me to go. One of the girls was on duty and couldn't go right away and they were going to come back and pick her up later on. I told them to check with me then, and I might tag along.

"When they came back, the ballgame was in the 11th inning and no one on the Braves had reached base. Harvey Haddix was pitching

30

a no-hitter, a perfect game. I told my friends there was no way I was going to leave that game.

"Well, they drank too much that night and they were in a terrible automobile accident. They went off the road and crashed into a tree. Four of them were killed, and one of them was disabled for life. She was just about to depart the States for Germany when she was hurt. It didn't take long for the word about the accident to spread on our post. Early the next morning, everyone in our barracks was talking about it, and everyone was so upset and sad. I'll never forget that night. Never.

"I live near Bradenton, and I saw Harvey Haddix a couple of times at Pirate City when he was coaching the Pirates. I felt like telling him what happened in Syracuse that night, but I never did. Now he's gone, too.

"I can also tell you where I was when Bill Mazeroski hit the home run to win the World Series in 1960. Maz was my favorite, and I was so excited. I was on my honeymoon when he hit the home run."

Pirates' left-handed ace Harvey Haddix was a big man back home in Ohio.

Harvey "The Kitten" Haddix was one of the Pirates' most popular pitchers and coaches. He signed autographs at the '94 Piratefest at ExpoMart in Monroeville shortly before his death.

Harvey Haddix

Suzie McConnell Serio
She's got Olympic spirit

"The one thing that sets her apart is her determination."
— Tim McConnell

A light rain fell as I drove from my home in Upper St. Clair to the home of Suzie McConnell Serio at the other end of the community, the southern tip along the border of Bridgeville. It had been a gray, dank day, April 15, 1999, suitable for the deadline for filing one's income tax reports.

The view was verdant everywhere, though, if you looked for a brighter scene. The grass and trees were rich green, spring flowers were in bloom, welcoming the April showers. There were lilies, daffodils, tulips, crocusses coloring the landscape, the forsythia bushes were bright yellow, the oriental cherry trees were in the pink. It was only a gray day if you failed to search for some sunshine peeking through the clouds on occasion. You could also brighten your day if you talked to Suzie McConnell Serio.

I arrived shortly before our scheduled six o'clock date, to get a head-start on our appointed hour together. Suzie had squeezed me into her ambitious schedule, after weeks of trying to work out a meeting.

She had been back and forth to New York and Cleveland and Orlando in connection with her pro basketball role, coaching her Oakland Catholic High School girls' basketball team to a WPIAL Class AAAA title, working out to get in shape for the training camp that loomed ahead in May, looking after her family. Busy, busy, busy.

Suzie and her husband, Pete Serio, shared the home with their four young children. They were both busy people. For them, every day is a taxing day, but they wouldn't trade it for anything. They had just finished their dinner when I got there.

The daily demands were great, as they sometimes swapped responsibilities. They were there for each other, and for their kids.

Whenever I spoke to Suzie on the telephone, there was always noise in the background, the sounds of a nursery or day-care center. "The volume always picks up when I pick up the telephone," said Suzie. "Real chaos."

They lived in a ranch-style home on a cul-de-sac. She said the address would be hard to make out on the curb in front, but I knew it was her place when I spotted three basketball hoops, each at a different height, at the bottom of the driveway. There was also a miniature basketball, a little bigger than a softball, resting against the front of the home. They have since moved to another home in the same community.

33

Their oldest child, eight-year-old Pete, came to the door when I rang the bell, but retreated quickly shouting, "There's a man with a camera at the door!" The three girls were gone, being looked after by Suzie's mother.

Suzie opened the door and led me into their living room. She was wearing a dark blue, white-trimmed warm-up suit, off-white sneakers, and her brown hair was in a pony-tail. She was ready to practice somewhere. I think she was planning on working out that evening at a nearby gymnasium.

Pete appeared a little later. He, too, was wearing a warm-up outfit. He, too, coaches a high school girls' basketball team. He's a physical education teacher at Boyce Middle School in Upper St. Clair. They are a perfect pairing.

It took awhile for Suzie to sparkle, and say the sort of things that give you insight into what she's all about, and why she has been so successful in her pursuits. Maybe she just has so much on her mind it's difficult for her to relax.

Suzie sat on a chair, and offered little at the start. She sat on the edge of the chair, and fixed her blue eyes on me. She didn't look that comfortable. She steeled herself for a series of questions. Her answers were usually as spartan as our surroundings. There were no nicknacks, no glass figurines, nothing her children could get into and destroy. No Olympic medals or any memorabilia about her storied basketball-playing career were in evidence either.

That was elsewhere, in the gameroom downstairs. There were a few family photos in the living room. I don't recall seeing any lamps. The room was dimly-lit, mostly from the natural light coming through the windows. The living room became an interrogation room. I pride myself on making my subjects comfortable, on having conversations. We simply talk to one another, swapping stories. Not this time.

Suzie wasn't talking with me. She simply answered my questions. She volunteered no stories, no tales. Suzie has quite a story to tell, inspirational stuff. She seemed almost shy, reluctant to tell it. I'm told she's not one to boast. She's best, with a basketball in hand, as a pro player and high school coach. She smiles the most when little Pete climbs up in her chair, hugs her, and kisses her on the lips before departing the room. He was wearing a WNBA (Women's National Basketball Association) jacket over the No. 8 jersey of the Los Angeles Lakers' Kobe Bryant, with Cleveland Cavaliers shorts hanging below his kneecaps, an eclectic getup which brought a smile to Suzie's face. Pete was so proud of his basketball wardrobe, and his mom.

Asked what she was proudest of, Suzie smiles and says, "My four children."

That's why she wears No. 4 for the Cleveland Rockers in the WNBA. She loves to play best when Pete and the kids are in the crowd at Gund Arena. Nearing her 33rd birthday (she was born July 29, 1966), she managed somehow to combine a basketball career with raising a family. So far, so great.

34

Suzie McDonnell Serio with son, Pete Jr. and her husband, Pete, are at home in Upper St. Clair, but both are Brookline natives.

Photos by Jim O'Brien

She helped lead the Rockers to an Eastern Conference title, while being named to the All-WNBA team and winning the league's Newcomer of the Year and Sportsmanship awards. She averaged 8.6 points and 6.4 assists, third best in the league.

Pittsburgh Post-Gazette sports columnist Lori Shontz scolded the Dapper Dan for picking Joe Paterno as Pittsburgh's Sportsman of the Year. She thought McConnell Serio would have been a better choice. McConnell ended up getting a True Grit Award at the Dapper Dan Sports Banquet.

McConnell Serio told me she really enjoyed the banquet.

When I asked if I could take a picture of her and her husband, she took a seat in front of Pete, then begged off for a moment. "Can I put some lipstick on?" she asked, running into the next room where her bag was on the kitchen table. When she smiled for the camera, her Irish eyes lit up, and she looked terrific.

Back in the living room, Suzie took her seat again. She appeared smaller than I expected.

"Would you like something to drink?" she asked me after I had been there about a half hour. She was trying her best to be a good host. She suffered interviews with the same enthusiasm as a former famed resident of Upper St. Clair, ex-Steelers coach Chuck Noll.

Late in our meeting, I mentioned Vivian Stringer, the women's basketball coach at Rutgers University, who had formerly coached at Iowa and Cheyney State. Stringer grew up in Germantown, Pennsylvania, in Fayette County at the southwestern end of the state, graduated from Slippery Rock State College (now Slippery Rock University), and became one of the most respected college basketball coaches in the country. I had spoken to students at her old high school a few years earlier, and had a file on her in my home office.

I hit one of Suzie's sensitive buttons.

"Do you know her?" snapped Suzie, her smile gone.

"I know of her," I came back. "I know her story. She's got a good story, too."

"She's the coach," said Suzie slowly and emphatically, "who looked me in the eye in '91 and told me I was too small."

Suzie said that she had been one of 15 finalists for the USA women's basketball team that year, the year before the '92 Olympic Games. "She was a good friend of my coach at Penn State, Renee Portland, but she didn't think I was big enough to be on her team," said Suzie.

"They wanted me to be on their alternate team, another traveling team, but I was just so disappointed I didn't make the top team. I didn't say anything. I just walked away."

That was at the Olympic training camp in Colorado Springs, Colorado. "I wanted to play in the Pan-American Games to get ready for the Olympic Games," said Suzie.

"I was never on our No. 1 team the year before either of the Olympic Games in which I competed. The only year I played No. 1 was the Olympic year. I was second-team before that, sometimes third-team.

"I remember the first time how I got to go to Seoul, Korea the year before the 1988 Olympic Games were held there, touring with our second developmental team. I saw the buildings going up, the venues, the Olympic Village. I knew I wanted to be back there in a year."

Suzie said this near the end of our interview. It took her that long to warm up. Maybe the mention of Vivian Stringer heated her up, or fired her up. In any case, the recollection of that snub, that disappointment, brought out the best in Suzie McConnell Serio.

Like so many successful athletes, she had overcome the doubts of others. So many great athletes were told at some time in their young lives that they were too small, too slow, didn't jump high enough, or didn't have what it took to be a big-time ballplayer.

"That's all I have to hear," said Suzie, "to get me going." In short, I'd gotten her Irish up.

"Someday she'll be in the Olympic Games."
— Dan Kail, grade school coach

Suzie McConnell had a special spark and spirit, right from the start. When she was the only girl playing on the boys' basketball team in grade school in Brookline, her coach predicted that someday Suzie would be playing in the Olympic Games.

Even the coach, Dan Kail, couldn't have predicted that she would do that twice or that someday she would be playing pro basketball. There was no pro basketball league for women in the United States when Suzie was in grade school.

Even Coach Kail couldn't have believed that someday, at age 31, following a six-year layoff as a player and while parenting four children and coaching a high school basketball team, that Suzie would be a star in the WNBA.

If you knew Suzie, like her family knew Suzie, you would never short-change this spunky kid and what she can do. Her story is an inspirational one for all of us. Early on, she was told she was too short and didn't jump high enough to play with the big girls in college. More recently, she was thought to be too old, too long away from the game, too much a mom to make it in the pros.

She's been proving critics wrong for a long time. She is living proof that all things are possible if you have a positive attitude, truly believe in yourself, and are willing to work hard and make the personal sacrifices necessary to realize one's aspirations. That's the sort of stuff Suzie tells schoolkids when she makes public appearances. They need the right stuff to succeed.

Tim McConnell, her 34-year-old brother, was the coach of the boys' basketball team at Chartiers Valley High School in Bridgeville during the 1998-99 campaign. He was a respected coach in his own right. His team posted a 20-8 record. They won the section crown and got as far as the WPIAL Quad A semi-finals and the PIAA quarter-finals. He was also serving as the dean of students, responsible for discipline, next door at the Chartiers Valley Middle School.

"I think the one thing that sets her apart is her determination," offered Tim, when I visited him at the school after I had spoken to a middle school assembly during National Middle School Month in late March, 1999.

School principal Betsy Steiner was spearheading a program to get her sixth, seventh and eighth grade students inspired to do more community service. She couldn't have found a better role model for these students than Tim's kid sister, Suzie McConnell Serio. Suzie had spoken to the students there on earlier occasions, and she had an open invitation from Mrs. Steiner to come back again. Ever since her Olympic days, Suzie has been a community relations representative for Highmark Blue Cross/Blue Shield.

Suzie's husband, Pete, moonlighted as a basketball coach of the girls' team at Canevin High School. With their four young children and the crazy demands of their school and sports schedules, the Serios led a strange existence.

"It's a family affair, it always has been," said Tim McConnell. "Everybody in our family pitches in when they can, and Pete is supportive of everything Suzie wants to do.

"Suzie has always been different. You see this person, small in stature, just 5-3, meek and very humble, and you'd never think she was such a strong competitor. She doesn't like to talk about herself. She'd rather talk about her family. She's a perfectionist, so demanding of herself. Her determination, her drive, they all serve her well. Nothing is impossible as far as she's concerned."

Tim McConnell gave away a family secret somewhere in there. Suzie McConnell Serio has been advertised as being 5-5 for many years, and is listed as 5-5 by the Cleveland Rockers. Tim knows better. He's 5-7½ himself. He insisted that Suzie is 5-3. I asked him when he first recognized that Suzie was something special.

"When she was very young, she played on a boys' basketball team at Our Lady of Loreto on Pioneer Avenue in Brookline, where we grew up," said Tim McConnell. "She made the team when she was in fourth grade. In fifth grade, she was good enough to start. Dan Kail was her coach. She was the star of the team in sixth grade, and that's when people made a stink about a girl playing on the boys' team.

"After her sixth grade season, when the team won a state title with a 37-0 record, they formed a girls' basketball team at the school because so many parents had complained about the situation. Suzie didn't get any special treatment. She took her lumps, but never took a backstep.

38

Suzie McConnell (No. 1) is in the center of both pictures of her 4th and 5th grade basketball team at Our Lady of Loreto in Brookline. She was the only girl on Dan Kail's club. She points out that she cut her hair in a more boyish cut her second year in order to fit in better with her teammates. She still stood out. Coach Kail predicted that someday she'd be playing for the U.S. Olympic women's basketball team.

"People don't appreciate how hard she worked to become what she became. When she was younger, we'd play two-on-two games at Moore Park near our home. One of my other brothers and I would play with her and our sister, Kathy, who's just as competitive.

"Suzie's friends would come by and say, 'C'mon, let's go swimming,' and she'd say, 'I want to play a little longer. I'll join you guys later.' And they'd walk away, wondering why she'd want to stay and play basketball instead of going to the swimming pool.

"After she was married and wanted to get back in shape for the '92 Olympic tryouts, she asked me to help her. She wanted to go back to the Olympic Games again. I'm big on conditioning and staying in shape, so she thought I could push her. She had one child, Pete, at that time, but she wanted to go to the Olympic Games. It had been one of her goals. I was a little surprised that she wanted to do it, but knowing Suzie I knew it was possible.

"The first night we went to Oakland Catholic High School, where she was coaching, and I had her working on sprint work. After she ran a few sprints, ten minutes into the workout, she stopped and threw up, right there in the gym. That's how out of shape she was. She went to the bathroom and she came out with some paper towels and she cleaned up the mess. Then she turned to me, and said, 'OK, what's next?' And we worked out for another hour and a half. That's when I knew she'd be able to do it again."

Suzie came home with a bronze medal in 1992, retired again and gave birth to three daughters, a little closer than she planned.

Then along came the WNBA dream and again she turned to Tim for some help in getting her act together. "She was not going to come back," he said, "if she could not be the same player she was."

He talked about how she ran in the early morning, sometimes during downpours, coached during the day and played basketball at night, her mother, husband and siblings taking turns looking after her children. She pushed herself too hard, too fast, and suffered a stress fracture in her foot. Even that didn't slow her down too much.

When she goes on the road with the Rockers, her family returns to Pittsburgh. In Cleveland, she has a long day. "It's always hardest to say goodbye," she said. "When we have practice, I have a half-hour drive home and that's my time to think about my kids. I really look forward to walking through the door and hearing each of them scream, 'Mommy!' They're giving me kisses and hugs. They help me keep all of this in perspective — win or lose, I'm still their mother."

Her children were often sleeping when she left the two bedroom apartment in the suburbs for practice. She returned in the afternoon to change diapers, play Putt-Putt or go to the swimming pool with the kids. Pete cooked many of the meals, did most of the laundry, bathed the kids and drove them wherever they needed to go. Suzie's parents, Sue and Tom, came to Cleveland the day before a home game and usually stayed for a week to help out.

Pete said she was able to come home only once, for two days, during the four months she was involved with the Rockers. "We also made one trip to Geauga Lake, an amusement park in Ohio, with the kids, and that was about it as far as breaks go," he said.

"Some days are easier than others," said Suzie. "Really, my kids are very flexible."

It must be in the genes.

"This is what she was put on earth to do."
— Kathy McConnell

March Madness is not something new. There was an item in the *Post-Gazette* the month of March, 1999 in a "Looking Back" feature calling attention to a sports event 15 years earlier. On March 10, 1984, Kathy McConnell had 24 points and sister Suzie 21, leading Seton-LaSalle High School (27-2) to a 71-59 win over Beaver Falls in the WPIAL Class AAAA girls' basketball championship game. That team, dubbed the "Runnin' Rebels" because of its fastbreak style, went on to win the PIAA title.

Kathy had come back home in February from Champaign-Urbana where she was the associate head coach for the University of Illinois women's basketball team to do some recruiting in the Pittsburgh area, and stopped to see sister Suzie. She ended up doing some baby-sitting in the afternoon at Suzie and Pete's home in Upper St. Clair, not far from my home.

"I just think she's so modest," commented Kathy when we started talking about her sister. "She doesn't realize the impact she's had on kids, her peers, older women, moms. I think she goes about like this because this is what she was put on earth to do.

"We're 13 months apart, and we've always been close, even though I live in Illinois. When I was at the University of Virginia (1985-1989) and she was at Penn State, we stayed in touch. She has the best kids, and I'm here, so I'm helping out.

"We're all willing to help her at any cost so she can achieve her goal. This is something she is definitely into. It was just a matter of timing."

Kathy, by the way, had been a candidate for the position of head coach of the women's basketball team at Pitt, but lost out to Traci Waites.

Suzie found time during the WNBA playoffs in August, 1998, to serve as maid of honor when her sister, Kathy, got married. Somehow they squeezed it in. The name is now Kathy McConnell Miller.

Teamwork has always been stressed by the McConnell clan. They didn't need to look past their kitchen or bedrooms to find heroes.

"I don't remember one person we watched or wanted to be like in sports," commented Kathy. "We wanted to be like our older brother,

Tommy. We wanted him to show us how to be like him. There was not somebody in sports we modeled ourselves after. Our role models were our parents and our brothers."

Kathy can remember when Suzie started to think about trying out for the new women's pro league.

"During the first year of the league, she started to think that she'd like to take a shot at it," recalled Kathy. "She was pregnant at the time with her fourth child. She watched it on TV and she told me, 'I could do this.' During the year, we talked about the possibility, and where she'd fit in.

"I'd say, 'Suzie, there are some good point guards coming out of college this year.' But that didn't put her off. They don't have the court awareness she has. They're not the same style of guard that she is. They're not as well-rounded. Suzie sees the whole floor.

"I believe her pregnancies made her tougher, more disciplined and focused. She still has her speed and quickness, and I think her personality has changed considerably from when she played before. The coaching aspects have helped her."

I asked Kathy if she thought her sister had a chance when she attended the WNBA's tryout camp in Chicago back in April, 1998. "I went to Chicago to the combine and stayed with her," recalled Kathy. "At the first workout session, I knew she was the best point guard there. She was in charge, right away."

Suzie was selected on the second round of the WNBA draft, the 16th player picked, by the Cleveland Rockers.

"When Suzie is on the floor, she doesn't think about Suzie," continued Kathy. "She's thinking about winning. She still wants to win at all costs. She gives it everything she has. She takes losses personally, like it was her fault.

"She plays like it's her last game, like she's never going to be on the court again."

Sounds like a mini-Michael Jordan. Sounds like the kind of player a coach like Kathy McConnell would like to recruit. "You hope you can find someone with her approach to the game," said Kathy. "They're hard to find. Suzie is special. She gives everything.

"Suzie's team is playing Fox Chapel, and I'm looking at a girl on her team. I know she'll understand the game."

The best basketball prospect, boys or girls, in the Pittsburgh area in a long time was Swin Cash, who led McKeesport High School to a WPIAL title in 1998, and was a freshman on the nationally-rated University of Connecticut team.

"She made a good choice," said Kathy. "If the coach stays and doesn't go pro, she'll be in a good program. She's a nice player, and she's a nice kid."

That's what they always said about her sister, Suzie McConnell.

"Her kids are her No. 1 priority."
— Husband Pete Serio

Suzie McConnell Serio has a resume that's unreal. Her full name, for the record, is Suzanne Theresa McConnell Serio. Her occupation is mother of four, wife, high school coach and professional basketball player. That'll keep a woman busy.

Her hometown is Pittsburgh, Pennsylvania. She's the only woman who grew up in the city ever to win an Olympic medal, and she did it twice, as a member of the 1988 gold medal-winning women's basketball team in Seoul, and as a member of the 1992 bronze medal-winning unit in Barcelona.

"Winning the gold was the ultimate dream come true," said Suzie.

She was saluted in a parade for "Pittsburgh's Hometown Heroes" in the summer of 1996 along with Kurt Angle, after he had won a gold medal in wrestling at the Olympic Games in Atlanta. Two other former Olympians, platform diver Dr. Richard Rydze of Mt. Lebanon, and ice skater Suzy Semanick of Bridgeville, were among those who were also hailed.

Suzie McConnell Serio's position is point guard, her height and weight are 5 feet 3 inches, 125 pounds, respectively. She is a graduate of Seton LaSalle High School and Penn State University, class of 1988. She wore No. 32 at Penn State.

She was a *Parade* All-America as a senior at Seton LaSalle. At Penn State, she set the NCAA career record for assists with 1,307.

She was the 16th pick in the WNBA draft in April 29, 1998. During her rookie season, she looked after her four children, three girls and a boy. Peter Jr., at 7, was the oldest, followed by Jordan, 4, Amanda, 3, and Madison, 1.

"Her kids are her No. 1 priority in her life," said Pete Serio. "We told each other before we had all four that we both wanted a lot of kids, but that we would not let having kids keep us from doing what we want to pursue. Some people questioned her judgment when she said she was going to try out for the pro basketball league. But she loves proving people wrong. She loves a challenge."

More than 1,000 women applied for the WNBA's pre-draft camp, and Suzie survived the cut and was among 76 who were invited to attend. Players ranged from 21 to 39 years old and from 5 feet 3 to 7 feet 2 inches tall. McConnell Serio was the only one who had four kids.

If there were any doubts about Suzie's size and skills, she erased those right away. In her pro debut in Cleveland, she had 10 points and 10 assists as the Rockers beat the New York Liberty 78-71 in the season opener.

"That is the role I am comfortable with — being a floor leader, making sure all the players are on the same page," McConnell Serio said afterward. "It was so exciting. This is what I remember basketball being like."

A near-sellout crowd of 17,911 at Gund Arena roared with approval, and McConnell Serio drew praise from the Liberty's Rebecca Lobo, an All-America performer two years earlier at the University of Connecticut. "She has all the respect in the world from me because, whether or not she has four kids, she's a great, great point guard," allowed Lobo. Consider her credits as a basketball player. In her first year in the WNBA, she was a first-team all-star selection and won two of the league's major honors, Newcomer of the Year and the Sportsmanship Award.

She was a tri-captain of the Cleveland Rockers, and represented the team on the WNBA All-Star Team that toured Brazil. She was named one of Cleveland's 50 Most Interesting People by *Cleveland Magazine*.

In 1988, she was named the Naismith Award Winner as the small player of the year. She was a 1987-88 Kodak All-American, and held the NCAA record with 1,307 career assists.

Equally impressive, she coached Oakland Catholic High School to a PIAA Quad A championship in 1993. Her school is just across the street from St. Paul's Cathedral, near where Duquesne Gardens once stood. It used to be called St. Paul's Girls' High School, a block away from Central Catholic Boys' High School. Girls who used to go to Sacred Heart High School and St. Rosalia's High School, both closed, attend Oakland Catholic as do students from other Pittsburgh Catholic grade schools.

"All that and a mother of four!" reads a banner at the bottom of the Cleveland Rockers publicity release.

"When I talked to Pete about it, he saw how excited I was."
— Suzie McConnell Serio

One of her big fans was Lori Montgomery, publicity director for the Cleveland Rockers, who wrote the following:

"Much like Superman, Rockers point guard Suzie McConnell had two different identities this past summer. Part of the day, she spent at home with her husband and four children, changing diapers, doing laundry, and just doing what moms do.

"The other part of the day, she played the role of standout point guard for the Cleveland Rockers, leading the team to its first-ever playoff appearance, a 20-10 record, and an Eastern Conference championship. In the summer of 1998, Suzie McConnell Serio took a leap of faith that she could do it all. She wound up flying."

She had all four of her children between 1991 and 1997, and seemed content with being a coach and mom and wife when she got the bug to give basketball another shot. She began to wonder if a comeback was possible.

She ran into Renee Brown, the WNBA's Director of Player Personnel, at a USA Basketball Committee meeting in August of 1997, and they talked about the possibility.

"Renee definitely planted the seed," said Suzie. "When I talked to Pete about it, he saw how excited I was and assured me that we could work it out if I wanted to pursue this new dream.

"It was my husband who finally said to me, 'What are you waiting for? Why don't you give it a try?' I figured I could do it. I coach during another time period of the year, and I do motivational talks on behalf of Blue Cross, so I decided I had nothing to lose."

Cleveland was close enough to Pittsburgh — a two-and-a-half hour drive — to make it logistically sensible to pull off this coup.

The WNBA's summer schedule suited Suzie and Pete's schedule because Pete, as a middle school teacher, had a long summer break. He played "Mr. Mom" all summer at the couple's Cleveland apartment while Suzie was playing ball.

"I am fortunate my husband gave me the opportunity of having the best of both worlds," Suzie said. "It was an opportunity that I wanted to take advantage of, and he's been incredible. I couldn't have done it without him."

Even though her first-year pro accomplishments were spectacular, Suzie wasn't satisfied. She wanted to lead the Rockers to a WNBA championship.

Even if she accomplishes that, she won't stand in the spotlight simply as a WNBA star.

"Everything I accomplish on the court means so much more to me because I have a family to share it with," she says proudly.

Suzie was also hopeful that she could get a boost in her paycheck. Because she was a second round pick, her compensation the first year was capped at $25,000, and she was scheduled to get $30,000 the second year. The 1999 schedule was threatened by a strike threat, but league officials and the players' organization managed to work things out.

Suzie and Pete believe, of course, that she merits more money because of her success on and off the court.

Pete appears to be a patient man who also appreciates the importance of him and his children seeing Suzie doing her thing. "I'll get to golf all I want after however many summers she plays," he said. "The upside of all this is I get to let my wife play basketball. The upside is watching Peter's face when his mother is playing."

> *"When Suzie is on the floor, she doesn't think about Suzie. She's thinking about winning."*
> — Kathy McConnell Miller,
> Assistant Basketball Coach,
> University of Illinois

Suzie was the fifth of eight children in the McConnell clan. They shared one bathroom in their modest home on Dunster Street in Brookline. Their father, Tom, 63, worked for the Port Authority as a bus driver. Their mother, Sue, 61, who was one of 14 children, managed the family team. As Sue McGrady, she was a fiesty member of several city championship volleyball teams in her youth. During the 1998-99 season, six of the eight children, (three men and three women) were basketball coaches in high school and Division I college programs.

Tom resigned as coach of the men's team at St. Francis of Loretto at the end of the 1998-99 campaign, and wasn't sure he wanted to coach again. Michael McConnell was coaching the girls' team at Carlynton High School. Maureen McConnell serves as an assistant for Pete's program at Canevin High and as a baby-sitter for Suzie.

Suzie has coached at Oakland Catholic since 1989-90, guiding it to an overall 201-58 record, including seven straight 20-win seasons. Suzie believes that playing pro basketball helps inspire her players at Oakland Catholic. "I think, for my players, they look at me and have something extra to aspire to," McConnell Serio said. "I've heard them say to reporters in the past that seeing me makes it (playing professionally) a more realistic goal for them. They watch me work out; I practice with them in order to stay in shape and they see what it takes to play at that level. Every team I've played on, including the Rockers, we've played a very uptempo style. That is how my high school team plays. I've tried to incorporate a little bit from every coach I've played for, and then add in my own experiences as a player.

"I really thought I'd be a different coach from playing in the WNBA, but I'm not. I realized that the difference between the levels of basketball is the talent and the little things, but basically, it is the same game. That is what I try and emphasize with my players — the importance of learning the fundamentals and basics and becoming a complete player, because those things will carry with you no matter where you play.

"Of course, I am probably a little more patient with turnovers now," McConnell Serio continued. "Being a point guard this past summer, I had my share of those. I try to be a bit more understanding when I talk to my players about protecting the basketball."

Playing in Gund Arena where the NBA Cavaliers also play has been exciting for McConnell-Serio. "I loved everything about it — the players on my team, the atmosphere in Gund Arena, the pre-game introductions, the incredible fans. I was very proud to have been a Cleveland Rocker. Everything was just first class."

She was asked if winning all-league and Newcomer of the Year honors were important to her. Her remarks were offered on a tape-recorded interview by the Rockers public relations office.

"Getting this award made me look back and think about how worthwhile all the hard work was. And taken together with going to the playoffs with Cleveland and being on such a great team, this made the WNBA one of the greatest experiences of my life.

"All my life I've had skeptics because of my size and my children. So proving that I could do this, that I could accomplish good things despite those obstacles, feels so good. And as long as I'm healthy, as long as my husband and kids continue to give me the support I need, I'll keep playing.

"My son is old enough to really understand the game, so he got into the whole thing. He even lives in my Rockers' gear — he wears it to school, to sleep, he has all of the player cards, he knows my teammates, watches other games on television. My daughters aren't old enough yet to get it, but they still loved coming to the games and seeing my face on the Jumbotron screen. And it's just exciting to have a family to share all of this with.

"Winning a sportsmanship award was good, too. Sportsmanship, and all of your values and morals, are taught to you by your parents. So, when I get out on the floor, I am expected by both my parents and my family to be a good sport. So being recognized for good sportsmanship was even more special to me than anything else last season.

"Now that I have one season under my belt in the WNBA, I know more about what's expected of me. I'll hopefully be in better shape and be a better scorer, a better shooter, and a better playmaker. And I want to take my game up another notch.

"I'll be coaching my high school team again, doing some promotional work for the Rockers and training a lot, so I don't think I'll have much time to relax. And, don't forget, I have four kids, so I keep pretty busy, even when I'm just at home."

"She was the only girl in the game."
— Tim McConnell

Tim McConnell told me during my visit at Chartiers Valley Middle School that his sister, Suzie, was coming to the high school gym that same night to scrimmage with some of his players and friends.

It would be like it was when she started playing at Our Lady of Loreto Grade School in Brookline. "She was the only girl in the game," said Tim when I telephoned him the following day for a report.

"There were 12 of us altogether," Tim said of their pick-up game at Chartiers Valley. "We played for two hours, from 6 to 8 o'clock. We played about ten games. Suzie got a good workout. We all got home in time to watch the NCAA final. It was a great game."

It was the morning after Connecticut had defeated Duke in a tremendous NCAA men's basketball championship. It was a few days after Purdue defeated Duke for the women's championship.

And Upper St. Clair, coincidentally enough, had won the PIAA Quad A girls' basketball title. "I watched their final game on TV and I was rooting for them," said Suzie. Her Oakland Catholic team had won the WPIAL Quad A title, but lost out in the PIAA quarter-finals.

I asked her about the potential of Beth Friday, the 6-1 senior star for Upper St. Clair. "She's a great player; she'll do well at Duquesne University," she said. "If she works hard and continues to improve, she could be in the WNBA someday."

"I knew all of the Steelers and Pirates."
— Suzie McConnell Serio

"I remember my older brothers were always playing games," said Suzie during my visit to her home. "All the kids in the neighborhood were into sports. That's what I grew up with. It wasn't just basketball. We played baseball and football and wiffleball in the street.

"We had a hoop in our backyard. I can remember trying to shoot when I couldn't even reach the hoop. My parents were fans of the Pirates and Steelers. They watched all the games on TV and everyone really got into it. Sports were always important in our home.

"When I was little, I knew all of the Steelers. I knew the players and their numbers. I knew most of the Pirates, Dave Parker, Willie Stargell and Omar Moreno. I really followed Pittsburgh sports. I knew them better back then than I do now.

"Dan Kail was the coach of a lot of teams, and he coached my brothers. He'd pick my brothers up for practice. I'd go to practice and shoot at the side hoops while they went through their drills. He'd let me do some dribbling drills with them. When I was in fourth grade, he asked my parents if I could play on the boys team. As I got older, the boys didn't want me playing on their team. You'd get looks, from some of the other players, from their parents.

"If you look at my fourth grade team picture, I have long hair and I looked like a little girl. In my fifth grade photo, I had a real short haircut, like a boy's haircut, trying to blend in.

"I just did it because I enjoyed it. We had to go home for lunch because we didn't have a cafeteria at our grade school. I'd come home and I'd go out in the backyard and shoot before I'd go back to school. It just became the sport I found myself playing more and more. The success I enjoyed was a motivational factor in itself.

"I hated to lose. I had a quiet personality. I wouldn't speak unless I was spoken to, but the competitiveness just came out of me.

"I don't remember the '76 Olympic Games. We boycotted the Games in 1980 as a political protest. I was in the eighth grade at the time. I remember watching the '84 Olympic Games when I was in high school. Cheryl Miller was the star of our women's basketball team. I remember the ceremony when they got their gold medals. It ignited my interest, for sure, in the Olympic Games, though I had no idea how I'd ever get involved. I just said, 'Wow. That could be incredible!' I remember watching Mary Lou Retton win the gold medal in gymnastics. She was from around here (Fairmont, West Virginia).

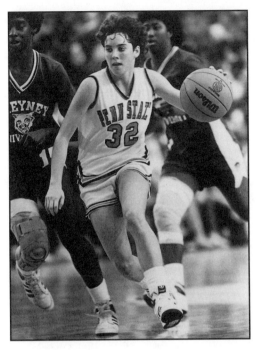

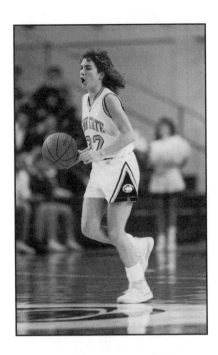

A little girl's dream can come true. Suzie McConnell got her start with Our Lady of Loreto in Brookline, and later played at Seton-LaSalle High School, Penn State University and the U.S. women's Olympic basketball team. She returned to University Park where her former coach, Rene Portland, at left below, was among those who paid tribute to her.

"At the end of my freshman year at Penn State, my coach, Renee Portland, began to talk to me about the possibility of playing in the Olympic Games. She changed our offense, things like that, to help me get ready.

"When I was in college, my ultimate goal was to be on the Olympic team.

"I never thought I was better than anybody else in my family, and I never tried to separate myself from them. Being one of eight children, there was always a competitive spirit. Growing up with a big family, you fought for everything. We had a small house and we were competitive about everything, not just sports.

"Getting good grades was important; you were competitive with yourself. Our parents encouraged us and supported us in school and in sports. We had high expectations of ourselves growing up. That's one of the things I talk about when I'm speaking to students at schools.

"Our parents always expected us to do our best, whatever we got involved with. My parents went to games seven nights a week. We played on Sundays, too. We played our home games at the Brookline Community Center. We'd be there from 8 a.m. till 5 or 6 p.m. Someone in the family was always playing in one of the games. My parents would do different things to help out, like my mother would work in the concession stands.

"I believe in striving to be better. There's always room for improvement. If you're comfortable where you've gotten, your game will suffer.

"My husband, Pete, was primarily responsible for me being able to do what I'm doing today. He gave me the opportunity to do this. He encouraged me to do it. We watched some of the WNBA games on television, and Pete could tell it piqued my interest. Pete said, 'If you get back into shape, you could do this.' And I said, 'Right. When am I going to get into shape.' I had all these kids and couldn't see myself getting into competitive shape again.

"I'm so glad we did this. Playing pro basketball has been an exciting experience. It's the opportunity of a lifetime. My son, Pete, really loves it and follows it closely. I had a chance to give him and Jordan a basketball at midcourt of our games in Cleveland, and they were so excited. Pete has all the cards. He has his own uniform that my mother made for him.

"Pete and I met through basketball. He's from Brookline and he played on the same basketball teams with my brothers. They'd play at Moore Park. He went to Seton-LaSalle. I couldn't do this without him. He's incredible. I don't think most men would do what he's done. He enjoys his children. He's done a great job. I always know my kids are being looked after. And I love my time with them, too.

50

"I'm looking forward to my second year in the league, my eleventh year of coaching. I'd like to stay in coaching, on the high school level. The WNBA schedule works out perfectly for Pete and me. I wouldn't have come back if it were a year-round season. May is the toughest month. I'm at training camp, and Pete isn't finished teaching yet. I really miss my kids. I talk to them twice a day on the telephone. It's hard being away from them. They don't like that I have to leave for training, but they like being part of the excitement. The children keep things in perspective. I'm very competitive and I hate to lose as a coach and as a player. But when you're a mother, win or lose, you're their mom and they don't care if you won or lost."

The McConnell family, clockwise, Suzie, Peter, Pete, Madison, Jordan and Amanda as they posed on midcourt logo at Gund Arena during Suzie's rookie season with Cleveland Rockers.

Mario Lemieux
Montreal's gift to Pittsburgh

"We try to help them realize their dream."

If you want to see the most sports heroes in one place at one time in Pittsburgh, then put a future Toyota Mario Lemieux Celebrity Invitational golf tournament in your datebook for a June outing in the new century.

Mario is the magnet, no doubt about it, that draws a galaxy of stars from all sports and some celebrities from other fields as well. The cast for the 1999 edition at The Club at Nevillewood, atop Pesto, Pa., about a 20-minute drive heading south from downtown Pittsburgh via U.S. 79, will be tough to outdo.

Mario managed to attract the likes of three of the most popular sports figures who had retired over the previous year in Michael Jordan, John Elway and Wayne Gretzky, to name just the head-liners. Mario and Dan Marino, the two most popular attractions the year before, were both back as was defending champion Rick Rhoden, a former Pirates pitcher who was finding a second pro sports life on the fledgling celebrity golf tour.

With the golf outing and a sports memorabilia auction at a dinner that kicked off the five-day gathering, nearly $1 million was raised for the Mario Lemieux Cancer Foundation. They raised over $500,000 the previous year.

"It's great to see everyone, to have some fun and to raise money for a good cause," said Hall of Fame Steelers coach Chuck Noll, winner of four Super Bowls in a six-year stretch during his celebrated 23-year career, summing it up as well as anyone.

Mario was as impressive as any of the sports figures in attendance. He's 6-5 and walks even taller. He's handsome, has a commanding presence, is respected by athletes in all sports. He was also being looked upon by many in the gallery as the one guy in town who might be able to put together a deal to save the Penguins and professional hockey in Pittsburgh.

He had saved the franchise once before, lifting it out of the doldrums and financial difficulties, as one of the great offensive players in hockey history, and leading the team to Stanley Cup championships in the early '90s. Now he had to do it again. The Penguins had gone into bankruptcy during the 1998-99 season, and the future of hockey wasn't a pretty picture in Pittsburgh or too many other places for that matter.

It needed a white knight like Lemieux and he was willing to assume the role. He and his associates were on the telephones talking to prospective investors and league and legal officials even while the golf tournament was going on. It's a wonder Lemieux was able to play golf as well as he did, even if it was below his personal standards. He mentioned to Michael Jordan and other celebrity entries that they could have a piece of the action if they wanted to join in the ownership group.

"I asked him on Wednesday," said Lemieux. "Michael's had offers from the NBA and the NHL to invest in teams. I don't think he's biting on this."

The weather was bright and sunny throughout the tournament, a tad too hot and steamy at times, but preferable to the heavy and frequent downpours that interrupted play on several occasions the year before.

It's a fan-friendly event, for the most part, though some marshalls and security officials are overzealous, and confuse the event with the U.S. Open. Most of the fans are there to see the sports stars, not to watch golf. They want to get some autographs, get some photographs of their own, and just get near these nationally-renowned sports favorites.

There are players for everyone, even tennis fans. One of the game's all-time greats, Ivan Lendl, is also quite a golfer, but hardly turned a head at Nevillewood. Rhoden, the best golfer of them all, and a pretty fair pitcher during his 16 years with the Pirates and Dodgers, doesn't draw that big a crowd, either, unless he's paired with Elway, the way he was on the final day of competition. They were the leaders going into the last round, and Rhoden required a 4-under par 272 to win by one stroke over Elway, who didn't surrender until the final hole.

Most of these guys are just gifted athletes and natural-born competitors. "I didn't think he would get nervous," Rhoden remarked about Elway after the event, in which he took home the top prize of $40,000, plus a few side bets. "But John's such a great athlete. I've never seen him play pingpong, but he probably plays that well, too."

Elway went for broke on the final hole with his drive, but ended up in a bunker instead of the fairway. "It's the first time I've ever been in a situation like that," said Elway, who is famous for his late touchdown and game-winning drives on the football field in his long and illustrious career. "It was a great learning experience. It took me three times (actually four) to get it right in the Super Bowl."

Rhoden was complimentary of both the golf course and the competition.

"This is the best golf course we've played so far," related Rhoden in the post-event press room. "Better players stick out on a course like this. It's demanding but rewards good shots. John was tough, which I expected him to be. He didn't make many mistakes. And he's quite the competitor. If he spends more time at this game, he'll get even better. I don't want him to get too much better."

Lemieux made quite a tribute to the repeat winner. "He's the best player on this tour," allowed Lemieux. "He's got a great mind; all pitchers do. He remains tough in difficult times."

Everyone had a caddy, but Lemieux was accompanied also by a young man from his home area of Quebec who is challenged by cancer. He has Hodgkins Disease, which is what Lemieux was threatened by during the latter years of his playing career.

The young man was Pierre Oliver Vear, a 13-year-old hockey fan who said his dream was to meet Mario Lemieux. The meeting was set up by a group in Canada that Lemieux likened to the Make-A-Wish Foundation familiar to Americans. Terminally ill youngsters are granted their wishes. It's contributed to an improvement in health for so many of those who have participated in the program, and has lifted nearly everyone's spirits and outlook. Mario has met other youngsters in similar straits.

A dedicated family man all the way, Lemieux said, "Our goal from the outset has been to raise a million dollars a year. We're trying to help young kids who have to undergo chemotherapy and radiation treatments, and we hope to cure this terrible disease.

"I just talked to him," continued Lemieux, referring to his new young friend from Quebec. "He came down here with his family, his two brothers, and walked down the fairways with me for three days. We want to help such kids enjoy what life they have left. Some of them don't have a long time to go. We try to help them realize their dream."

Lemieux said there were meetings scheduled the very next morning relating to his group's bid to buy the Penguins and improve the pro hockey picture in Pittsburgh. "We're trying hard to do the right thing," he said.

"It's been hectic the last six months. If I can make some deals and get the team straightened away, I'd like to spend more time at my golf game and participate more in these celebrity tournaments. You need to get used to this. It's different from playing your buddies for a Nassau over the weekend."

Lemieux's tournament is a real treat for local sports fans. The price is right, that's for sure. Adult tickets are just $10 for the day, with children under 12 admitted for $5. Parking and air-conditioned shuttles are free.

Many local non-profit children's organizations were invited to attend the golf outing as guests of the sponsoring companies. They included Children's Hospital of Pittsburgh, Allegheny County Children & Youth Services, DePaul Institute, The March of Dimes, the Burger King Cancer Caring Center, Pittsburgh Youth Golf, Easter Seals, Multiple Sclerosis Service Society, Muscular Dystrophy Association and Youth Guidance, Inc.

The event begins with a two-day pro-am, where sponsors are paired with a celebrity for prizes and trophies awarded Friday evening. The weekend features celebrity-only competition, 54-hole medal play for a purse totaling $250,000. The winner received $40,000.

There were many Hall of Famers and outstanding former stars in the field. Some of the biggest names were Johnny Bench, Mike

Schmidt, Emmitt Smith, Joe Morgan, Stan Mikita, George Gervin, Digger Phelps, Pierre Larouche, Eddie Johnston, Bill Fralic, Andy Russell, Mike Wagner, Grant Fuhr, Lynn Swann, John Brodie, Andy Van Slyke, Rollie Fingers and Chris Chandler.

TV actors such as Jack Wagner and Alan Thicke were there, too.

Giant Eagle sponsored an autograph-signing tent at the 18th hole, the UPMC Health System sponsored the celebrity auction gala in The Strip, and Mellon Bank sponsored a winner's circle party at The Club at Nevillewood.

"The field was great," said Lemieux. "Having people like Michael Jordan, Wayne Gretzky, John Elway and Danny Marino really helped us quite a bit. Hopefully, they all had a great time and, hopefully, they'll accept our invitations to come back again next year. The crowds were great, too. To see all those people lining the fairway as you came down 18 was tremendous." Talking about Jordan, Rhoden remarked, "He's the Pied Piper; he's like Elvis."

Mario Lemieux remained the cover boy for the tournament. If he pulls the Penguins out of their plight, he'll really be a hometown hero in Pittsburgh.

Jim O'Brien

Two of the greatest superstars in sports, Mario Lemieux and Michael Jordan, enjoyed a weekend of golf at The Club at Nevillewood in mid-June, 1999. They attracted record crowds for an event that raised nearly $1 million for the Lemieux Cancer Foundation.

Roger Kingdom
Still clearing hurdles

*"I'm proof that dreams
do come true."*

The Roger Kingdom Story is not an easy one to tell or understand. It is both inspiring and disappointing and, like too many aspects of Kingdom's career, unfinished. It is complicated, controversial, confusing, wondrous, definitely worth reviewing. On a wing and a prayer, Kingdom became an international track & field sports star.

He is one of the greatest sports performers to call Pittsburgh home, right up there with Roberto Clemente, Mario Lemieux, Franco Harris and Jack Lambert, Honus Wagner, Ralph Kiner and Willie Stargell, Connie Hawkins and Billy Knight, Billy Conn, Harry Greb and Fritzie Zivic, yet seldom mentioned in the same breath as those legendary figures.

That's unfortunate and unfair. Gaining proper recognition in Pittsburgh for his feats is one hurdle Kingdom has yet to clear. Kingdom had the credentials and looks to capture hearts, in the way that Lemieux and Clemente and Harris had done, but track & field failed to attract as much attention. For the record, though, he was named the Dapper Dan Man of the Year for 1989.

Kingdom had as many comebacks from injury and adversity and the ravages of time as the 1960 Pirates or the 1979 Steelers, or the Penguins of the '90s who won two Stanley Cup championships, and he should be a source of inspiration for all of us. Kingdom's confidence and determination and competitive spirit are the stuff of giants in any game. He won gold medals in two different Olympic Games, in 1984 in Los Angeles and 1988 in Seoul, South Korea, a remarkable feat, by twice winning the 110-meter high hurdles. He set records at the University of Pittsburgh and across the world. He's had a remarkable run on a big-time level.

He even takes pride in having a 2-0 record against former Purdue University and Steelers star Rod Woodson in hurdles competition. "I beat him as a freshman," recalled Kingdom, "and I beat him after he was drafted by the Steelers."

Roger was the first Pitt athlete to win a gold medal in the Olympic Games since John Woodruff of Connellsville claimed the 800-meter race at Berlin in 1936, the Games best known for Jesse Owens winning four gold medals in track events. Kingdom has kept company with Woodruff as well as Herb Douglas, a bronze medalist in the long jump at London in 1948, the only other Pitt trackman to medal in the Olympic Games. They have been assembled for special recognition events on the Pitt campus. Douglas was from my hometown of Hazelwood, and has grown from a boyhood hero to become a good friend and counselor.

It was Douglas, a retired business executive, who founded the Jesse Owens International Trophy Award in 1980 in honor of his boyhood hero, and was so proud when Kingdom claimed the award as the world's most outstanding athletic competitor at a dinner at the Waldorf-Astoria in New York City in 1990.

The year before, Kingdom was named the athlete of the year by *Track & Field News*, and "hurdler of the year" in 1990. It remained for the panel of judges who annually select the Jesse Owens International Trophy Award to go one better. It's not restricted to track & field. It covers all areas of athletic endeavor.

Kingdom cruised to 22 victories in 27 starts in 1989. He did it once in a world record time of 12.92 seconds. The record he shattered was by his own idol, Renaldo Nehemiah, who had done the distance in 12.93, a mark some experts thought could never be bettered. At the time, Kingdom, in fact, was the only man other than Nehemiah to dip below 13 seconds, and he had done it three times.

He was only the second man in Olympic annals to capture high hurdles gold twice, and was designated the hurdler of the year five times. He failed in his bid to win three gold medals, not qualifying at Barcelona in 1992 or Atlanta in 1996. In advance of Atlanta, Kingdom said, "No one's ever won three before. This would be history."

Kingdom came to Pittsburgh from Vienna, Georgia in the early '80s to play football, but became a track star instead. Pittsburgh was still known as "The City of Champions" when Kingdom came to town, and he fit right into a picture he still praises and cherishes. He never got into any trouble, or triggered any bad publicity, and was a good kid.

Kingdom's boyhood heroes were NFL running backs Tony Dorsett and Walter Payton, not Olympic hurdlers, and they have since been inducted into the Pro Football Hall of Fame. There's a touch of football player in his hurdling style as Kingdom can hit hurdles and not lose his balance or break stride.

"As a football player, he has that aggressiveness that comes from hitting people," said Elbert Kennedy, his coach with the New Image Track Club. "He's got that mentality and it carries over to how he attacks the hurdles.

"He's such a big hurdler, he can hit a hurdle, regroup and still catch people. It's got to do with an attitude that you just can't coach."

Track & field has never captured the interest or hearts of Pittsburgh sports fans or the media, however, and Kingdom's love affair with the city and his university has too often been one-sided, a case of unrequited love. He's more recognized and fussed over in Philadelphia, New York and LA, or even Paris, London and Berlin than he has been in Pittsburgh.

"I'm better known in Europe than Danny Marino," said Kingdom. "I've always been asked why I stayed in Pittsburgh."

Kingdom was always comfortable in Pittsburgh, had good friends there, and chose to remain there. He has lived half his life in

Pittsburgh. He became an adopted son, sort of, maybe a step-son, and Pittsburgh became his hometown. Except for a few occasions, a sports banquet or parade, he was seldom heralded as a hometown hero. Yet the city has been better for his regal presence.

"This is my career," said Kingdom. "That nobody cares can create a lot of frustrations."

He said he still gets more attention and publicity, for instance, when he returns to Miami, where he lived as a youngster, before the Kingdoms came back home to the family farm in Georgia. It was in the Peach State, at a high school near the family homestead, where Roger Kingdom first gained national attention as an athlete of great ability and promise.

Kingdom has cleared more hurdles than he had to in his outstanding career. Some he put there himself, though he seldom suggests as much. More of them were put there by others, some who sought his attention and an association with his international celebrity, some because they didn't know what to do with him, or refused to cater to his every whim. Kingdom was known as a power hurdler, someone who was as apt to run through a hurdle as he was to cleanly clear it, and sometimes he stumbled. No one was faster between the hurdles.

He overcame so many obstacles to continue his success, some physical, some imaginary, but he never stopped running. He didn't seem to ever want to stop running. At times, he seemed to be running away from the real world. He may have stayed too long at the fair.

He reminded me of Wilt Chamberlain, feeling under-appreciated — "No one loves Goliath," Chamberlain once complained — and under-utilized. Kingdom had many athletic gifts, and spoke often, as Chamberlain did, of wanting to be a decathlon performer. He spoke often, as Chamberlain did, of becoming a great football player. Chamberlain also considered becoming a boxer to challenge Muhammad Ali. Kingdom's dad had been a pretty fair baseball player, and Roger thought, as Michael Jordan did, that he might've been quite the baseball player if he had picked that sport. Whereas Jordan toyed with being a golfer, Kingdom, like the Steelers' Jerome Bettis, thought he could be a pro bowler. He is a fair golfer. Great athletes are like that. They're good at most games, and they like to compete, and they dream about what might have been. Don't we all?

In track & field, for instance, Kingdom has cleared seven feet as a high jumper.

Who could blame Roger Kingdom for considering other sports? After all, just prior to our meeting, he had bowled a 640 series at Wissman's Forward Lanes in Squirrel Hill, one of his favorite haunts. He didn't tell me that. His pal, Bob Wissman, whom he calls "Uncle Bob," told me of Roger's latest feat. I had known Wissman, a 75-year-old sportsman, since I was 14, and frequented his bowling lanes and billiards establishment, The Hazelwood Recreation. Kingdom likes to shoot pool and play ping-pong, but Wissman still has his way with him in both games. Even so, Kingdom is truly a man for all seasons.

Roger Kingdom and his bowling, pool-playing, ping-pong playing buddy, Bob Wissman, enjoy each other's company at lunch session at Oxford Athletic Club in Monroeville on Feb. 9, 1999.

From Roger Kingdom photo collection

Roger Kingdom clears another hurdle enroute to first place finish in 60 meter high hurdles at World Indoor Championships in 1989. His time of 7.43 seconds was two-hundredths of a second faster than Colin Jackson, seen at right.

His voice was as rich and warm as Wilt Chamberlain's as well. His memory for dates was uncanny, whether it was for personal highlights, injuries or the birthdays of his grandparents. With his mind, he should have been a better student.

He was religious and prayed regularly, yet he had a 17-year-relationship with Joy Shepherd, whom he met during his student days at Pitt, and they had an eight-year-old daughter, Jierra Brianne, yet they had never married. Joy was back home in New York with their daughter as Roger and I spoke in the winter of 1999. They had parted, but remained cordial and in contact, he was quick to point out. The home they long shared in Monroeville had been up for sale for nearly a year. Roger was residing at an apartment in Oakdale, out in the direction of the Pittsburgh International Airport. Why Oakdale? It seemed to make less sense than Pittsburgh. Why have an apartment if you still own a home?

I first met Roger Kingdom and his loving mother, Christine, in 1983, a year before Kingdom collected his first Olympic gold. I liked him from the start. I had no idea — no one at Pitt did — just how great he was going to be. That was part of his problem at Pitt. He didn't have the early support he sought to bring out the best in him, as a football player, as a track & field man, as a student, as a young fellow looking for love and guidance. Or, at least, that's the way he saw it.

Kingdom keeps coming back to the track. "He gets it mostly from me," said Christine Kingdom. "It's not so much that I'm stubborn as that I don't give up easily."

Kingdom provided a clue as to what was possible in the summer of 1983 when he won the gold medal in the 110-meter high hurdles at the Pan American Games in Indianapolis.

After being a sportswriter in Miami, New York and Pittsburgh, and meeting and interviewing the greatest athletes in all sports, I switched sides and accepted a position as assistant athletic director for sports information at my alma mater, the University of Pittsburgh, just before school started in 1983.

Kingdom was one of the athletes who was a frequent visitor to my office at Pitt Stadium. He liked to visit and talk to many members of the Pitt athletic department. He was an office favorite on one level, a constant challenge to the powers on the level above, where Dr. Edward Bozik, the director of athletics, and Dean Billick, his top assistant, held sway. Kingdom didn't care for either of them, and didn't think they had his best interests at heart.

There was always a power struggle for Kingdom's attention and services during his days as a student-athlete at Pitt. With the football team, the offensive and defensive coaches vied for his services on their side of the ball. Sometimes no one seemed to want him. The men's track & field coaches wanted him, but the women's track & field coach, who also directed an amateur team for men and women in the community, enjoyed a better relationship with Kingdom. That was always a messy situation, and Kingdom was often called on the carpet to find out just where he stood, and whose colors he was wearing in his next track meet.

Kingdom came to my office for kinder counseling. Maybe he liked hearing my stories about Muhammad Ali or Dr. J, or the Steelers and Pirates. There was a couch in my office, and Kingdom would stretch out on it and just talk with me. The couch wasn't long enough for Kingdom, or basketball players like Curtis Aiken or Joey David, or strong enough to hold football behemoths like Bill Fralic and Craig "Ironhead" Heyward, also frequent visitors. Sometimes I felt more like an amateur psychologist than a sports information director, but the most satisfying part of the Pitt job was the interaction with the athletes, and helping them sort out their young lives. I was probably repeating some of the things Pitt coaches and administrators had told me during my own student days there in the early '60s, when I was the sports editor of *The Pitt News* or something Art Rooney or Chuck Noll or Red Holzman or Casey Stengel had said somewhere along the way. During my student days, I often visited the office of Dr. "Red" Carlson, a Hall of Fame basketball coach who was then the head of the student health services. I learned more from Doc Carlson than most of my professors.

You can learn a lot in different places on a college campus, not always at the most likely places.

Kingdom was a handsome, charming rogue. He was ambitious as an athlete, loving as a son, somewhat lazy as a student, and not quite sure of what he really wanted out of life, or Pitt. Kingdom was good company, a great conversationalist, and a convincing story-teller.

His mother told me at that first meeting that, above all, she wanted her son to graduate from the University of Pittsburgh. She wanted him to get his degree.

Kingdom was 35 years old, and would soon be 36 and was still competing in track & field when we met — sometimes at local school-boy competition when coaches would permit him to race — and reflected on his career at the Oxford Athletic Club, formerly the Monroeville Racquet Club, on a rainy, gray Tuesday, February 9, 1999. More than 15 years had passed since our first meeting in my office at Pitt Stadium. It was good to see him.

He was still 14 credits, or a semester's work, shy of his degree in economics at Pitt, still talking about going back to school to finish what he started, still talking about what might have been, about what he wanted to do when he finally hung up his spikes. He'd had a chance to check out a coaching opportunity the year before with the track & field program at the University of Miami, but never applied because he wanted to continue to compete. He had allies there willing to boost his candidacy. Linda Venzon Britton, an assistant athletic director for sports information at UM, had been a member of my staff at Pitt, and tirelessly promoted Roger Kingdom when he was running for the Panthers. Coaching a track & field team in Miami sounds like an idyllic situation, but Kingdom didn't jump at the chance.

Now he was having second thoughts about his decision. When he was a student at Pitt, he talked about being a business executive someday. Now he thought coaching was something he'd enjoy more. "I could still compete," he explained. "I could hug one of my guys or girls, and say 'we won' and feel good about that. That idea appeals to me."

At least it did at that moment of that gray day in February. At the close of our reunion, a five-hour conversation, I reminded Kingdom of something I had said to him during one of our one-on-sessions in his student days.

"You're a con man, Roger Kingdom." I scolded him softly one day in my office at Pitt Stadium. "Just make sure that the last man you con isn't Roger Kingdom."

Roger remembered. He smiled when I repeated the remark. What a smile. What a face. You wanted to adopt him on the spot and take him home for dinner.

But he had other plans. "It's time for me to work out," he said, checking his wristwatch, before we parted company. "I can't believe we've been talking for five hours. I've got to go out to Pitt to work out."

On my way home, I pictured Roger Kingdom in his sweatsuit, prancing about the track at Fitzgerald Field House, looking like a proud stallion. Mixing and talking to anyone else on the track. The warm smile. He was nursing a slight injury, and was passing up a track meet in Montreal he had on his schedule the coming weekend. It was unlikely he'd be putting up any hurdles in his path at Pitt that night. He wasn't up to it.

"It was like falling in love with a girl for the first time."
— Roger Kingdom

There are two moments in sports involving Pitt athletes I will long cherish. I witnessed both in the comfort of my family room at our home in Upper St. Clair. The venue is important because I could behave like a fan, and let my feelings come forth honestly. As a sportswriter, one is conditioned to showing no emotion while watching a sports event. There's an accepted rule that there is no cheering in the press box; it's considered bad form. It can even lead to eviction in some stern places. This is harder for some than others. I have always rooted for Pittsburgh teams and athletes to be successful, with few exceptions, but I can appear as cool as the next guy or gal in the press box. I know how to behave there.

I remember Danny Marino firing a 33-yard touchdown pass to tight end John Brown with just 35 seconds remaining in the game to give Pitt a pulsating, come-from-behind 24-20 victory over Georgia in the 1982 Sugar Bowl. Kingdom was a freshman on that Pitt football team. Kingdom would earn a letter the following season, as a reserve defensive back, before leaving the football team to concentrate on his track career.

"They beat Georgia in '76, too," recalled Kingdom, knowing the pain felt by his friends back home, "when Tony Dorsett led Pitt to the national championship."

I jumped off the couch when Marino connected with Brown and bounced around the room in pure merriment. No one else was in the room.

It was a similar scene in 1984 when I watched Kingdom surprise the world by winning the 110-meter high hurdles at the Olympic Games in Los Angeles. When Kingdom took the lead from the favored Greg Foster, I jumped off the couch and started shouting to my wife, Kathie, in the kitchen. Roger Kingdom, the kid who came to see me in my office at Pitt, was going to get a gold medal in the Olympic Games. It didn't get any better. I couldn't have been happier.

"The Lord reached down and touched me, I'm convinced," recalled Kingdom. "I was talking to The Lord from start to finish, and I just had a burst when he touched me."

Being a bit of a doubting Thomas, I asked Kingdom why he thought the Lord was looking out for him rather than Foster and the rest of the field. Kingdom smiled and shrugged his shoulders. "I have always asked for his help in everything I do," he said.

Kingdom, at age 21, and in only his second season of big-time competition as a hurdler, had set an Olympic record with a 13:20 clocking. I saw him win a second time, four years later in Seoul, but I have no special memory of it.

Roger Kingdom didn't look much different when he was having lunch at the Oxford Athletic Club than from his student days. I had last spoken to him, along with Jerome Bettis, at a Professional Bowling Association tournament in Harmarville two years earlier, and waved to him while passing at a sports banquet a few months earlier. His skull was shaven clean, ala Michael Jordan or Mel Blount, with some dark stubble on his chin. In between, the mustache remained, but was less evident. When I asked him to pose for pictures, he apologized for not shaving. There was still the same glint in his eyes, the same smile and stories on his lips. There was a familiar ring to Roger's reflections. The dreams and schemes sounded familiar, the problems and promises and complaints hadn't changed much.

Kingdom still carried himself with the unmistakable look of the proud athlete. He might have been short on money, but not ego and enthusiasm and dreams. "Yes, I still dream of what I'm going to do," he said with a smile, "and I'm proof that it's good to dream, and that dreams do come true."

Kingdom began by explaining why he picked Pittsburgh in the first place. After all, he could have gone anywhere he wanted in the United States. He had twice been named the Georgia Athlete of the Year, as a junior beating out a senior named Herschel Walker to win such honors.

He had gained national attention and *Parade* magazine mention as a running back in football, and was a state champion in three events in track & field — in the high hurdles, high jump (6 feet, 10 inches), and discus (164 feet) and the anchor man on winning relay teams. He would clear seven feet in the high jump during his days at Pitt.

"I could have gone to Alabama, Auburn, Georgia, Tennessee or Florida State," he said. "There was one thing those cities could never match — that's the view of Pittsburgh when you come through those tunnels. Once I saw the view, I was sold."

This comment reminded me of Simmie Hill, another hometown hero. Hill had been a schoolboy basketball star at Midland High in the 1960s, leading Hank Kuzma's team to a PIAA title. He went to Wichita State University. When I asked him why, he once told me, "You know when you're a kid and you went to see the cowboy movies. Well, they always seemed to be in Wichita." You never know what moves a teenager.

Kingdom continued about his enchantment with the city's unique skyline, framed by its three rivers. "It was like falling in love with a girl for the first time," he said.

"Football was my first love. It was more of a challenge for me than track & field. You had to work with ten other guys. You have their back, and they have your back."

He liked Pitt Stadium, and even knew its history. He had read where it was built (it opened in 1925) to eventually be able to hold 100,000. The foundation could support a second level. "There's a long tradition of outstanding football at Pitt," commented Kingdom. "Oakland is the University of Pittsburgh, as a lot of the alumni see it. You can't beat that. If you have a major game, like when we played North Carolina at Three Rivers, that's fine, but football at Pitt belongs at Pitt Stadium.

"The talk about going to the new stadium where the Steelers will play, or new facilities, is just trying to keep up with the Joneses. They see what Syracuse and Tennessee and Connecticut are doing, and they want something similar.

"I still like to stop at Pitt Stadium or the Field House, when I can find a parking space. I still like to work out there. I like to spend time with Buddy Morris in the weight room."

He remembered when he worked out there at the same time as one of his former Pitt football teammates, Jerry Olsavsky, who was rehabilitating from what some regarded as a career-ending injury at Cleveland. "Jerry definitely has the heart of a champion, and he could inspire anybody with his work ethic," recalled Kingdom.

"I remember when I first came to Pitt, I was shown Heinz Chapel, the Walk of Fame where the athletes are remembered on the sidewalk between the Chapel and the Cathedral of Learning. I remember bouncing in and out of all the Nationality Rooms, and I went as high in the Cathedral of Learning as they'd let us. I loved the

Roger Kingdom kept company with two other Pitt Olympic track & field medal-winners, getting together at campus luncheon with, left to right, Herb Douglas of Hazelwood (bronze medal in long jump in 1948 Games in London) and John Woodruff of Connellsville (gold medal in 800-meters in 1936 Games in Berlin).

Kingdom keeps after Pitt to remind him when the football players are having a reunion. Here he enjoys good times with former teammates from the '80s, left to right, Troy Hill, Bob Lawson and Bill Fralic, along with Nick Bolkovac, who played for Pitt and the Steelers in the early '50s.

view. That's the first thing I do when I'm in a tall building, look out the window.

"I used to do that when I'd visit my agent at the USX Tower. That's why I chose the room I had for two-and-a-half years in Tower C, one of the student dormitories. I could see Downtown Pittsburgh from my room.

"Why did I stay in Pittsburgh? I just loved the city. I've had a love affair with Pittsburgh. Tony Dorsett played here. I roomed with Craig Heyward and Lee McCrae; you think that wasn't a challenge. I still see Julius Dawkins, who was a good friend of mine on the football team. It's hard for me to leave. I wouldn't mind if a job came open here."

He said he had recently visited Heyward in a hospital in Indianapolis following surgery to remove a tumor attached to the brain of the running back of the Colts. "They couldn't get it all," said Kingdom. "It was starting to mess with his vision, and they didn't want to risk that."

McCrae had been an NCAA indoor sprint champion and a world-class runner. He'd come to Pitt from Pemberton, North Carolina. I visited his parents' home in 1983, and know first-hand of his humble beginnings. McCrae and Clinton Davis, a world-class sprinter from Steel Valley High School in Munhall-Homestead, were at Pitt at the same time. Davis did not compete for the Pitt track team, however. "I had two more years to go at Pitt when they were both here," recalled Kingdom. "If we were all running for Pitt, we could have had an NCAA championship team just with the three of us."

He said he had spoken to Steve Pederson, the Pitt director of athletics, about allowing him to return to Pitt as a grad assistant to help with the track teams or in the weight room with the football team, in exchange for student aid to complete the requirements for his degree. That had been five to six weeks earlier. He said he had not heard from Pederson since their conversation. He said he still attended a lot of alumni outings, even when he was not invited, such as golf outings for former football players.

"They tell me they think of me as a track guy," said Kingdom, with a shrug of his wide shoulders.

As a high school senior in Georgia, Kingdom recalled that he received scholarship offers from all the SEC schools. At that time, the SEC had its own letter-of-intent, which was in addition to the national letter of intent.

Kingdom signed an SEC letter-of-intent with Tennessee that meant he could not go anywhere else in the SEC. It was not binding outside the conference, so he was not penalized when he opted for Pitt. He was quite impressed with John Majors, who was the head coach at Tennessee at the time. "He was a great recruiter," Kingdom said. "He sent Bobby Jackson down twice a week to talk with me. Coach Majors flew down a couple of times in a private jet. He made me feel really important.

"Willie Gault, the great trackman, who later played for the Chicago Bears, was my host during my visit to Tennessee. I later broke his record in the hurdles.

"Reggie White was there at the time, too.

"When I competed in the Jeep Superstars competition in Bal Harbour, Florida in 1990, I spent some time with Reggie White. Reggie came up to my room at the hotel and he called Buddy Ryan from my room. Ryan was the head coach at the time with the Philadelphia Eagles. Reggie told me, 'You're the man, Roger. Come up and play football for us. We need you.' I was impressed that he called Coach Ryan right from my room.

"My high school coach, Richard Powell, kept a lot of correspondence from schools away from me. He wanted me to go to an SEC school, somewhere close. He helped me a lot, God bless him. He passed away in 1981. I was brought to Pittsburgh by Jackie Sherrill. I respect the ground he walked on. He treated us as young adults. We didn't have curfews and stuff like that.

"I had an attitude and was impatient to play in my freshman year. One day, Sherrill stared me down, and told me to take a knee. He always believed you should look a man in the eye when you're talking to him, and he did just that.

"He said, 'I understand your frustration. We can't all be freshman all-stars. You can't be like Herschel Walker.' He called out names, one after another, who had to wait their turn to play, who turned out to be great. He mentioned Danny Marino, among others. I told him I felt good about being there, and I said, 'Coach, you'll never have any problems with me.'

"After that, I hit Caesar Aldisert with a block to spring Bill Beach in a spring drill. Sherrill chased after me and he grabbed me and picked me up and hugged me. He was praising me for a big hit. If I could have transferred to Texas A&M when he went there — heck, I didn't have the grades — I'd have gone with him. Sherrill let me skip spring drills at times to work on track. Foge Fazio was never in favor of that when he took over. He wanted me to be completely devoted to football. He told me I had to be dedicated to football year-round. I was running first team as a defensive safety for awhile, but I was ten minutes late for a practice, and I was put back behind everybody at my position. Tommy Flynn got in there, and I was never going to get my job back. That's when I decided to give up football for track. I could have more to say about competing in track. You're more on your own in track; you can show what you can do."

"To all of you young people in the audience, be all that you can be. Share your talent, determination and leadership, and you will leave a legacy."
— Ron Peduzzi,
Former principal at
Norwin High School

"Perseverance is the key."
— Roger Kingdom

For every Roger Kingdom in sports there is a Clinton Davis. Kingdom mentioned that he had just spent some time with Clinton Davis. Kingdom said that Davis was in charge of the shipping dock at the new Wal-Mart in North Versailles. "He's doing pretty good," said Kingdom. "He has a wife and four kids, and they're fine."

I'd forgotten about Clinton Davis, but as Kingdom related what had happened to the one-time track & field phenom, it had a familiar ring to it. "He was in a bad car accident," said Kingdom. "He broke one leg and crushed the other one. He was 19 or 20 at the time, getting ready for the Olympics in 1984. As a 17-year-old in high school, he was beating senior sprinters in national track meets.

"He could've gone anywhere in the country on a track scholarship. During his visit to Southern Cal, he went to O.J. Simpson's house.

"He was kinda rushing somewhere in his car one day in McKees Rocks," continued Kingdom. "He was going too fast for conditions, but he wasn't speeding. He went to make a turn and he slid into a bridge embankment. He was rushed to the emergency room at Allegheny General Hospital with multiple injuries."

Kingdom said he visited Davis at the hospital, and it really hit him hard. "When I left the hospital, I went across the street into West Park, and I just ran around there to burn off the anxiety I felt," said Kingdom. "I just ran and ran.

"There were bad signs before this that Clinton Davis didn't see that should have made him more careful, more cautious. There was a chain of events, but he didn't get the picture. That whole spring he wasn't running well. We later learned he had an '82 Saab in 1984, and he had a fender bender accident. Then his house burnt down. Everything was lost but his Bible, which was singed on the edges. That chain of events all occurred in a two-to-three month period.

"That was the end of his bid to make the Olympic team. That was the end of his track career period. He was lucky to be able to walk again. At the same time, I was an optimist about my chances of making the team. I was thinking about it all the time, but I also recognized that I knew that I had to go out and work for it."

I mentioned to Kingdom that our friend, Herb Douglas, had once talked to me about how many athletes were devastated when they didn't make the Olympic team, and that some never got over the disappointment.

"It's crushed so many people, I know," Kingdom came back. "You sacrifice four years of preparation, maybe more, and then you miss. You fall short. You miss it. Personally, I think you have to keep chasing your dream. Perseverance is the key. Some don't make it the first two times they try, but make it on the third try. That's perseverance.

"Mike Connelly, the long jumper, is a perfect example. He made it in 1984, and he didn't win it. Willie Banks was the favorite, but an unknown named Al Joyner won it. Connelly didn't make the team the next time. He didn't give up. He made the team again in 1992 and won it. I was also inspired by Edwin Moses, who stayed at it as long as he did, about 35 or 36, and was still as good as anybody in the 400 meter hurdles. He twice won the gold medal and also the bronze in his event in the Olympic Games. He dominated his event, winning 122 straight times. He proved that if you stayed in shape, mentally and physically, you could continue to compete at what was considered an advanced age. That's what keeps me going.

"People's respect is what motivates me more than anything. When you come see me run, you want to see a good race. I want to give you a good show. I'm a performer, and I love to perform for you."

When he won the Dapper Dan Man of the Year Award in 1989, he expressed his sentiments about his adopted hometown.

"The award feels good because it's a Pittsburgh award," Kingdom said. "I compete all over the world and I try to represent Pittsburgh well. People see me race and ask, 'Where is Roger Kingdom from?' It makes me feel good when they associate me with Pittsburgh. I'm from a little town in Georgia, but I consider Pittsburgh my home."

Michael F. Fabus/Pittsburgh Steelers

Roger Kingdom was cheered by the crowd at Pittsburgh Steelers game at Three Rivers Stadium upon return from gold medal-winning effort in 110-meter hurdles at the 1988 Olympic Games in Seoul, South Korea.

Billy Conn
"The Pittsburgh Kid"

"Billy was not meant to be in public life."
— Mary Louise Conn

Billy Conn can rest assured that his family is still fighting for his honor and glory. The family fealty is unwavering. Conn, a world champion boxer back in the late '30s and early '40s who helped put Pittsburgh on the sports map, is best known for nearly winning the heavyweight title from the great Joe Louis.

He lacked a knockout punch and patience, and he was Irish, otherwise he might have ruled the boxing world. As it was, he did win the light heavyweight boxing title in 1939 and kept the crown until 1941.

The Conns do not want anyone to forget that their man, William David Conn, was the biggest, toughest and most popular Pittsburgh sports hero of his time. That's all-time, as far as the Conns are concerned.

He was a handsome, dark-haired, brutish, hard-hitting hometown hero, an even six feet, but bigger than the Steelers and Pirates in those days. He was cocky and strident, for sure, but he could do no wrong with his family and followers. He came out of a poor neighborhood in East Liberty to steal the hearts of fight fans and women everywhere with his immense boxing skills, speed, courage and Hollywood looks.

His dark Irish eyes positively danced during his heyday. They even made a movie about his life, called "The Pittsburgh Kid," and he played himself. A poster from that movie is on display in the Conn's family room.

His picture was plastered on the wall of every bar in Pittsburgh back then, and can still be seen in some, like Conley's in Lawrenceville. He was even portrayed on a mural, along with two other local fight game favorites, Harry Greb and Fritzie Zivic, on the wall of Pete Coyne's Irish Pub in Oakland, just below the Irish Club. He was a hero at the Hibernian Club in my hometown of Hazelwood.

There was a boxing show somewhere every week in the Pittsburgh area in Conn's era. Boxers fought frequently in those days. The purses weren't that big and boxers had to be active to make a living at it. Then, too, the best fighters fought the best fighters, most of the time. And there were some rivals who would fight each other as many as five and six times. They had a primal passion for combat, and there were some absolute backyard brawls and feuds.

Conn, for instance, fought Teddy Movan of McKeesport five times (Conn won the last two after two defeats and a draw). No

BILLY CONN

Marty Wolfson

ballplayer was ever bigger than Billy Conn in the eyes of Pittsburgh sports fans. There was no television when Conn was a celebrity. Newspapers and radio ruled the day. The prize money paled by comparison to today. Even so, Conn once figured that he'd made about a million dollars during his fighting days.

After his boxing days were over, important people everywhere liked to keep company and have their pictures taken with Billy Conn. He was a big shot in New York. He was a big shot in San Francisco. He was a big shot and paid to shake hands with customers at the Stardust Hotel & Casino in Las Vegas. He rubbed shoulders with giants.

Joe Louis and Billy Conn became friends and they became, as time passed, two of the most beloved sports figures in this country. They were routinely seen with U.S. Presidents, showbiz and sports celebrities.

A friend once arranged for Conn to meet President George Bush at a social event. "Be sure to address him as Mister President," the friend kept telling Conn. When it came Conn's turn in the receiving line, however, Conn offered a firm hand and a bright smile and said, "Hi, George." And President Bush, not missing a beat, replied, "Hi, Billy? How are you?"

Before long, Conn was heard to say, "George, I'm going to tell you how to run this country..."

Pittsburghers boasted that Billy Conn was one of their own, indeed, a favorite son. For better or worse, he was always his own man.

Billy was 75 when he died May 29, 1993 after a 10-month stay at the Veterans Affairs Medical Center (still referred to as the VA Hospital), the one in Oakland, overlooking Pitt Stadium. In his last months, Billy didn't recognize the best of friends. It was a sad time for oldtimers in Pittsburgh who remembered him as a battling young man who once carried their banner so brilliantly.

His name still shows up in boxing books and magazines as one of the Top 50 fighters of all time. His family feels that he's too often overlooked or forgotten in Pittsburgh, where his image matters most. It's a popular complaint with the families of many local sports personalities of the past.

Roy McHugh and Pat Livingston, both former sports editors of *The Pittsburgh Press*, point out that Pittsburgh first merited the nickname of "City of Champions" during a ten-year span from 1934 to 1944 when six fighters from the Pittsburgh area were champions of the world.

There were never more than three at the same time, but they included Conn, Teddy Yarosz, Sammy Angott, Fritzie Zivic, Billy Soose and Jackie Wilson. In the same decade, Pittsburgh had other top-notch fighters: Charley Burley, Al Quaill, Harry Bobo and Zivic's brothers, Pete, Joe and Jack, to name a few.

It was often referred to as "the golden age of boxing" in Pittsburgh. Earlier, there were great boxers from the area such as

Harry Greb, a world champion known as "The Pittsburgh Windmill," who grew up in Garfield and was an idol of Conn from the neighboring community in the East End. Then, too, there were champion boxers like George Chip and Frank Klaus.

Spending an evening with members of the Conn family — his wife of 52 years, Mary Louise, and sons, Tim, and Billy Jr. — was like a scene out of a movie, an opening act in a tragicomedy or, at least, the stuff of sitcoms. We sat around and talked about Billy Conn, at least that was the idea.

It was a sit-Conn, for sure, on a Wednesday night, February 10, 1999, a rare winter's day in Pittsburgh when the sun broke through the clouds and warmed the sidewalks of Squirrel Hill, where the Conns have long resided.

Mary Louise lives, along with her middle son, Billy Jr., namesake of the great boxer, on the second and third floors of an attractive duplex home at the north end of Murray Avenue. She had moved there in March of 1998, figuring their former home had become too big for their current needs. They had previously lived on Denniston Street in Squirrel Hill. Billy Conn lived most of his life in Squirrel Hill, and loved to dine at the old Weinstein's Restaurant with friends.

After four frenetic hours in their delightful company, a visitor feels like he has been sparring four rounds with the ghosts of Billy Conn, Harry Greb and Fritzie Zivic. You come away with some scars, but also with a smile on your face. It was so much fun, we got together a second time. These are real people. This is the way you felt when you had a spaghetti dinner with Danny Marino's family in their South Oakland home in his junior season at Pitt. Or when you twice visited Milene and Bill Mazeroski in their home along farm fields in Greensburg.

The Conns are so passionate about their husband and father, respectively, that they zealously scrap for air time. It's not always fair. One starts to tell a tale about Billy Conn, and the other butts in and interjects an additional item, or something someone once said, or an anecdote about Billy or his fabled father-in-law, "Greenfield Jimmy" Smith, or something that had nothing to do with the discussion topic. The boys are swapping stories originally related to them by "Dad" and "Pap," and they remember them well. They're a positive joy. They never run out of steam or stories. Boom-boom-boom. Get the idea?

The Irish prefer a good argument to a good conversation, or they figure they are one and the same.

"Isn't this supposed to be about Billy Conn?" snaps a perplexed Mary Louise at one point in the free-for-all. "Let Jim ask the questions..."

It's like being in a gym where someone is banging into the big bag, while two others are working out simultaneously on speed bags nearby, skipping rope with one hand and tattooing the small black bag with the other hand. "Hey, guys, let me talk," begs Mary Louise, exasperated by the rat-a-tat-tat discussion.

"Hold on," Tim retaliates, "I just wanted to tell him..."

"This is about Dad, isn't it?" comes back Billy Jr. "How about the time...?"

"Can I get back to my story?" cries Mary Louise.

"Yeah, Mom, you can tell it best," yields Tim. "Why don't you...? He's looking for stories..."

"Hold on...," blurts Billy Jr.

It's spirited, combative, festive, a true Irish wake that would have delighted Billy Conn or his best friend, Art Rooney, the late owner and patriarch of the Pittsburgh Steelers. All that was missing was cigar smoke. Art Rooney, by the way, was Tim Conn's godfather.

For the record, Billy Conn wasn't everybody's cup of tea or brand of beer. Conn could be churlish, argumentative, a bit of a bully, though Mary Louise insists he went out of his way to avoid a spat, and would defend him to the death. Some thought he had a huge chip on his shoulders. Let's just say he was easily annoyed. That's why he fought in the first place.

His detractors describe him as fast with his hands in a fight, but slow with his hands when it came time to reach for his wallet. They called Conn "America's guest" derisively. He only offered complimentary drinks when someone else was picking up the tab. Be sure to duck if you tell that to his wife or kids.

His name and remarks were always popping up in the daily sports column of Al Abrams, the sports editor of the *Pittsburgh Post-Gazette*. Mary Louise once telephoned Abrams to complain about him constantly quoting her husband saying words like "dem" and "dose" instead of "them" and "those" in his column. "To me," Abrams said in his own defense, "he's a Damon Runyan character, and I want to portray him like that."

She was even more incensed when Abrams reported that Billy Conn "went ga-ga" over singer Phyllis McGuire when she and her sisters were singing at The New Arena Club in downtown Pittsburgh.

"I'll give you ga-ga," she scolded Billy when she next saw him, flashing a fist of her own. *Gaga*, by the way, is from a French word for foolish old man.

Mary Louise is still a looker, still fiesty, even well into her 70s. "Don't put my age in there! Just say I'm 39," she firmly directed me. She's fun to be with, a natural. She was wearing form-fitting black slacks and a black jersey top, gold earrings, full makeup and a warm smile. She kept her hair blonde. Her figure and sense of humor remained intact. On another visit, she wore a light blue v-neck sweater and was positively smashing. Mary Louise looked after me like I was a rich uncle, keeping me contented with Diet Cokes, peanuts, corn curls and, eventually, a share of the pork chop dinner she prepared for herself and the boys. Being Irish didn't hurt in being welcomed in their company. They even offered critical thoughts about a few of Pittsburgh's icons, but that was off the record. Before long, you felt like family, and you were thinking about your own crazy

Jim O'Brien

Two of Billy Conn's three sons, Bill and Tim, and his wife, Mary Louise, were lots of fun in reflecting on "The Pittsbugh Kid" at home in Squirrel Hill. The room is like a Boxing Hall of Fame.

family and how they once talked with the same pace and fury as the Conns.

"I hope these photos turn out OK," she said more than once. "I'd hate to look good in the photos from my early days, and look like a haggard old woman now. Look after me, Jim. Be kind."

It was funny, informative and, quite often, difficult to comprehend. Taking notes could not have been more difficult if I had been wearing boxing gloves. And Tim handed me a huge scrapbook of newspaper clippings that felt as if someone had shoved a medicine ball into my belly. Mary Louise praised Tim for the job he had done in restoring the scrapbook to its current cleaned-up state. It was great to see how much Mary Louise still loved her late husband — he could be a difficult man in or out of the ring — and how her boys were still banging the drum for the old man.

He was a great boxer, a great provider, and he cared deeply about them all, even if he didn't display it much publicly. "He wasn't meant to be a family man," Mary Louise allowed more than once. "He wasn't meant to be a celebrity. He was somewhat shy, and wanted to be left alone. Billy was not meant to be in public life."

They still have a room, a family room, devoted to Billy Conn's career and achievements. There aren't as many photos and framed letters from Presidents and political leaders as there were in the last house — which once prompted *Sports Illustrated's* ace writer Frank Deford to declare it the best collection of boxing photos he'd ever come across. DeFord wrote a classic article in *SI* about Billy and Mary Louise Conn called "The Boxer and the Blonde." A copy of the article, which first appeared in June of 1985, was framed on a wall just outside the Conn's cramped kitchen. Deford has told other writers that the story attracted more mail than any other piece in the magazine's history.

"I'm as fond of that story as any I've ever done," said Deford for a story written by Gene Collier on the occasion of Conn's death that appeared in the *Pittsburgh Post-Gazette*.

"The thing about that story was the love interest," said Deford. "It was really two love stories. His wife, the whole family really, and his mother. His mother was dying when he was falling in love and trying to win the heavyweight championship of the world while the world was falling apart. You just can't scare up that kind of thing. Against the whole tapestry of history, and of boxing, it was so compelling."

Conn's mother, Maggie McFarland Conn, died in 1941, just after Billy departed Pittsburgh for the Louis fight in New York. On parting, he told his mother, "The next time I see you, I'll be heavyweight champion of the world." To which she said, "The next time I see you will be in paradise."

Talking about his mother once, Billy said, "She was really from the ol' sod. She came over third-class steerage from the old country." His father, William Robert Conn — note they had different middle names — was born in Pittsburgh, and worked 40 years as a steamfitter at Westinghouse Electric Corporation.

Billy Conn is joined in May, 1946 at training camp in Pompton Lake, N.J. prior to his second championship fight with Joe Louis by former heavyweight boxing champions, James J. Braddock, left, and Jack Dempsey.

Champions' dinner gathering includes, left to right, Billy Conn and son, Tim, Rocky Marciano, Jack Cargo, Mary Louise Conn and Joe Louis.

There are photos everywhere in the four-bedroom complex, even in the stairway leading up to the third-floor attic retreat of Billy Jr., of some of the greatest boxers ever to grace the ring world, especially Pittsburgh favorites like Zivic and Greb, but also Sugar Ray Robinson, Joe Louis, Rocky Marciano, Jack Dempsey, James J. Braddock, Max Schmelling, Barney Ross, Sonny Liston, Rocky Graziano and Tony Canzoneri and you name your favorite celebrity.

"My father and Billy both loved Harry Greb," said Mary Louise, as we scanned the photos.

They tested me on identifying individuals in some of the photos. I made a breakthrough with my hosts when I correctly identified a lineup in one photograph, from left to right, Billy Conn, Craig Morton, Bob Mathias, Hank Stram, Keith Morris (a press representative from *Sports Illustrated*), Carl Eller, Billie Jean King and Tony Kubek. Tim said they couldn't remember Keith Morris until I mentioned his name.

The biggest photo in the room shows Conn chin to chin and nose-to-famous-nose with comedian Bob Hope. "Here's where I can tell you something that only two other sportswriters in Pittsburgh would know," I boasted.

"In his early days, Bob Hope fought professionally under the name of Packy East in Cleveland."

"Yeah, Roy McHugh told us that," said Tim Conn.

Yeah, I was right on both counts. Myron Cope, a sportscaster who grew up in Squirrel Hill, would also have been able to offer the information about Hope's boxing background.

Conn enjoyed the company of Bob Hope, Frank Sinatra, Jimmy Durante and Jayne Mansfield ("she was so big she hurt me when she sat on my lap," he told Mary Louise), as well as John F. Kennedy and Robert Kennedy, George Bush and Ronald Reagan, and they all pop up, along with personally signed correspondence which the Conns keep on display. There is a signed photo to Billy Conn from Stan Musial and others showing Billy with Joe DiMaggio and Bob Feller at his side. It's a mini-Hall of Fame and a great backdrop for a discussion about "The Pittsburgh Kid" with his kids and the ever-loyal lady in his life.

Pictures of Mary Louise in bathing suits at the beach with husband Billy in their prime are reminders of what a handsome couple they were.

There are also pictures of her family, including her youngest son, Michael, 46, a successful executive at Morgan, Stanley, Dean Witter brokerage house in the World Trade Center in New York City. "He's my forgotten son," Mary Louise allowed. She misses Michael not being around like her other two sons.

There are many photos of her daughter, Suzanne Robinson, who had died of breast cancer six years earlier at age 45. There's still a hole in the heart of the family over Suzanne's difficult illness and passing. She was an attractive woman and Mary Louise proudly

"The Boxer and the Blonde" frolic at Atlantic City

"Held in abiding affection, Billy Conn was to a generation of Pittsburgh kids, the symbol of excitement and romance."
— Phil Musick
The Pittsburgh Press

pulled framed photos off mantles and such to show me. "Don't you think she has Billy's looks?" she asked. There's also a photo gallery of grandchildren and relatives.

There's a signed portrait of Bishop Fulton J. Sheen ("To Billy Conn, God love you, Bishop Fulton J. Sheen").

Bishop Sheen of Catholic University in Washington D.C. had a nationally-popular TV show back in the '50s and '60s called "Life Is Worth Living." Bishop Sheen was a face from my childhood. I remembered those deep-set, dark steely eyes, the winning smile, and his scribblings on a chalkboard to emphasize his lesson points. Talk about TV from another era. He was even better than Billy Graham, the evangelist not the boxer from New York City, or so we thought at St. Stephen's Grade School.

"Billy just loved Bishop Sheen," said Mary Louise. "He never asked anyone for autographs, but he got one from Bishop Sheen, and we all treasured this."

Billy Conn Jr. was 54 years old at the time of our visit, but he had boyish good looks, brown curls falling on his forehead, a bit of "The Dead End Kids" in his mug and demeanor. He was a dead ringer, I thought, for Dick McGuire of the New York Knicks organization, the older brother of Al McGuire and a member of the Basketball Hall of Fame. Billy Jr. doesn't look that much like his dad, but he carries himself with the same take-your-best-shot surly facade, leading with his chin. His dad liked to loaf and so does Billy Jr. He has worked as a sales rep for a local brewery. "Billy never wanted any of his sons to be named after him," said Mary Louise. "He said it wouldn't be good for him, that it would scar him for life."

I hadn't taken a seat in the Billy Conn Memorial Room when his namesake started peppering me with lead left jabs, just to feel me out.

"Do you listen to the sports talk shows here?" began Billy Jr. "They had a show last week where the callers were encouraged to call in and vote for the greatest athletes in the history of Pittsburgh.

"Of course, Roberto Clemente was mentioned. So was Mario Lemieux, which is fine. Someone said Honus Wagner. But there must be a lot of Penguins fans who listen to this show. People are mentioning former Penguins you never heard of. Like Dave Burrows. Did you ever hear of him? (A positive nod did not deter Conn from continuing his complaint.) Some of the names were insane. They're trying to come up with a top ten. Rocky Bleier was mentioned. That's OK. Everybody liked him.

"But nobody mentioned Dad. That's nonsense. He's the No. 1 guy. He was 21 when he won the light-heavyweight title. He was the toast of the town. That was in 1939. The Steelers were just starting — Pitt football was bigger than pro football here in those days — and the Pirates weren't drawing that well.

"Boxing was the No. 1 sport in Pittsburgh. If you were a boxer, you were the big star," Billy Conn Jr. continued. "New York was No. 1 in boxing. And thanks to Dad, Pittsburgh was No. 2.

80

"Billy Conn was the No. 1 guy here. He wasn't just a boxer, he was a star. He looked like a matinee idol. Look at that picture...does that look like a boxer? If you're going to talk about charisma, Billy Conn had that and more."

Tim Conn, 56, was also looking after his dad. A few weeks earlier, the Saturday sports section of the *Pittsburgh Post-Gazette* carried a letter-to-the-editor written by one Tim Conn of Point Breeze. It read:

"The original intention of the Dapper Dan award was given 'to the athlete who did the most to publicize the City of Pittsburgh during the year.' This is the inscription that was on the first award given in 1939 to my father, boxer Billy Conn. He was a two-time winner.

"Unless the original intention of the award has changed over the years, I can see no reason that Joe Paterno should be so honored. He has done nothing that I know of to bring attention to Pittsburgh.

"I am sure there's an athlete whose accomplishments were more in tune with the original purpose of the award."

"He can run, but he can't hide."
— Joe Louis

Some background on Billy Conn is called for here so younger readers can better appreciate how big a name he was in sports, and so older readers are reminded of the magic moments.

He was born William David Conn on October 8, 1917 in East Liberty. There's a Giant Eagle store standing where his home at 6327 Shakespeare Street once stood, not far from the present-day Reizenstein Elementary School and Mellon Park. Aurelia Street is the nearest street to his old home that remains.

He began his pro boxing career in 1934. He never fought as an amateur. He was advised to go straight to pro boxing by his trainer and manager Johnny Ray, a former boxer.

Ray had a solid reputation in local boxing circles. Ray's most memorable bouts were against a deadly rival from the South Side, Johnny Kirk. When they fought, the police department always assigned extra officers to keep order, but they weren't always successful in maintaining peace.

Conn caught Ray's attention in the first place because Billy was a tough street guy who could lick all the kids who hung out, or loafed, at the neighboring drug store. When the youngster started turning up, at age 14, at a gym that was Ray's hangout on Penn Avenue, putting on gloves and sparring anyone available, Ray began to see possibilities in this scrawny, but game kid. There was a toughness about him that appealed to Ray.

He adopted him as his favorite prospect. In a few years, Conn was fighting Joe Louis for the world's heavyweight championship and came within a mental lapse of winning it.

"My dad wanted to be a boxer after his dad took him to see where he worked at Westinghouse Electric out at their big plant in East Pittsburgh, right there in the Turtle Creek Valley," said Tim Conn. "Their family was real poor. 'You're going to spend the rest of your life working in the mill,' his dad warned him. That put a fright in my dad."

Conn was a lightweight when he started, but gradually gained weight that put him in Louis' class, or close to it. He fought professionally weighing from 135 to 187 pounds. Ray trained him for over a year before Conn, at age 16, had his first four-round prelim on a fight card in Fairmont, West Virginia. He lost a decision to a fellow named Dick Woodward. The purse was a whopping $2.50 — that's right, $2.50 — and Johnny Ray gave his fighter 50 cents for his share. "Where's the rest of the money?" demanded Conn. To which Ray responded, "You ate, didn't you? Plus, you lost."

Ray thought it was a waste of time to fight amateurs, believing Conn couldn't learn anything fighting amateurs, and he convinced Conn that he needn't worry about losing bouts in the beginning. "It's not important until you get good," Ray told Conn. "Right now, you've got to learn how to fight."

Conn's first good payday was $2,085.50 when he won a close decision over Fritzie Zivic. That was on Dec. 28, 1936 at Duquesne Gardens. There were 5,163 in attendance. Zivic's take was $2,502.60, according to newspaper accounts.

"Dad wanted to get paid in $20 bills," said Tim during my visit to his mother's apartment, "because it would seem bigger. He said you could buy 20 good hamburgers for a buck back then. A new Chevy for $800. So it was good money. They had to turn away people."

A good gate at a boxing show in those days was $10,000, and it had to be split among the fighters, trainers, managers, officials, promoters, and probably some promotion-friendly sportswriters. So it wasn't easy for anybody to make a buck.

Ray's real name was Harry Pitler; he was the brother of Jake Pitler, a coach with the Brooklyn Dodgers. It was better back then to be Irish rather than Jewish in boxing circles, so Harry Pitler adopted the name of Johnny Ray. It was not uncommon for athletes, especially boxers, to change their names in those days. Some changed their names and ethnic identity frequently, according to the ethnic makeup of the community where the fight was staged, to help sell tickets.

The first time Ray spotted Conn in the gym, he reportedly said, "I hear you're a thief." To which Billy came back, "What's here worth stealing?" Ray had Conn sweep the gym after workouts to keep him from getting a big head. Conn lost six of 18 fights in his first year, fighting mostly in Pittsburgh, at Motor Square Garden in East Liberty and Duquesne Gardens in Oakland.

He also boxed in Pittsburgh at Hickey Field in Millvale, Greenlee Field in the Hill District, Forbes Field in Oakland, North Side Arena,

> **"Billy Conn was ours, a cocky Irish kid with hands and a grin that were both quicksilver."**
> — Phil Musick
> *The Pittsburgh Press*

Boxing figures at Eagles Rest Training Camp in Shaler in September, 1939, included, left to right, Billy Marquart, Rich Gregory, Emil Josephs, Glenn Lee, Barney McGinley, Billy Conn, Art Rooney, Sammy Angott, Fred Apostoli and Jimmy Leto.

Art Rooney is flanked by the Conn brothers, Jackie, left, and Billy, at Eagles Rest Training Camp.

Kissing and making up once again were Billy Conn and his fiesty father-in-law, "Greenfield Jimmy" Smith.

From the Billy Conn family collection

Billy Conn

the Armory in East Liberty, South Side Market House and the Islam Grotto on the North Side.

He also fought in places like Parkersburg, Wheeling and Johnstown. He was undefeated in 19 bouts in his second year, including a decision over Fritzie Zivic of Lawrenceville. That victory came on December 28, 1936.

He defeated four other ex-champions in 1937: Babe Risko, Vince Dundee, Teddy Yarosz of Monaca and Young Corbett III. Conn won the world light heavyweight title, vacated when John Henry Lewis retired, with a 15-round decision over Melio Bettina on July 13, 1939 at New York's Madison Square Garden. Conn also won the rematch later that year, and twice defended his title with 15-round decisions over Gus Lesnevich.

Lesnevich and Bettina were two of five other former title-holders that Conn beat, including Fred Apostoli, in one of Conn's toughest fights, Solly Krieger and Tony Zale. Some of those were wars.

From 1935 through 1937, Conn had 24 consecutive fights in Pittsburgh before he fought in San Francisco. Then he had seven more fights in Pittsburgh before returning to San Francisco.

"He seems like a clean-cut fellow."
— Opponent Vince Dundee

Checking through clippings in the Conn scrapbook, there were mentions of opponents like Red Bruce, "a Hill colored boy," and Honey Boy Jones, "a local colored boy," in a story by Havey Boyle, and Oscar Manning, "a colored boy from Jersey," in a story by Bert P. Taggert. It was a different era, for sure.

Other nuggets mined from the family's scrapbook:

Jake Mintz, who later managed and promoted heavyweight Ezzard Charles of Cincinnati, and matched him with Archie Moore in a classic title fight at Forbes Field, promoted some of Conn's fights.

Conn was cited for having good manners in the ring by one of his opponents, Vince Dundee. "He kept calling me 'Mr. Dundee' throughout the fight," said Dundee, "and he seems like a clean-cut fellow. I wish him well."

Interestingly, Conn and Fritzie Zivic both had reputations as mischievous but fairly good guys outside the ring. They could be downright nasty in the ring. Zivic was notorious for punching on the break, and for scraping the laces of his gloves across the face of his foe. In short, he was a dirty whatever-it-takes fighter.

The Pittsburgh sports writers got on the bandwagon early in Conn's career, and predicted great things for him. Conn could do nothing wrong, as far as the writers were concerned. Often, they wrote that Ray may have put the young Conn in against an opponent who

John Gamble of Coraopolis,left, a fight fan who promoted public memorial in honor of Billy Conn, joined Tim Conn at street-naming in Oakland on June 18, 1998.

Billy Conn is flanked by boxing friends, Bunny Buntag, left, and Natie Leff.

One of Billy Conn's dearest friends and fans was Art Rooney, seen in his Steelers office in the early '80s. Rooney's collection of sports photos now fill the walls of a library that memorializes him at Three Rivers Stadium. They were checking out photo from first Conn-Louis championship fight.

was too experienced and rugged for him, and feared the worst, but then they'd credit Ray afterward for doing such a great job of bringing Conn along wisely.

Conn started out under the guidance of Johnny Ray and Barney McGinley, father of Jack McGinley, a long-time minority partner with the Rooneys in the ownership of the Steelers, and one of the grand gentlemen in the sports world.

Conn grew from a lightweight to the heavyweight ranks, and was always drinking milk shakes, trying to put on weight.

Ray often cried out to Conn from ringside to deliver the "Jo-Jo punch" — a left hook to the stomach and a right cross to the head.

Conn started out at Sacred Heart School in the East End and attended the adjoining Sacred Heart Catholic Church. He and the nuns were seldom on the best of terms. Even so, his religion was important to him, and Father Coughlin was his favorite radio personality and Bishop Sheen, of course, his favorite TV personality.

Conn's father was Irish, his mother English. In his teen years as a fighter, Billy turned over most of his purses to his mother. He was the oldest of five children, and had two brothers and two sisters. One of his brothers, Jackie, was also a fair club fighter.

"They used to have some awful scraps in the gyms and bars around town," said Tim. "One time when they were about to begin a sparring session at Eagle's Rest, a fight camp out in Shaler, Uncle Jackie sucker-punched Dad before he was ready. Dad chased Uncle Jackie down the highway. They were running with their boxing gear on past the cars. What a sight they must have been."

Billy and Jackie fought an exhibition once that was refereed by the great former light heavyweight champion, Georges Carpentier.

Other big sports news in Pittsburgh in 1939, the year Conn fought Louis the first time, was the resignation of Jock Sutherland as the football coach of the highly-successful Pitt team because of differences with Chancellor Bowman over University commitment to the program.

Conn was a football fan, but his favorite team was Notre Dame. He was talented as an artist, and once sent a drawing he'd done of Knute Rockne to the Notre Dame coach and it was returned to him from South Bend with the coach's signature on it.

Asked why he didn't pursue a career as an artist, Conn said he liked boxing better.

His first main bout was outdoors at Greenlee Field, the home field for the Pittsburgh Crawfords of the Negro Baseball League. His first appearance at Madison Square Garden was a narrow victory over Fred Apostoli on January 6, 1939. Conn's face was all cut up and black and blue after that bout, and he hardly looked like a winner when pictured in the next day's newspapers. That fight drew 11,000 fans, and about 300 Pittsburghers made the trip to root for their hometown favorite.

Not since the days of Harry Greb had so many Pittsburghers followed a local fighter to New York. And they'd be back in greater numbers for future fights.

The New York press went wild for Conn, and predicted great things for him, saying he'd surely be fighting Joe Louis for the crown someday.

"If he hadn't been Irish, he would have won."
— Caswell Adams,
N.Y. Herald-Tribune

Billy Conn challenged Joe Louis for the heavyweight title on June 18, 1941, in a scheduled 15-rounder before 54,486 fans at the Polo Grounds. An estimated 6,000 fans from Pittsburgh traveled to New York to cheer on Conn. He was 23 years old and weighed in at 174½ pounds compared to Louis, who was 27 and weighed 199 pounds. Some reports say Conn weighed only 169 pounds. In any case, it would be a boxer versus a puncher. Legendary sports columnist Grantland Rice said it was one of the finest fights he ever covered.

Conn gave Louis a lot of trouble right from the start, moving and sticking, in and out, quickly, flashing his left jab, and retreating. He danced away from Louis' punches and landed a few speedy blows when Louis was off-guard. After 12 rounds, Conn was ahead on two scorecards, even on the other.

Trainer Jack Blackburn in Louis' corner told his fighter after 12 rounds, "You've got to knock him out to win."

Conn couldn't be satisfied to stick and run, or to stay away from Louis the last three rounds, cover up, hold and win a decision. He wanted to knock out Louis. So he got bolder and more aggressive and came after Louis. When Louis tagged him a few times, instead of escaping, Conn kept coming and fought back.

It was just what Joe Louis needed to pull the fight out of the flames. Here's a report on that fateful 13th round:

"Conn sent a left and a right to the head and Louis sent a left to the face. Conn hooked a left to the body and then brought the same hand to the head. Joe smashed two rights to the chin and body and exchanged lefts and rights to the body. Conn came back to outfight Louis in a fierce exchange. Louis nailed Conn with a right to the chin and sent Conn's head back with another right uppercut. Louis hurt Conn with another right to the jaw. Louis dropped Conn with a right to the jaw and Billy was kayoed. The time was 2:58."

After the fight, Conn was reported to have said in the locker room, "I lost. So what?"

A scheduled rematch was postponed due to family problems that demanded Conn's attention. Next, Conn broke his left hand — in a family dispute that's a legendary story in itself — which delayed the rematch until the end of World War II.

Both men went into the military service, mostly entertaining troops with exhibitions and appearances. The United States was battling Germany in Europe and Japan in the Pacific.

Five years later, the war was over, and Conn and Louis finally met again in a rematch at Yankee Stadium. Before the fight, Louis said of Conn, "He can run, but he can't hide." The Louis remark has gone down in history. It's in popular songs still heard these days, and it's an oft-repeated phrase. The rematch was held on June 19, 1946. The second time around wasn't much to look at. This time the bout was a farce. Conn hardly connected on a punch. Conn was KOd in the 8th round.

Conn fought only two legitimate bouts after that before he retired. He won both by knockouts in the ninth round, but he was never quite the same after blowing that first bout to Louis.

He and Louis boxed a six-round exhibition in Conn's final ring appearance on December 10, 1948. He was finished.

Altogether, Conn's record was 63-11-1, including 14 knockouts. He was elected to the Boxing Hall of Fame in 1965.

If there was a rap against Conn it was that he was head-strong. Caswell Adams, a sports writer with the *New York Herald-Tribune*, wrote of the first Conn-Louis fight:

"It was nationality that cost Conn the title. If he hadn't been Irish, he would have won. But being Irish, he wanted to finish it the way all Irishmen want to finish a fight. He wound up on the floor, hoping Irish legs would save what Irish spirit had thrown away, the heavyweight championship."

In the dressing room, Conn said, "What's the use of being Irish if you can't be thick?"

Louis later said it was one of the toughest fights of his storied career, and credited Conn for pushing him to the limit.

During our visit, Tim and Billy talked about how their dad, after some early bravado, cried in the dressing room. He realized how he'd let it all slip away when the world title was within his grasp. "He left the locker room by himself and went for a walk," said Billy. "He ended up walking a few miles, right through Harlem. The black people there all cheered for him when they spotted him. Joe Louis was their man, their hero, but they had a place in their heart for Billy Conn, too. He showed them something.

"They say my Dad was the only fighter who ever talked to Joe Louis during a fight. He told him, 'You're in a tough fight tonight.' And Louis said, 'I know.' Dad was into trash talking before it was fashionable."

Billy Conn lands a hard right to the head of champion Joe Louis during their championship fight June 18, 1941 at New York's Polo Grounds.

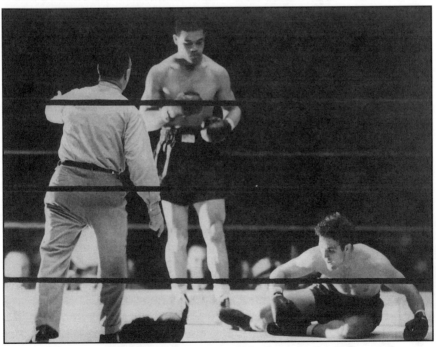

"The Brown Bomber" from Detroit KOs Conn in the 13th round.

"My grandfather was a bench jockey."
— Tim Conn

There was a photo of Mary Louise's father in a baseball uniform on the wall of the family room. "Greenfield Jimmy" Smith was one of the more interesting matchups for Billy Conn.

Billy Conn and Mary Louise Smith met for the first time at Ocean City, New Jersey, where her family had a vacation home. Billy was no day at the beach, but he cut a handsome figure in a swim suit.

Even so, Mary Louise was less than impressed. "I was a senior at Mount Mercy Academy (where Carlow College is now located in Oakland), and my father had a summer home on the beach," she recalled. "My father was a sportsman and he had money. He owned one of the biggest speak-easies in the city, in East Liberty, and we had a beautiful beachfront home.

"Some people around here try to hide the fact that their family was in the saloon business, horse racing and gambling, but I think you should be honest about your heritage. I'm proud of my dad; I'm proud of Billy. They weren't saints.

"I was 16 or 17, and I was no more interested in Billy Conn than I was the man in the moon. I was just interested in the lifeguards at Ocean City. He didn't appeal to me at all. He wasn't preppy. He did not go to Villanova like many of the guys there."

Just then Billy Jr. was back in the conversation. "Can I interrupt?" he said, holding up his hand like a kid in school. "Did everybody make a big fuss...?"

Just then Tim had a thought. "He asked you out, didn't he? Didn't he ask you to marry him on the first date? Didn't you think all fighters were a little punchy?"

Mary Louise shook her head and closed her eyes. "No, that happened three months later when I met him again.

"Billy took a liking to my dad. My dad's place was called Bachelors, and it was located at Penn and Shady. Billy came there and I was there. The second time he ever saw me, he said, 'Someday I'm going to marry you.'

"My dad didn't want me marrying any fighters, or having anything to do with ballplayers or professional athletes. He'd been a major league baseball player, and he didn't think much of ballplayers and their behavior. He didn't like their lifestyle.

"My dad wanted to be respected. He wasn't out front with his after-hours club. He was behind the scenes. Gambling was illegal, and so was booze during Prohibition. My dad made money from gambling and drinking. We had a nice home on Beechwood Boulevard in Squirrel Hill."

"He was supposed to take over Honus Wagner's job when Wagner retired," interjected Tim. "My grandfather played with the Pirates in 1916 (two years before Wagner retired). He played in the

Federal League with Chicago and Baltimore before that. Even before that, he played on a Triple A team in St. Mary's (Pa.) with Art Rooney and Dan Rooney, the one who became a priest. My grandfather was a bench jockey — you don't hear that phrase anymore — but he was very vocal and got on guys a lot from the bench. He was traded a lot."

He was in the big leagues for seven years and played with seven different teams, including the Pirates, the New York Giants, the Boston Braves, Cincinnati Reds and Philadelphia Phillies. He must've been tough to live with, judging by the number of teams who dealt him elsewhere.

"He played with Cincinnati in the 1919 World Series against the so-called Chicago Black Sox," said Billy.

"Have you read that book about them?" asked Tim. "I did. It was called *Eight Men Out*. My grandfather hated Judge (Kenesaw Mountain) Landis, the baseball commissioner, for banning all those guys from baseball. He said all of them didn't deserve that kind of punishment."

Jimmy Smith is listed at 5-9, 158 pounds in the *Baseball Encyclopedia*. "He had a great arm," said Tim. "He was a great fielder. He was always ready to fight people. They'd let you fight in those days."

It was Mary Louise's turn. "He liked to talk," she said of her father. "But he was good to us. He was more of a father to these boys than Billy was. Billy was not meant to be a family man.

"When Billy wanted to take me out in the beginning, my father was upset about the whole thing. Pap took a dislike to him, whereas he had liked him in the beginning, before he showed an interest in me. He didn't want me to get involved with him. He sent me away to Rosemont Catholic Girls School outside Philadelphia.

"Billy was fighting Gus Dorazio at Shibe Park (which was later called Connie Mack Stadium) in Philadelphia (August 14, 1939). He told me he'd have tickets for all my girl friends. No one showed up. We had a school curfew and had to be in by 9 o'clock every night, and we weren't really interested in going anyway."

I asked Mary Louise what Billy was like as a husband. "He was wonderful," she replied. "In those days you were a mother and a wife. We were an old-fashioned family. I was not competing with him like they do today. I was home and he took good care of me. He provided well for me and our kids. He liked being with his friends. I didn't run with him; I wasn't in his shadow. He and my dad were always at odds, though, for one reason or another. Mostly their personalities."

Jimmy Smith warned the priests at St. Paul's Cathedral that they were not to marry his daughter and Billy Conn under any circumstances. So Billy and Mary Louise criss-crossed the state trying to find an obliging priest.

They found one in Philadelphia. They were married July 1, 1941, about two weeks after Billy's much-ballyhooed loss to Louis. They were married at St. Patrick's Cathedral. "The charwoman at the church was the maid of honor, and Gabby Ryan, who was my dad's driver, was the best man," Tim related.

Tim told his mother to tell me the story about what happened on the day (April 12, 1942) that Tim was christened. She begged off, so Tim told it himself.

There is no story too embarrassing for the Conns to keep to themselves. "My grandfather was always working out, and he was in great shape," said Tim. "He was way ahead of his time in that regard.

"They were in the kitchen at Pap's house, and Pap's drinking. Dad's sitting on a stove, and Pap's lecturing Dad. He's telling him, 'If you're going to be in this family, I'm going to tell you what you need to do. You've got to go to church. You've got to...'

"My Dad told Pap that he was tired of him telling him what to do, that he'd heard enough. My Pap said, 'Boxing champion or no boxing champion, I could beat the hell out of you every day.' My Dad said, 'I've had enough of your bullcrap.' And they really went at it. They were swapping shots."

Mary Louise blushed at the retelling of this story. "I didn't see it," she said. "I was in the living room dancing. It was Timmy's christening and we had the rug rolled up in the living room. It was catered; we had champagne, and I guess Billy was sitting out there on the stove with his legs dangling off it. Pap liked to pick at Billy. Criticize him. I guess Billy had just had enough. I still remember Art Rooney saying, 'I can still see Billy coming off that stove.' "

Billy Conn suffered a broken left hand in that brawl with his father-in-law. He was pictured in his military uniform in the newspapers that week, sporting a black eye, a scraped nose and a cast on his broken hand. It proved a costly flareup for the family, as Conn had to call off a title rematch with Louis. Then they both went into the military service.

"A rematch with Louis was set for September of 1942, so Dad's fight with Pap cost him a million dollars in the long run," said Tim. He showed me a photograph of his grandfather and father shaking hands to make up soon after their altercation.

It was four years before Conn and Louis would fight again. The same couldn't be said for Conn and his father-in-law.

Everyone laughed at that story, so Mary Louise felt compelled to add a few more of a similar vein.

"Billy didn't want any trouble, but someone was always challenging him when he'd be out in public. I remember this one night at the Hollywood Social Club in Shadyside when I was there with Billy. Some little guy came up to him and said, 'You're not so big. I could take you.' Billy smiled at the guy and said, 'OK, you beat me. Have a drink and I'll put you in the record book for beating me.' The guy wouldn't let it go. He kept tormenting Billy.

"He pulled out Billy's chair, and when Billy went to sit down Billy fell on the floor. Everyone in the place laughed. That was it for

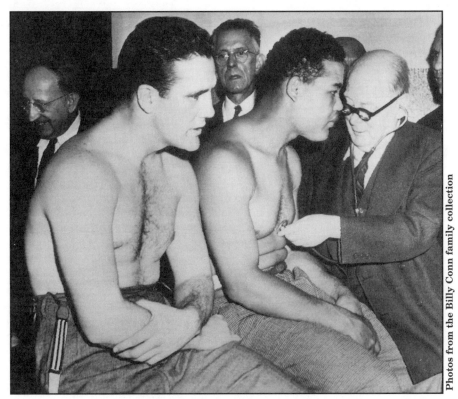

Billy Conn and Joe Louis are given physical exam May 3, 1946 prior to their second championship fight in New York.

Private Conn and Corporal Louis fought exhibition match for benefit of Army Emergency Relief Fund on Oct. 12, 1942 at Yankee Stadium.

Billy. He snapped, 'OK, wise guy, the last laugh's on you.' He punched the guy out with one shot. Then Billy got a drink from the bartender and poured it on the guy's face to revive him. Then he turned to the crowd and said, 'Everyone can laugh about that.' Somebody was always challenging him wherever he went. When he went into a bar, it was like in the western movies. He was the fastest gun, and everybody wanted to test him.

"There's another story...Billy was with his buddies, Joey Diven and Jack Cargo, one night at the Gaslight in Shadyside. The next day was Mother's Day. In the newspaper on Mother's Day there was a story about Billy Conn and his friends being in a brawl at the Gaslight. The story said they tore up the place. Billy blamed it on Joey Diven and Diven blamed it on Jack Cargo. I asked Billy how I was supposed to go to Mass that day with everyone knowing my husband had been in a brawl the night before."

Another Gaslight Club story...

Dave Figgins, a Pittsburgh construction icon, loved to sing Irish ballads at local bars and restaurants, and never needed much prodding to perform. Figgins is from Ireland, and Conn liked the way he was singing one night at the Gaslight.

"Do they know me in Ireland?" Conn asked Figgins.

"They not only know you in Ireland," replied Figgins, "they revere you."

Mary Louise remembered how Billy Conn suffered his fans, for the most part. "Someone would come up and say, 'Hi, Champ. Can I have your autograph?' It killed him.

"He hated sports banquets, or any crowds. Bobby Kennedy would call and invite him to Forest Hills for the tennis matches. Billy didn't want to go. I'd say, 'Let's go, Billy, just to be with the Kennedys.' He still wouldn't budge."

That brought a story to Tim's mind. "Don King paid for him to fly to Manila for the 'Thrilla in Manila' fight (September 30, 1975) between Ali and Joe Frazier," said Tim. "King wanted to introduce Dad in the ring before the fight, to add to the show. Dad got as far as San Francisco, and he decided he didn't want to go. He came home. Don King is still mad at him over that to this day."

That brought a story to Billy's mind. "Al Abrams used to say Dad was about as subtle as a bulldozer," said Billy. "One time the Irish government paid to have Dad go to Ireland for some celebration. When he was there, the Irish officials asked him at a public gathering what he thought of Ireland. Dad took the mike and said, 'I'm glad my grandparents didn't miss the boat.' He was no politician. He spared no one."

There's a story Tim likes to tell about his dad. It happened when he entered the Army during World War II.

"There was this sergeant, a big Southern guy, 6-4 or something," he said. "He has them lined up, all the new privates, and he's hollering at them, 'If any of you guys think you're tough, just step out of line

94

right now and I'll show you how tough you are, and that goes for every last one of you.' Many of the guys were aware of who my father was, and were aware of his boxing record. They look at my dad and, sure enough, he steps out of line. The sergeant comes over to him and growls, 'Who are you?' Dad says, 'I'm Billy Conn.' The sergeant recognized the name. He turns to the rest of the troops and says, 'Like I said, that goes for every last one of you, except this guy here.'"

"He drew a crowd wherever he went."
— Billy Conn's son, Tim

Pittsburgh is a big small town. That's part of its charm. Tim Conn was a contemporary of mine. We were students at Central Catholic High School and then Taylor Allderdice High School during the same four-year span, starting out at the private school in Oakland and then transferring to the public school in Squirrel Hill. I switched schools midway through my sophomore year and Conn did so after his junior year.

"I flunked out," he confessed.

"I quit," I told Tim.

I had a spat with one of the so-called Christian Brothers hellbent on showing me who was boss. I telephoned my mother and told her I'd had it and I wanted to go to Allderdice, where I had wanted to go in the first place. In truth, I was a better student as grades go under the disciplined environment at Central Catholic — on the honor roll all six terms — but learned much from some special teachers at Allderdice that serves me well today. So I sampled the best of both. It was easier to play hooky with my buddies at Allderdice, so I had opportunities to study local characters in downtown entertainment sites, pool halls, the Casino Burlesque Theater, et al. That was good for an aspiring writer.

Tim looked even better than he had in high school. He had aged well. He was a pleasant fellow. He was selling real estate for Prudential Realty. He lived about a mile from his mother in the Point Breeze section of Pittsburgh, not far from his father's boyhood home, with his wife, Veronica, and their son, Ryan, a 19-year-old sophomore at Washington & Jefferson College, and Milena, a 17-year-old senior at Oakland Catholic.

He was a tall, about 6-2, left-handed pitcher on the Dragons' baseball team. He could still throw a high hard one past your ear.

He remembered his dad came to see him pitch on a few occasions when he was playing high school and sandlot ball. "He drew a crowd wherever we went," said Tim. "I remember him coming to see me pitch at Burgwin Field. I remember Chief Bennett was the groundskeeper there and he took such great care of that field. I remember Hazelwood had a good player named Tony Sacco." Yes, it's a small world. I remembered them, too.

"Billy was never crazy about the place."
— Mary Louise Conn on Las Vegas

Mary Louise told how the Conns got to Las Vegas: "Milton Jaffe, who once owned a nightclub in Pittsburgh and was always involved with gambling, was running the Stardust Hotel & Casino in Las Vegas. He invited us to come out there. He put Billy in charge of the lounge, and he had that job from 1961 to 1964. Billy had a lot of jobs when we were married.

"John F. Kennedy was running for President and he came to the Stardust one night. He wanted to see the Lido Show, the French revue. Lots of beautiful nearly-naked women parading on stage.

"Billy called Milton Jaffe in the office and said, 'Milton, you're not going to believe this, but the next President of the United States is in the lobby and wants to see the Lido Show.' Kennedy wanted to sit in the back, out of the way, but Jaffe insisted he have a front row table.

"Billy started talking with John Kennedy, and Kennedy mentioned that David L. Lawrence, the governor of Pennsylvania and former mayor of Pittsburgh, wasn't backing him for President. Billy told Kennedy that Lawrence was a close friend of Art Rooney. 'And he's my best friend and my oldest son's godfather.' He told Kennedy he would talk to Art Rooney and have him talk to David L. Lawrence on his behalf. Billy promised Kennedy that would change everything, that he didn't need to worry anymore. He'd have Lawrence's support in the election.

"We stayed in Las Vegas for 2½ years. Billy was never crazy about the place, but he was making good money. He called it Devil's Island. Bob Hope chased us home. Bob told Billy it wasn't a good place to raise a family."

"The world's battlefields have been in the heart chiefly; more heroism has been displayed in the household and the closet, than on the most memorable battlefields of history."
— H. W. Beecher

Jim O'Brien

Pierre Larouche,
Former scoring star for Pittsburgh Penguins:
*"My hero was Stan Mikita. He played for the
Chicago Blackhawks, and I liked their uni-
forms. I liked that Indian logo. I liked the way
Mikita played. I was a right-handed shot and so
was he. I wanted to be able to play like him."*

Korie Hlede
The Kid from Croatia

"She was a natural."
— Dan Durkin

Who is the only basketball player in the history of Duquesne University to have their number retired? Well, it wasn't Chuck Cooper, Dick Ricketts, Sihugo Green, Willie Somerset, Billy Zopf, Moe Barr, Barry or Garry Nelson, Mickey Davis or Norm Nixon.

No, it was Korie Hlede. How's that? Yes, Korie Hlede.

That name may not be familiar even to some of the city's more passionate basketball fans. I'm not sure how many could tell you her uniform number was 25. Duquesne did its best to get the word out about Korie Hlede (pronounced Ha-LAY-day), but women's basketball has never been an easy sell in Pittsburgh.

Korie Hlede was never a household name on the Pittsburgh sports scene. Some still look puzzled when you mention the name to them. She was better known in her homeland as a member of the Croatian National Senior Team which earned two Croatian championships.

It was Nellie King, the former Duquesne sports information director and one-time Pirates pitcher and broadcaster, who shared that trivia gem about Hlede and having her number retired.

I must confess I saw her play only once, at the Civic Arena in the opener of a doubleheader that matched Pitt and Duquesne during her senior season. Shame on me. I wish I had seen her more. *She can play.* She's the first real pro turned out by Duquesne, unbelievably, since Nixon was drafted by the Los Angeles Lakers in 1977, over 20 years earlier.

She was also the only Duquesne University basketball player I ever asked for an autograph. Earlier in the day when I saw her play, someone asked me if I could get some autographs for his ailing mother who was a big sports fan. Hlede was heading my way near the locker room after the game, so I asked her to sign the cover of the game program. She was the cover girl for that game's issue. Hlede offered a smile as well, and thanked me for asking.

I liked her already.

As a senior, Hlede was the third-leading scorer in the nation among women's college basketball players, averaging 27.1 points as well as seven rebounds a game. She helped lead the Lady Dukes to a 19-9 record in 1998, which was the most successful season since the 1982 squad went 19-6.

She was the fourth player selected in the 1998 WNBA draft, the first-ever player drafted by the Detroit Shock.

Korie Hlede
Duquesne
University
5-9
Guard
Zagreb, Croatia
VII Gimnizija

She had a great rookie season in the WNBA. At age 23, she was the Shock's second-leading scorer, averaging 14.1 points a game. She also averaged 5.2 rebounds, 2.7 assists, all ranking in the Top 20 in the league, as did her three-point (.391) and free throw (.806) shooting percentages. With the Shock, she wore jersey No. 7.

She suffered a season-ending knee injury at Sacramento on August 11, and was busy early in 1999 rehabilitating to be ready for the next season.

In her senior season at Duquesne, despite her relative local anonymity, she was a candidate for the Pittsburgh Dapper Dan award as the athlete who did the most to call attention to the city. She was on the ballot with the likes of Jerome Bettis, Mario Lemieux, Gene Lamont, Walt Harris and Kordell Stewart. Bettis was the eventual winner.

Korie came from Croatia as an 18-year-old student to play basketball on The Bluff. It was Dan Durkin, the women's basketball coach at Duquesne, who made the arrangements to bring Hlede to Pittsburgh. Back in Zagreb, where she was born March 29, 1975, she was Koraljka Hlede and her high school was VII Gimnizija.

It was a boon to both parties. It got Hlede out of Yugoslavia, which had been torn apart by political and religious feuds more than usual in the eight years since the former Communist country was divided into independent states.

Croatia gained its independence in 1991, as did Bosnia, and soon the bloodshed began as Serbian-led ethnic cleansing ripped apart a culture. Hlede had a cousin who was disabled from shrapnel wounds in his head. She had a teammate with the Detroit Shock, Razija Mujanovic, a Bosnian for whom Hlede acted as an interpreter.

Hlede was sympathetic to Mujanovic. "She has gotten the worst end of the stick," said Hlede, a reference to the intensity of the battles that made Bosnia, with its greater ethnic mix, such a horrific battleground compared to Croatia.

Then blood was spilled in Kosovo, where Serbs and ethnic Albanians clashed.

Kosovo came to the attention of most Americans in March, 1999 when NATO and President Clinton called for a NATO-sponsored series of air strikes on Kosovo to stop the blood-letting. It only sparked more of the same. It was a controversial decision. Now there was March Sadness to go with March Madness, the term associated with the NCAA basketball tournament that seizes our attention at that time of year.

Most Americans couldn't have pointed out Kosovo on a world map or globe. They could sooner tell you where Gonzaga was located.

"A piece of land is not as important as one human life," Hlede told Lynn Henning, a writer for *The Detroit News*. Hlede was upset by the inhuman campaign being conducted by Serbian leader Slobodan Milosevic. "He and his followers see only one thing — nationalism. They see nothing beyond that. They deny humanity."

"Americans are so enthusiastic."
— Korie Hlede

Korie Hlede arrived at Duquesne University during the thick of Bosnia's ordeal. She found the free-spirited, high-energy scene on the Duquesne campus as such a contrast to the sober scene in her homeland. At first, she found it amusing. Then invigorating.

What a different life Hlede has in Detroit that she wouldn't have enjoyed if she weren't a gifted student and basketball player. Her academic and athletic talents transformed her life.

"What I love about the United States is that it is so individualistic," she said. "I treasure things in my own country, I appreciate that things are more interpersonal there. But here I want to learn to grow — not in a selfish way, but through self-expression."

Hlede is a writer of poetry and personal reflections. At Duquesne, she had a double major in psychology and communications. She's a serious reader, drawn to philosophers such as Sartre, Camus and Kierkegaard, even Zen Buddhism.

She is the daughter of divorced journalists, Bojan Hlede and Ljerka Milkovic-Hlede, both of whom work for newspapers in Zagreb. She speaks three languages — Croatian, German and English — and speaks them all with great passion. Nowadays, she prefers to speak in English.

"Americans are so enthusiastic about life," Hlede said. "They get up in the morning and it's, 'How are you doing?' There's just such a vibe to them. I think it shows you that you can be busy and still mindful of others."

She was lucky to have the opportunity to come here from Croatia. One of her friends back home spent time in America as an exchange student in Pittsburgh. Her name was Ali Topic, and she was a center for the Lady Dukes.

Topic began telling Dan Durkin at Duquesne about this kid back home in Croatia who could really play basketball. Topic did Hlede and Durkin a favor by sending him a video tape showing the considerable basketball skills of a blonde guard from Zagreb. It was the best tape Durkin ever screened.

"I want you to know this tape is two years old —the person you're watching is only 16 at the time," Topic told Durkin.

He let a week go by before he watched the tape, and he couldn't believe his eyes. "She was a natural," he said.

He managed somehow to make arrangements for Hlede to come to Duquesne. He did this two weeks before classes started in 1994. The next five years would be a dream for this wonderful warm young woman with a winning smile.

She was able to smile even while undergoing difficult rehabilitation in February of 1999. She was trying to come back from a torn right anterior cruciate ligament (ACL) that caved in the previous August late in Hlede's first season in the WNBA. It was the end of the season for her.

It was an injury known to Pittsburgh sports fans because it had happened to Rod Woodson of the Steelers, among others, and he was able to come back and play. As athletes who have shed ACL tears will vouch, the road back is a long grimace.

It takes about nine to ten months to heal, and Hlede had the proper attitude, according to Laura Ramus, the Shock's head trainer. Ramus thought Hlede had a good chance to be ready when the Shock opened their 1999 training camp in May.

"Mentally and emotionally, she's had a great attitude from the start," remarked Ramus. "A lot of times, even in my position, it's difficult to give encouragement. I found some days that she was picking me up. She's an inspiration, a pleasure to work with."

Ever since her injury, Hlede began harping on the need for athletes, especially women, to stretch before physical activity. It was necessary to loosen those hamstrings. She spoke at many clinics throughout Michigan.

"It's not about never failing, it's about getting up and coming back," she said about the need to respond properly to such setbacks.

Hlede likes to talk, on any subject. There's a sweetness about her, and a lilt to her Eastern European-edged voice that appeals to anyone who meets her.

A check of her personal files from Duquesne University and the Detroit Shock offers some interesting insights into this exceptional young woman.

She was a Chicago Bulls fan because of her admiration for Michael Jordan and fellow countryman Toni Kukoc. She considered Jordan and the late Drazen Petrovic as her role models in basketball.

She began playing basketball at age 13.

She has one brother, Svebor, 22, who was still living in Croatia, but would like to come to America.

She prefers playing tennis to basketball because it's an individual sport and one can determine the outcome of a contest more often. She also enjoys soccer and swimming.

She's a dreamer and would love to travel to the Himalayas, Mt. Everest and Tibet and go mountain climbing. If she wasn't a basketball player she'd be a tennis player, or a tour guide. She'd like to try a triathlon competition. When she's finished with her ballplaying career, she'd like to be a writer.

She regards the defining moment in her life as coming to the U.S. to attend college, and regards her greatest achievement as graduating from college. She didn't just get by, either. She was a fixture on the Dean's List and Director of Athletics Honor Roll.

"Getting an education is the most important thing you can do for yourself," Hlede likes to tell the young people she addresses at clinics and school assemblies. "The reason why I left home was not to play basketball. It was to get an education. I put that first."

102

She's a lean, mean 5-9, 155 pounds, but admits to having a passion for all kinds of foods, especially Italian and Chinese, with ice cream as the ultimate treat.

She tells young players that they have to work at their ball-handling skills and not just shooting.

"Without ball-handling skills, you can't shoot," she said. "When someone passes you the ball, you're usually being guarded, so you still have to get past them to make a shot. If someone gets two open shots in a game, they're lucky."

"She wants to be well-rounded."
— Nancy Lieberman-Cline

One of her biggest fans is Shock general manager/coach Nancy Lieberman-Cline, one of the most celebrated individuals in the history of women's basketball. "She's the type of kid who cares, who wants to learn, not just about her craft, which is basketball," said her GM and coach. "She wants to learn about life. She wants to be well-rounded.

"Korie is a tremendous scorer. She excels in a variety of areas, distributes the basketball well and can play defense. Her skills are exceptional. She is a floor leader for Detroit and gives us versatility in our lineup."

I had met and gotten to know Nancy Lieberman when she was an All-American performer at Old Dominion in Norfolk, Virginia back in the late '70s. She was from the Queens section of New York City, and she would come home each summer to see her mother, Renee.

I had lunch each summer for three years running in Manhattan with Nancy and her mother. It was one of the highlights of the summer, when I would be in the midtown section working on the next *Street & Smith's Basketball* annual, the No. 1 selling magazine of its kind in the country.

Our magazine was one of the first to devote a section to women's basketball. Lieberman was one of the best known women players of her time. She and her mother were both talkers.

I remember her telling me stories about playing basketball with the guys at the playgrounds in her native Far Rockaway, also Al McGuire's hometown. They were the sort of stories I'd later hear about Suzie McConnell, the first woman in Pittsburgh to bring back Olympic medals.

Any young woman who makes her mark in basketball had to be a gym rat, had to spend the kind of time "Pistol Pete" Maravich and his father, Press Maravich, brought to the task. There were two Serbs, by the way, who could play basketball.

Dan Durkin, who coached Hlede at Duquesne, remembers when he discovered her one day working out in a dark campus gym. She was shooting hoops in the dark when Durkin came upon her, sticking his head into the A.J. Palumbo Center. He recognized the shadowy figure in the distance.

"You want me to put the lights on?" Durkin asked his Duquesne dandy.

Korie cried out in response, "No, no, don't turn them on."

Durkin didn't get it. He pressed her as to why she wanted to continue shooting in the dark.

"Michael Jordan shoots in the dark," she said. Yes, she'd seen the Nike commercials which said so.

And Michael Jordan was her favorite player. She modeled herself after Michael Jordan, not another more celebrated college women competitor.

In time, Korie Hlede would score more points (2,631) than any previous performer, man or woman, on the Duquesne campus. She also held Duquesne women's records for steals (334) and assists (570).

She led the Atlantic 10 in scoring and was all-conference each year. She was a four-time Kodak honorable mention All-America, and a two-time GTE Academic All-America.

It wasn't easy for Hlede to get to Duquesne in the first place. There was little time to maneuver by the time Durkin decided to offer her a scholarship.

She had to take the Scholastic Aptitude Test, the SAT, which was a requirement for admittance. No SAT centers were open in her war-torn country. The nearest test site was Vienna.

So a road-weary Hlede returned home to Zagreb on a Friday after touring Europe as a member of Croatia's national team. She visited briefly with her family, then boarded a bus that evening for a nine-hour overnight journey through Slovenia and Hungary and into Austria. She arrived in Vienna cramped and bleary-eyed from the uncomfortable sojourn.

"That was some trip," recalled Korie. "We traveled all night and I was like squished in a seat, trying to sleep. I found my way to the American Academy and I took the test, without any preparation at all. Fortunately, I passed."

She enrolled at Duquesne two months later, and immediately made her mark in pickup basketball games at Palumbo Center.

"I wasn't allowed to watch her live because that's the NCAA rule," said Durkin. "So I'm in my office drooling about what other people are reporting to me.

"One of the maintenance guys comes in and he says, 'Coach, did you see this kid out here? Man, she plays like Maravich.' She was out there dribbling two balls at once, doing 360s, all that stuff. The men's basketball team and their staff would come in and say, 'This kid can play, Coach.' I couldn't wait until October 15 so I could see for myself."

Durkin didn't have to wait long to see how good Hlede was. She adjusted to a new country, a new culture, a new campus, new teammates, and she averaged 24.2 points per game, eighth-best nationally and No. 1 among all Division I freshmen, male or female.

She was the complete package, however, not just a scorer. She led the Atlantic 10 in steals, was second in assists and, even more impressive as a 5-9 guard, was third in the league in rebounds. It would be like that throughout her collegiate career.

She won the *Women's Basketball News* Freshman of the Year award which was presented to her at the NCAA Final Four in Minneapolis. She and Penn State's Suzie McConnell were the only two freshmen ever to be named to the Atlantic 10 first-team all-conference list.

She was featured by local newspapers, radio shows and TV sports segments, received national attention on CNN Sports and ESPN and was featured in *USA Today, The Sporting News* and *Basketball Weekly*. Even so, the Lady Dukes didn't draw big crowds to see the Croatian Sensation, as she was tabbed.

"That first season," declared Durkin, "I kind of marveled at how many good things she did on the floor — the passing, the jump shot that was extremely good as far as stopping on a dime, the strength and distance she had with her shot, her nose for the ball and her instincts."

In only her ninth game, she became the first woman in school history to score as many as 40 points in a game.

She could have scored points that way routinely, the way Maravich did at LSU, but she didn't want her teammates thinking of her as a ball hog. Durkin told her she was unselfish to a fault.

"The object of the game is to win," Durkin told Hlede. "If you score 40, maybe we win tomorrow."

The next day she pumped in 41 points, a school record for women, by connecting on 18 of 26 shots, but the Lady Dukes were defeated.

"For me, it's great to score or lead the team in whatever," she said back then. "But honestly it means nothing if we don't win."

In her senior season, she set a new single game scoring record at Duquesne with 42 points against Dayton.

She said one of her goals was to represent her homeland in the 2000 Olympic Games. The kid was hoping she'd have a homeland to return to at the start of the milennium to make good on her goal.

She was praying for her people.

"Despite our fears and worries — and they're very real to all of us — life continues...it goes on."
— Robert Frost, poet

Arnold Palmer
The ultimate pro from Latrobe

*"I could never repay golf
for what it has meant to me."*

Arnold Palmer is one of those people I appreciate more than most in the world of sports. He has always been special. He remains the most important person ever in the game of golf, but he also remains the humble son of the groundskeeper and club pro at the Latrobe Country Club. He now owns the club, but he has kept the same respectful stance and good manners he learned as a child. He remains a good guy, natural to the bone, the greatest ambassador his sport has ever known.

I got my first up-close look at Palmer when I was nearing my 20th birthday and had volunteered to write cutlines for a photographer from *The Pittsburgh Press* at the 1962 U.S. Open at Oakmont. I wore a media pass that allowed me to watch from inside the ropes. Having that kind of insider's view of sports was something that appealed to me a great deal about pursuing a career as a sports writer. I liked the up-close and personal approach.

I have had several opportunities since then to see and talk to Arnold Palmer. It has always been a positive experience; it's always been a memorable time. Such meetings, helter-skelter as they have been, are the meat of this personal reflection.

The last exposure to Palmer occurred in a clubhouse room at that same Oakmont Country Club in the summer of 1997. He had come to a press conference after playing in the Family House Invitational put together by the irrepressible Frank Fuhrer.

What struck me was Palmer's serious yet affable approach to this press conference, an informal gathering of local newsmen. Palmer appeared as if he were fielding questions at Augusta following a Masters victory.

He looked every questioner directly in the eyes, as he has always done. He gave every question serious consideration, and did his best to offer a thoughtful response, something useful for the next day's newspaper, radio or TV report. Palmer usually provides good sound bites.

Sportscaster Stan Savran said it was his first exposure to Palmer, and he came away impressed. "He was everything I'd heard about him, and then some," said Savran. "That was reassuring." Goose Goslin, Bob Pompeani, Gerry Dulac and Marino Parascenzo had interviewed Palmer prior to this day, Parascenzo the most by far, but all of them appeared to appreciate Palmer's pleasant nature and spirit as well.

"I'm always aware of who he is, and what he's done," said Pompeani. "So I appreciate the opportunity to do something with him."

Dulac caddied for Palmer at a fund-raising event and enjoyed that experience, but said he never was caught up like a fan might be with talking to any sports personality.

Palmer talked and smiled easily, poking fun at himself at times, being honest with his emotions, offering thoughts about his goals and approach to the game. He has always been self-deprecating. He was working the press conference the way he had just worked the course. He was still out to win. He reminded me of coaches and managers I had dealt with through the years — Chuck Noll, Red Holzman and Gil Hodges come to mind — who weren't particularly colorful, but were decent individuals, cordial and cooperative, doing their best to work with you.

He had the ability that Bob Prince and Art Rooney had, of making every one in the room feel important. He posed for some pictures, signed some programs for anyone who asked, and wanted to know if everybody had what they needed before he exited the room. Then he paused in the hallway to field yet one more question and request. His eyes, so expressive, are critical to his communication skills.

Members of the media, veterans and newcomers, exchanged observations about how impressed they were with Palmer. They always do this. He's too good to take for granted. Their world would be a better place if everybody took a cue from Palmer in that regard.

It's that quality that sets Arnold Palmer apart from the pack. He has always made a point to treat the gallery with the same respect — always making eye contact, usually offering a few kind words, that killer smile that can still weaken women's knees — and it's one of the main reasons he remained one of the most popular golfers in the game. He hadn't won a major tournament since 1964, almost unbelievable enough, yet he was still "The King" of golf. His last American triumph on the regular PGA Tour was in 1973 at the Bob Hope Desert Classic at Palm Springs.

This afternoon at Oakmont was one of many memorable days in the presence of Palmer that have formed a personal reference of what Palmer appears to be, and it's always pleasant for this reporter. I have seen him angry, when a reporter let a locker room door fly into his right hand at the Oakmont Country Club. It smarted and so did Palmer. He flashed a fierce look at the writer, muttered something, and walked away. It was good to see Palmer deal with a difficult moment the way you and I might have. He never said he was perfect.

During his press conference that afternoon, Palmer spoke about his efforts to make Pittsburgh a regular stop on the PGA Tour. He thought it possible. If it was, indeed, he was the reason. "We'd love to have a tournament here," he said. "If we could pull it all together, it has real potential. If I had anything to do with it, it would be at Laurel Valley."

Bob Prince and Arnold Palmer somehow ended up in a swimming pool at the Pittsburgh Field Club after one of the Ham-Am Golf Tournaments in the late 1960s.

Arnold Palmer plays at Oakmont.

Arnold Palmer is flanked by two of his favorites, the late Del Miller of harness racing fame, left, and Stan Musial, a Hall of Fame baseball player from Donora, at a golf event in Florida in early 1990s.

He is a member at Laurel Valley, not far from his own Latrobe Country Club. He is also an owner of the Bay Hill (Florida) Club. He still lives and works out of an office at Latrobe Country Club, but winters at Bay Hill.

He spoke of the need to get proper sponsorship, local and national, to make a Pittsburgh-area tournament a reality.

"You have to be aware of sponsors first of all," added Palmer. "Without them, you have no tour."

That's a lesson often lost, along with a lot of other lessons, with the young pros these days.

"My game is a question mark at this time," said Palmer, age 68 at the time. "But I'm feeling a little better."

Palmer had been operated on earlier that year for prostate cancer, and had just begun a comeback.

"If I can't play and play up to my own standards," he continued, "I'll cut back on my activity. I've cut back already, to be sure, but I try as much as I can to help the tournaments. I keep getting asked to play, and I'm still appreciative of that. I don't like to say no.

"Playing with those three guys I was with on Monday gave me a terrible inferiority complex. I wanted to hide in the closet. You see a guy like Tiger Woods and the way he can drive a ball...he can outdrive everyone else (except John Daly) by 40 to 50 yards. I still hate to be outdriven by anybody."

Some writers were paying tribute to Palmer with their comments, and he seemed uneasy for the first time. "I don't think too much about that," he said of his status in the sport. "I hope I've helped the game. I could never repay golf for what it has meant to me.

"I love the game. That's why I'm still here. If I can help the game by showing up, I'll do it."

He spoke about his passion for the game, his belief that it was important to uphold certain traditions, to know and respect the history of the game, and to pay proper tribute to those who played in the pioneer days of the sport.

He also talked about, and this is something that always blows my mind about the man, his search for something that would improve his game. He always gives the impression that he thinks that if he keeps working on his approach shots, regains his touch with a putter, and trims his clubs just so, he can get better. Yeah, better.

I've seen Palmer at pro-ams where he's often the lone entry practicing chip shots while everyone else is blasting away with tee shots. He works at his weaknesses, not his strengths, as most tend to do. Chuck Noll noted such activity at a pro-am once at Latrobe Country Club, and used it to make a point with his players at a clubhouse meeting that week.

In short, if Arnold Palmer is still practicing, and working at his weaknesses, doesn't that tell you something? Palmer told me he had heard that Noll did that.

After he turned 70 on September 10, 1999, Palmer was probably still working to improve his game.

"I want more distance," he said at Oakmont. "I don't like to be outdriven. As long as I work the course, I want to be able to get good distance on my shots. That's why I spend so much time in my shop. I want to find something to add 20 yards. Maybe I'll find it today."

He was optimistic about what lies ahead for the game of golf, and he hopes he can continue to be a part of its development and progress. I've been in his workshop, and it contains more golf equipment than you can find at some sporting goods outlets. He alters some of his irons on lathes, working like a machinist, which was my dad's occupation. "I think golf will continue to make fantastic strides," he said. "I think there are 27 million homes now on golf channels. The media is bringing it to the attention of more people than ever before. We're all over the Internet, you name it."

He was asked what he did during his time away from golf activity, when he was recovering from his prostate cancer treatment. "I did some writing and some reading; I was bored to death," he said, grimacing at the memory. "I had lots of time and I didn't want it.

"I'm designing several golf courses now, and that keeps me busy. I want to see if I can get it going again. I want to remain active, at my own pace, in all aspects of golf. I still can fly anywhere I want in my own plane right near my club at the Westmoreland County Airport in Latrobe. I like it when I can play here and still stay at home. I like to sleep in my own bed. Hey, it's a nice day, nice weather, nice people. Now if I could just get a few breaks." In May of 1999, it was announced that the airport would be named after Arnold Palmer. That was quite a tribute to a local aviator.

"I like to sleep in my own bed."

Arnold Daniel Palmer cut back on his activity during the 1998 season, yet his schedule was still impressive. He spearheaded the Senior Tour for the Cure program, a national campaign to promote prostate cancer awareness, and along with Jim Colbert, similarly challenged, he helped to raise $4.3 million to combat the disease.

He was off the circuit for 11 weeks during the fall due to seven weeks of radiation treatments for prostate cancer. He returned at the Pacific Bell Senior Classic in Los Angeles in late October.

He made 13 appearances on the Senior Tour for the second straight year. His best outing was at the Upper Montclair Country Club where he tied for 47th in the Cadillac NFL Golf Classic.

He made his 18th appearance at the U.S. Senior Open at Riviera Country Club, breaking Miller Barber's record for the most appearances at that prestigious event. He joined the Senior Tour in 1980.

Palmer played in his 44th Masters and tied Sam Snead for the second longest streak in the history of that event, behind Doug Ford's 46. He teamed with writer James Dodson to produce an autobiography called *A Golfer's Life*. These lines are from the dust jacket of that book: "There has never been a golfer to rival Arnold Palmer. He's the most aggressive, most exciting player the game has ever known...His rise to fame was meteoric, and by the 1960s he had emerged as one of the few American athletes the public truly cared about — a vibrant, daring, handsome sports celebrity who attracted wild crowds and enormous television audiences whenever he played and whose charisma propelled the explosion of enthusiasm for golf in the sixties."

Palmer provides interesting insights in this well-written book, including one about his mother, Doris, who once worked as a bookkeeper at the Latrobe Country Club, and was responsible for getting Arnold out to play golf initially, before his father, Deacon, began to teach him how to play.

"She was a classic 'people' person," offers Palmer, "interested in just about everyone and everything, always enthusiastic in her approach to life, and she never met a stranger she didn't like. I'm deeply flattered when people who knew us both say I inherited her personality, for she was magnetic and charming and nobody ever had a bad word to say about her. No aspiring golfer ever had a greater, more nurturing golf mom." Along this same line, Palmer once told Orlando sports writer Larry Guest the following reflections on his mother:

"When I was a kid, my mother used to take up for me when my dad was getting on me. She's the one who used to take me around to all the golf tournaments. Dad was working. She drove me all over — Philadelphia, Detroit, Pittsburgh, every place I had a tournament.

"My wife, Winnie, likes to say I got my 'ham' from my mother. And it is true that my mother enjoyed being in the limelight. For example, she loved talking to reporters, and when she and Pap went along for some television appearances in New York, he was happy to remain backstage while my mom wanted to be on camera.

"She was always rooting — she never had a negative thought. She was such a positive, upbeat influence, always encouraging me. My father, on the other hand, was always on my side, but he was tough. He was always, 'You didn't do it as well as you should have.'

"I needed a little of that, no question, but my mother was the warm, caring influence that a child absolutely has to have if he is going to make it. I can't express the importance of having her in my life, of how important she was to everything that I have become."

> *"I needed no crystal ball to perceive that young Bob Jones was to become an immediate hit with the galleries — the ladies particularly — with his dark blue beret, his big blue eyes and his winning smile."*
> — Grantland Rice, 1954
> *The Tumult and the Shouting*

"The King" credits his mother, Doris, for his people skills.

Arnold's brother, Jerry; age 55 as of June, 1999, serves as general manager of Latrobe Country Club.

Arnold Palmer

Arnold and his dad, "Deacon," work on expansion of Latrobe Country Club from 9 to 18 holes in the mid-1960s. Harry Saxman, who was president of the club at the time, looks on.

"I'm just being myself."
— Arnold Palmer

Back in the summer of 1992, I was invited to speak, along with Jim Meston, a former Westinghouse official, to customers of AEG Westinghouse Transportation Systems, Inc., more recently known as ADTranz. The customers were from all over the country, a few from overseas, and they were being housed at the Mountain View Inn in Greensburg, where Meston and I offered our talks. Then the guests went to the nearby Latrobe Country Club for a golf outing.

A gentleman from New Orleans told me about his excitement. "I can't believe," he began, "that I'm going to be playing at Arnold Palmer's own country club. And that Palmer will be playing with us! You don't know what a big fan I am of Arnold Palmer. If I were to die tomorrow, after playing with Palmer, I'd be able to say I've had a full life."

Meston and I were invited to accompany the guests on the trip to Latrobe Country Club. I don't play golf, but I realized it had been several years since I had last visited with Palmer at his club. I thought I should take advantage of the opportunity.

So I drove over to the Latrobe Country Club on my own, unannounced. For starters, I stopped by the office of Palmer's assistant and Man Friday, Donald "Doc" Giffin. I had first known Giffin when he was a sportswriter who covered college sports and golf and worked the desk at *The Pittsburgh Press.* This was back in the early '60s when I was a student at Pitt, and was the sports editor of *The Pitt News,* a position Giffin had held in his own student days when he was growing up in Crafton. Giffin went to work for Palmer in 1966, after a brief stint as the second full-time publicist/traveling secretary for the PGA.

Giffin was always a good guy. He always looked after old friends. I'm not sure he even said hello to me when I peeked my head into his office that day. "C'mon, come with me," he directed me as he passed me and tugged at my sleeve.

I dutifully followed Giffin out of his office and across a walkway and into another area of the clubhouse. The next thing I knew I was in the men's grill, and I was being introduced once again to Arnold Palmer, who was having lunch with another gentleman. I joined them and was given a menu. I pulled out my notebook — never leave home without one — and began interviewing Palmer. It was a Pavlovian response. I see somebody like Palmer, I pull out the notebook.

As I said earlier, I'm not a golfer. As I sat next to Palmer, and had his complete attention for 30 or 35 minutes, I kept thinking how my father-in-law, Harvey Churchman, might feel if he were in my seat. Ol' Harvey loved to play golf and bowl and enjoy the company of other men in a setting like this — play some cards after 18 holes perhaps — and he'd have thought he'd died and gone to heaven. His son, Harvey, and his friends down in North Carolina would be just as excited. I thought of a lot of serious, but not-so-good golfers I knew, and what it would mean to them to share a sandwich and conversation with "The King" in the clubhouse as I was doing.

Phil Newcamp, the pro at the St. Clair Country Club, once escorted Palmer for 36 holes in the Family Invitational when it was held at Oakmont Country Club. Newcamp was so excited to be with his idol, and cherishes the memory.

"I was on the rules committee, and my job was to keep people from hounding Palmer," recalled Newcamp. "He told me not to worry. He said, 'No one will bother me.' So I just walked with him for two days. At the No. 9 hole at Oakmont, he asked me for some advice about his swing, and I thought that was kinda neat. He was great with everyone."

When I asked Palmer one particular question, relating to the way by which he treated his fans, he seemed stumped. Giffin came in from the bullpen. "You're just being yourself, right?" said Giffin, feeding Palmer his next line. "Right, Doc," said Palmer. "I'm just being myself. That's the only way I know how to be."

Palmer is a lot like another guy who loves to play golf from that neck of the woods in Westmoreland County, namely Bill Mazeroski, who lives on a lonely road off the beaten path in Greensburg. They both can't understand why people insist on fussing over them. Like why all the fuss? Treat me with respect, but don't treat me special. Dick Groat, a Pirates hero in 1960 like Mazeroski, operates Champion Lakes Golf Course near Ligonier, and he's like that, too. That's why Palmer and Mazeroski get along so well, and why they're apt to appear, without advance notice, at a neighborhood restaurant like DeNunzio's in Jeannette or Mr. P's in Greensburg, and feel right at home. The other guests are glad to see them, and will tell friends about it, but they don't bother Palmer or Maz when they are eating with friends and family. There are framed photographs of both on the wall in the bar area, taken by Tony DeNunzio, the father of Ron, who runs the restaurant, and at Mr. P's as well.

It was time for Palmer to appear before the group that was going to play golf and dinner that day at the Latrobe Country Club. As we came out of the grill room together, Palmer and Giffin flanking me, I spotted the fellow from New Orleans I had been talking to earlier. He wasn't looking up, and didn't notice Palmer making his official appearance. The man from New Orleans was looking at his shoe tops.

I asked Palmer if it would be all right for me to bring the guy over to meet him, telling Palmer how much the man admired him. Palmer gave me the green light. I went over to the man from New Orleans and asked him to come with me. He walked, still looking at his shoetops, or as if he had dropped the dime he'd brought to mark his ball.

Now we're standing in front of Arnold Palmer, the man himself. When I introduced the two, as I mentioned Palmer's name, the guy's eyes grew wider, like he was watching a Mardi Gras parade on

Bourbon Street. I was hoping the guy wouldn't faint. He couldn't believe he was saying hello and howya doin' to Arnold Palmer. Palmer shook his hand, said a few things, and made it look like we had just made his day. The man felt like he'd been marching in with the saints.

Palmer posed for photos with everybody later that evening before dinner. He talked off the cuff, and made everybody feel right at home. It was his home, but now it was their home as well. Palmer is the perfect host, and he doesn't even work at it. He was, as Palmer put it earlier — or was it Giffin? — just being himself.

"Everybody is important."
— Deke Palmer,
Arnold's dad

Arnold Palmer always appreciated everybody associated with golf. He had learned his lessons well in fan appreciation from his father, Deacon or Deke Palmer, who worked at the Latrobe Country Club for 50 years.

His father taught him how to play the game, of golf and of life. His father stressed practice, and taught him the fundamentals. He told him to hit the ball as hard as he could. He told him nothing could take the place of getting out and hitting golf balls.

He taught him a game that became a lifetime joy to play. He taught him to be deferential to everybody he encountered at the country club, where his father was employed. "Everybody is important," his dad told him.

That carried over to the uncommon patience Palmer had with the press and with the fans in future years.

He captured the public imagination with his all-out, hell-bent playing style. He became the embodiment of "the nice guy next door."

The Palmer image was created in 1960 when in the space of a few months he won both the Masters and the U.S. Open from positions that seemed hopeless.

His Masters win was capped by back-to-back birdies on the final two holes. Going into the final round of the 1960 Open, he was seven strokes behind.

Such strong come-from-behind finishes became known as "the Arnold Palmer charge" and the fans who followed him across the course became known as "Arnie's Army."

Palmer was named the *Sports Illustrated* Sportsman of the Year and the Hitchcock Athlete of the Year. The Associated Press would hail him as the Athlete of the Decade for the '60s.

"We have to play our foul balls."
— Sam Snead

116

"He that lives to live forever,
never fears dying."
— William Penn

Arnold Palmer was approaching his 70th birthday when I began writing this book. I remember that I had visited him one day at the Latrobe Country Club to do a cover story for *Roto*, a Sunday magazine in *The Pittsburgh Press*, when he turned 50. It appeared in the September 23rd issue, about two weeks after his birthday. It was hard to believe 20 years had passed since that day.

That was back in 1979, soon after I had moved back to Pittsburgh after spending ten years away, one year at *The Miami News*, and then nine years at *The New York Post*. I was covering the 3rd annual Press Old Newsboys Celebrity Golf Tournament hosted by Palmer at Latrobe Country Club. Ray Kienzl was then the lead golf writer at *The Press,* following Giffin and Bob Drum on that beat, and I was there looking for feature and column material.

Among the sports celebrities who participated in that outing were several members of the Steelers, Chuck Noll, Ray Mansfield, Matt Bahr, John Banaszak, Rocky Bleier, Jack Ham, Cliff Stoudt, Mike Webster, along with Jim Hart of the St. Louis Cardinals, Paul Warfield, Dick Anderson and Nick Buoniconti, former members of the Miami Dolphins, and Jackie Sherrill of Pitt. Gregg Sheppard represented the Penguins.

One can see the outline of a can of chewing tobacco in the back pocket of Palmer's slacks on the *Roto* cover shot.

It is difficult to imagine a more beautiful setting in Penn's Woods than the Laurel Highlands of Westmoreland County. I remember a radio commercial for Rolling Rock in which the beer's virtues were extolled. You could hear the pure mountain spring water splashing down from the mountains to the fertile valley below. You could almost taste it striking your tongue.

The Mellon Family could afford to live any place in the world, yet it chose to build estates, and summer there. The same also holds true for Arnold Palmer, a native son who travels the world, yet always returns home to restore his energies.

He was weaned on that pure mountain spring water and you'd swear his forearms were forged at Latrobe Steel. His home and office at The Latrobe Country Club, by the way, just for the record, are located in Youngstown, Pa., along the Latrobe borders. Palmer did graduate, however, from Latrobe High School. He has always called Latrobe his home.

He spoke at a reunion of his high school class and said, "When you're from this area, it's not just where you're from, it defines who you are."

He was one of Western Pennsylvania's greatest natural resources, one of the world's most popular and respected professional athletes, an international salesman for every product you can imagine and then some, but he's never felt the need to leave his Latrobe diggings. For over 20 years, however, he has been wintering in Florida. Who could blame him? The way Palmer sees it, he enjoys the best of both worlds.

Palmer learned to play golf in the Laurel Highlands, his dad, Deacon, teaching him to hit as hard as he possibly could, and he's never forgotten where he came from.

A few weeks earlier, between trips to Germany and North Carolina, Palmer came home again. On one of those rare days when he doesn't have some kind of business commitment somewhere, and when he only had to spend half the day on the telephone looking after his worldwide interests, talking with that rich, resonant voice of his, he did what he loves to do best — he went out and played golf with family and friends on his Latrobe Country Club course.

It is located right across the street from his private estate, where his home, office and workshop are situated within a high-walled compound.

There had been six inches of rain a few days before that threatened to wash away Westmoreland County and closed down a horsepulling contest at its fair, and a chilling breeze the night before, but the day came up bright and warm, as if the Mellons had it made to order. The greens were lush and the sky was as blue as Palmer's eyes. Those eyes are a blue that can only be seen in the clubhouse, when Palmer isn't squinting as he must in the sunlight, or in Paul Newman's head or the center of a glacier in Alaska, as I can personally attest.

He was playing with Roy Saunders, one of his two sons-in-law, who was in for a visit from Gainesville, and club champion Chris Adams and his father, Al.

"When I want to relax," said Palmer, who seldom does, "I like to play golf with friends. They try to hustle me. These guys are good amateur golfers and they always want more strokes than I should give them. We have a good time, though."

It was difficult to imagine anyone outhustling Arnold Palmer, who loved to shoot pool almost as much as he liked to play golf.

He smiled often, and enhanced the day for everybody, as only he can. "Arnold Palmer likes people," said Doc Giffin. "He's in the people business." Palmer, as I see it, would have made a great bartender if he hadn't been such a great golfer.

It struck one how much Arnold Palmer looked like Arnold Palmer. He acts, looks and is the part. He seemed to enjoy being Arnold Palmer, despite the demands. His whole life is golf, his family, his airplane and his business.

His wife, Winnie, was at home across the road. Like her husband, she has since been challenged by cancer herself. His daughter, Peggy, was married to Doug Reintgen, a fine golfer who became an even better doctor. Palmer's other daughter, Amy, was married to the Saunders fellow playing golf that day with Palmer.

Arnold and Winnie Palmer are at home in Latrobe.

Arnold Palmer and his wife, Winnie, both are challenged by cancer. "The very word...used in the same sentence as Winnie's name, has struck cold terror in my heart," said Palmer.

Palmer can look across the way from the clubhouse and see Latrobe Senior High School and remember like it was yesterday, when his girls were in school there. It's been reported that Arnold cried at his daughters' weddings, just another example of his humanness.

He seemed to gain strength from the moist Mother Earth as he strode the course, as only he can — he looks like he's charging even when he's playing for fun — and it was difficult to accept the fact that the man was charging toward his 50th birthday. (Now that I'm 56 and Palmer 70, I have different thoughts about his age and go-get-'em approach. Back then, I wondered how he could still walk as well as he did.)

It aged all of us. It bothered us. But did it bother Palmer? "Oh, no," replied Palmer. "Not when the alternative's so bad."

Palmer was going gray at the time. He was now officially in the classification of "senior" players on the Professional Golfers Association Tour, but he wasn't worrying about that. The Senior Tour was a start-up situation then, not as big a deal, or paying the kind of prizes it does today.

An argument used to be made that Latrobe was the birthplace of pro football, but it was later determined that the first pro, or paid performer in the game, was actually a member of the Pittsburgh A.A. team. His name was Pudge Heffelfinger. A better argument could be made that Latrobe, and not some green patch in Scotland, is the birthplace of pro golf as we know it. Arnold Palmer put professional golf where it is today.

He came along at the right time, when television was seeking a sports hero with whom the public could identify, and Palmer was perfect for the role.

Dan Jenkins, the best golf writer who ever sat in front of a typewriter or word processor, captured the early Palmer in print this way:

"He first came to golf as a muscular young man who could not keep his shirttail in, who smoked a lot, perspired a lot and who hit the ball with all of the finesse of a dock worker lifting a crate of auto parts. Arnold Palmer did not play golf, we thought. He nailed up beams, reupholstered sofas, repaired air-conditioning units. Sure, he made birdies by the streaks in his eccentric way — driving through forests, lacing hooks around sharp corners, spewing wild slices over prodigious hills, and then, all hunched up and pigeon-toed, staring putts into the cups. But he made just as many bogeys in his stubborn way. Anyhow, a guy whose slacks are too long and turned up at the cuffs, who matched green shirts with orange sweaters and who sweats so much is *not* going to rush past the Gene Littlers, Ken Venturis and Dow Finsterwalds to fill the hero gap created by the further graying and balding of Ben Hogan and Sam Snead."

Get the picture? Palmer, at 50, was a different matter. He'd matured gracefully and there was a more polished Palmer that met the public at this point in his career.

Dr. Jonas Salk, who discovered the anti-polio vaccine at Pitt in the mid-1950s, and opera diva Beverly Sills join Arnold at a fund-raiser in the 1960s.

Dow Finsterwald and Dick Groat get together with Arnold at Pebble Beach in the 1960s. Groat was the NL MVP in 1960 when Pirates won the World Series and Palmer was the PGA Golfer of the Year.

"He's the Muhammad Ali of golf."
— Fuzzy Zoeller

He was a Mark McCormack creation — molded and schooled to be more marketing-smart by his agent in Cleveland — larger than life, yet still so down to earth. What a combination — a lot more classic than those green shirts and orange sweater match-ups.

Palmer was prepared for another season of questions alluding to his age. He got testy at times about it, which Jacqueline Kennedy could appreciate as the former First Lady was getting the same treatment at the time. "I see a lot of stuff in the paper," said Palmer that same summer during the U.S. Open at Inverness outside of Toledo, "telling me that I should do this or that with my life. I don't think anyone should make a judgment about what I should do with my life."

It seems funny now, writers being concerned about what Palmer ought to be doing at 50. Like he really listened. They are still asking him the same questions 20 years later.

"There will come a time when I quit, but when I do, it will be forever," said Palmer. "I won't be back. But I'm not ready to quit. Look at that guy on the screen (Byron Nelson was on television.) Byron quit at 30. I've heard him say lots of times he wished he hadn't. But that was his life.

"If winning was the whole thing, there'd be a hell of a lot of disappointment in the world. Sure, it's hard not to win when you've once won. But it's also hard not to be there playing. When I stop playing golf, I'll have to find something else competitive I can do. I might start racing horses, who knows?"

He smiled at the idea. He already had an interest, though, in some harness racing horses with his good friend, Del Miller of The Meadowlands. Ed Ryan, Jack Piatt and Joe Hardy had horses out in those Washington, Pa. barns as well. Stan Musial, a buddy of both Miller and Palmer, used to show up for special promotions.

Palmer could no longer play as he did in his glory days, those red-hot years from 1958 to 1966, when he was winning everything in sight, with the exception of the PGA.

He had won 92 tournaments worldwide. His 60 Tour victories trailed only Sam Snead (81), Jack Nicklaus (70) and Ben Hogan (63) on the all-time list. He was the first player in PGA Tour history to reach the $1 million mark in official earnings, achieving that feat in 1968. He led the PGA Tour in earnings in 1958, 1960, 1962 and 1963.

He was one of only four men to win the first official Senior Tour event he entered, the 1980 PGA Seniors' Championship. His victory at the U.S. Senior Open at Oakland Hills one year later made him the first man to claim both a U.S. Open and U.S. Senior Open title. Palmer was one of the reasons the Senior Tour was instituted, according to Dean Beman, the PGA Commissioner.

He won the Masters four times and finished runner-up three times, he won the British Open twice and was runner-up, he won the U.S. Open once and was runner-up four times, and he was runner-up three times in the PGA.

In more recent years, he was always the sentimental favorite. "My golf isn't good enough to be anything else," he said. "I don't resent it. I'm glad that people think enough of me to make me a sentimental favorite. But I didn't spend my life working to that goal.

"I realize I'm not 28 or even 35 anymore. Obviously, I've lost something physically, but every time I go out to play I have to think in my mind I can still play the way I used to."

It's a known fact that when a golfer gets older, the first thing he loses is his putting stroke. Putting was never one of Palmer's strong suits, even in the days when he was the best player on the Tour. "I had to putt boldly to score," he said. "But the rest of my game was strong, and that helped my putting because I didn't have to make too many long ones."

Bobby Jones once said, "If my life depended on a putt, I'd have Arnold Palmer putt it for me."

Reminded of that, Palmer responded, haltingly, "There was a time...there was a time...there was a time when I felt like I could make every putt — particularly if it meant something. But I don't think I was ever a great putter."

His peers appreciated his importance to the game. One of them, Fuzzy Zoeller, said few players had Palmer's charisma. "We have some players who are characters and some who can play well," said Zoeller, "but none of them has the charisma of Arnold Palmer. He's the Muhammad Ali of golf."

"He's probably the greatest people-person in the history of golf."
— Mark O'Meara

Arnold Palmer was described by one of his biographers, Larry Guest of Orlando, as "one of the most compelling men of our times." Guest painted Palmer as a "man's man" and as "a swashbuckling risktaker who enjoys life to the fullest, a champion of the so-called moral majority, perhaps the most compelling athletic hero of the 20th century." They don't come any bigger than that.

Guest goes back to Palmer's early days, when he was 17 and won the Pennsylvania state amateur championship. On one hole, there were trees blocking his approach to the green. He told the gallery he was going to put the ball through a two-foot opening and onto the green, and he did.

"That was always my joy," said Palmer. "That put more pressure on me to do it. Sometimes I didn't, but when I did it was a great thrill for me and the fans."

What makes the story even better is that Palmer was playing in front of a half-dozen friends and relatives. Yet it was the start of his signature "go-for-broke" style.

Palmer also performed in a few high school plays back in those days, and even sang in the church choir. It helped keep him well-grounded.

He became a disciple of the game, and worked hard to improve at every facet of his game. He had a hell-bent drive for first place or nothing. It pleased Palmer to win with a flair, coming from behind, or with a spectacular shot on the 17th or 18th. He had a bold playing style, and it appealed to the golf writers who began to build his legendary reputation.

The late *Los Angeles Times* columnist Jim Murray once compared Arnie's arrival at any PGA Tour event to a swashbuckler jumping onto the deck of a pirate ship, knife clinched between his teeth.

British writer Louis T. Stanley wrote in *Legends of Golf* (1997): "No individual elevated the status of a golf professional as much as Arnold Palmer."

He had some of the best writers trudging behind him, from Bob Drum and Doc Giffin in Pittsburgh, to Dan Jenkins, Bud Shrake and Herbert Warren Wind writing about him on a national level, and they liked this guy from Latrobe right from the beginning. He was always accessible, and he took pride in being a regular guy.

He was a hero, and he knew his lines. Once, when he was speaking before the Downtown Athletic Club in Orlando in 1988, he was asked if he ever thought about running for the Presidency.

"I thought seriously about the Presidency," he said with a wide grin, "but I decided I couldn't afford the pay cut."

Guest, a golf writer and columnist for the *Orlando Sentinel*, kept a close watch on Palmer, and even played a round or two with him from time to time. They got along well. Guest positively gushed over Palmer in print.

"He is an exemplary figure," wrote Guest, "an eminently commendable sports hero for our times."

Guest was among the writers who appreciated the way Palmer responded to their needs. "He looks at you when you ask him a question," said Guest. See, that's something that everyone notices right away about Palmer.

It's something any teacher appreciates in a student, something a wife appreciates in a husband, something anyone should strive to emulate. It's pretty difficult to mimic Palmer while playing golf — though many do: "What would Arnie do if he were in this spot?" they ask themselves — but it makes more sense to study his sales skills, and follow his lead in that regard.

Arnold Palmer was one of the first pro golfers to get his own airplane. He prided himself on his piloting skills. They named the airport near his home in Westmoreland County in his honor in 1999.

Broadcaster Jim Simpson interviews three of the game's greatest players back in the 1960s, left to right, Arnold Palmer, Gary Player and Jack Nicklaus.

"I'm damned proud of my efforts."
— Arnold Palmer, from his
autobiography *A Golfer's Life*,
written with James Dodson

There are many how-to-play-golf books reputed to be Arnold Palmer's approach to the game, but there ought to be a book about his approach to people and to life in general.

The current stars paid Palmer proper tribute. Mark O'Meara, an Orlando golfer who really came into his own in the late '90s, said, "Arnold Palmer is the greatest at what he does. He knows how to deal with people. He's a people person, probably the greatest people-person in the history of golf."

He won so many friends for golf. He and President Eisenhower, one of our most popular military and political leaders, combined to popularize the game in America. Palmer was always flirting with disaster, and his game seemed most like everyman's in that regard, but it's what he did on the next shot that made him a superman.

Super agent Mark McCormack often gets credit for shaping the Palmer persona, but McCormack knew better. He knew that Arnold Palmer was a product of his father, Milfred "Deacon" Palmer.

"Deacon taught his son the straight and narrow of life," said McCormack, "and wanted to make darned sure his son stayed on it. He had a huge influence on Arnold throughout his career. We all are trying to prove ourselves to somebody or get the approval of somebody, and in Arnold's case that somebody was his father."

There were many Scottish-Irish values instilled in Palmer by his "Pap," as he liked to call his dad.

"Deke" Palmer went to work for the Latrobe Country Club in 1921, and he was still working for the club when he died in 1976. His ashes where strewn by the 18th green. He was the father of four children, and he paid as much attention to the others as he did to his best-known son.

"I have two daughters and two sons and Arnold is just one of them," Deke declared. "I'm proud of them all."

Arnold knew his place and it helped him keep things in their proper perspective. "Pap didn't just teach me how to play golf. He taught me discipline." He always acknowledged that "Pap" would always be with him.

Deke believed in all the right things — God, country, hard work, respect for others, Lawrence Welk, a shot-and-beer at the bar and, most of all, humility.

He was quick to scold his son if he thought he was getting too big for his britches. When he saw Arnold throw a temper tantrum on his course as a kid, he screamed, "If I ever see you throwing clubs on a golf course again, your golfing days are over!"

Palmer never knocked his opponents in the papers. "My father taught me when I was a boy to be a gentleman," said Palmer. "It's a lesson that I have never forgotten. I've always wanted to win as much as anybody who ever played this game. But I never wanted to win so badly that I would hurt somebody else. I never did see how it would help my game to be mean to another player."

He had an unfailing sense of thoughtfulness. He never made excuses for a bad round. Honesty was his best policy.

"I blew it," he would say.

Palmer took pride in his behavior as a pro and the way he comported himself every time out. He liked to drop in neighborhood pool halls or bars and compete with the locals. "It's fun to sometimes be down here with some people that are down-to-earth and different," he once said. "I enjoy that. I enjoy hearing them and talking to them. They are just nice people who are going along and want to have a little fun and drink a little beer and enjoy life."

As Guest put it, "He had a commoner's touch. He grew up as the son of a humble greenskeeper during The Great Depression. His playground was the country club. He was three years old when Deke started to teach him how to play golf."

He hitched his pants and took all the shortcuts and challenged the course and captured the fans' imagination. In 1971, he bought the club where his dad worked all those years. His success and the money that came with it surprised him.

"I was having fun," he said. "I was enjoying it because I didn't think there would be that much money to play for. And I enjoyed the people. They rooted and screamed when I hit it through the trees. And I still like to play for that reason. The fellas today are a little different in that they are real businessmen, right from the beginning. I had to win the Masters twice before I could afford my own plane. Today, these guys can get one after a few weeks on The Tour.

"I wanted to be one of the great players who hit it in the woods over here, and then in the ditch over there and got it in the hole on the next shot. And I didn't care how that happened. And that's what people liked. They enjoyed that, and I enjoyed that."

"Go get 'em, Arnie!"

I was still 19 when I was rooting, like so many Western Pennsylvanians, for Arnold Palmer to win the U.S. Open at Oakmont June 14-17, 1962. He was the biggest man in golf at the time, and looked like a natural to win. He would be playing in front of people who knew him, rooted openly for him, and worshipped him. He knew the course; he had played it many times as an amateur.

Palmer had been the British Open champion the previous July, and had won the Masters in April for the third time in five years. He was at the top of his game.

It was the first time I was ever at a country club in my life. One of the waitresses at the Oakmont Country Club was a sister of one of my aunts. That was almost the only way anyone in my family was going to get into a country club back then. I was on my best behavior.

I ran into two fellows from my old neighborhood, Jack and Ronnie Fite. They lived in my house at 5410 Sunnyside Street before I did. I wondered how they got in. For the rest of my sportswriting career, no matter where I went, I always ran into guys from the old neighborhood. They knew how to crash the best parties, with or without credentials or invitations.

Jack Nicklaus had just joined the pro Tour after many successes as an amateur out of Ohio State University.

Oakmont was regarded as a monster of a course, a true test for veterans and downright unfair and unforgiving for rookies. Its greens were glossy, and it had those infamous furrowed sand bunkers — "the church pews" — that made it different from every other course in this country. They have since been eliminated from the course.

"Go get 'em, Arnie!" fans were yelling, right from the start. There was no question as to who was the hometown favorite. The gathering loved Palmer's bold, attacking style, plus he was from nearby Latrobe.

They played 36 holes on the last day of the scheduled tournament then. Palmer had 73 in the morning and 71 in the afternoon, and finished in a tie with Nicklaus. They had an 18-hole playoff on Monday and Nicklaus carded a 71 and Palmer a 74, and the outcome never seemed to be in question. Palmer should have won. He was the better golfer at the time, but he did not. I still have color photos I took that weekend of all the top pros, including Palmer, Billy Casper, Gene Littler and Gary Player.

He lost a playoff the following year to Julius Boros in the U.S. Open.

He won often enough, however, to retain his position as the premier player in golf. He became a multi-millionaire, the first to fly a plane of his own, and he showed the way for others to follow.

Some of the more enlightened young pros of this era are in awe of Palmer. Jeff Sluman, who competed in the Family House Invitational at Oakmont in 1997 and went on to win the British Open, said, "We all grew up watching Arnie and rooting for him. But the real magic comes when you meet him. There's just no one like him."

The grind of the tour and the toll it can take on family life never seemed to affect Palmer.

He won seven Grand Slam titles and the U.S. Amateur title when that was something special.

In his terrific book, *A Good Walk Spoiled,* John Feinstein wrote, "No one has ever been loved and revered and *worshipped* like Arnie. Palmer has been the single most important player in the history of golf."

Arnie has always been one of the guys, but he's never stopped wanting to win.

"That's why we still tee it up," he says.

He hopes he's gained the respect of the players, young and old, and that his feelings merit their attention.

"I don't want to be some old man going on about the old days," he said, "but I still have some strong opinions about the tour and what goes on around the players in the game today."

There are things that have changed that Palmer doesn't appreciate much. "Anyone who would charge for an autograph ought to be ashamed of themselves," he has said. "It's an honor and a privilege to be asked for an autograph. I just don't know what's wrong with these people.

"A lot of players just don't understand how lucky we all are to be doing what we do. I look at my life and all I can do is be thankful for everything I've been given by so many people over so many years. It's just too much damn fun to ever stop."

Palmer can see the end coming, however, to playing competitive golf. In July of 1999, he was particularly frustrated after shooting rounds of 81 and 84 and failing to make the cut in the U.S. Senior Open for the first time since 1991. Palmer was pleased that he was still the biggest draw for a record crowd in West Des Moines, Iowa, but not with his play. "Well," he said, "I guess everything has to come to an end somewhere."

A month after he said Arnold Palmer should stop playing in the Masters, Mark Calcavecchia apologized to the King. And he planned to apologize a few more times.

Calcavecchia, who was playing in the group behind Palmer the first two days at Augusta National in 1999, said at the time that Palmer should "surrender" after a first-round 83. Calcavecchia later wrote a letter of apology to Palmer, who graciously accepted.

"The next time I see Arnold I'm going to apologize in person," Calcavecchia told Golf World magazine. "Then, the next time I see him after that I'm going to apologize again. I don't know what I was thinking when I ripped him other than I wasn't thinking.

"I was mad at the world and I took it out on Arnold. I was totally out of line. We're not talking about just another golfer here, you know. We're talking about a legend. I took some heat for my dumb remarks, mostly from my wife."

Sam Huff
Ambassador from West Virginia

"The game came easy to me."

There was no hesitation in Sam Huff's cheerful voice. "Let's do it now," he said, when I told him I wanted to schedule an interview with him. He was at home at Sporting Life Farm, a 22-acre horse farm he owns in Middleburg, Virginia.

We were talking over the telephone, and I was explaining why I had called. I told him I was writing this book about hometown heroes, and he was one of those I had in mind. He was always a personal favorite.

Sam Huff excelled as the prototype middle linebacker for 13 pro football seasons, the first eight with the New York Giants from 1956 through 1963 and the final five with the Washington Redskins. During his days in New York, he became one of the most publicized of all pro football players.

I told him some of the other people I was profiling. "I'm honored," he said. "That's pretty good company."

Huff prides himself on not procrastinating, and this was proof of it. So many ballplayers today are always putting off interviews for another day, so Huff, as always, was a breath of fresh air. He'd come up the hard way, and he appreciated anybody who wanted to hear and write his story.

He picked up the telephone himself after only two rings at his horse farm, which is about 45 miles from Washington, D.C., and what followed was an enriching experience. It was such an easy conversation. To him, it comes naturally. He couldn't have been a better ambassador for his sport.

"I always thought the writers were an important part of the league," explained Huff. "I always had time to talk to the reporters, and got along with everybody in New York and Washington when I was playing. They were good to me and I tried my best to be decent with them. It was no big deal."

I had last interviewed Huff in Hawaii at a National Football League owners' meeting, and that was 17 years earlier. It hardly seemed that long ago. He had all the time in the world for me then, when he was basking in the sun of a paradise in the Pacific as a sales and marketing representative for the Marriott chain. He was just as cooperative and cordial this time around. I had interviewed Huff a half dozen times in my career, and they were all entertaining and enlightening experiences. After all these years, I still get pumped up when somebody like Sam Huff had an hour for me, and seemed so naturally helpful and pleasant.

I'd had a similar experience a year earlier talking on the telephone to Don Maynard, one of Joe Namath's favorite receivers, when

I called him in Texas to reflect on the New York Jets' victory in the 1969 Super Bowl for a 30th anniversary piece for *Street & Smith's Pro Football*.

Robert Lee "Sam" Huff knows his history well, loves to talk to people, has a great sense of humor, a down-home outlook on life, and is eager to share his blessings and stories with anyone who'll listen. Maynard, the pride of El Paso, was like that, too.

An hour with Huff is better than reading a self-help book. He is so glib, so positive, so proud of what he has accomplished, yet he doesn't boast about it. He's happy for the life he's led, the long association with sports and special people. There is a light in his brown eyes as he speaks, I recalled. He had his own ideas of how to succeed in this world, how to excel at something. He talked about the coal mining camp in West Virginia where he grew up, and the memories of those days — when his father and neighbors came home from work with blackened faces and hands — kept him humble. He was born there during The Great Depression, and it was a demanding life for everyone in the family.

His father, Oral, gave him the nickname of Sam at an early age. If it hadn't been for football, Huff might have ended up as a coal miner like his father, and so many of their relatives.

"I'm one of the most fortunate people in the world," he went on as he talked about those early days and his good fortune to become a pro football player. "I wouldn't trade it for anything. I look back and I can't believe it."

Huff said his health was outstanding as we talked the evening of April 13, 1999. He would be 65 come October. "I'm in such good health," he added, "I think I could play one more game. If they could send that old guy — astronaut John Glenn — up in space, why not me?"

Huff talked about his activities. He was still providing analysis and color for Radio WJFK broadcasts of the Washington Redskins, which he had been doing since 1973. He had retired after 27 years in marketing for Marriott, pitching them to pro and college sports teams throughout the country as the best place to stay for road contests, but still helped them with special events.

He raised race horses, and was particularly excited about a five-year-old thoroughbred filly named Bursting Forth, which had some Northern Dancer blood in her. "She runs on grass very well," he said, pointing toward an upcoming racing date for her. He did a syndicated five-minute horse racing report that was beamed everywhere by satellite, as well as on the Internet. He'd been doing the show for 15 years.

He was looking forward to July 6, 1999 when he would be inducted into the National High School Sports Hall of Fame in nearby Washington, D.C. "I've just been elected, and I'm excited about that as much as anything I've ever gotten," he said. "When I think back, playing ball at a Class B school in little ol' Farmington, we didn't have a stadium. No grass. I used to help put down lime to line the field. To come from that and be inducted into a national hall of fame... When you think of all the kids who played sports and graduated from high schools, there's more competition than there is to get into the Pro Football Hall of Fame."

Farmington is only seven miles from Fairmont, the hometown of Olympic gold medalist Mary Lou Retton, another of America's most popular athletic figures.

Huff was enshrined at the Pro Football Hall of Fame in Canton, Ohio back in 1982. He was inducted along with Doug Atkins, Merlin Olsen and George Musso.

"I cried like a baby when they told me I had been elected to the Pro Football Hall of Fame," Huff said at the time. "When you realize how few people are in the Hall, it's just an indescribable feeling."

Huff has come back for other induction ceremonies, and I've been lucky to catch him there a few times, as I make an annual pilgrimage to Canton. He was one of the most famous football players of his time, one of the first to gain national exposure on television. There was no ESPN in his day, no nightly highlights in every hamlet in the world. TV and pro football found each other in his heyday. It was the beginning of a beautiful relationship.

He benefitted greatly from playing in New York, the nation's media center. He was the subject of a 1960 TV documentary called "The Violent World of Sam Huff," and he made the middle linebacker position one of the most coveted and glamorous this side of playing quarterback. He was wearing a miniature microphone — the first pro football player to do that — and everyone heard most of what Huff had to say as he went about his work, terrorizing his opponent. It was great theater. Huff was hardly a violent man, however. He was a teddy bear, a fun fellow with a quick smile, a quick story or joke, and a warm manner. On the football field, however, he was one of the fiercest competitors. If you had a football in your hands, he was coming after you. He followed the ball, it was that simple. He was famous for making tackles from one sideline to the other.

At the age of 24, Huff was also featured on the cover of *Time* magazine. His number 70 became known to youngsters across America. Those were different days, however, and kids weren't wearing football jerseys to school with the names and numbers of their favorite players.

In Huff's eight years in New York, the Giants reached the NFL title game six times back when it was the ultimate game, in the pre-Super Bowl era. They won the championship in 1956.

His Giants played against the Colts in the celebrated sudden-death championship contest in 1958 that was heralded as "the greatest football game in history." Since the Giants lost out to the John Unitas-directed Colts, Huff had mixed emotions about the game rating that all-time tag.

It may or may not have been the greatest football game in history. It was, indeed, the most important game in the NFL up until that time. This was the game that did it for NFL football. It seemed that everyone was watching this game on television. This game sold the sport to America.

In an NFL-produced book, *The First 50 Years*, this summary of that game's impact appears: "Pro football had risen from the sandlot days through a stage as Sunday pastime. Now it was launched as a significant portion of the mass culture of America... And it started with sudden death."

"Football...it's America's game."
— Sam Huff

He was born October 4, 1934 in Morgantown, West Virginia, 30 miles from the coal mining camp where his father worked and where the family lived.

"My dad was a coal miner, and he weighed about 155 pounds," said Huff. "I was raised in a coal mining camp, where the owners owned the mines, the company store, the houses where the miners lived."

You can hear Tennessee Ernie Ford singing about the company store, and Jimmy Dean singing about Big Bad John in the background as Sam Huff talks about his early days.

He was a two-way All-America lineman at West Virginia University in 1955, and the No. 3 draft pick of the New York Giants in 1956. He also had a fling as a catcher with the Cleveland Indians, at their Class A minor league club in Reading, Pennsylvania, before reporting to play in the College All-Star Game in Chicago.

The Giants initially played him at tackle and guard on the offensive line, then switched him to the other side of the ball. He initially signed with the Giants for $7,000 a season. There was no bonus, and you had to buy your own shoes and make sure they were broken in before you reported to training camp. Landry was developing a 4-3 defense which was taking the place of the then fashionable five-man line.

"I felt as if I had been born to play middle-linebacker," said Huff. "I, for one, knew hardly any of these ballplayers when I reported to camp. I had heard of Dick Modzelewski, out of Maryland, but he was in his first season with the Giants after having played at Washington and Pittsburgh. I knew Rosey Grier, another tackle, because I had played against him when he was at Penn State. But basically I had not seen the Giants play. Remember, this was before televised football became so popular."

Huff did not appear to have great speed or great strength, but he had enough of both — plus a tremendous enthusiasm for the game — to become the ideal middleman in the intricate and highly-effective Giants' defense.

134

The middle linebacker's role was to be big enough to handle the power runners, fast enough to overhaul swift linebackers and to protect against passes. Sam had a nose for the ball and a heart to do whatever was necessary to stop the opposition.

"You play as hard and as tough as you can," said Huff, "but you play clean. We hit each other hard, sure. But this is a man's game and any guy who doesn't want to hit hard doesn't belong in it."

Opposing coaches had great respect for Huff's ability.

"It's uncanny the way Huff follows the ball," said Green Bay's fabled coach, Vince Lombardi. "He ignores all the things you do to get him away from the play and he comes after the ball wherever it's thrown or wherever the run goes. He seems to be all over the field at once."

Huff was an inspirational leader, a brilliant diagnostician with great instincts and tackling ability. During his 13-year NFL career, he was noted for hard-hitting duels with premier running backs like Jim Brown of the Cleveland Browns, Jim Taylor of the Green Bay Packers, Alan Ameche of the Baltimore Colts, Rick Casares of the Bears and Ollie Matson of the Cardinals.

"We tried to kill each other every play," Huff said.

After the 1962 NFL title game, Taylor accused Huff of piling on, and Jim Brown defended Huff, saying he played hard but not dirty. Huff had more success in stopping Brown than Taylor in their storied clashes.

"We knew Jim Brown would carry the ball 25 or 30 times," Huff recalled. "By sticking with him, I was in front of the play most of the afternoon. That was a tough assignment, covering Brown. When you hit him, he lunged like a bull, sometimes he lunged right out of the tackle. I loved nothing better than playing against Jim Brown. There's something special about facing the really great backs."

Their rivalry began in their college days when West Virginia and Syracuse regularly played one another. Huff had great respect for Brown on and off the field, and the feeling was mutual.

"I see Jimmy Brown every year," said Huff, when we spoke in April, 1999. "Bobby Mitchell has a golf tournament in Washington, and Brown comes. He tells everybody he put me in the Hall of Fame. Bill Russell comes, Oscar Robertson — the Big O — comes. It's great to be with those guys."

They should be just as happy to be in Huff's company. Huff had 30 career interceptions — only two less than Jack Ham's league-leading 32 among linebackers — played in six NFL title games, five Pro Bowls and was All-NFL four years. He was named the top NFL linebacker in 1959. He was a player-coach with the Redskins in 1969, coming out of a one-year retirement to help Lombardi revive the Redskins after that legendary coach-general manager departed Green Bay to become the boss in D.C. Lombardi had been an assistant, along with Tom Landry, on Jim Lee Howell's staff when Huff broke in with the Giants. Lombardi improved the Redskins right away, posting their first winning season (7-5-2) in 14 seasons, but died the next summer. Huff had no desire to continue after that and retired again.

"Vince Lombardi was a motivator of men," said Huff. "He was some person. He really had charisma. The first time I ever heard that word, he used it. Charisma. Geez, Lombardi had it."

So does Huff. Huff always had a glad hand and was good company at the NFL owners' meetings, one of the highlights of covering the Steelers and the NFL for *The Pittsburgh Press* (1979-1983) at resorts in Maui, Palm Springs and Phoenix.

He said he had missed the 1999 meeting in Phoenix because of an airplane problem in Miami. "I didn't mind, really," he said. "The Redskins ownership situation was still up in the air, and I didn't want to get caught in the middle of that. That's the first one I missed in a long time."

With all his activities, Huff said football was still his primary passion. "Always has been. I've been fortunate. I love the game and I've been very successful at it. Football comes hard to some guys, and easy for some guys. It came very easy to me. I loved the grind, the teamwork, the discipline. I thrived on it," he said.

He knew how lucky he'd been. He spoke about Consolidated Coal Camp No. 9, his home when he was young. It was in a place called Edna Gas. "It doesn't exist anymore," he said, a hint of sorrow in his voice. "There was a big coal explosion there in the '60s (1968), when I was playing pro football with the Redskins. There were 78 miners trapped and killed. Five of my relatives, including three cousins, were among those who were killed. It could have been me if it weren't for football."

He still carries a lot with him from his Farmington days. "When I was young, I worked for an Italian family at a furniture store in Farmington," he recalled. "The owner's name was John Marchin. He also had a grocery store. He was a real salesman, and he taught me how to treat people.

"He gave me a job when I was 16 and 17. I was playing football at West Virginia and I'd come home from the games and work there. Mr. Marchin had a two-story building, and it burned down when I was playing pro football. They never had a ladder in the local fire department that went up as high as two stories in that little town of 700 people. They lost four people in that fire; it was a terrible tragedy."

Sam married Mary Fletcher when they were 17, and they had quite a run together. They had, however, been divorced 12 years when we spoke. I remember how he had boasted about Mary and her impact on his life when we last spoke in Hawaii. I still remembered her name, one of those things that remains in the back of your brain. Huff had not remarried, but he told me his "significant other" was Carol Holden.

When he left a Class B high school to play for Pappy Lewis at West Virginia in 1952, his class included four other fellows who would

Sam Huff returns to WVU campus to be honored at halftime.

Sam Huff

Huff lines up for Mountaineers in early 1950s.

The freshman recruiting class of 1952 was one of the finest in WVU history, including, left to right, Bobby Moss, Sam Huff, Bruce Bosely, Joe Marconi and Fred Wyant, who all went on to play pro ball.

later play professional football. He not only remembered their names, but their hometowns as well.

They included Bruce Bosley, of Green Bank; Bobby Moss, of East Bank; Joe Marconi, of Frederickstown, Pa., and Fred Wyant of Weston, who played in the National Football League, the Canadian Football League, and later served as an NFL official. "Pappy Lewis taught us all how to play football," said Huff. Marconi, who is now deceased, was his roommate. Huff was a three-year starter and a captain his senior season.

Huff was discovered by Giants' scout Al DeRogatis when he went to a West Virginia game to rate Bosley. "Bosley is great...but there's another guard there who will be even greater," reported DeRogatis. "His name is Sam Huff."

Huff was a senior when Jerry West was a freshman at WVU, and remains a big fan of his as well as Hot Rod Hundley.

Huff nearly returned to West Virginia to work following another tragedy. He was a strong candidate to coach at Marshall University in December of 1970, shortly after a November 14 chartered jet airplane crash that killed 37 Marshall football players and eight athletic department members, including head coach Rick Tolley. Somehow that didn't work out.

He even staged an unsuccessful campaign for a Congressional seat from West Virginia after he retired from football. He kept some ties to his home state, however. He remained a driving force behind the West Virginia Breeders Classic in Charleston.

"I looked up to Ernie Stautner."
— Sam Huff

When Sam Huff played for the New York Giants their defensive unit was the first to command national attention. Their ends were Andy Robustelli and Jim Katcavage, and tackles Roosevelt Grier and Dick Modzelewski. Huff played middle linebacker between two mobile wings, Harland Svare and Bill Svoboda. The backfield was good and experienced, with Lindon Crow and Carl Karilivacz at corners, Jim Patton and Emlen Tunnell at safety. "Tunnell was the best safety of his time," said Huff.

So Huff had a strong affinity for the Steelers of the '70s, and started talking about them when Pittsburgh came into the conversation. "That was some team," he said, admiringly. "I watched those linebackers work. When they had Andy Russell, Jack Lambert and Jack Ham in there together they may have had the best threesome ever. That was a helluva football team. Their angled pursuit was perfect, their tackling ability was second to none. Chuck Noll was quite the coach, and they had solid schemes."

Huff said he was a big fan of Pittsburgh and its teams, since he grew up only 85 miles away. "I was a Steelers' fan, a Pirates' fan," he said. "I loved the Steelers; I loved the Rooneys. I looked up to Ernie Stautner — there was no tougher player in football — and we became friends later on. I remember Dale Dodril, their middle linebacker. I never met him, but I heard about him.

"When I played college football, I was hoping that someday I could play for the Steelers. I told Art Rooney once that I wished they had drafted me, and he said, 'Sam, you're just damn lucky we didn't draft you, the kind of team we were then.' When I think about the Rooney Family and the Mara Family in New York, I think of some great people. I didn't get to know George Halas, but I have respect for all those founding fathers of our game.

"When I think of Pittsburgh, I think of Danny Marino. Dan's one of the truly great people I've ever met. I watched Marino play when he was at Pitt. He's not only been a great player, but better still, he's one of the best people of all time.

"Back in the 1973 season, I was watching Pitt play West Virginia at the old Mountaineer Field in Morgantown. They beat us pretty good (35-7). When I saw (Giants' owner) Wellington Mara, I said, 'I just saw the greatest running back since O.J. Simpson.' He said, 'Who is he?' I said, 'He's only a freshman, and his name is Tony Dorsett. I saw him run and this kid's sensational.'

"I loved the Pirates with Danny Murtaugh and Dick Groat. I loved Bob Prince. He used to work with Rosey Rowswell, and then Jim Woods and Nellie King. Those were all great people. Prince and Rowswell...that shows you how far back I go with the Pirates. Prince was truly one of the great sports announcers of all time. I always thought the Dapper Dan banquet in Pittsburgh was the best sports banquet in the country. Prince was peerless as the emcee. It was fun. They always treated you great. When you talk about Pittsburgh, you're talking about a city I love."

Even so, he loved playing in New York. The low point in his pro career came when the Giants traded him to the Redskins in 1964. Huff has never gotten over it. He blamed Allie Sherman, the Giants head coach at the time.

"I cried," said Huff, recalling how he felt at the time. "That was the worst thing anyone could ever do to a guy who loved a team and performed for it as I did. People ask me, 'How could you still carry a grudge?' I answer, 'You never forget pain.' Next to a death in the family, it was the most painful thing that ever happened to me."

"We are all of us, it has been said, the children of immigrants and foreigners . . . What a man is and what he becomes is in part due to his heritage."
— Western writer Louis L'Amour

"I want to be somebody."
— Rev. Jesse Jackson

When I asked Huff to reflect on his personal philosophy, he said, "It's to be somebody. Be proud of the uniform you wear. Try to excel. Get your education. Nobody can ever take that away from you. Don't procrastinate. When somebody asks me to do something, I get it done. I don't just think about it. I do it. Word gets around. Credibility is a key word. Good coaches are always preaching about accountability and credibility. You gotta have pride in yourself. Jesse Jackson put it all together for me when he said, 'I want to be somebody.' If you have that in your mind, in this country where you have so much opportunity, you can accomplish great things.

"I never bragged about myself. I always thought there were better ballplayers. I never said I was No. 1. I never ran around saluting the sky, or holding up my finger to say I was No. 1. I hate that stuff.

"That's what I liked about football. It was a team game. I like the team."

I mentioned to Huff that he provided quite a contrast to someone like Kordell Stewart, the Steelers' quarterback who had come under criticism in his third pro season.

Two years earlier, I attempted to interview Stewart for a book I was writing about the Steelers. He was in the team's clubhouse when I approached him. "Don't you know the new rule?" Stewart asked me when I pulled out my pen and notebook. "I only do interviews on Wednesday." Oops, it was Thursday.

I told Stewart he was telling me something I had never been told by Terry Bradshaw, Franco Harris, Jack Ham, Mel Blount, Henry Aaron, Wilt Chamberlain, Dr. J, Muhammad Ali or anybody else in sports. Tony Parisi, the team's equipment manager, scolded me for scolding Stewart. "Besides, he doesn't even know who the hell those guys are!" said Parisi.

Huff had a thought about that, too. "Kordell has all the talent in the world," he said, "but you have to be a team guy to be a good quarterback. That might help explain why he's been having problems. He was just getting started, and he was already talking about being in the Hall of Fame someday.

"If Ernie Stautner were still playing for the Steelers, or if Art Rooney were still there, Kordell Stewart would have a different attitude. They'd straighten him out in a hurry.

"Nobody was as tough as Ernie on the field, and as much fun off the field. We played in the Pro Bowl together. One year I had Bob Lilly of the Cowboys and Ernie Stautner of the Steelers as the tackles in front of me. It was the only time I went a whole quarter without making a tackle. I finally hollered at them in the huddle, 'Would you let

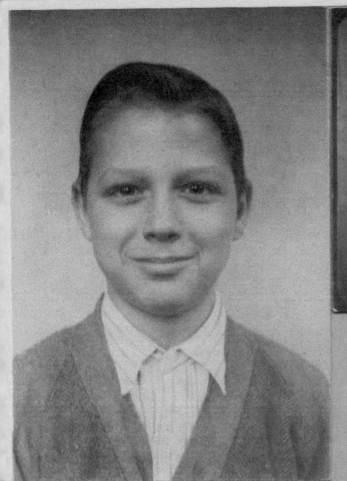

SCHOOL DAYS

1940-1941

Sam

somebody through so I can tackle somebody!' You appreciated people like that. Jack Lambert was a tough guy. He was a beer-drinking tough guy. I'll tell you something, though. He wouldn't fool with Ernie."

"I always got along well with bartenders."
— Sam Huff

That last observation took me back to Maui where I had my last meeting with Huff. That was in 1982, and Huff was 47 and I was 40. I can picture Huff like it was yesterday. His hearty laugh punctuated his story-telling, and it came off like a television beer commercial. I checked a story I had written back then for *NFL Gameday* to get the details.

"I always got along well with bartenders," Huff said. "I'd come in and sit on a stool, and more often than not the guy would give me a look, like he was eyeing a diamond and say, 'Hey, you're Sam Huff, aren't you?' And I'd smile and he'd draw me a beer.

"But, just as often, there was always some wise guy in the bar who'd hear that and come over and needle me. 'So, you're Sam Huff,' he'd say. 'Well, you don't look so tough to me. I think I can kick your butt.' Most of the time, I'd talk my way or walk my way out of those situations.

"I wasn't looking for trouble. But, because of football and the reputation I had, they always found me. I was a marked man after CBS did that half-hour documentary on me called 'The Violent World of Sam Huff' and after Jim Taylor of the Green Bay Packers said I was a dirty player who piled on a lot.

"One day I went into this bar, and this guy got on my case. 'I think I can whup you,' he said with a snarl as he put his face into my face. He caught me in a foul mood that day, and I grabbed the front of his shirt, and I gave him this look — just like I'm looking at you now — and I said to him, like I used to say to Jim Taylor all the time, 'Listen, are you ready to make a commitment? Because if you are, I'm gonna kill you right here!'"

Huff smiled, perhaps to provide some comic relief, and said, "With that, the guy smiled and said, 'Hey, Sam, you're my man!' He bought me a beer."

Sam Huff was telling his tale in the atrium lobby of the Hyatt Regency at the Kaanapali Beach Resort in Maui during the National Football League's annual owners' meeting.

He had come a long way from the coal mining town where his father labored near Farmington, West Virginia. He had come to Maui in his role as vice president in charge of special marketing for the Marriott Corporation, for which he had been working for ten years at the time. His job was to spread goodwill among the many owners, general managers, front-office officials, coaches and sports writers in attendance.

Huff had to make sure Marriott maintained its hold on NFL teams — all 28 of them at the time — that stay at its hotels sometime during the season. He was in Maui to point out the Marriott hotel under construction just across the road on Kaanapali Beach, to pitch it as the site of the NFL owners' meeting which was going to be held in this same outpost in 1984.

This entailed playing golf with NFL coaches (Tom Landry, Bart Starr, Mike McCormack and Ron Erhardt), and owners and officials (Billy Sullivan, Gil Brandt, Tommy Prothro and Ernie Accorsi) and enjoying a drink and conversation with many others, including sports writers.

He also hosted a western-style party sponsored by Marriott and United Airlines which I attended with my wife, Kathie, one night during the activity-filled week.

He was living at the time in Alexandria, Virginia, a suburb just outside Washington, D.C., with his wife, Mary, and their three children.

As we spoke in April, 1999, Sam Huff Jr. was 47, Catherine Huff was 42 and Joseph Huff was 40. All were doing well, according to their dad.

"Certainly, I miss playing football," he said. "You don't know how much. I'm not one of those guys who thinks football owes me something. I owe everything to it — my college education, all the material things I have — friends, such as players, coaches and sports writers."

Huff reminded me of one of his own early favorites from the Pirates, Dick Groat, when he talked that way.

"The best part of my job is the people I deal with," said Huff. "I'm a sports lover. It's been my whole life."

He never embraced the tough-guy image the media created. "I never wanted that image off the field," said Huff. "I wanted people to think of me as an intelligent businessman.

"I was lucky, in so many ways, to be associated with the sort of people that were with the Giants, both for football and for business reasons.

"We had two of the greatest coaches in the history of the game — Vince Lombardi on offense and Tom Landry on defense — and a head coach, Jim Lee Howell, who really believed in discipline. The personnel just blended beautifully, the way it has for the Steelers in recent seasons.

"We had guys like Frank Gifford, Chuck Conerly, Andy Robustelli, Pat Summerall, and Kyle Rote, and they were all involved in business pursuits on the side. They set a good example. Their priorities were straight. Football came first, but they were looking to their future careers at the same time.

"But those were in my early days, when Bert Bell was the commissioner. He used to go around the league and lecture everyone that pro football was just a stepping stone to another career. It was not the end-all it is for so many young guys today who are making so much money they don't worry about tomorrow.

"All athletes, no matter how much money they make for playing, should think of the future, get into something while they're playing. When you're finished playing, the phone quits ringing. Sam who? Dave who?

"We all get twenty-four hours a day. It's the only fair thing. It's the only thing that's equal. It's up to us as to what we do with that twenty-four hours. I got on the merry-go-round of success, and I don't want to get off. I know what it's like to be poor. Rich is better.

"I appreciate great talent and great games as much as when I played. When I'm broadcasting a game, I try to be as professional as I can. Above all, I want to be professional."

"I want Lambert in there all the time."
— Sam Huff

Back in the '80s, Huff was critical of what had become of the pro game he loved. Huff hated special situation substitution, which is used even more these days.

"I don't like what they've done to football," he said. "I like the blocking, tackling and hitting. Most teams have gone to the small, quick-hitting backs. They don't have the bruising fullback anymore.

"That's why all the teams can afford to play 3-4 defenses (most of them have since switched back to the old 4-3). The offensive linemen are allowed to push and hold these days. The defensive line has a helluva job today. A defensive lineman can't hand slap or do much to shed the offensive lineman.

"Now it's a run-and-gun game. It's like the NBA with an odd-shaped ball. When I played, I liked to get down and get dirty and grunt it out. I liked the way they played in the '50s and '60s."

Mention "situation substitution" to Huff, and move back a few inches so you don't get caught in the fire from his nostrils.

"I believe you put your best athletes on the field all the time," Huff said. "I saw the Pittsburgh Steelers pull Jack Lambert in passing situations. I want Lambert in there all the time. Let them catch the ball over the middle and let Lambert tag somebody. I disagree with what they're doing. They're overcoaching, as I see it.

"It was Landry's thinking to develop a defense with responsibility, where everyone has a responsibility as they do on offense. Even today, some NFL defenses don't have that responsibility.

"Everybody has a key, to react to what the offense was doing. I think Landry was ahead of everybody else. He was the first guy to apply a computerized system to a pro football team. There are strengths and weaknesses to every formation, and he came up with schemes to combat them.

"There was a Brown formation, for instance, with a flanker right and a split end left, with the fullback in the regular position with the halfback beside him. The fullback is right behind the quarterback. A lot of people call it a pro set. But we gave them colors for our defensive calls. We named that formation after Jim Brown. In his honor.

"As an athlete, Jim Brown was the greatest football player who ever put on a uniform. Great competitor and good natured. I really respected him, as a person and as a ball player.

"When the fullback was split, that was a sweep formation. We called it Red. We played automatic defense against those formations. You set the strength of your defense to the strength of the offense. It was simple: when they run this offense, we run this defense."

It's more difficult today, however, because teams often disguise their offensive and defensive sets and move people at the snap of the ball.

"I can still read keys," said Huff. "Today, they're using computers to chart tendencies. They watch films so much. It's so sophisticated. But hell, we were sophisticated for our era — in 1957 and 1958 — most teams were all playing man-to-man. People were just starting to use the 4-3 defense. Middle linebackers were the center of attention and the defenses were set up for them to make most of the tackles. Detroit had Joe Schmidt and Chicago had Bill George and Green Bay had Ray Nitschke and the defensive units started attracting attention from the fans and media.

"Our defensive unit was the first ever introduced at the start of an NFL game. It happened at Yankee Stadium. Our offensive team hardly scored any touchdowns and they started getting booed during the introductions. So they switched to us for a change of pace. The fans loved it.

"There was some resentment. The defensive guys were getting their pictures taken for the papers. Frank Gifford would say, 'You guys are getting your picture taken; we make the money.' That still hasn't changed much, but the defensive players get more respect these days. I feel good about that."

> *"When we attribute greatness to these Americans of the past, we are, in reality and largely unconsciously, making a standard of conduct for ourselves. The next step is for us to make our own lives into the kind of effort which we think our chosen heroes would applaud."*
> — John Foster Dulles,
> Lawyer and statesman

Armon Gilliam
Son of a preacher man

"If I had played football,
I'd be a hometown hero."

At last, Armon Gilliam was going to be a hero in his hometown. He had always been one of the biggest men in Bethel Park, a suburb ten miles south of Pittsburgh, and often turned the heads of passersby. After all, there aren't many people who stand 6-9 and weigh 265 pounds, not even with the Pittsburgh Steelers. "Must be a basketball player," someone might say when they see Armon Gilliam. "Who is he?"

Gilliam was often taken for granted in his own backyard. He had never been a high profile high school athlete, and it took him awhile to find himself in the college ranks. No one paid him any mind, for instance, when I interviewed him over lunch at the Eat'n Park Restaurant at South Hills Village in Bethel Park on a Tuesday, August 4, 1998.

In March, 1999, however, at age 34, he was playing in his 12th season in the National Basketball Association, a reserve forward with the Milwaukee Bucks. He had been a starter and a scoring and rebounding leader, in turn, for the Phoenix Suns, Charlotte Hornets, Philadelphia 76ers and New Jersey Nets. His contract called for $3.2 million a season, but the 1998-99 campaign had been cut nearly in half by an owners' lockout, and so was player compensation. He had a year remaining after that on his four-year contract. There hadn't been an NBA team in Pittsburgh since the league's first year — the Pittsburgh Ironmen of the 1946-47 season — so NBA awareness often stopped at Michael Jordan, Magic Johnson and Larry Bird for a lot of the local citizens.

Armon Gilliam (pronounced Ar-men Gill-yem) had asked Bill King II, the publicity director of the Bucks, to change his name to Armen in all the team's official guides and releases during the 1998-99 season so that people would quit mispronouncing his first name as Ar-MON.

He had averaged 14.3 points and 7.2 rebounds for his first 11 NBA seasons. His best season in both categories came with the Nets during the 1995-96 campaign when he averaged 18.3 points and 9.1 rebounds. His best playoff performance came with the 76ers in the 1990-91 season when he averaged 16.9 points and 6.5 rebounds in eight starts. He played in only 21 playoff games in 11 years, so he was seldom with real contenders. During the 1996-97 season with the Bucks, he grabbed a personal high of 22 rebounds against the Phoenix Suns.

Armon Gilliam

Phoenix Suns/NBA

Armon Gilliam established himself as strong rebounder in rookie season with Phoenix Suns.

Photos courtesy of the Milwaukee Bucks Inc.

No one approached our table at Eat'n Park Restaurant for an autograph. And that suited Gilliam just fine. "It's one of the reasons I like to come home," he said. "It's easier to move around here than it is in Phoenix, Charlotte, Philly, New York or Milwaukee."

He learned in March that he was going to be one of the charter members of the Bethel Park High School Sports Hall of Fame, and would be invited to induction ceremonies before the October 1, 1999 football game between Bethel Park and neighboring rival Mt. Lebanon. This would certify his status as a hometown hero, an honor he had long merited.

The class included Dave Piontek, class of 1952, who played in the National Basketball Association from 1956-1963 for the Cincinnati Royals (with Jack Twyman and Maurice Stokes), the St. Louis Hawks and the Chicago Packers (now the Washington Wizards).

It also included Steve Previs, class of 1968, who starred at the University of North Carolina and for two seasons as a guard with the Carolina Cougars (with Denny Wuycik of Ambridge), and Tom Skladany, class of 1973, who played at Pitt and from 1977-1984 for the Cleveland Browns, Detroit Lions and Philadelphia Eagles.

The Bethel Park High School Sports Hall of Fame was an idea promoted by former athletic director Joe Lodge, and was implemented by Paul Zolak, who succeeded him.

Zolak had spent over 20 years at Ringgold High School, which may have the most star-studded high school sports hall of fame of any school in the tri-state area. Ringgold was a merger of the Donora and Monongahela school districts, and its alumni included Stan Musial, Joe Montana, Ken Griffey Sr., Arnold "Pope" Galiffa, "Deacon" Dan Towler, Fred Cox, Rudy Andabaker, Scott Zolak, Ron Necciai, Mike Buchineri, Bap Manzini and Anthony Peterson among others. There is also a hall of fame for other students who succeeded in their careers and it includes military leaders, judges, educators, entertainers and business figures. Every school should have a hall of fame for both categories. Lou "Bimbo" Cecconi should be up there somewhere at Ringgold, even if he never played pro ball.

"I would have been a hometown hero," said Gilliam, "if I had gone to Pitt or Robert Morris. I don't think a lot of people here are aware of UNLV. It's not something popular in Pittsburgh. If I had played football I'd be a hometown hero.

"In July of 1986, I was on the U.S.A. team that won the gold medal in the World Championships in Madrid, Spain. David Robinson was the star of our team. Our team included Mugsy Bogues, Sean Elliott, Kenny Smith, Steve Kerr and Derrick McKay. When I came back to Bethel Park, they had a program in my honor. Mayor (Reno) Virgili gave me a certificate of recognition, and they had a special day for me. Mayor Virgili was a beer distributor in our town, and I went to school with his daughter. My parents and one of my brothers were there. It's always nice to be recognized in your hometown."

148

When Gilliam was a student at Bethel Park High School, he had difficulty with math. "What do I need this for?" he complained on one occasion to his math teacher.

"Because if you keep getting better as a basketball player, you might be a rich man someday," she told him. "And you'll need to know how to count your money."

When Gilliam returned for a special assembly at Bethel Park High School some years later, as a high-priced performer in the NBA, he spotted the math teacher and lifted her off the floor and hugged her. Now he realized she knew what she was talking about.

"I got into basketball because I got fed up with wrestling."

During our luncheon meeting in August of 1998, Armon Gilliam said he had bought a house of his own nearby in Bethel Park about seven years earlier. "I stay there during the off-season, and I come back there during the season, too," he said.

His brother, Javan, 32 at the time, lived there with his wife, two sons and a daughter.

There were two familiar sports people at Eat'n Park that day, but neither was aware of Armon Gilliam. One was Jim Meston, a retired Westinghouse executive and humorist on the sports banquet circuit, and the other was Dr. Hank Zeller, an Aliquippa-based physician who had played basketball for Dr. "Red" Carlson at Pitt and had been a close friend of former Robert Morris College basketball coach Gus Krop. "Who's he?" they asked when I pointed out Armon Gilliam across the room.

"Pittsburgh's not really a basketball town," said Gilliam. "I spent most of my early pro career out west. It's nice to be here and not be recognized, rather than being harassed and bothered for autographs. If I go into the inner-city on the east coast, I get a little more attention. I played in Philly and New Jersey. The kids are more tuned in to pro basketball there."

He said when he was traveling through airports and in the lobby or elevator at a hotel, people asked him if he was a basketball player. "Older people ask me how the weather is up there," he said with a roll of his bright eyes. "That must have been a running joke somewhere back then."

I told him an NBA story about how Walt Bellamy, a big man in the NBA in the '70s, was holding a drink in his hand when he entered an elevator during his days with the Atlanta Hawks.

A man on the elevator asked him "How's the weather up there?" Worse yet, the man laughed at his joke in a crowded elevator. Bellamy simply tipped his drink over the man's head, and spilled it on him.

"It's raining, my man," came back Bellamy. "Yeah, it's raining in here."

Gilliam could see someone doing that, if not himself.

Armon was accompanied for our luncheon meeting by Norisa Lynch, 9 years old, whom he introduced as his god-daughter from Philadelphia.

Armon left the New Jersey Nets two years earlier when they were unwilling to offer him a new long-term contract. He was in his option year with the Nets, but decided to take his chances as a free agent. He could have played for John Calipari, who hailed from Moon Township and had been an assistant coach at Pitt under Roy Chipman and Paul Evans and then head coach at the University of Massachusetts before getting a nod from the NBA.

"He was a Pittsburgh guy, too," said Gilliam. "I was disappointed with him, frankly, and so were a lot of our guys." So it wasn't a surprise when Calipari was fired after the Nets got off to a pitiful start in the lockout-delayed season. Calipari had been successful as head coach at the University of Massachusetts and as an assistant coach at Pitt, and would surely bounce back.

Gilliam could have remained with the Nets on a one- or two-year contract. The Knicks offered him a three-year deal, and the Bucks offered him a four-year deal. "I wanted a long-term commitment," said Gilliam.

Gilliam was, no doubt, in the twilight of his career, but 12 years in the bigs wasn't bad for a guy who got such a late start in the sport.

He's still trying to play catch up, in many ways. "I started real late," he explained. "I got into basketball because I was fed up with wrestling. I didn't want to do it anymore.

"I was a poor basketball player, but I just kind of fell in love with the game. I just decided that basketball was what I enjoyed the most, so that's what I pursued.

"As a junior, I didn't start most of the year. Then I attended the 5-Star Summer Basketball Camp at Robert Morris College conducted by Howie Garfinkel. There were a lot of outstanding basketball players there, and that's where I learned how to play the game. I got some good coaching."

He mentioned how Rick Bell, the boys basketball coach at Peters Township High School, grew up in Bethel Park and played for the team there. "I hadn't played much organized ball and Bell put me in a ballgame in a summer league my junior year against Chartiers Valley. I didn't understand all the rules of the game. I kept getting three seconds called on me for being in the paint too long. Bell told me I was in there for three weeks. He got his point across."

"Nobody loves Goliath."
— Wilt Chamberlain

Armon Gilliam enjoys company of his godchild, 9-year-old Norisa Lynch, during luncheon interview in his hometown of Bethel Park.

"The Lord just blessed him so much."
— Alma Gilliam

To fully appreciate Armon Gilliam, you have to visit his boyhood home on Elm Street in Bethel Park, as I first did in the summer of 1989, and meet his parents, Rev. James T. and Alma Gilliam. They were still living at the same address in the summer of 1999. They are good people.

They believed in Armon when no one else thought he had a prayer of ever playing big-time college basketball, let alone pro basketball. No one was prouder when the Phoenix Suns selected him as the second player taken in the 1987 draft out of the University of Nevada at Las Vegas. He was named to the NBA's All-Rookie team.

Back then, they called him "The Hammer," or an enforcer, which made his parents flinch. This is a nickname that was once associated with pro football stars Mike Ditka and Fred Williamson. Gilliam had learned the game from Jerry Tarkanian, one of the winningest college basketball coaches in history, with a lot of help from his top assistant, Tim Grgurich, who grew up in Lawrenceville and made his mark at Central Catholic High School and the University of Pittsburgh, the latter both as a smart backcourtman and as a coach.

The Gilliams' home was a modest one, but pin-neat and full of love and pride, and just about all the trophies and medals ever awarded Armon in his athletic and academic pursuits. It was his home and his Hall of Fame at the same time.

As soon as you stepped inside the bright red door, you saw a bronzed size-15 sneaker once worn by Armon, which was his award as the MVP at UNLV. There were also various All-America certificates, a glass case full of trophies (there were more that filled a small room on the second floor), and then his mother proudly displayed the gold medal he won for playing for the victorious U.S. team in the World Games in Spain, and a beautiful ring marking UNLV's Final Four appearance in Armon's senior season of 1986-87.

If Armon Gilliam is rock solid, as he is in so many ways, it is because of what he gained from his family. It's in the genes. The rap against him is that sometimes he's too soft, doesn't come at you hard enough, and lacks a fiery disposition. That comes from his family as well. In some respects, Armon Gilliam is too good for his own good.

The expectations at home were always high, the best possible personal conduct was demanded, respect for a higher authority was preached, and thoughtfulness and concern for your fellow man was stressed. Plus, there was enough food and love to go around among Armon and his three brothers.

From his father, a Baptist minister and former career postal worker and amateur boxing champion, Armon got his size and strength. From his mother, who plays the piano at her husband's Shiloh Baptist Church in nearby Library, he must certainly have gotten his confidence, iron will and determination.

152

Both parents would dispute these observations. "He's just been so blessed," said his dad during our visit. Or, as his mother put it, "The Lord just blessed him so much."

Armon's father, a two-time Pittsburgh Golden Gloves heavyweight boxing champion (1957 and 1959) and Eastern champion (1957), stands 6-1, 210 or so pounds. He speaks softly and smiles easily. There's a warmth and pleasantness about him. But you wouldn't want to mess with him. He embraced me with a bear hug and a blessing.

Armon's mother makes her points as directly. She was quick to show you certificates and clippings heralding the achievements of her three other sons as much as those of Armon. There's Gralan, Jerrel and Javan, too. Javan was just 5-7, by the way. "We called him Spud, like in Spud Webb," said his dad, a chortle turning to a cough he quelled with the back of his fist.

Armon was quick to point out that Gralan was a high school All-American in track & field in the triple jump event at Bethel Park High School, and that all his brothers attended college.

Alma Gilliam also popped a video tape into the television's VCR unit to show some TV features that were done about Armon and the Gilliam family following the NBA draft in 1987, when only Navy's David Robinson was selected (by the San Antonio Spurs) ahead of their son.

"How do you like what my son is doing?"
— James T. Gilliam

One day in 1988, I was having lunch with my wife, Kathleen, at a sprawling, casual Italian restaurant in Bethel Park called Grisanti's (now the Olive Garden) when my head was turned by the sight of a large man moving past our table. Just from his broad back that filled a beige sportcoat, I swear, I recognized him as an old friend, James T. Gilliam.

I'd come across him a few years earlier, working behind the counter at a post office in nearby Mt. Lebanon, and recognized him as a man who had been a terrific amateur boxer back in my boyhood days. At age 14, I was the sports editor of my hometown bi-weekly newspaper, *The Hazelwood Envoy*. The highlight of the year back then was covering the Golden Gloves Boxing Tournament because our Glen-Hazel Boys' Club team was the best in Pittsburgh, winning the team title 11 of 12 years in one stretch. And James T. Gilliam was the granddaddy of the team, its heart and soul and spiritual leader.

Gilliam had begun boxing when he returned home from the military service at age 23, and competed on an amateur championship level until he was 31. "Until I was saved," he said, reflecting back to when he was won over by God.

153

In 1999, he was 68 years old, and he had been the pastor at the Shiloh Baptist Church for 26 years. He had retired from the postal service in 1984 after 33 years of government service, including four years in the military service. He and Alma had been married 45 years.

After a little reminiscing that day at the restaurant, Gilliam tossed a playful and soft (praise the Lord) right-handed blow into my shoulder, and said, "Hey, how do you like what my son is doing these days?"

I was stunned, not by the blow to the shoulder, but because he had caught me completely off guard with his question. I didn't know what he was talking about. I apologized for my ignorance. "My son, Armon, is playing for the Phoenix Suns in the NBA!" he said with a big smile above his neat goatee.

I was embarrassed. I'd never made the connection. And I was supposed to be a basketball expert, as the editor for nearly 20 years of *Street & Smith's Basketball Yearbook*, the so-called "Bible of Basketball." It only points up the fact that Armon Gilliam was never that well known when he was playing basketball as a schoolboy in the Pittsburgh area.

It suddenly made sense that Armon's father had been a big, husky athlete himself, a heavyweight boxer who was always quick on his feet.

The elder Gilliam had goals, too. He wanted to be a professional boxer. But he started late at the sport, just as Armon did at his, and waited too long to turn pro. Plus, he was told he had everything a boxer needed back then, but that he lacked a killer instinct.

"After somebody told me that," recalled Rev. James T. Gilliam, "I got into my head before my next fight, the next-to-the-last fight I ever fought, and turned myself into an angry demon. I couldn't wait to get at my next opponent. I was shaking and heaving before the bout even began. As soon as the bell sounded, I was all over him, hitting him at will. When he went down on his knees, I was over him, and I wanted to hammer him into the canvas.

"The referee knew me well because I'd been boxing so long, and he forced me into a corner, and even forgot to keep counting. He gave me a strange look, like he didn't know what had gotten into me. I nearly killed that guy. I didn't like the way I felt that night.

"In my next fight, I tried to tone myself down, but it wasn't any good. I just didn't like being a boxer anymore. I didn't want to hurt anybody. It wasn't a sport for me anymore. And then I found the Lord."

"After all, he is still our father. We belong to him, and he belongs to us."
— Peter Taylor,
"A Summon to Memphis"

UNLV senior Armon Gilliam accepts John Wooden Award as outstanding college basketball player as namesake listens at left.

Armon Gilliam

Gilliam was billed as "The Hammer" in publicity campaign at University of Nevada at Las Vegas.

Alma and Rev. James T. Gilliam are proud parents.

Jim O'Brien

"He wanted to be successful."
— Red Ryan

Red Ryan was the basketball coach at Bethel Park High School when Gilliam was a student there. Ryan had been a good, hard-nosed guard on some pretty good teams at Duquesne University (1957-59) at the same exact time that James T. Gilliam was a Golden Gloves champion in Pittsburgh.

Ryan coached the boys basketball team at Bethel Park for 21 years and retired after the 1997-98 season with a 1989 WPIAL Quad A championship to his credit. Ryan recalled that Gilliam asked to try out for the Blackhawks basketball team during his junior year. He'd been on the football team, and had also tried his athletic skills in track & field and wrestling.

"He didn't really understand the game," said Ryan. "He thought you had to score, like most kids, and he didn't worry much about rebounding and passing. He was 6-5 or 6-6, and skinny compared to what he is now. He was throwing up 25-foot shots as soon as he showed up at the gym, and I told him I didn't want to see any of that stuff.

"In his junior year, he just made our cuts. He seldom played in a varsity game. It was jayvee for him that year. He started every game as a senior. He was very inconsistent. He wanted to win, and he wanted to be successful, but he was far behind most of the other kids basketball-wise. He didn't make the section all-star team.

"In one game against McKeesport, he scored 27 points and pulled down 20 rebounds and blocked a lot of shots, and in the next game against Norwin he had five points and three rebounds. We got knocked out of the playoffs in the quarter-finals."

Some college scouts checked out Armon as a prospect. As a senior, he averaged 13 points and 10 rebounds. "Most of them didn't give him a second look, though," recalled Ryan.

Gilliam's academic record posed a problem, too, according to James T. Gilliam. "Armon had done well as a student in his last two years, but very poorly in his first two years and his overall grade point average wasn't so hot. Coach Ryan and some other people thought he'd be better off going to a junior college."

Ryan remembers Gilliam's parents telling him that Armon's ambition was to play pro basketball some day. "He told us how difficult that would be, and how the percentages of such success were so stacked against Armon or anyone else at that stage," said Mrs. Gilliam. "But I told Coach Ryan that Armon would fulfill his dream. He had God-given talent, and I knew God would give him the resources to succeed. I had faith all along."

Said Ryan, "I remember the father telling me, too, that Armon would make it. I told them the kid had a long way to go to get to that point. They weren't convinced. They really believed in him. Based on what he did in high school, no, I never thought he'd be the No. 2 pick in the NBA draft and a star with the Phoenix Suns or anyone else. Believe me, it was beyond my wildest dreams."

Joe Lodge, the athletic director at Bethel Park High School at the time, said of Armon, "He was an average football player. Who knows how good of a wrestler he'd have been, because he didn't stick with it. He was a very large young man. He stood out. People knew who he was. He was a big guy, but we had no idea he'd be that good."

One of Gilliam's teachers, Jack McKay, was a nationally-respected evaluator of high school talent. His ratings were reprinted in *Street & Smith's Basketball*. McKay admits he graded Gilliam on his high school performance, not his enormous potential.

James T. Gilliam gives you a good-hearted laugh when he looks back. "Armon played basketball to stay in shape for football, at first. But then he said, 'Hey, I like this game. You can be indoors and you don't have to be out in the snow and the cold.' And he settled down to play basketball."

Ryan said he saw Gilliam in a local playground tournament two months after the end of his senior season in high school and could not believe the improvement. "He must've been playing a lot, and really working at it," said Ryan.

Tim Grgurich had strong Pittsburgh ties, and was close with all the area coaches, but he never thought of recruiting Gilliam out of Bethel Park High School.

Gilliam went to Independence (Kansas) Community College and got better, athletically and academically. He averaged 17 points and 11 rebounds for Coach Bob Kivisto's club which finished with a 33-5 record. Grgurich explained how Gilliam ended up at UNLV.

"One of our other assistant coaches, Mark Warkentein, went to scout a player named Frank James at San Jacinto (Texas) Junior College, and saw Armon playing against them. One of my former teammates at Pitt, Billy Shay, who coaches at Allegheny Community College in Pittsburgh, told Mark that Armon was as good as anybody. I said, 'Geez, I saw him, but I didn't think he was that good.' But we got him here and he worked so hard.

"We had another Pittsburgher at the same time, Melvin Bennett, who had played at Pitt and in the ABA and NBA, and was our volunteer assistant coach. He and Armon worked together. We also had Keith Starr of Sewickley, who had played for us when I was with Buzz Ridl at Pitt and with the Chicago Bulls. He was a coaching intern in our program. We also had Jim Bolla from Canevin with us. He became our women's coach. Then Cleveland Edwards came out from Pittsburgh in December of Armon's first year. Armon sat out his first year at UNLV — that was a big key — and then played three years for us. And he graduated from our school. He's tough as nails; you can't be any tougher. And he's a good kid. His family is fantastic; they've been a good influence."

Recalling his early years at UNLV, Gilliam said, "We had five guys with connections to Pittsburgh when I was in Las Vegas, so that kept me from getting too homesick. Mel Bennett was a big help. I was hard-headed and Mel was real patient with me." Plus, Joyce Aschenbrenner of Brentwood, who had been an assistant sports information director at Pitt for years, was the head of the p.r. department at UNLV. She took an early interest in Gilliam, and got him some ink back home.

"Grgurich was the 'big man coach' at Las Vegas," said Gilliam, "and he really worked with me. Tark worked with the guards."

Tark's handsome son, Danny Tarkanian, was a smooth senior guard at UNLV during Gilliam's red-shirt season. "Tark's wife, Lois, used to be at courtside for all our games, and she was always saying a rosary," said Gilliam. "She prayed extra hard whenever her son, Danny, had the ball. She was real emotional. You looked at her face during the game, and you thought the world was coming to an end."

Gilliam gives Grgurich credit for turning him around. "One day he told me I could be a good player," said Gilliam. "He told me I could be in the NBA. I didn't have a clue about whether I could or couldn't.

"He started waking me up at 6 a.m. to go to the gym, whether I wanted to or not. He spent a lot of time with me. He did it with a lot of guys.

"I've seen him in recent seasons when he was coaching with George Karl in Seattle, or now with the Portland Trail Blazers. I'd see him and his wife. They were always good to me. I always talk to Coach Gurg. He's a very likable guy, not a flashy guy. Real down to earth. He has no ego; he wasn't looking for the spotlight. He was a big help to Coach Tark. He was the driving force behind the team. If there were any problems, he snuffed them out. He convinced me that it was worth it to work hard. Life's funny. Now George Karl is my coach in Milwaukee."

"You have to know who you are."
— Armon Gilliam

I had been to the Pro Football Hall of Fame induction ceremonies in Canton, Ohio the week before my get-together with Gilliam. Tommy McDonald, a former wide receiver with the Philadelphia Eagles, had been outrageous and stole the show with his shenanigans during the nationally-televised ceremonies.

"He's wild," said Gilliam, closing his eyes at the memory of McDonald. "I was on the dais with him at several sports banquets in Philadelphia. He said some things that were funny, but he went a little overboard a couple of times, as far as I'm concerned. Some things were almost blasphemy. He's a wild guy to be around."

Gilliam usually sits on the dais for the annual YMCA banquet at the Hilton Hotel in Pittsburgh to honor more than 200 of the top high school scholar-athletes in the area. He sits through a long program, just to pay tribute to the kids in his own subdued way. I've sat next to him and he's good company, and a young man with his priorities in proper order. It's easy to determine that right away. Gilliam makes a good impression.

"I have a value system, and I know what's most important in life," he said. "Going to church, being a part of that type of community, helps put your life into perspective for you. I don't know if that's in line with the MTV (Music Television), BET (Black Entertainment Television), the Generation-X crowd, the hip-hop crowd, but it works for me.

"God's blessed me. Now it's my turn. I've got to love him back.

"If you do it right, you'll get enough rewards. If you do it wrong, there's a payback for that, too. My mom was always telling me, 'Don't break the rules!' every time I left the house. She still says it. My Dad made his points, more or less, simply by example. I learned what it is to be a man, dedicated to your family, to be there consistently, standing up for the right things, having principals and values. It's not like he preached to us at home.

"When I was growing up, my dad was like in his late 30s, or early 40s, and he was still an athletic-looking guy. We'd go to Corrigan Pool, and he'd entertain the crowd with flips off the diving board. He was in the Navy, too, so he knew his way around water. He had people clapping for him. He used to be a big man at Corrigan Pool."

Armon also remembers hearing about his dad doing similar shenanigans at Sully's Pool, a swimming pool for blacks only in South Park in the late '60s.

Gilliam stands out in the team photo from his basketball playing days at Bethel Park High School. He's standing in the center of the back row, the tallest player, and the only black player. "See if you can find me in there?" asked Gilliam with a grin when he showed me this photograph.

"I didn't even know what racism was when I was growing up," he said. "Not in my neighborhood, anyhow. Some kids from the other side of town thought it was OK to be snobbish and rude because their dad had a big job. But they were the same way with whites from the other side of town.

"I have no complaints. God has been good to me. I've been blessed with a lot of opportunities. A lot of people blow it, and don't take advantage of what's afforded them. I like to help young people grow and be what they can be if they work hard at it. It hurts to see what happens when guys go the wrong way.

"You have to define yourself, and not let other people define you. Guys you play with, for instance. Others might have expectations for you. You have to know who you are, and not give in to peer pressure.

"I'm secure financially. I don't plan on doing anything crazy. I'm not going to be the next Dennis Rodman. That sort of stuff doesn't appeal to me."

"That's why he's Michael Jordan."

Throughout his pro playing career, Armon Gilliam has always given a share of his salary to the Shiloh Baptist Church. When he was playing at Phoenix, he provided his father with the money for an expansion program at his church that included a recreation center for the youth of the church. It was named after Armon Gilliam, at his parents' insistence.

"Armon didn't like us making too much of his helping out to build this gym for the kids. You know, Armon was playing the organ at our church since he was 15. He can play the organ, the piano and the guitar. And I mean really play."

Once again, she sounded like a scout trying to convince a disbeliever that Armon Gillam can really play. By now, it's an old song.

Michael Jordan had not yet made up his mind about whether he would retire or not when I spoke with Gilliam in August. Jordan waited till the lockout was over before publicly announcing that he was calling it quits.

Jordon set the standard for everyone in the NBA, and Gilliam admired him greatly. He said, however, that some of his teammates found Jordan difficult to please.

"He expects everyone to be like him and they can't be," said Gilliam. "That's why he's special. That's why he's Michael Jordan. His persistence, competitiveness, and desire to grow as a player is unmatched by anyone else in the league.

"When he first came into the league, he wasn't a good shooter. So he worked at it and became a good shooter. His athletic ability has gone down as he gets older, but he's such a student of the game that he more than makes up for that by how he plays the game.

"The guy shows up every game. For a guy who's achieved so much, he's hungry all the time. He has all the accolades, but he remains just as competitive, like he's flat broke. That competitiveness...it's just a part of him. I can admire him, and I can look up to him for what he stands for. Michael is the man. His dedication to the game is impressive.

"Lots of guys are talented, but they don't work as hard as he does. He's demanding of everyone on his team. He expects you to play as hard as he does. That's why good things happen for him. That's why he does so much."

> *"Some of God's greatest gifts*
> *are unanswered prayers."*
> — Song by Garth Brooks

Former Steelers receiver Randy Grossman, now a Pittsburgh investment counselor, was reunited with Coach Chuck Noll at 1997 National
Collegiate and West Penn Tennis Championships in Mt. Lebanon.

Snapshot:

**Chuck Noll,
Hall of Fame coach, Pittsburgh Steelers:**
*"Kenny Keltner was my favorite ballplayer. I
was a third baseman and he was a third baseman for the Cleveland Indians. I didn't wear
his number, or anything like that. I just
watched him more than anyone else. I can't say
I was a real big fan. I'd listen to Jack Graney's
broadcasts, that's about it."*

Jim Leyland
Yogi Berra was his man

"Hey, this game is for all shapes and sizes."

W hen Jim Leyland was growing up in suburban Toledo, Ohio, he was a Cleveland Indians fan. That was in the mid-50s, the days of Al Rosen, Luke Easter, Jim Hegan, Bob Lemon, Early Wynn, Vic Wertz and Bobby Avila. Leyland's favorite ballplayer back then, however, was Yogi Berra, the catcher and clutch hitter for the hated New York Yankees.

"He always struck me as a very interesting guy," allowed Leyland, looking relaxed as he sat at the end of a couch in his cozy den. This was at Leyland's home in the Mt. Lebanon suburb of Pittsburgh in January of 1999. "His physical structure...he looked different," Leyland said of Berra. "I thought, hey, this game is for all shapes and sizes.

"He was a notorious bad-ball hitter, and I liked that because I swung at a lot of bad pitches, too. Didn't we all? And I was a catcher. I heard so much about him, and saw him on TV a lot. I can still see him jumping up in the arms of Don Larsen when Larsen pitched the perfect game (on Oct. 8, 1956) in the World Series. And baseball was my favorite sport, so I sorta adopted him."

In short, Berra wasn't handsome and he wasn't perfect, and Leyland looked at himself that way, too. He still does.

"In 1981, I saw Yogi Berra up close for the first time," related Leyland. "When I went to the World Series with Tony LaRussa, I saw Yogi Berra at a post-game party. I had just joined the White Sox and LaRussa wanted me to meet people. Yogi was wearing pink, yellow and white pants, and a yellow sweater, and he really stood out from the crowd. I got to meet Yogi Berra and that was a great thrill for me. I finally got to meet my childhood idol.

"I came up to the major leagues in 1982 with the White Sox, as a coach with LaRussa. We got rained out and snowed out in Chicago on the opening weekend. So I made my debut at Yankee Stadium. Yogi was in the outfield during the pre-game warmup, flagging down balls behind a screen out by second base. He was a coach with the Yankees that year.

"We had been rained out of the first game in New York, too, so we had a doubleheader there on Easter Sunday for starters. I got to meet Yogi again. I really enjoyed him. I found him refreshing, down to earth. They like to tell you all these dumb sayings of Yogi Berra — 'nobody goes there because it's always crowded' — but he's dumb like a fox. He's kept his money. To this day, I think the world of him."

162

Leyland's boyhood hero was Yankees' Yogi Berra

Leyland was not only excited about Berra being out on the field. The whole scene captivated the kid in Leyland. He also went out to the deepest part of the outfield at Yankee Stadium to check out the monuments that offer tribute to some of the Yankee greats. "Whenever I go to Yankee Stadium, I still go out there," said Leyland. "I'm still like a kid in a candy store."

Leyland's hometown outside of Toledo is Perrysburg. In his early days in the minor leagues, as a player and manager, he always went back home to Perrysburg. In more recent years, he comes back home to Pittsburgh. A lot has happened to him — good and bad — since he went from Perrysburg to Pittsburgh, but he remains the same guy, he insists. He never thought he was a big deal. He prides himself on being a regular guy. His home in Mt. Lebanon was less than a mile from Atria's, a popular neighborhood bar-restaurant, and he enjoyed debating sports and politics or whatever with anybody who cared to join him and his close buddies around or near the bar. "Is this off the record?" he barks continually when he's mixing with media types. Leyland liked to let his thinning hair down when he was with people he trusted. He liked to speak his mind on many matters. "It's my turn now," he'd snap, holding a finger to his lips to silence someone who went over their time limit to make a point. He also lowered his eyelids and sealed them when he wanted to shut up someone.

When the Colorado Rockies came to Pittsburgh for a series at the end of April and the start of May, Leyland and his good friend, Bucs' broadcaster Lanny Frattare, showed up both nights at Atria's after the games at Three Rivers Stadium. They were joined by Gene Lamont, briefly, the second night following a 9-3 matinee victory by the Pirates. Leyland and Lamont had worked together in Chicago and Pittsburgh. He is loyal to old friends.

He has a self-deprecating way about him that is appealing. He'll put himself down, go on about his humble beginnings, mention some of the family tragedies he endured during what the public may have perceived as the best of times in his life, because of what was going on in baseball at the same time. At age 54, Leyland's life was pretty good. He'd more than paid his dues with low-paying jobs as a player and manager in the minors much of his pro career, but he was now among the elite in his profession and doing his best to find some balance in his life, and to keep his priorities straight.

There's a World Series trophy in the living room of his home in Mt. Lebanon, a reminder of how it was in 1997 when he managed the Florida Marlins to the championship. There were more reminders of his 11 years (1986-1996) as manager of the Pittsburgh Pirates. His key players in Miami were dumped in a payroll slashing for his second season there, and he decided to resign after the team fell from first place to last place in a year's time. Soon after, he signed as the manager of the Colorado Rockies. He signed a $2 million contract, $1.5 up front, and $500,000 deferred compensation. He wasn't planning on moving to Denver, however. His family was comfortable in Pittsburgh.

164

When Jim Leyland is at home in Mt. Lebanon, he likes to relax at nearby Atria's Restaurant &Tavern with his wife, Katie, and their good friend, Pirates broadcaster Lanny Frattare. World Series trophy Leyland won with Florida Marlins in 1997 is on display in his home along with other personal plaques and awards.

Photos by Jim O'Brien

Once H. Wayne Huizenga revealed his plans to sell the Marlins in the midst of Leyland's first season in South Florida, Leyland moved his wife, Katie, and their two children, Patrick and Kelly, back to their home in Mt. Lebanon. It was a nice old manse, but it wasn't anywhere near the biggest house on a block of beautiful well-maintained classic residences. There was a basketball hoop in the back yard, and some kid-size homes on a terrace below where his daughter liked to play with her dolls. It was a nice set-up, but Leyland said the family was looking to buy a bigger home somewhere in the same community "so we have more space for the kids."

Money wasn't his main motivation, he assured anyone. In fact, he tended to get a bit riled whenever anyone brings up the subject of how much money he makes. "What the hell difference does that make?" he'll scold. "Why's that important?"

Just being in a big league uniform, in a big league ballpark or dugout is enough to make Leyland's day.

"My love for the game is still in me," he said. "For me, it's something that will always be there. My motivation is to be there. My motivation is to compete in some form against the best. I wasn't good enough as a ballplayer to do it. Some people must think I'm good enough as a manager to do it. Some don't think I'm a good manager. What the hell...

"I'm still amazed by what goes on in this game. The home run race between McGwire and Sosa was something we all were excited about. It was a thrill. McGwire hit four of his 70 home runs against us in the last series at Pro Players Stadium. It wasn't so good for us, but I was still glad I saw it, that I was a part of it.

"This flunky backup catcher in Double A...and you're a part of it. The McGwire-Sosa battle, and the way they both handled the whole thing, was baseball at its best. I felt the same way when I went out on the field at Shea Stadium and there'd be 56,000 in the stands. A lot of people think it's the money factor. That's a bonus. That's not what matters the most.

"When we were playing in the 1997 World Series, we had a team meeting every day. I talked to my players about Muhammad Ali. To me, that was a slam dunk. I used Ali as a model. My theory was that Ali was always at his best for the big fights. He welcomed the challenge and he worked harder to get ready. I wanted my team to play harder. Some people think that getting to the World Series is the most important thing. That the pressure is off once you get to the championship series. It might be fun for the fans and the owners, but it was not fun for me. It was a challenge, and I loved it, but it wasn't fun.

"When Ali got ready for big fights, he pushed himself even more. He prepared himself more. He was more focused. He had a passion to be a winner. We made a call to Ali and he was going to walk through our clubhouse. We thought it would make a big point with our players. Then we thought about it some more, and we thought it might turn out to be a media circus, and that it wouldn't be fair to him. So we called it off.

166

Jim and Katie Leyland relax in his den at Mt. Lebanon home.

Jim O'Brien

"Players have a tendency to relax a little, and ease up, when they get to the World Series. I used Ali to motivate them. Once we got there, I was worried. We were up against Atlanta in the National League playoff, and Atlanta had been a thorn in my side when I was in Pittsburgh. So it was difficult to get to the World Series. Believe me, as the manager, you're *working* in the World Series. It's stressful."

When Leyland was growing up in Perrysburg, he said there were older boys he respected and wanted to be like, but they weren't heroes.

"This sounds corny, I know, but I looked up to my father and my mother more than anybody else," he said. "When I was growing up, I never came home that my mother wasn't there. My dad worked swing shifts, from 8 to 4, or 4 to midnight, or midnight to 8. I think $16,000 was the most money he ever made.

"There were seven of us. My dad was one of 16 and they grew up in western Pennsylvania. Our family lived in Butler and Kane and Zelienople. My grandfather worked for American Plate Glass. We looked up to him. My father moved the family to Ohio before I came along. It was a different time in those days, and my mom stayed home and did all the work. My dad's name was James and my mother's name is Veronica. My dad was a semi-pro pitcher, and he was supposed to have been pretty good."

(Butler sports broadcaster Jim Lokhaiser offers a tidbit that American Plate Glass imported glassmakers from Belgium and France to work there, and did special curved plates that were used in the Statue of Liberty. He added that Leyland's relatives up that way pronounced their name Lay-land rather than Lee-land, as Jim does.)

I suggested to Leyland that I had the feeling that even when he was managing in the minors he thought he was a lucky bird to be making a living that way. "No question about it," said Leyland. "I never was in a place I didn't like. Most people think my biggest thrill was winning the World Series, but that's not so.

"My biggest thrill was being named manager of the Pirates. My dad was still alive. We opened the season against the Mets at Three Rivers Stadium. Doc Gooden was pitching for the Mets, I remember that, and we lost by 4-2, I think."

One of the nicer plaques displayed on the wall of his den is one that was presented to him by the Pirates. He is pictured along with Chuck Tanner, Danny Murtaugh, Fred Clarke and Frankie Frisch as members of the "500 Club," managers who had won 500 or more games as the bench boss of the Bucs. Leyland is keeping pretty good company. There are several Manager of the Year awards from *Baseball Weekly* and *The Sporting News*. Then, too, there are family photos.

Leyland is not a name-dropper, but there are a lot of special moments he remembers well. He got to meet Michael Jordan when Jordan was playing baseball with the White Sox organization. Most of all, he was impressed with Jordan's work ethic and the way he comported himself.

Jim Leyland meets President Reagan at Wrigley Field.

Leyland has some framed photographs of himself with some celebrities in golf outings. He has a six-photo sequence of him with President Bill Clinton on such an outing. Leyland is also pictured with President Reagan at Wrigley Field, and there's another with President George Bush. There are pictures of him with golfers Fred Couples and Arnold Palmer.

"One of my bigger thrills," said Leyland, "and this is going to sound corny, was when I got to play golf with Arnold Palmer. Vince Sarni, who was the chief executive officer at PPG at the time, and headed the Pirates board of directors, had me and Cam Bonifay playing a round of golf with Arnold Palmer at Laurel Valley. Arnold Palmer did more for golf than any man alive. Walking down the fairway with Arnold Palmer was a particular thrill. Hey, it doesn't get any better.

"I went to dinner with him, too, and during the conversation the sense that I got was one of the best lessons for me. It was an insight into his ability to compete. That's the most amazing thing about Palmer.

"I asked him about that. He said, 'I don't think, Jim, that I was the best golfer out there, but I could get the ball in the hole.' As good as Palmer got, he never saw any reason to leave his roots, which is another thing I like about him. He divides his time, I realize, between Latrobe — where my wife, Katie, comes from — and Orlando, where he owns another golf course.

"I don't see any minuses to Pittsburgh. I don't know too many sports figures who wanted to move on. Economics were the main reason. Most people like to play here. The fans are fair, the media are fair.

"I get in trouble because I'm sometimes too honest, but one of my concerns about Pittsburgh is if it's big enough now to support pro teams in a first-class manner. The economics of our game have hurt cities like Pittsburgh. And Montreal, Milwaukee, Minneapolis-St. Paul, places like that. If you give Kevin McClatchy, Cam Bonifay and Gene Lamont a level playing field, they can win. They nearly had a miracle year here two years ago when the Pirates, despite having one of the lowest payrolls in the league, made a nice run of it for most of the season. But you can't keep losing big-time players, whether you're the Pirates or the Steelers, and stay in contention. It's very frustrating.

"I'll tell you what I always loved about Pittsburgh. It's big enough to get lost, but it's small enough to have good friends. When we lived in Ohio in my youth, I remember my father talking about western Pennsylvania, and the charm of it. I knew about western Pennsylvania even though I had never lived here. My wife is from this area, and she has family nearby. She's one of 11 children. She has a sister in Mt. Lebanon, and a sister in Pittsburgh. It's one of the reasons we're still here. It's a great place to raise a family. Chuck Tanner kept his home in New Castle, near his hometown, no matter where he

Photos by David Arrigo

managed. You can do it. I'm content to sit in this little den. I've got young kids in school. I enjoy being with them. I want to stay home. I miss them.

"When you're on the road, getting your butt whipped, you would rather be home with your wife and kids. Most everyone who'd hear that would bring up the financial package. 'You're getting well-compensated for what you do.' That's true. No argument there. I've seen both sides. It doesn't change missing your kids, or worrying about them."

Sports gets some bad raps, and deservedly so in many instances, for the ill behavior of some of its participants. Leyland looks around, however, and sees some people he's impressed with.

"At 54, it sounds funny, but one of the most impressive professionals, to me, is Barry Sanders of the Detroit Lions. He just does it, like the Nike commercials. That's the best way. Don't talk a better game than you play. Just do it!

"One of the most impressive guys I've met in recent years was Pat Riley, the coach of the Miami Heat. He's not what you might expect after seeing him on TV. His dad was a minor league manager. He almost got the job with the Phillies. So we had a bond of sorts in that regard.

"Bobby Knight, the basketball coach at Indiana, is totally impressive. He and Tony LaRussa are good friends. That's how I got to know him. I've played golf with him. He's a competitor, in every sense of the word. He likes to compete. But he has high standards for the kind of players he recruits.

"I still drive down the road once in a while and I look at my (World Series) ring, and it's still hard to believe that you were a part of it. A small part, mind you, but a part. It's hard to believe. The World Series is our Super Bowl. It's big.

"That brings somebody else to mind. Chuck Noll, to me, and I don't know him that well, may be the best of all time. I admire him. He was in the Super Bowl four times and he won it four times. He won every time he was there. He doesn't get enough credit. They say Terry Bradshaw was the difference, and some of the other great players get most of the credit. But Noll must have known what he was doing.

"I've met several United States Presidents because of my position in baseball. That's meaningful to me even though in this day and age there are people who'd poke fun at you for feeling that way. I'm not a hero-worshipper. We're all people; we all put our pants on the same way. The game has given me a chance to meet some special people, that's all. For that, I'm grateful to the game."

> *"I like people who stick their necks out."*
> — James Michener

Jim O'Brien

At age 38, Andy Van Slyke paid a visit from St. Louis to play in 1999 Mario Lemieux Celebrity Invitational. He overcame thyroid cancer challenge earlier in the year.

Andy Van Slyke (signature)

Snapshot:

Andy Van Slyke, former outfielder for Pirates (1987-1994)
At the Mario Lemieux Celebrity Invitational Golf Tournament at The Club at Nevillewood:
"I was a pitcher and catcher when I was a kid, so my heroes were Tom Seaver and Johnny Bench. I had a poster of Seaver on the wall next to my bed at my home in Hartford, New York. My second big league homer came off Seaver my rookie season (1983) with the St. Louis Cardinals. When I left home after I was drafted, I didn't even have time to clear up my room. The poster of Tom Seaver was still on the wall when I hit that home run. That's when I knew I'd arrived."

Billy Knight
Braddock's gift to Pitt

"College is the best time of your life."

Image Point

Brian Generalovich with Knight at Pitt Field House.

B illy Knight never seems to change, which is part of his charm. At age 45 in the winter of 1998, Knight remained pleasant, good-natured, modest, polite and down to earth. He was more sophisticated and polished than he was as a teenager out of Braddock High School when he first reported to Pitt to play basketball back in 1970, but it was a subtle change.

Knight returned to the Pitt Field House on February 24, 1998, to scout the talent in his role as vice president of basketball operations with the NBA's Indiana Pacers. The son of a Braddock steel mill worker had done well for himself.

He brought his old ballclub some good luck, too, as he witnessed a comeback 65-61 victory over Villanova in the final regular season game for the Panthers at Fitzgerald Field House.

Knight, the most successful pro player to ever come out of the Mon Valley and Pitt's basketball program, was welcomed home with a standing ovation by fans when he was introduced at courtside. He was a halftime guest with Bill Hillgrove and Dick Groat on WTAE Radio, and he had a reunion with Pitt alumni and boosters.

"He was the most level-headed kid I can remember," said Hillgrove. "He had a great sense of humor. There are not too many like him who come around."

"I still love to come here," acknowledged Knight, beaming from ear to ear. "I see my mom and a lot of old friends. It brings back a lot of great memories. College is the best time of your life, as I see it, and I'd come to Pitt if I had to do it over again."

Pitt had only one winning season in the seven years prior to Knight's arrival. In three years, the Panthers would become a Top Ten team and were only one game away from reaching the NCAA Final Four.

He was recruited by Georgetown, St. Bonaventure, North Carolina State and Arizona, among others, but he chose to stay home. "I'd never been away from home," said Knight. "We had a large family, and I wanted to be near them."

There were 11 children in the Knight family, and his kid brother, Terry, followed Billy to Pitt. So did a lot of local players, which prompted some to tab him "The Pied Piper of Pitt basketball."

Knight sat out his freshman season — freshman couldn't play varsity ball then, anyhow — to concentrate on getting up to snuff academically. Even so, before he had played a single varsity game, *Street & Smith's Basketball Yearbook* tabbed him a pre-season honorable mention All-American prior to his sophomore season.

174

There was a reunion during the 1998-99 Pitt basketball season of the highly-successful 1973-74 Pitt basketball team on the 25th anniversary of their exciting NCAA tournament run, reuniting, left to right, assistant coach Fran Webster, the late Buzz Ridl's wife, Betty, and the team's top two players, Billy Knight of Braddock and Mickey Martin of Baldwin.

l-America Billy Knight's No. 34 jersey was retired eb. 20, 1989.

Billy Knight was one of ABA's top scorers, right behind Julius "Dr. J" Erving.

"There's no question Billy Knight will be a great basketball player," remarked Buzz Ridl, the head coach of the Pitt basketball team then. "It's just a matter of how long it will take." Ridl regarded him as the ultimate team player. "Everything was always done within a team concept," Ridl said during Knight's tenure at Pitt.

Among those who left their seats to speak to Knight during his visit to Pitt in 1998 were former local schoolboy coaching legends, Hank Kuzma of Midland High School fame and Jerry Conboy of South Hills Catholic. Billy was happy to see auto magnate Bill Baierl, one of the biggest benefactors of the Pitt athletic program.

"My family still buys its cars at Baierl's dealerships," said Knight. "Bill is a great guy; I see him every year at The Big East tournament in New York."

Former Pitt multi-sport performers Frank Gustine, Jr. and Brian Generalovich gathered around Knight with Eddie Ifft, Dr. Stan Marks, Keith Fammartino, et al. It was a real reunion for all concerned. Knight was also introduced to some familiar faces at courtside, including former Pitt basketball standouts Curtis Aiken and Joey David, and Pitt football coach Walt Harris and former Penn State and Steelers Hall of Famer Franco Harris.

It was celebrity night at Fitzgerald Field House.

Knight remains one of the most popular Pitt athletes of all time, and he was comfortable with the company he was keeping. He signed autographs for anyone who approached him.

He was excited about the idea of hot dogs and fries for dinner before the game at the "O," at the corner of Forbes and Bouquet, and he was disappointed to learn that the concession stands at the Field House no longer made fresh popcorn at the counter. "It was one of the last places where they still did that," Knight said with a theatrical sigh.

Nicknamed "Mooney" during his schooldays, Knight's No. 34 jersey is one of three that have been retired at Pitt. Don Hennon's No. 10 and Charles Smith's No. 32 are the others so honored. Knight is also a member of the Western Chapter of the Pennsylvania Sports Hall of Fame.

Knight averaged 22.2 points and 12 rebounds as a three-year starter, leading the team in both categories each of his three varsity seasons. The playoffs and NCAA tournament make for March Madness and Knight's appearance at the Field House had long-time fans reflecting on one of the school's most exciting and successful seasons.

The 1973-74 season was a special one in Pitt's basketball history. Knight keyed a 22-game win streak during the season. The Panthers received an at-large bid in the 32-team NCAA Tournament and made it to the Eastern finals before bowing in a dramatic contest to eventual NCAA champion North Carolina State, 81-78, led by All-American David Thompson.

George Gojkovich

Knight was the star of a team that had a strong Pittsburgh area flavor, with most of the players coming from within an easy commute of the campus. It was heralded in a full-fledged feature by *Sports Illustrated*.

Knight was the No. 1 draft choice of the Los Angeles Lakers of the NBA and the No. 2 draft choice of the Indiana Pacers of the ABA. He signed with the Pacers and was the ABA's Rookie of the Year in the 1974-75 season, and finished second in scoring in the league the next year, averaging 28.1 points per game for the Pacers. That was one point less than the leader, Julius Erving.

He played ten years in the ABA and NBA and one year in Europe, playing for a team in Limoges, France. He averaged 16 points a game for his pro career. I had followed his pro career closely because I was covering the ABA for many publications, including *The New York Post*, *The Sporting News* and *Street & Smith's Basketball Yearbook*, and always paid special attention to hometown ballplayers.

Billy Knight was a delight to deal with, then and now.

Off and on, he had been with the Pacers organization for ten years. Asked to explain the first-year success of Larry Bird as coach of the Pacers, Knight said, "He has the respect of the players.

"That's a big key in the NBA. There have been some incidents that point up a lack of respect for coaches with certain teams. Larry's approach and attitude are right. He's been a recent player and that helps. He doesn't get into yelling and screaming. He doesn't get into coaching every nuance of every possession. The guys like playing for him. They like the rapport they have with him."

Knight never gave any of his coaches a problem, on any level. Respect was his middle name. "That's the way my mother raised me," he said, referring to Addrallace Knight who made her home in the Penn Hills suburb east of Pittsburgh.

He mentioned the late Moe Becker, Andy Zezza and Ralph Campanone from his days at Braddock High when he helped them win some WPIAL B section titles, and another threesome, Buzz Ridl, Fran Webster and Tim Grgurich during his stay at Pitt. That he mentioned assistant coaches in both programs is another tip-off to Knight's recognition of how many people contributed to his success. He doesn't forget anyone.

I toured Braddock and North Braddock one day in the winter of 1998, and the building where Billy once played was pointed out to me. Billy smiled when I told him I had seen his old gym just a few days before his visit to the Field House.

Knight takes pride in staying in touch with his old coaches and their families. "For me, it was always different than just a coach-player relationship," recalled Knight.

"I always had a personal relationship with them."

He sees and checks in with them from time to time. "Coach Webster called me this season and asked me if he could buy ten court-side seats for our game with Michael Jordan and the Bulls," noted

Knight. "I told him, 'Hey, Coach, I'm working for the Pacers. I don't own them.' But I did the best I could and helped him out."

That wouldn't surprise anyone who knows Billy Knight.

When the Seattle Supersonics came to Indianapolis, Knight would hear from one of his former coaches, Tim Grgurich. He was a highly-respected assistant to George Karl, who came out of Penn Hills to star at North Carolina and with the ABA's San Antonio Spurs.

"I still have contact with Coach Grgurich all the time, and I talk to Mrs. (Buzz) Ridl on the telephone," said Knight. He said he had talked that same afternoon with Moose McCullough, a fixture in the equipment room at the Field House, and with Kirk Bruce, a Pitt athletic department official who had been a college teammate.

"I saw Keith Starr in Las Vegas and I run into Joyce Aschenbrenner, who worked in the sports information office when I was at Pitt, in my travels around the league," he said.

I used to bump into Billy when I was covering the ABA and the NBA and he was right up there with Dr. J, in my book, with class acts in the leagues. Any league they were in was a big league by their presence.

Knight was glad to hear that Pitt had unveiled plans to build a new convocation center that will be the home court for the Pitt basketball team. "We're building a new arena in Indianapolis that will seat 19,000 for basketball," noted Knight. "We're just as excited about that."

"If you like the sunshine, you've got to accept the rain."
— Billy Knight

The University of Pittsburgh invited the members of its 1973-74 men's basketball team to return to Fitzgerald Field House to be honored in January, 1999.

It was a mixed blessing. It was great to see all those guys again, but it also pointed up what a difference there was in the make-up of that team and the fifth and final lineup fielded by Ralph Willard.

Willard was beset with all sorts of problems. One player missed several games while undergoing alcohol rehabilitation, another had been suspended for being arrested in a burglary while the team was visiting Villanova.

They didn't have any problems like that with the Pitt basketball team fielded by Buzz Ridl, a soft-spoken, country gentleman who came in from Westminster College in 1968 to boost the Panthers' program.

Ridl had to be one of the classiest coaches ever to work in Pittsburgh on any level. He had good kids, mostly home-grown kids,

179

on his club, and they became good citizens. They also formed a pretty good basketball team.

One of the team's most successful players was Tom Richards, a point guard from Moon Township. He came back to Pitt from suburban Chicago, where he was an executive vice-president at Ameritech, a big, big job.

I got to know Richards a few years earlier when he was living in Upper St. Clair and playing basketball on weekend mornings with an over-the-hill gang. He was easily the best shooter on the floor, and could still bury the ball from the backcourt more consistently than most of the present-day Pitt players. Everybody liked playing with Tom Richards. He got everybody into the game, even a no-shot guard like myself. Everyone respected Richards. He had a confident, yet humble manner about him.

He remained a big fan of Billy Knight. "It all began with Billy, and he made us all look better," remarked Richards. "He was a classy competitor, and he hasn't changed much. It was just a wonderful experience. It was a great lesson of people understanding what their role is in the success of a whole unit."

Richards revered Ridl, and respected his assistants, Tim Grgurich and Fran Webster. "Coach Ridl always remained calm, no matter how chaotic things were," said Richards.

Richards was honored in his hometown on May 1, 1999 when he was inducted into the Western Chapter of the Pennsylvania Sports Hall of Fame at a dinner at the Sheraton in Warrendale. Mrs. Ridl was his guest and was present, along with Fran Webster. Both knew how much Richards and the rest of the players respected Coach Ridl.

"We looked at him as a father figure," said Knight. "He treated us like we were his own."

It was a home-grown ballteam. Knight, of course, was from Braddock. Jim Bolla was from Canevin Catholic, Mickey Martin from Baldwin, Kirk Bruce from Knoxville. The sixth man, Keith Starr, was from Quaker Valley, and another top reserve was Ken Wagoner, from Beaver Falls.

"There are no hotheads at Pittsburgh," Ridl, 53 during that 1973-74 campaign, told Curry Kirkpatrick of *Sports Illustrated*. "No grouches. I try to get the type of player who relates to me, not the other way around."

And they could compete against just about any team in the country. "The nice thing," said Martin, the team's No. 2 scorer at 12.2 points a game, "was that not only were we close as a team, but our parents were at every game, cheering as a unit."

"We had mostly Pittsburgh kids," remarked Richards, who had set scoring records at Moon Township, "who grew up watching the Pirates and Steelers, kids who had similar roots. That helped from a bonding perspective."

Bruce may have been closer to Knight than any of the other Pitt players. "His friends were everyone," said Bruce. "There was never any of that star mentality. He got along with everyone."

Billy Knight
enjoyed
30th year
reunion of ABA,
which began in
1967-68 season,
in Indianapolis
in summer of
1997. He shared
good moments
with Charlie
Scott, above, and
Connie Hawkins.

Knight never questioned his decision to go to Pitt and turn down some programs that enjoyed higher national profiles at the time.

"If I had to do it all over again, I'd go to Pitt," said Knight. "It was a great experience and I learned quite a bit. I made so many friends here, with the coaches and the players and the alumni and boosters, and we keep in touch.

"I look back at the time I played here and remember great times. There were setbacks, but it's like I always say: If you like the sunshine, you've got to accept the rain."

Bob Smizik, a Pittsburgh sports writer, made this observation about Knight: "He is the best college player around here since at least Willie Somerset at Duquesne. In fact, he's probably the best since Jerry West at West Virginia."

Knight never let his press clippings or public pronouncements about his ability swell his head.

"There are a lot of nice people in this world," said Ridl, "but none better than Billy Knight."

Even during his schooldays at Pitt, Knight knew that he had been blessed in many ways, and had a mature perspective about his place in the campus environment.

"I think that without college basketball, I'd be a completely different person now," he said back then. "I'm sure I wouldn't be in college if it wasn't for basketball. But I'm thankful I got the chance to come here.

"I've met a lot of people, some good, some bad, and I've learned a lot about life, the public, money and society. I like to travel, but without basketball I probably never would have left Pittsburgh. And I'm also thankful to Braddock.

"Seeing the people in Braddock has helped me see how people live in the streets. I've got an overall view, you know, both sides. It's helped me keep my balance."

---

*"I tell young people all the time:
Disappointment and failure are part of life.
The only thing you want to do with them is
examine them, see what you did wrong — not
what somebody did to you that caused them —
and learn from that. Then bundle it all up,
wrap it up and throw it away."*
— Gen. Colin Powell

Penguins reunion
Oldtimers return to South Hills

"Pittsburgh is where I had fun."
— Syl Apps

As kids in Canada, they didn't dream of someday playing for the Penguins in Pittsburgh. They grew up in cities like Montreal and Toronto and wanted to skate with the Canadians or the Maple Leafs.

If they were out in the boondocks, living on the bitter cold prairies or the dreary mining towns, they listened on the radio to "Hockey Night In Canada," and the Penguins were not an NHL team yet.

If they had to play in the U.S.A., they'd rather play in big cities like Chicago, Detroit and New York, where there were long-established franchises in the National Hockey League. As they got older, and the league doubled in size, they didn't want to play in L.A., either. It was too warm and it wasn't a hockey town.

Jack Kent Cooke, the original owner of the Los Angeles Kings, said he saw census figures that indicated there were 300,000 former Canadians living in the Los Angeles area, which prompted him to invest in an NHL franchise there. After struggling at the gate for years, Cooke said, "I think they all moved here because they hated hockey."

Pittsburgh had been a hockey town for years, but a minor league hockey town, where the Maple Leafs and later the Red Wings had farm teams. There's some history that hints that the first professional hockey league might have been established in the Oakland section of Pittsburgh, but the city was never looked upon as a hockey hotbed.

When they learned they had been drafted, purchased or picked up somehow by the Penguins, hockey players were less than thrilled about the prospects of reporting to Pittsburgh. The town was shaking its smoky city image somewhat, but its hockey image still needed some improvement.

They came when the National Hockey League expanded from six to twelve teams for the 1967-68 campaign, and Pittsburgh was one of the new franchises, and they came during the '70s when every other team in town — the Steelers, Pirates and Pitt — were winning championships.

"That was tough," said Syl Apps. "It was fun to be here and follow that, and to interact with some of those guys. We had a good team, but never good enough. We had money problems and we were never really a part of the City of Champions picture."

Apps was among the 31 former Penguins who appeared to play in a golf outing on July 27, 1998 at the South Hills Country Club in

Whitehall, about six miles from the Civic Arena traveling south on Rt. 51. That was fitting for, at that point, it had been 31 years since the Penguins came into being. It was to raise money for youth hockey in the Pittsburgh area, but it was also just a good excuse for a reunion.

No one enjoyed the get-together more than Tom "Scoop" Saulsbury, who had been associated with pro hockey teams in Pittsburgh for 30 years, from the Hornets at Duquesne Gardens in 1952 to the Penguins at the Civic Arena when he called it quits in 1982. Saulsbury and his wife, Arlene, live across the way from her mother in West Mifflin. Saulsbury was an insurance adjustor who moonlighted as a minor official at Pittsburgh hockey games.

Saulsbury, who was a month away from his 70th birthday, thought he had died and gone to heaven. "It's great to be with these guys again," said Saulsbury. Tom and Arlene sat on a bench by one of the holes and couldn't have been happier.

The Penguins from the past were happy to see "Scoop" as well. "He was always there," said Apps. "I lived with him for one year. He kept us out out of trouble." There were others who could say the same.

Saulsbury boasted that, in addition to Apps, he had housed Val Fonteyne, Jimmy Morris, Wally Boyer, Dean Prentice, and Al Smith among others.

"The Century Line" of Apps, Jean Pronovost and Lowell MacDonald was reunited at the South Hills Country Club gathering. They formed one of the best lines in the league, scoring 107 goals in the 1973-74 season to earn their nickname.

Les Binkley, the "original Penguin," was there as well. Ron Schock, who played for the Penguins from 1969 to 1977, was 54, but easy to recognize. He still held the club record for the fastest two assists in Penguins' history. Back on March 5, 1970, he was credited with two assists in a six-second span on goals by Wally Boyer.

Dave Burrows, 49, who put in two stints with the Penguins (1971-78, 1980-81), was one of the best defensemen in the league.

Yes, there were some outstanding players in the Penguins' line-up before Mario Lemieux came to town. But life with the Penguins was never a day at the beach, unless you were a sportswriter covering the club. All admitted they weren't keen on coming here originally. But they came, they saw, they liked the place and its fans. They hated leaving. They were happy to have a reason to return.

"There's a lot of history here," said Jack Riley, the original general manager of the Penguins, who still resides in Scott Township.

"He's still the best guy who ever worked for the organization," Saulsbury said of Riley. Of course, he was prejudiced. It was Riley, after all, who informed Saulsbury of the Penguins' reunion and told him it would be OK if he showed up, invitation or no invitation.

Most of the players lived in the South Hills in those days, when the Penguins practiced at the rink in Rostraver Township and then for ten years at the Mt. Lebanon Recreation Center. That was convenient

Long-time Penguins' fans Arlene and Tom Saulsbury are flanked by former players and good friends, Dave Burrows, left, and Les Binkley, at Penguins' alumni golf outing on July 27, 1998 at South Hills Country Club.

"The Century Line" is reunited, left to right, with Jean Pronovost, Syl Apps and Lowell MacDonald, as they once lined up in the NHL. They combined for 107 goals in 1973-74 season.

for Eddie Johnston, the coach, who lived in neighboring Upper St. Clair.

They seemed like regular guys back then. They were making a lot more money than the average mill worker, but they didn't seem any different. They fit in like snug hockey boots.

Anyone who thinks the Penguins' recent plight — front-office turmoil and financial shortcomings, bankruptcy and the NHL threatening to fold the franchise — is a new development doesn't know the history of this hockey team. Apps and Pronovost swapped stories about the season when they were limited to one pair of skates a season, one hockey stick a month and one towel per game.

"If you had a good stick, you didn't practice with it for fear you'd break it," said Apps. "Sometimes I felt like giving up my towel so the visitors would have at least two towels per man. It was embarrassing for them to see stuff like that, and know what we were going through. Some people would have said it was crummy. Even so, it was a great place to be at that time in my life."

Pronovost simply nodded when he heard Apps' appraisal of the situation.

"I can still remember coming to the Civic Arena one day to pick up my paycheck and the doors were locked," said Pronovost, the Penguins' most productive player until Mario Lemieux came along.

That was in the summer of 1975 when the IRS padlocked the doors of the financially-strapped club. The Penguins had won the first three games of a best-of-seven series with the New York Islanders that winter, only to lose the next four. It was a year these Penguins won't soon forget.

That was broadcaster Mike Lange's first year on the job. What a way to break in, huh? He had reason to believe his hockey broadcasting career had been aborted before it really got underway. So he had war stories to share with the Penguins alumni as well.

Les Binkley, Ron Schock, Vic Hadfield, Denis Herron, Bryan "Bugsy" Watson, Dave Burrows, Paul Gardner and Mark Recchi were among the most familiar of the Penguins who attended the reunion.

Watson was a real pest in his playing days, quick to annoy, quick to anger, quick to toss his gloves aside and start throwing punches. He smiled at the memories. "The thing about being an agitator," Watson once said, "is to get the last word in and, above all, don't make sense. That really confuses them."

Watson was still witty. He still made fun of his own face. It had a map of his hockey travels stitched across it.

Many of the Penguins lived in apartments in Green Tree in those days. Some remained in the South Hills. They included Joe Mullen, who put this event together with the help of publicist Cindy Himes, George Ferguson, Dave Hannan, Randy Hillier, Duane Rupp, Kim Clackson, Rick Kehoe, Peter Taglianetti and Lange, "The Voice of the Penguins." They remained in Mt. Lebanon, Upper St. Clair, Peters Township, Bethel Park, Bridgeville and Canonsburg.

186

Penguins of the past pose for team photo at July 27, 1998 reunion at South Hills Country Club. Close-up below, left to right, shows Syl Apps, Lowell MacDonald, Jean Pronovost, Joe Mullen and Jack Riley.

Hannan, who made his home in Peters Township, was helping promote youth hockey in the South Hills. He was coaching a championship Double A team. His 9-year-old son, Jeff, was playing the game with great zeal. Hannan was helping with the construction of hockey rinks in the area.

Jay Caufield came, as did Mario Faubert — "I'm the other Mario," he said on meeting. Troy Loney, Eddie Johnston and Doug Shedden were there, and they had a great time.

They said they would be back again for future reunions.

"We made the best of it."
— Syl Apps

Syl Apps played for the Penguins from 1970 to 1978. He was one of the first players named to the team's Hall of Fame. He was a handsome, classy individual with a terrific hockey pedigree. His father had been a star with the Toronto Maple Leafs, and was a member of the Hockey Hall of Fame.

The Penguins traded Glen Sather to get the younger Apps, and obtained him and Dave Schultz from the Los Angeles Kings. Schultz had gained notoriety as a goon with the infamous Broad Street Bullies of the Philadelphia Flyers. Apps was one of the Penguins best-paid players, making $125,000 for the 1974-75 season.

"I was happy to be traded to Pittsburgh where I had a chance to play in the NHL," said Apps. "We had a lot of fun in Pittsburgh despite the problems we had in the front office. The owners were good guys; they just had a case of the shorts. Tad Potter was in charge and he couldn't have treated us nicer on a personal basis. They were doing their best; they were trying. We were going through some financial problems, but we made the best of it."

Apps was living in Unionville, a suburb of Toronto, where he had worked in the financial investment business the previous 17 years. He said he had just left the business — he felt he needed a break — and wasn't sure what business pursuits he would get involved in, but said he had several options.

Apps was so approachable and agreeable. Hockey players remain the most down-to-earth of all professional athletes in this country, but the players from the past particularly made life for a sportswriter so much more of a pleasant task. Being around Apps and some of his old linemates on a sunny afternoon reminded one of just how great they had been. They didn't know any other way to behave.

It was hard to believe that Syl Apps was now 51. His hair was silver-streaked, otherwise he seemed, at first glance, to look the same as when he skated for the Penguins. He was a solid 6-1, 195 pound player with a strong right-handed shot.

DENIS HERON
Former goaltender

VIC HADFIELD
Hard-nosed goal-getter

Eddie Johnston enjoys reunion with Bugsy Watson, one of most combative pests to play in the National Hockey League.

He wore No. 20 and played center on a line that had Pronovost at right wing and MacDonald at left wing.

"I didn't have a great shot," said Apps. "I wasn't going to take three steps over the blue line and beat anybody. I didn't think so, anyhow. Lowell wasn't a big shooter, either. Prony had the best shot of the three. Psychologically, maybe we just thought 'we'll get a little closer and we'll have a better chance of getting the puck in the nets.' Prony knew if he could get to a certain spot, I'd look for him. And he'd look for me the same way. Lowell laid back a little, and covered for us both defensively. We were accused of passing the puck too much. That's team play. It serves one well in life.

"It's nice to be appreciated for what you've done," added Apps in a lengthy interview. "If you've been in a place long enough, you'd like to think that you made a contribution to that sport in that city. I had so much fun here. I enjoyed that situation so much, despite the difficulties. I started out in New York, and finished up my career in Los Angeles, and Pittsburgh is where I had fun.

"When I look back on it, I led a charmed life. I was lucky to get a college education, and I was lucky to be traded to Pittsburgh where I had an opportunity to play in the NHL, and to play with some pretty terrific guys. I have friends who wonder what it was like, who wish they could have experienced what I experienced. My friends say, 'I'd like to just warm up in Chicago Stadium.' Millions of people would love to be in your shoes just once."

His father, who starred for Toronto in the '30s and '40s, once gave him this bit of advice: "A job worth doing is worth doing well."

Apps said his dad was retired when he started playing himself, and that his father seldom came to see him play. "There were kids who used to say I only made the team because of my dad, and I'd go out and score three goals, and say, 'Yeah, that must be it.' My dad quit playing hockey the year I was born. I remember when I was about 7 or 8 years old, and I remember I couldn't take the puck away from him on the ice, and I wondered why I couldn't do it.

"I enjoyed being his son. He never pushed me in hockey. I was two or three years old when I started to play. But he pushed me in school. There was an expectation to do well in school, and to go on to the next level. I went to Princeton for a year and then to Queens College for two years. Dad always said to keep your nose to the grindstone, your shoulder to the wheel and your ear to the ground, and all will be well. But you can't do everything at once. My dad used to tell me there are a lot of opportunities in this world.

"It was inevitable that people were going to compare me to him. Although it didn't bother me that much, I'm sure I worked harder to succeed in hockey because my father was such a famous player.

"I didn't dream of being a professional hockey player. There were five of us kids, and we all played a number of sports. There weren't any pictures of my dad in the house. He has a lot in the house now; that all came later. Dad was a very private person, and he didn't boast about being a hockey player or anything like that.

"I remember going to Maple Leaf Gardens with my dad, and he'd be asked to do a radio show. I remember going to the studio with him. My dad arranged for me to go on with him. But he rarely went to any of my games. My dad's focus was on education. Our house was balanced.

"What he did stress about hockey was that it was a team game. That's probably why I passed more than I shot. It was a kick just to be playing. It was more of a game than a business back then.

"We had some close teams in Pittsburgh. We had some good players. We had a lot of fun together; I have some fond memories."

"Pittsburgh has always had a special place in my heart."
— Lowell MacDonald

Lowell MacDonald had just moved back to Pittsburgh from Milwaukee. He had worked at the University School, a prep school, in Milwaukee, and now he was going to be directing the hockey program, and helping out with the golf team, at Shady Side Academy in Fox Chapel.

He and his wife, Joyce, had maintained friends in Pittsburgh and were looking forward to their return. Joyce had worked as a nurse at the University School. They would be living in a home right on the Shady Side campus.

Their two sons, both terrific amateur hockey players in their schooldays, were grown up now and on their own, so the MacDonalds were moving into a different passage in their lives.

MacDonald had played for the Pittsburgh Hornets and twice with the Penguins (1970-71, 1972-78). He had played for the Hornets when the team was revived with the opening of the Civic Arena in 1962, and played for them for three seasons.

"My two boys both grew up here," MacDonald said of Pittsburgh. "So Pittsburgh has always had a special place in my heart."

MacDonald had surgery performed on his knees on several occasions. He waddled as he walked the golf course.

"I can't be compared to Lemieux."
— Jean Pronovost

Jean Pronovost said he was no longer coaching at McGill University, which he had done for nearly a decade. Ol' No. 19 was a good guy, too, easy to talk to, over the telephone or in person. He was a devout Christian, and practiced what he preached.

He played for the Penguins from 1968 to 1978, and his name remained among the all-time leaders in every offensive category. It was hard to believe it had been 20 years since he last played for the Penguins, or 30 years since he first reported as a French-speaking kid from Quebec.

Back home, he was better known as the kid brother of Marcel Pronovost, already an established star in the National Hockey League. "The thought of doing anything else besides hockey never entered my mind," said the younger Pronovost.

The Penguins purchased him from the Boston Bruins in a steal of a deal negotiated by Jack Riley.

Jean Pronovost played more games (753) than anyone else in Penguins' history. Rick Kehoe (722) was the closest. Only Lemieux scored more goals than Pronovost, and only Lemieux and Kehoe had more points as a Penguin. When the talented but ill-fated Michel Briere played his rookie season (1969-70) with the Penguins, it was Pronovost who looked after him.

They could talk in French to each other, and they had a lot in common. Pronovost still mourns the death of Briere, who died months after being injured in an auto accident in Canada during the summer months following that promising first season with the Penguins.

Pronovost was the first Penguin to score 50 goals in a season. He led the team in goal-scoring five times and in point scoring twice. He was inducted, along with late coach Bob Johnson and Kehoe, into the Penguins Hall of Fame in 1992.

His best season was 1975-76 when he had 52 goals and 52 assists for 104 points.

"I can't be compared to Lemieux," Pronovost once told me. "I don't have the same talent. I wouldn't want to compare myself to him. He's more of a natural goal-scorer. I was more of a hard worker."

During his ten-year stay with the Penguins, Pronovost played under five different coaches, three different general managers, and three different ownership groups. It was hard to get any consistency that way.

"Everyone knows you don't build a team from the ice up," Pronovost pointed out. "You build from the front office down, from management down."

He was married to his wife, Diane, over 30 years. "She should have a medal for courage," he kidded. They have four children and, yes, they were now grandparents.

Asked about his popularity among his teammates and the fans at the Civic Arena, Pronovost said, "I try to treat people the way I want to be treated, which is another way of stating the golden rule, I suppose. You'll only get back what you put in."

Though he was now living in Terrasse Vaudrevil, Quebec, Pronovost said a piece of his heart remained in Pittsburgh. "Even though I am away," he said, "I am there in spirit."

Former GM Jack Riley reminisces with former Penguins defenseman Duane Rupp at team reunion.

Former Penguins George Ferguson and Russ Anderson swap war stories.

"I think they were embarrassed to pay me that."
— Les Binkley

Les Binkley, the original Penguin and a goal-keeper who played without a facemask those first few years, was very visible at the South Hills Country Club.

Binkley was the first player ever signed to play for the Penguins. The team purchased his rights from the Cleveland Barons the year before the franchise actually competed in the NHL.

So Binkley prepped for the Penguins by playing another season in the American Hockey League, and competed against the Hornets in their last AHL season. The Hornets won the AHL's Calder Cup championship that last season.

Binkley replaced Gil Mayer in Cleveland and won rookie of the year honors while doing so. Mayer had been the goalie for the Hornets in their last years at Duquesne Gardens. Freddie Glover was the star of the Cleveland Barons, and was a familiar foe to Pittsburgh hockey fans.

Binkley was paid $15,000 that first season with the Penguins. "I was originally signed for $12,500, but I think they were embarrassed to pay me that," he said. He played without a mask his first two seasons in Pittsburgh. He lost some teeth doing so and picked up a few facial scars. He set a team record with 11 shutouts as a goalie for the Penguins.

He was so happy to be playing in the NHL. When he came up through the ranks, there were only six teams in the league. The six goalies played nearly every game. They never sat down unless they were hurt. "All six goalies are now in the Hockey Hall of Fame," said Binkley. "There were no openings."

One of them, Harry Lumley of the Detroit Red Wings, lived next door to Binkley's home in Owen Sound, Ontario. Lumley left his old goalkeeper sticks at Binkley's home whenever he visited his parents. Imagine two NHL goalies growing up next door to each other, even though they were a generation apart. Binkley said he still kept in touch with Lumley, and that he was doing fine.

Then again, Binkley said he was doing fine, too, though he had hip replacement surgery on July 8, 1993 in Toronto, and said he was bothered by athritis in his knees. His smile and great sense of humor were still intact. I had seen him at a Penguins' golf outing at the Fox Chapel Country Club shortly after he'd had his surgery and he, understandably, was having a difficult time getting around on the veranda that day.

Binkley and Watson shared a table with Eddie Johnston and me in the men's grill at the South Hills Country Club. It was great to hear them swap war stories.

"I think of myself as a Penguin."
— Ron Schock

Vic Hadfield was a late arrival at the reunion. He was the 31st player to appear, and was not present when a team photo was taken on the patio behind the South Hills Country Club. He thought he was lucky to be there at all. He had been struck by another automobile as he was driving a month earlier, and his back was bothering him. He showed up with Mike Lange, the Penguins' broadcaster, and they lay on a grassy knoll, drinking some beer and greeting the golfers as they went by the clubhouse.

I had first known Hadfield when he was playing for the Rangers, and I was writing for *The New York Post*. I covered the Rangers now and then, and during the playoffs in the early '70s. We had the same agents in New York in Steve Arnold and Marty Blackman, and had benefitted from the association.

Hadfield held out one year in tandem with teammates Brad Park, Rod Gilbert and Jean Ratelle, and they all received huge pay increases as a result. It was when agents were really making an impact in pro sports.

Hadfield was always a fun guy. He had more creases in his face, and in his smile when he showed up at the South Hills Country Club. I told him he was starting to look like Tom Berenger, the movie actor, though he probably would have preferred reminding one of Robert Redford.

Ron Schock played for the Penguins from 1969 to 1977, and was always an aggressive frontliner. Jane, his wife of 33 years, recalled when they used to get together with the other Penguins and their families when many of them lived in an apartment complex in Green Tree.

"I didn't want to play in Pittsburgh," said Schock, "but I grew to like it very much. Yes, I like Pittsburgh. I think of myself as a Penguin. That's where I played the longest."

He roomed with Eddie Johnston when he played for the Boston Bruins in his early days in the NHL. He called him "Downtown Eddie." Asked to explain the nickname, Schock said, "He really liked life, and he enjoyed it to the fullest."

Paul Gardner was one of those Green Tree guys. I remembered having drinks with him on a few occasions at the Jamestown Inn, a once popular supper club where Banksville gives way to Dormont on Rt. 19. It was a hangout frequented by several of Chuck Noll's assistants, and members of the Pirates, Steelers and Penguins, sportswriters and suburbanites who got sidetracked on the way from Downtown to their homes after work. In more recent years, I bumped into him at Vincent's Pizza Pub, just off the Parkway in Green Tree, when he was in town as the coach of the Portland, Maine team in the short-lived summertime deck hockey league.

195

Gardner made his mark with the Penguins by becoming the first player in team history to score four goals in a game, that performance coming on December 13, 1980, against the Philadelphia Flyers. He did it in his 10th game with the team, and it made him an immediate hit with his teammates and the fans.

Gardner also had strong NHL bloodlines. His dad, Cal Gardner, had played 12 seasons in the league, and was with two Stanley Cup championship teams in Toronto. Paul's older brother, Dave, played seven seasons in the NHL.

Paul and Greg Malone had played junior hockey together in Oshawa, and ran together when they were rejoined as teammates in Pittsburgh. Malone was the head of the Penguins' scouting department.

"I loved playing hockey."
— Dave Burrows

Dave Burrows lived in Parry Sound, Ontario, better known as the birthplace of Bobby Orr, perhaps the greatest hockey player ever. Burrows managed a youth center there.

When Burrows played in Pittsburgh, he rented a home in Green Tree that had been previously owned by Roberto Clemente.

Burrows was one of the most popular Penguins. He wasn't an offensive force like Orr — who was? — but he was a stay-at-home guy who protected goalies like Les Binkley and Denis Herron.

He and Pronovost were both proud to tell you they were Christians. He and his wife, Carol, thought they had it made in Parry Sound.

"There is a wonderful life after hockey," said Burrows. "At the peak of your hockey career, you can't think anything could be better. I loved playing hockey, but I love what I'm doing now."

He was happy to be back with his old teammates and they reminded him of why he liked playing for the Penguins in the first place.

"You can have a team with talent, but if the guys don't get along in the dressing room, it shows up on the ice. If you don't get along, man to man, or as friends, I don't think it helps you on the ice.

"Prony, Syl and Lowell MacDonald proved that. Those three guys were the most unselfish players I've ever seen. If they had a fault, it was passing too much to let the other guys get the goal. It was a pleasure to play with those guys."

> *"The greatest tragedy in life is that most people spend their entire lives preparing to live."*
> — Paul Tournier

Penguins lineup includes, left to right, Rick Kehoe, Eddie Johnston and Ron Schock.

Former teammates, left to right, are Les Binkley, Dave Burrows and Syl Apps.

Herb Douglas
Boyhood hero at Olympic Games again

"Jesse Owens has always
been my hero."

A boyhood hero of mine, Herb Douglas, went to the Olympic Games in Atlanta in the summer of 1996. Douglas won a bronze medal in the long jump in the 1948 Olympic Games in London. To my knowledge, he was the only athlete to be born and bred within the city limits of Pittsburgh to win an Olympic medal until Suzie McConnell of Brookline came along as a member of the women's basketball team that won medals in 1988 and 1992.

When I was in 7th and 8th grade, I used to pause when passing the boyhood home of Herb Douglas at 160 Hazelwood Avenue. His home was sort of a shrine, because someone told me that a man had lived there who had won an Olympic medal.

When I went to Allderdice High School, where Douglas had been a four-sport star, I loved to read books in the school library about Olympic heroes. Now I write books like that. It had all sorts of inspirational stories about track & field stars such as Jesse Owens, Bob Richards, Bob Mathias, Glenn Cunningham, Archie Sam Romani and Babe Didrickson Zaharias.

Track & field was one of my favorite athletic interests. Parry O'Brien, an Olympic shot-putter from Southern Cal, caught my eye for obvious reasons, as did female sprint star Wilma Rudolph. I remember reading about sprinters like Bobby Morrow of Abilene Christian and Dave Sime of Duke. I read stories about them in *Sport* magazine. Then there were weight men like Al Oerter and Harold Connolly.

I met Douglas for the first time in 1980 on an airplane trip to Philadelphia, near where he has been living for many years. We have been friends ever since. Whenever he came back home to see his mother, which was often, he called on the telephone. We met for lunch on the Pitt campus.

At age 76, he was staying for extended periods because his mother, Ilessa Mae Douglas, who was 96, was in failing health in a nursing home in the city's East End. I had spoken to her many times. She was a woman of great spirit and a wonderful sense of humor. She took credit for her son's speed. It hurt to hear she wasn't doing well.

Douglas didn't know whether he should go to the Olympic Games in 1996, something he had done every four years with few exceptions since 1948.

His family and friends convinced him that he couldn't do anything for his mother and that it would improve her spirits if he was in Atlanta among people who were aware of his accomplishments.

All-star lineup at 1997 Jesse Owens International Trophy Dinner in New York, left to right, includes Dr. LeRoy Walker, vice-president of International Amateur Athletic Assn. (IAAA); Mrs. Jesse Owens, award-winner Michael Johnson, award founder Herb Douglas and emcee Bob Costas of NBC Sports.

Herb Douglas visits Pittsburgh Athletic Association (PAA) to host luncheon meeting. He was named in 1999 to Board of Trustees at his alma mater, the University of Pittsburgh.

"Your mother will be so proud to tell people that her son is at the Olympic Games," a friend told Douglas.

Herb's mother was always his biggest fan, and he returned the adoration. It was his mother who took him, when he was a student athlete at Gladstone Junior High, to the Hill District to meet the great Jesse Owens who was on a national tour after winning four gold medals at the 1936 Olympic Games.

Douglas spoke to Owens that day, and Owens praised him and encouraged him to continue his running and jumping efforts, saying he was doing better than he had at the same age.

"I later learned that Jesse would stretch the truth if it suited the occasion," said Douglas. "Jesse Owens has always been my hero. Even today, he inspires me."

When Douglas became a vice-president at Schieffelin & Somerset, a leading wine and spirits company — he boasts that he was one of only three African-Americans who had risen to such a lofty position in corporate America at the time — he created one of the most prestigious international athletic awards in memory of Jesse Owens. He founded and served as president of the International Amateur Athletic Association, Inc. He gained attention from *Ebony* magazine for his business accomplishments.

Douglas was 26 and a student at the University of Pittsburgh when he participated in the Olympic Games. He had started out at Xavier University in New Orleans, but had to drop out when his father suffered a stroke and went blind in his mid-40s. Douglas went to work in Shadyside with his father for three years before entering Pitt.

His father became a huge business success — after he went blind — prompting the son to say, "My dad was the real hero in our family."

Herb was only the second black, behind Jimmy Joe Robinson by a few days in 1945, to play for the Pitt football team. That was two years before Jackie Robinson broke the color barrier in major league baseball.

"Back then, young African-American athletes thought they could improve their lot by going to the Olympic Games," said Douglas. "They saw how famous Jesse Owens became. The 1948 Olympics were particularly significant because there hadn't been any Olympic Games in 1940 and 1944 because of World War II. There were only eight African-Americans on our track and field team back then, and only one African-American — Don Barksdale — on our basketball team."

How things have changed. The USA track and field teams are dominated by black athletes, and our basketball team — the "Dream Team" in 1996 — had only one white player, John Stockton.

Douglas and I spoke on the telephone during the Olympic Trials that preceded the 1996 competition and we were talking about how some gymnasts and divers were making mistakes in their routines that ruined their chances of going to Atlanta.

"Getting to the Games is so difficult," Douglas said. "That's the most important thing, just getting there. You can train for a lifetime and not be at your best on one day and the dream is gone. I've seen it ruin people's lives."

That's why Douglas was excited by going to the Games again. But he had mixed emotions this time. "My heart," he said, "will be back here with my mother."

As it turned out, Herb had to cut his stay short in Atlanta to return home to Hazelwood upon learning that his mother had died. I had the honor of speaking at her funeral service at Grace Memorial Presbyterian Church in the Hill District.

Douglas still returns to his home in Hazelwood when he comes to Pittsburgh on business or to see friends and relatives. In 1999, he was named by Mark Nordenberg to Pitt's board of trustees.

He still prefers to stay at his home, which is looked after by his life-long friend and "brother" Carl Redwine. He sleeps in the bed he slept in as a boy.

"I have a $400,000 home in Philadelphia, but I can't sleep there like I can sleep here. There's no place in the world where I can get a good night's sleep like I do here. This is still home."

Jim O'Brien

Herb Douglas admires a framed photograph of one of his Olympic heroes, Pitt's John Woodruff, which he was responsible for having displayed at school's Hillman Library.

Peggy Michel
Wimbledon champion

"It's nice to be important, but it's more important to be nice."

Evonne Goolagong with Michel

A Wimbledon champion ought to attract attention at the Martin Tressel Tennis Center in Mt. Lebanon, a suburb eight miles south of Pittsburgh.

It's a nationally-acclaimed 10-court complex — with Har-Tru surface courts — and it attracts many of the area's long-time tennis enthusiasts. Eavesdrop on some of the courtside conversations and you'll realize that many of the fans really know their tennis.

Yet few paid Peggy Michel any mind when she attended the National Collegiate & West Penn Tennis Championships at midweek, July 27, 1998. Before year's end, she would be inducted into the ITA Women's Collegiate Tennis Hall of Fame.

Michel sat with some old friends on a grassy knoll, sunning themselves and scanning the courts to catch the kids in competition.

Some of the best collegiate and high school tennis players in the country, including some home grown talent, come to Mt. Lebanon each summer to show their stuff. They are brought there by Dr. Donald Mercer, the tournament director.

The West Penn aspect of the tournament was 111 years old in 1999 — it may be the oldest continuous amateur tennis tournament in the country — and once attracted the likes of Bill Tilden, Roscoe Tanner, Harold Solomon, JoAnne Russell and Vitas Gerulaitis. One never knows what's to become of these kids, and who will be the next Vitas Gerulaitis. Most of the entries are teenagers or young adults, at best, and those names etched on the tournament trophies mean little to them. These names were more familiar to their parents and the officials, who were sad to learn of the deaths the day before Michel's visit of two of their favorites, astronaut Alan Shepard and TV father and doctor Robert Young, but those names meant nothing to the competitors, either. It's a generation thing.

Peggy Michel was never a marquee tennis player like Billie Jean King or Chris Evert, but she has a distinguished history. Back in 1974, she teamed with Evonne Goolagong to win the women's doubles title at Wimbledon. In 1969, when she was just 18, Michel made it to the finals of the women's doubles at Wimbledon.

"It was always my goal to win at Wimbledon," said Michel, still looking terrific at age 50, and retaining the sunny disposition that made her so popular when she played in the mid-'70s for the Pittsburgh Triangles in World Team Tennis. Her brown hair was cut short and highlighted and it looked as if she had just stepped out of a

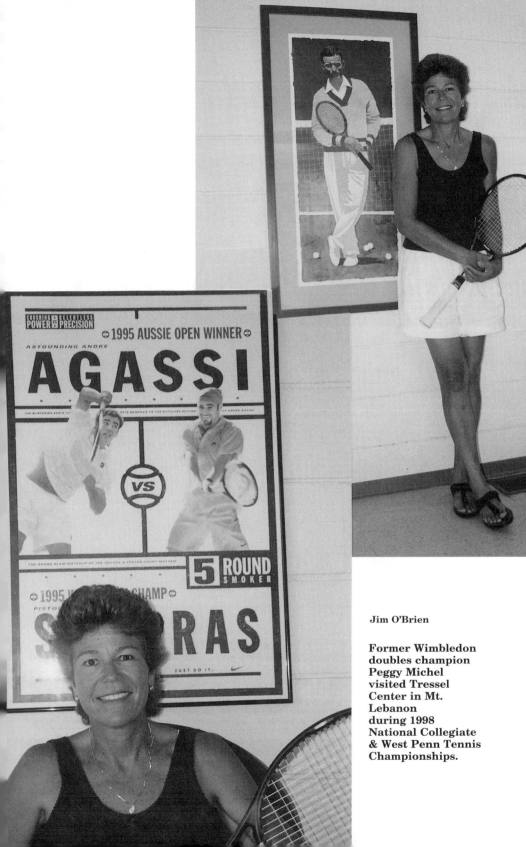

Jim O'Brien

Former Wimbledon
doubles champion
Peggy Michel
visited Tressel
Center in Mt.
Lebanon
during 1998
National Collegiate
& West Penn Tennis
Championships.

styling salon. She wore a short-sleeved violet jersey, beige shorts, open-toed sandals, large sunglasses and a bronze tan that had to be the envy of everyone around her.

This was a woman who had won eight tournament titles in doubles — Australian, New Zealand, New South, Canada and Wimbledon — and was still adding to her impressive resume.

She and Goolagong were also doubles partners in Pittsburgh when the Triangles won the World Team Tennis title. The Triangles, owned by successful businessman and sports entrepreneur Frank Fuhrer, played at the Civic Arena for three seasons — 1974, 1975 and 1976 — and were a vital part of "The City of Champions."

The Pirates, Steelers and Pitt were winning championships with regularity during that decade, and Michel took in and enjoyed the whole scene. The Triangles attracted big crowds for a while. Pittsburgh demanded and delivered winning teams at this time. Dan Rooney, the Steelers president, believed that one team's success rubbed off on the other. The passion for tennis waned in these parts, however, and a frustrated Fuhrer folded the tent.

Michel returned after her WTT experience, following a stay in Cleveland, to teach tennis at South Park. "Pittsburgh grabbed a piece of my heart," she said. "I grew up and continue to live in southern California, but I'm now here six months a year. The people here really took to us, and I've always liked the people; they're so genuine. I would say Pittsburgh is my home."

She and her friends were watching a women's doubles match pitting Jacqueline Bunting of Upper St. Clair and Kate Lutgert of Evergreen, Colorado against Leigh Ann Totty of McMurray and Stacy Voelker of McGuffey High School in Washington, Pennsylvania. Michel remained a good friend of Leigh Ann's mother, Judith Totty, the tennis pro at Rolling Hills Country Club.

"I wish I had come here to play when I was in college," said Michel. "My little sister, Christine, played here when she was on the junior varsity at Stanford. Tennis is a great sport for young women to take up. It's fun to play, it gets you on a team, and if you have the talent and work at it you can get to college with it. If you stay with it, and you're good enough, you can travel the world with it, as I did.

"I watch these kids today, though, and there's little style or shot placement. There's no grace. They're all trying to knock each other out. They get into bad habits. They'll find out that the pros not only can hit it hard, but they can hit it with control.

"I haven't seen a drop shot yet and this is clay."

She said she still played tennis, but had taken up golf, and that was her latest passion. This was true with a lot of women who took up tennis in the '70s.

While driving with friends to Mt. Lebanon, Michel was reminded of one of her former students when they passed through the neighboring community of Dormont. "I taught a deaf girl named Mary Jean Shanen from Dormont and she went on to finish third in the Deaf Olympics," said Michel. "I hit with her a couple of times on those courts in Dormont. I wondered about her when we went through there today. Working with her was a special thrill."

"I loved Maria Bueno."
— Peggy Michel

Peggy Michel started playing tennis at age 14 in her hometown of Pacific Palisades, a southern California community she says was as good as it sounds.

"I remember the first time I ever went to see a pro tennis exhibition at the Sports Arena in Los Angeles," said Michel when we met at the Mt. Lebanon Tennis Center. "It was one of those tours that Jack Kramer coordinated and promoted. I remember seeing Lew Hoad of Australia, Andres Gimeno of Argentina and Butch Buchholz Jr. of the United States."

She was particularly captivated by Lew Hoad. "He was one of the best tennis players I'd ever seen," she recalled. "He and Roy Emerson were two of the best players at that time. He had quite a physique and talent. They say he loved the night life, and never realized his full potential as a player.

"He made such an impression on me. He just seemed to play the game differently than everyone else."

As she spoke, I could remember as a teenager reading about Hoad and Buchholz in *SPORT* Magazine. I could still see them as they were pictured in the favorite magazine of my youth. I knew that Buchholz had grown up in St. Louis. He was America's best hope for tennis at the time when it was otherwise dominated by Australian players. He and Dennis Ralston were two of the best American players of that period.

Tennis was in the midst of a revolution at the time. It had always been an amateur sport, with the top players getting appearance fees and perks under the table. Kramer formed his own pro tour and those who joined him were unable, in the early years, to compete in the major tennis tournaments. The established tournaments, in time, gave in because they needed the best players to attract attention and attendance. That's when open tennis was born. Everyone was eligible.

Michel came along when the women's political movement was picking up steam, and tennis and women's tennis, in particular, were making great strides. It was a struggle, at first, but it was championed by the likes of fiesty Billie Jean King, and every young woman today, whether or not she plays tennis, has benefited by the gains that were achieved.

Michel remembers that the first women tennis players who caught her eye were Margaret Court, Ann Haydon Jones and Maria Bueno. Billie Jean King, Rosie Casals and Francoise Durr were all doing well when Michel came along. Althea Gibson and Darlene Hard were gone by the time she was playing.

"I loved Maria Bueno," said Michel. "When I was 16, I was told I had her style of game."

That was quite a compliment. Maria Bueno, of Sao Paulo, Brazil, was a ballerina on the court. She was 5-6, 118 pounds, and known popularly as "La Bueno." She won Wimbledon and U.S. Open singles titles at age 19. Altogether, she won three Wimbledon titles, four U.S. titles and three Italian titles. There was an absolute artistry about her game, and she wore beautiful swirling dresses designed by Ted Tinling, the same man who came up with the controversial lace panties for Gussie Moran.

In 1958, Bueno won a Wimbledon double's title, playing with Althea Gibson, a Harlem-born woman who was the first black to make an impact on the international tennis scene, way before Arthur Ashe of Richmond made his mark in the game.

Tennis wasn't that big in Bueno's native Brazil, but she was honored by parades, statues and airmail stamps.

Then there was Margaret Smith Court. She was bigger, stronger, more athletic, with long limbs, and she could reach everything. Between 1960 and 1975, Court won 62 Grand Slam titles in singles, women's doubles and mixed doubles. She won 24 Grand Slam singles titles and won all four events (U.S., Wimbledon, Australian and Italian) for a Grand Slam in 1970.

"She was an all-around tennis player," remembered Michel, "and she was a lady on and off the court. That appealed to me."

Margaret Smith Court was the first woman tennis player to use weights, working out five days a week to build herself into a powerful athletic force. Talking about her tennis talent, she once said, "It was a gift from God that I had. I just loved it. I loved all sports."

Billie Jean King was that way, too. She was only a year younger than Court, but she went to college and Court was on the international circuit for five years before King entered the fray.

"Billie Jean and I played at the same time," said Michel. "I competed so much with Billie Jean, so I didn't really idolize her. When I was 18 or 19, I got to play my dream match. I teamed with Patti Hogan to play Margaret Court and Maria Bueno, who were No. 1 in the world, at Piping Rock, New York. We lost, but it didn't seem to matter.

"Patti Hogan was my only other partner besides Evonne Goolagong, except when I was teamed with Pam Richman at Arizona State University in my school years. Patti was my partner when we lost in the women's doubles finals at Wimbledon in 1968."

A graduate of Arizona State University, Michel is a member of the Sun Devils Hall of Fame. In 1998, she was also named captain/coach of the USTA Young Cup Competition.

Michel said she had been working for former pro Charlie Pasarell in southern California since 1985. She handled corporate sponsorships for his Newsweek Champions Cup in Indian Wells, California, one of the most respected tennis tournaments this side of the Big Four. "We have a $7 million budget and it's a big-time affair," said Michel. "You have the four grand slam events, the Lipton and then Newsweek. It's about the sixth most important tournament in the world."

I remembered Pasarell from his playing days with the Los Angeles entry in World Team Tennis. I got interested in tennis in the mid-70s when it became so popular as a recreational sport, and covered the WTT in New York, with the team first called the Sets and later the Apples. We lived in Baldwin, New York, not far from Nassau Coliseum, and I arranged for the visiting WTT teams to work out at the Baldwin Tennis Club. We had clinics there hosted by the likes of Billie Jean King and Virginia Wade and Fred Stolle. Vitas Gerulaitis brought his kid sister, Ruta, and they conducted a clinic. He had flown in a day early from Pittsburgh to do this.

WTT players who played in virtually our backyard in Baldwin were the Armitraj Brothers from India — Vijay, Anand and Ashok — Kathy Harter, Francoise Durr, Rosie Casals, Mark Cox, Greer "Cat" Stevens, Sandy Mayer, Fred McMillan, Rayni Fox, Betty Stove, Renee Richards, Wendy Turnbull and Marty Riessen. They were fun to be around, and to hit with on occasion. In 1978, my last year in New York prior to returning home to Pittsburgh to work at *The Pittsburgh Press*, I covered the New York Apples for *The New York Post*. That team's roster included player-coach Fred Stolle, Mary Carillo, Vitas Gerulaitis, Billie Jean King, Ray Ruffels and JoAnne Russell. I also had opportunities to interview Jimmy Connors, John McEnroe, Chris Evert and Tracy Austin.

Russell and Gerulaitis had played with Michel and Goolagong for the Pittsburgh Triangles a few years earlier. I had traveled back home to Pittsburgh to cover the Triangles and Sets in playoff action. Back then, the Sets also had Virginia Wade, one of the all-time greats from England, Charlie Owens, Sandy Mayer and Phil Dent.

Sharing stories with Michel about those WTT days brought a smile to her winsome face.

"I just like the people here."
— Michel on Pittsburgh

"I come back and visit my friends here in the summertime," said Michel. "I don't like to stay in the desert at this time of the year; it's too hot. I'd like to come back here and live permanently.

"I just like the people here. I think there's a lot of potential for tennis here. When I was with the Triangles, I just enjoyed the people; they were so genuine. I don't think it mattered if you were a good tennis player. It was more important that you were a good person.

"They really took Evonne and me in. I remember we had 10,000 people at the Civic Arena for our first match, and a couple of times over the three years. After our first match at the Arena, I went shopping with my mother the next day in downtown Pittsburgh. We went to Horne's.

"When we there, some people stopped me and said, 'You're Peggy Michel. You play for the Triangles.' After they passed us, I said, 'Mother, I've never been noticed before. I like it here.'

"I had come to Pennsylvania the first time when I was 18. I played in the nationals in Philadelphia, and I thought that was so beautiful, too. Pittsburgh has been in my heart ever since the Triangles. I keep coming back.

"When I was growing up, they had this tournament here, but I never got to play in it.

"I enjoyed playing at the Arena here. We had quite a following. Vic Edwards was our coach."

Edwards was not only the coach, but he was also the legal guardian for Goolagong in her early years on the tour.

"I liked playing for Pittsburgh," said Michel. "I always thought of myself as a team player. I liked playing for a team, I liked playing for a city. And there was so much going on here. I remember going to see the Pirates in the playoffs, and even in the World Series (1979) when I was teaching tennis out at South Park and at the Longview Country Club.

"We went to every Steelers game. All the teams were doing well. We were here when (1976) Pitt won the national championship in college football, and I went to their games, too. It was great fun. Pittsburgh is a tough town. They love winners. You better win. They take sports very seriously here.

"They used to really get into it at the Arena. We were a family — the team and the fans — and we did well. Evonne and I won the women's doubles title at Wimbledon in 1974 — I can't believe that was 24 years ago — and they gave us a standing ovation at the Arena when we came home for our next match.

"So what happens...we go out and lose our doubles match. I think we were playing Pat Bostram and Janet Newberry. I think we were up, 5-2, and we lost the set. The fans booed us. Evonne was so furious. 'I can't believe they'd do that,' she said to me on the way to the dressing room at the break. I said, 'Well, you definitely know how you stand in their eyes.'"

Goolagong was a great tennis player, but she lacked the killer instinct of King, Evert and Navratilova. She lacked the steely reserve and focus of that fearsome trio. She used to have what her coach called "walkabouts," spells when she lost concentration and went for nomadic strolls like her ancestors, the Australian Aborigines.

King once said of Goolagong: "She walked onto the court with a smile on her face, and it was apparent to all that, win or lose, tennis was a sheer joy for her."

Chris Evert echoed those same sentiments. "She's the nicest champion you'll ever want to meet," said Evert.

"I never wanted tennis to be everything," said Goolagong, explaining her approach.

So Michel matched up well with Goolagong, for they shared the same sunny outlook on life, and thought there was life beyond the boundaries of the tennis court.

Michel always kept things in their proper perspective. She never regarded herself as a tennis star. She wasn't that successful as a singles player, and knew her strengths as well as her weaknesses. She needed a good partner. She and Goolagong could have been mistaken for sisters.

"My mom and dad were responsible for my outlook," Michel said. "I was one of six children. I don't think they ever allowed me to be cocky. No one was special in my family; we were all special. They urged us to be kind to others. I grew up on the public courts; I wasn't a country club kid. I liked playing tennis with men on the local courts.

"I never felt like a big deal in my hometown. My family was well known before I came along. When I won at Wimbledon, some attention was showed me. My tennis got my family involved in so many things. I traveled and learned about the world first hand.

"My ultimate goal was to win Wimbledon, so I achieved my goal. I was always a very goal-oriented person. I was nationally ranked when I was 16. I got to go to college for my tennis. That was great.

"I always had a good time. Vitas had such great spirit and was so much fun when we were together on the Triangles. He hosted some great parties. We encouraged people to go out with us after our home matches. We all had groups. The community was involved. No one on the team was a snob."

I asked Michel what it was like to play tennis for Frank Fuhrer, a strong-willed Pittsburgh businessman who also bankrolled indoor soccer and some major golf tournaments in Pittsburgh. Fuhrer was famous for delivering some salty pre-match talks to the Triangles when they weren't playing up to their potential.

Michel smiled. "He was an owner," she said, "and he hated to lose. He felt he had an investment, and he wanted us to perform. I don't think he understood that you didn't have to win every single point. He was rough on us at times, especially on us women.

"But he was a good businessman. He had high expectations for us, and it was tough to please him. He meant well. Pittsburgh wouldn't have had World Team Tennis except for Frank Fuhrer's financial backing. You can't forget that."

Gerulaitis, who died tragically because of a faulty gas heating system in his Long Island home in the mid-'90s, feuded with Fuhrer, who chastised him often for partying too much. Gerulaitis defended Fuhrer, however, "because Fuhrer's fair, generous and the most competent owner in the league. That's why we win. I can live with his temper."

The Triangles were well paid and they traveled first class, according to Mark Cox, one of their stellar performers.

The most magic night of all, as far as the Triangles and their fans were concerned, had to be the night of July 8, 1976, when 13,492 turned out at the Civic Arena to see the Triangles take on Chris Evert and the Phoenix Racquets. Evert had just defeated Goolagong in a three-set showdown for the women's singles title at Wimbledon and this was the first match of the second half of the WTT season. They took a break for Wimbledon each year.

There were other magic times at the Arena. Some of the game's greatest players came to Pittsburgh to play during that period. They included Ken Rosewall, the first player-coach of the Triangles, Billie Jean King, John Newcombe, Jimmy Connors, Bjorn Borg, Rod Laver, Virginia Wade, Diane Fromholtz, Martina Navratilova and Marty Reissen, among others.

The honeymoon didn't last, though, and in December of 1976 Fuhrer tossed in the towel.

World Team Tennis had its ups and downs everywhere, and has come and gone, in one form or another, through the years. I asked Michel what she thought of the senior tennis circuit. "It's not catching on like senior golf and it may not," she said. "Jimmy Connors is still very good. He's still in great shape. But that's not true with everyone, and it's especially not true with the women. They're not in as great shape.

"In golf, you don't have to run after the ball. Age doesn't show as much on the golf course as it does on the tennis court. Plus, you can fix the golf courses to make the players look better, and to keep the scores down. You can't change a tennis court or the demands of the game. You start missing volley shots because you're not getting to the net as quickly. That half step shows up dramatically. People see John McEnroe miss shots he never missed and they can spot it right away.

"Connors is in the best of shape. He hasn't changed one bit. Senior tennis hasn't taken off because there aren't enough like him. The women can't move anymore. The fans remember that Chris Evert never missed that shot. The image changes."

Image has always been important to Peggy Michel.

"My philosophy is take the racquet away and what's left. When they strip you of everything, if you're still a good person then you've accomplished something of substance. I don't think you'll get through the pearly gates because you're a good tennis player. Being nice is more important. You might get through as a good person.

"I don't know what's with a lot of these athletes today. I met guys like Terry Bradshaw and Joe Greene, and I watched Willie Stargell and Roberto Clemente, and they were good guys. They were great with people. Jerome Bettis seems to be like that, too. Bettis has that big smile and he seems to be enjoying life. That impresses me more than anything else."

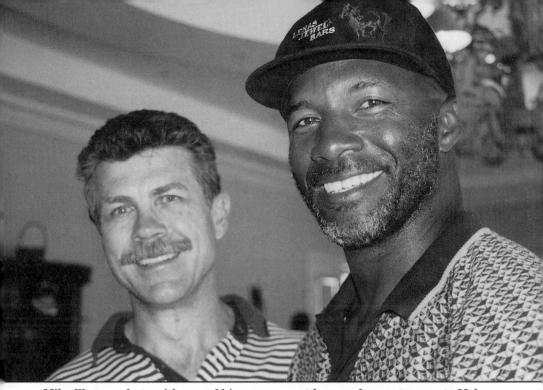

Mike Wagner chats with one of his more recent heroes, former teammate Mel Blount, before they teed off at Andy Russell's annual children's benefit golf tournament.

Mike Wagner, Former Steelers Free Safety:
"Bobby Hull was one of my first sports heroes. WGN Radio broadcasted the Cubs and Blackhawks games, and I used to listen to them religiously. We lived about 50 miles away. My dad had played a little bit of hockey when he was a kid. There were only six teams in the NHL back then. There were some great hockey players. Stan Mikita was another great Blackhawk. I never got to see any hockey or basketball games at Chicago Stadium. I got to see about four Cubs games, and I saw Kenny Holtzman pitch a no-hitter. That was so exciting. As far as football went, my hero was Larry Wilson of the Cardinals. I always wanted to wear No. 8 when I played because of him. I was such a late-round draft choice (11th round out of Western Illinois in 1971), I couldn't go around asking for a special number. Wilson was a late round pick himself, so he was an inspiration to me. If he can make it, I thought, I have a shot at the pros. I was lucky to go to the right team where Chuck Noll was playing a zone defense where a slow safety could fit in."

Jim O'Brien

Snapshot:

Dr. John Gaisford
He plays a different "skins" game

"He's impressive, quite a guy."
— Dr. Ross Musgrave

There is a calmness, indeed, a sweet serenity about Dr. John Collyer Gaisford that must be comforting to his patients and peers and maddening to those who play golf with him.

Dr. Gaisford grins a great deal as he discusses his work and his play. He is so enthusiastic about both, his research and his recreation, his hospital projects and his golf game, and he is to be envied. He balances both with his dextrous hands and keen mind.

He is closely identified with the Burn/Trauma Center at West Penn Hospital in Bloomfield, where he served as its chairman from 1970 to 1987, and where, in the summer of 1999, he continued to conduct research, counsel young doctors and amuse himself. He's been the director of burn research since 1987. He was also the chairman of the department of surgery at West Penn from 1970 to 1984.

Whether he was wielding a scalpel or a 9-iron, Dr. Gaisford's deftness and skills have always set a high standard for his colleagues and playmates. His zest and passion have worn out many who have tried to emulate him. At the height of his ability on the golf course and at the hospital, few could beat him in the "skins" game.

He has slipped on surgical gloves and golf gloves with equal care and confidence, and has captured more than his share of honors and awards for both.

I visited with him at West Penn Hospital three times over a nine-year period, and he was a great host every time.

Dr. Gaisford was 83 when I last visited him for an interview for this book, back on September 23, 1998, at his office at West Penn Hospital. "I still give talks to residents," he said. "We have resident doctors coming from other institutions to observe what we're doing here. They are young people who are coming for a short period of time. They are not coming because they're going to be burn doctors or surgeons. But at least if they come in contact with a burn condition they'll know what they're dealing with, and what to do to seek proper care from specialists."

He was still on the board of directors for Mylan Laboratories, which had a corporate office at the Century Building in downtown Pittsburgh.

Dr. Gaisford was 77, and marking his 50th year as a physician, when I visited him the previous time in the summer of 1992. It was the second of my three visits. When I mentioned how long he had been at it — he performed plastic surgery on my lip at Children's Hospital

212

Matthew B. Ridgway, a retired 4-star general, was a long-time neighbor of Dr. John Gaisford in Fox Chapel. Dr. Gaisford has been a pioneer in plastic surgery and burn treatment at West Penn Hospital in Bloomfield.

when I was nine years old back in 1951 — he smiled and said, "I'm still working. Ain't that awful."

He still comes to West Penn Hospital nearly every day, and he says he plays golf, even if it's just striking at balls in the backyard of his home in Fox Chapel, every day as well. He has netting in his backyard to keep the balls he strikes from going into the neighboring yards.

On the June day on which I visited him in 1992, he planned to play in a golf tournament that afternoon at the Longue Vue Country Club in Verona. It was the West Penn Seniors, which he had won a few years earlier.

He won the Fox Chapel Golf Club championship six or seven years earlier, he recalled, and was beaten in the finals in 1991. "By a young patient of mine, of all things," he said, shaking his head at the irony. "His name was Mike Foster, and he was the captain of the Harvard golf team. He's a superior young boy.

"I usually shoot less than my age," he said. "But if you get this old that's not that difficult."

I told Dr. Gaisford that a friend of mine, who was in his 80s, boasted to me about shooting under his age, and telling me, "I'd like to see Tiger Woods do that."

Dr. Gaisford also spoke about his friendship with the late Bob Prince, the "Voice of the Pirates" from 1948 to 1975, whom he got to know because of their mutual interest in golf.

"I had a lot of heart-to-heart talks with him about caddies," said Dr. Gaisford. "Bob was so involved in promoting the Ham-Am Golf Tournament to raise scholarship money for West Penn caddies. He was so great to promote things for these boys, these caddies, and he was so successful at it."

At his best, Dr. Gaisford was nearly a scratch golfer, playing to a 1 handicap back in 1932. In the early '90s, he was, even more amazingly, playing to a 4 handicap. When we spoke over the telephone in the summer of 1999, he said he was now playing to a 5 handicap. He came from Chicora, Pennsylvania, 10 miles north of Butler, up near East Brady, about 50 some miles northeast of Pittsburgh along the Allegheny River — where he was born June 11, 1915 — and he came by his work ethic honestly.

"There were only 11 in my high school class in Chicora," recalled Dr. Gaisford. "We had to be versatile, and fill a lot of roles.

"A golf course was built one and a quarter miles from where I was born. It was called the Riverview Golf Club. I caddied there the day it opened in 1928. I was 12, and I went there to make some money. You were paid 40 cents for nine holes, and 75 cents for 18 holes, carrying a bag. Then I got a job watering greens, and became the caddy master when I was 14. I'd never been out of the town. My dad had a little store, and we had all we needed right there.

"I was playing up in my home area one day and I was told a doctor wanted to see me. His name was Dr. McCall. 'I'm the headmaster at Kiski Prep,' he told me. 'If you'll come to Kiski Prep and play golf for us, it won't cost you any money. If you don't make the team, you'll have to go back home.' My dad wouldn't let me quit high school at the time. Eventually, I went to Kiski for two years starting in 1934. Obviously, I made the golf team.

"I'm going up to my old home area Friday to play at Dick Fuhrer's golf club, the St. Jude Country Club," offered Dr. Gaisford. "I worked there, at age 15, caddying for Dick's father. I played a lot with Dick and his brother, Frank Fuhrer. Frank's put together some great golf tournaments through the years and raised a lot of money for Family House. Now there's a competitive guy."

Dr. Gaisford has been a tough competitor himself, whether he was playing golf or performing surgery. When we first met at West Penn back in 1989, he had been in an auto accident the week before. He had been rear-ended by a cab in Chicago, and suffered fractured vertebrae.

Yet, following our interview back then, he was scheduled to perform head surgery on a cancer patient.

"It's always an emergency situation."

I have other vivid and warm impressions of Dr. Gaisford from that earlier visit to a different office at West Penn, a fourth-floor cubicle crammed to the ceiling with books and medical journals, and a small, cluttered desk. "It's out of the way, and I can get a lot done there," he said, when I mentioned it to him this time. "I still do my serious work there. I still have that; it's an excellent place to work and read and such."

I had come to see him on that first visit with my daughter, Sarah O'Brien, then a freshman at Upper St. Clair High School. In doing library research for a paper for her science class, she had noted in *Newsweek* that research for a living skin project was being done at West Penn Hospital.

I always think it's best with such projects or assignments to demonstrate some creative spark, and interview the individual on your own rather than relying solely on stories in publications or, today, from information found on the Internet.

I had heard an administrator from West Penn speaking to a church group a month earlier, and he had urged us to contact him if we ever wanted to tour West Penn. I suggested to Sarah that she would get a much more insightful view of this living skin project if we were to go to the hospital, and talk to someone involved in it.

That's how we got to see Dr. Gaisford. I thought the name sounded familiar. I checked with my mother and, yes, he was the doctor who had operated on me at Children's Hospital way back when. The story served as an ice-breaker.

Dr. Gaisford made us instantly comfortable, a real trick with a teenager who was nervous about interviewing a scholarly-looking physician in a well-starched white lab coat in a formidable, strange setting.

He understood, from the start, and Dr. Gaisford guided Sarah about the burn/trauma unit at West Penn, steering her past babies and young children who were being cared for after suffering burns of one nature or another. Nurses and staff members smiled as Dr. Gaisford passed.

He kept a comforting hand on Sarah's shoulders, and spoke softly to her, explaining what it was we were seeing, and properly preparing her so she would not be shocked by what she saw next. He also showed her some expensive new equipment that had just been purchased to treat burn patients. It was a tough tour, but Dr. Gaisford was sensitive to that, and he took the time to do it right and with compassion. You just knew his bedside manner was a model for others on the staff.

He showed her several slides, out of his collection of thousands of children and adults with various kinds of burns. They were not easy on the eye, and they could cause queasiness in the stomach, but he was assuring in his commentary. He didn't want it to be a horror show-and-tell.

"It's just the worst kind of injury you can suffer," he said more than once. "It's always an emergency situation."

My daughter received an "A" for that paper, getting extra credit for going beyond the library to personally research her subject. She wrote about that experience in one of the essays she wrote with her college applications in 1992.

The next time I visited him, three years later, I told Dr. Gaisford that Sarah was going to the University of Virginia, and Dr. Gaisford found it satisfying to learn of her academic performance. "Maybe we got her off to a good start," said Dr. Gaisford, always the teacher.

When I visited him the last time, again three years after the previous visit, I told him Sarah was a third-year student at the University of Pittsburgh School of Medicine, and that she was interested in pediatrics. He smiled. "I'm delighted to hear that," he said.

Dr. Gaisford had given up surgery in 1990, and had cut down his surgical activity the year before that when he turned 75. "The other fellows are doing the hard work here now," he said. "My work is restricted to research projects. I'm too old for that foolishness."

He was then in his seventh year as a member of the board of scientific advisors for Organogenesis, Inc., a medical research and development firm headquartered in Cambridge, Massachusetts.

Organogenesis was a world leader in the biomedical field of tissue engineering, the creation of living tissue and organ equivalents and collagen matrix structures capable of being remodeled into functional tissue by the body's own cells, according to the company's annual report.

"We're able to grow living skin," said Dr. Gaisford, good at breaking through the language barrier so a layman can understand and appreciate his project. "We're able to take man-made skin, like the cuttings in circumcisions, and grow more skin, at various thicknesses and so forth. We believe they can be used to replace skin lost to burns, for instance, or surgical procedures and skin wounds."

It was hoped that tissue engineering products could be used as supplements or replacements for diseased or damaged human organs.

He disclosed during our last visit, however, that the "living skin" experiments didn't pan out satisfactorily.

"In the end, it just didn't work," said Dr. Gaisford. "It was an interesting project, but it didn't do what we thought it might do. It had some applications, but not the way we thought it could."

Dr. Gaisford was sitting at one of several desks in a large, handsomely appointed office area on the third floor (Room 340) at West Penn Hospital. "I share this with Dr.(Harvey) Slater and Dr. (I. William) Goldfarb," said Dr. Gaisford. "They're doing all the hard work in the burn center. And it is hard work."

Just then, as if on cue, Dr. Goldfarb came through the door. No sooner did he see Dr. Gaisford than he grabbed for an imaginary driver from a golf bag, and he began swinging his arms, and emulating his efforts off the tee that weekend.

"I didn't miss one drive, I didn't slice the ball once," Dr. Goldfarb cried out in ecstasy. "I couldn't get any help from a pro for my $500," he said to me before we were even properly introduced. "I had a horrible drive; I was constantly slicing the ball. But the golf doctor here (he pointed to Dr. Gaisford) fixed me up with a band-aid for my game. I did what he told me to do, and I hit my drives straight, and chipped well."

Dr. Gaisford, in the way of an introduction, told me, "Dr. Goldfarb is quite a young man. He was one of my residents; now he's my boss."

Dr. Goldfarb regained the spotlight, going on about his golf game. Dr. Goldfarb sounded like Tom Kite explaining his U.S. Open triumph that weekend. "I watched that on TV; I wouldn't miss it," said Dr. Gaisford. "I have played that course at Pebble Beach; it's just great. I know that course well. It's a very different golf course. It's great to play. Golf is a real passion of mine.

"I knew Arnold Palmer's father. He was Mr. Palmer to me. Tom Watson is the one I looked up to the most."

Strangely enough, as we were talking about golf, Dr. Gaisford got a telephone call. It was a friend calling him from the Fox Chapel Golf Club. He was calling to tell Dr. Gaisford that Sam Depe III, the club pro at the South Hills Country Club who had played in a tournament at Fox Chapel, was hospitalized in serious condition as the result of an auto accident on Route 28, as he was traveling home from the event. His legs were crushed when he lost control of his car and struck several obstacles on the side of the road.

Dr. Gaisford grimaced as he related the telephone conversation to me. "He's lost one leg, and he's probably going to lose the other," he said. "That's a real shame."

"He's the greatest man I ever knew."

He also had quite a neighbor next door. That's General Matthew B. Ridgway, a retired four-star general and one of the nation's most decorated military figures. They swapped war stories, and they had traveled together to distant places like South Africa and East Africa.

General Ridgway had died, at age 98, in July of 1993. "He was the most brilliant man I ever met," said Dr. Gaisford. "He was doing fine right up until his last year.

"He was the overall commander of the allied forces in World War II. He replaced General MacArthur when President Truman took MacArthur out of the Korean War.

"Back in 1992, he was awarded one of the nation's top honors for his service to our country. Senator Sam Nunn and Gen. Colin Powell both came to his house, and made the presentation."

Dr. Gaisford helped in putting together a documentary film called "Ridgway — The Unsung Hero." Ridgway was included in a series that also profiled three other distinguished American generals, namely John J. Pershing, George C. Marshall and Colin L. Powell, which is keeping pretty fast company.

Ridgway had a remarkable military career, and Gaisford knows the highlights by heart. He parachuted into Normandy on D-Day. On April 11, 1951, Ridgway was appointed Allied Commander in Chief of the UN Command in Japan, succeeding General Douglas MacArthur. In May, 1952, he was named Allied Supreme Commander in Europe (SACEUR) succeeding Dwight D. Eisenhower. Thus, in 13 months, he had replaced two of the greatest generals — MacArthur and Eisenhower.

On August 15, 1953 he was appointed Chief of Staff of the U.S. Army. He retired September 15, 1955 and lived in Pittsburgh until his death. There is a center in his name at the University of Pittsburgh.

"He was absolutely magnificent," said Dr. Gaisford. "He's the greatest man I ever knew and probably my greatest friend. He was my mentor. I was his next-door neighbor for 27 years. He and his wife, my wife and I were together countless times. We traveled together; he always made our travels more interesting.

"He'd never bring up any story about the war, but he'd answer any question in a very, very interesting, honest, fashion. He'd never criticize an individual. He might not approve of another commander's decision, but he'd never get into personalities. One of the military leaders he respected the most was Germany's General Rommell. He thought he was the greatest general he ever fought against.

"General Marshall was his idol. General Marshall was from Uniontown. The only picture of an Army person that General Ridgway had in his home was of General Marshall and his son. I asked him what he thought of General Patton. He said, 'He was the best damn general as long as he kept his mouth shut.' He also liked General Omar Bradley.

"I asked him about General MacArthur. He'd never criticize him. General Ridgway, when he was a young officer, taught history at West Point. One day he was called by the commandant who told him, 'Tomorrow you'll be in charge of the French Department. And you're going to be an assistant football coach.' He said he didn't even know French at the time, or much about football for that matter. Do you know who the commandant was? It was MacArthur.

"I asked General Ridgway, 'What did you do?' He said, 'I found the smartest young student I could find to help me. He spent the weekend with me teaching me French.'

"I never met anyone who influenced the way I thought or the way I dealt with people as much as General Ridgway. I tried to copy the way he handled people in certain situations. He was so gracious. He never started a conversation.

"He held everyone's attention when he answered a question. It was always related to the military. I'd put him in a genius category. He knew how to treat people. He didn't do it for any other reason than he was a gentleman.

"He pulled no punches when it came down to specific decisions. Shortly before he died, he was sent a couple of letters by a nine-year-old boy and a 12-year-old boy. They were telling him who they were and what they were doing. He sat down and wrote notes to them. I have copies of those letters. I thought it was great of him to do that. Could he have been a doctor? No, he was an army general all the way. You had to be fascinated by being around him. He was always interested, and it was a sincere interest.

"That's what was so good about him. He was always interested in the other guy. In 1971, his son, a wonderful young boy, was killed just after he had graduated from Rutgers. He was at a boys' camp in Canada. They were carrying a canoe over their heads when a freight train hit them and killed him. He was the only one killed. He was 25 at the time. General Ridgway had been married three times, but this was the only child he'd had, to his third wife. He was devastated by his son's death. We saw them every night for six straight months, never missed a night."

"We were hunting alligators."

Dr. Gaisford was a captain in the U.S. Army and served with the 92nd Field Hospital at Luzon on the Phillipine Islands, where he was assistant chief of surgery, chief of surgery and chief of anesthesia. He also was stationed at the 118th Station Hospital at Fukuoka, Japan, where he was the assistant chief of surgery. He was awarded the bronze star.

"I had been trained in pediatric surgery at Children's Hospital in Pittsburgh, and I was in a M.A.S.H. (Mobile Army Surgical Hospital) unit before I was trained in adult surgery. But if you can operate on children, where everything is in miniature, you can go to adult surgery. But you can't go the opposite route. I learned a lot in the Pacific. And I learned that I needed to learn a lot more.

"As a side note, the man who started the M.A.S.H. show on TV about Korea, was Dr. Richard Hornburger. He died just a few months ago. I played golf with him several years ago in Maine. The golf pro at his club is a personal friend of mine."

I asked Dr. Gaisford if he had gone to see the movie, "Saving Private Ryan," which would win the Academy Award. It was a spellbinding but brutal retelling of a story within the story of D-Day by Steven Spielberg. "My two granddaughters recommended the movie," he said. "Two weeks ago, I took my wife to see it. I lasted two minutes. I absolutely could not handle it. My granddaughters really liked it. They went back and saw it again."

He showed me some photos that showed him with natives, called Negritoes, when he was stationed in Luzon, near the South China Sea, 400 miles north of Manila. "They were spotters for us," he explained. They were wielding bow and arrows in the photo. "We were hunting alligators with them that day. I had a hunting rifle, and I was carrying a couple of hand grenades. That was sometime in 1945. It was the summer they dropped the bomb.

"They'd throw this dog out in the swamp, and alligators would go for it. They never got the dog. I couldn't stop an alligator with a high-powered M-1, but those guys could kill it with their bow and arrows. There were guys in our outfit who weren't strong enough to pull that bow."

"You were one of my guinea pigs then."

I asked Dr. Gaisford how he came to Pittsburgh in the first place.

"I came to Pittsburgh strictly by accident," he said. "When I graduated from the Georgetown University Medical School in 1942, I had signed a contract to intern in Hawaii. On Pearl Harbor Day, the hospital I was to work in there was hit by aerial bombs. Suddenly, I had no job.

"So I came to Pittsburgh, and shopped around until Presbyterian took me in. Eventually, I performed surgery in just about every hospital in town.

"I was the first resident in plastic surgery at the University of Pittsburgh in 1948, at the beginning of the training program there."

When I mentioned that it was only a few years later, in 1951, that he performed plastic surgery to remove a scar from my lip that resulted from an auto accident six years earlier, he smiled and said, "You were one of my guinea pigs then." I wasn't sure how to take that.

When he saw a certain look on my face, Dr. Gaisford was quick to add, assuredly, "No, I had a lot of training before that."

In February of 1999, I was talking to Dr. Ross Musgrave, another doctor who still comes to the office most days, looking after medical alumni from an office at the School of Medicine of the University of Pittsburgh in Scaife Hall. He was a contemporary of Dr. Gaisford.

"Ah, the golfer," said Dr. Musgrave, a marvelous high-spirited individual who has a habit of summing up people and stories so succinctly. "He was the first resident in plastic surgery here, and I was the second. He had an interesting military experience in the South Seas. He's quite a guy."

During that same time frame, my daughter, Sarah, was doing a rotation with a plastic surgeon at UPMC as part of her School of Medicine training. She asked the doctor if he knew Dr. Gaisford. "Asking a plastic surgeon if he knows Dr. Gaisford is like asking an Italian if they know the pope," he replied.

Dr. Gaisford said his career had been a rewarding one, and he had no plans to retire completely. "The most significant thing is that people accept major problems they're faced with in a most courageous fashion," he said.

"I've dealt with a lot of head and neck cancer surgery, and burns, and the many problems that children have. Parents seem to be able to accept and deal with these difficulties. There's an acceptance. Particularly in areas that affect speaking, eating, talking. Burn patients never complain.

"The greatest thing is the untiring help we get from nurses. None of the work in surgery can be completed without the help of your colleagues, especially the anesthetists, and the hospital laboratory personnel.

"It would be impossible to carry on adequate surgery without the backing of people who run the hospital itself, the administrators and board, or any of the extensive research projects I've been involved with if we didn't have the financial support of a rather large cross-section of corporations in the city of Pittsburgh. They have been magnanimous in their help to me, as well as some individuals who have helped out of the goodness of their heart without any thought of gain on their part.

"We have been helped in many ways. One of the continuing interests I've had with surgical work here at West Penn has been the development of young doctors, and with the trainees we've been involved with. Many young men and women have gone through training here in general surgery, plastic surgery and burn/trauma work.

"We learn from these young people as well. They bring their own ideas.

"I started out officially at West Penn in 1950, but I worked here long before that as a resident. I was a resident in pediatric surgery. Dr. George Foster, the chief of surgery at Children's Hospital and U.S. Steel, was also the chief of surgery at West Penn.

"I recall going to West Penn in the early '40s to work with Dr. Foster on babies, but I was not actually on the staff. I joined the staff here in 1950. I was made chairman of the department of surgery in 1970, and that same year we founded the burn unit here."

"It's extremely difficult work."

I asked Dr. Gaisford to discuss the burn/trauma unit, which has been a special baby of his.

"Most burn centers have a continuing problem," he said. "Nurses working in burn centers usually elect not to stay for a long period of time. It's extremely difficult work. Many children are admitted to burn centers and, unfortunately, the mortality rate among seriously injured individuals is high. It becomes very difficult to work in burn centers.

"We here have been most fortunate. The turnover rate here seems to be much lower than it is at other similar facilities we know about."

I asked him about the smell of the burn/trauma unit. "It isn't a bad odor these days," he said. "You don't smell the burnt flesh anymore, or you shouldn't anyhow. It's just an odor of more medicine than anything else. The odor often associated with burns in the past isn't there today. There should not be any odor of burned tissue or open tissue.

"These young people have to work a shift that is generally eight hours. The doctors have the same problem. But the doctors can come in and attend to the problems and leave. The nurses can't leave.

"Most doctors don't become involved in burns, for which I can't blame them. It's difficult work, to begin with. It's all emergency work, seven days a week. And the income derived from the care of burn cases is not commensurate with that of most other types of surgery. It was one of the must unacceptable types of work there was in surgical practice.

"Things are done differently today than they used to be. Patients are not kept in bed waiting to have dead skin removed and skin grafted. Now they're operated on within 24 hours. We're constantly changing dressings. That prevents any odor. One can walk through the burn unit now and there's absolutely no odor.

"Back in the '40s, in the pioneer days, the odors were extremely bad. The accepted approach was not to change dressings for five, six or even seven days. That made it worse.

"There were not the types of drugs that could be used locally in burns that could keep the odor down.

"One might wonder why there are not more burn centers. Most hospitals don't want to be involved with burn centers. The financial responsibility is very high. The work is cyclical. Those beds are not going to be filled every day like they are on the medical or surgical floor.

"This is one of the largest units in the country, with 18 beds, but we sometimes have only five patients to look after. This institution has been magnanimous in its support of this unit. We've never had a problem getting equipment, or coverage by nursing personnel and housekeeping. We've had the complete backing of the administration and the board since we opened it in 1970. That's the reason I'm still working.

"There is one at Mercy Hospital and it preceded us. They do a great job over there, too."

One of the keys to whatever success he has enjoyed, says Dr. Gaisford, was his wife Frannie. "She's been completely supportive," he said. "She recognizes that I would never be able to stay home and do nothing.

"She has been very supportive of all my surgical problems and work. She recognizes that burn work has probably been most inter-esting for me and most satisfying, yet burns bother her more than anything in the world.

"That's the only type of problems I've managed that she does not want to be involved with. I have put together a lot of my papers and lectures at home. Having thousands of two by two Kodachrome slides of burn patients...it's one problem that my wife doesn't particularly like to look at."

There has been quite an evolution in the career of Dr. Gaisford. He has gone from pediatric surgery in Pittsburgh, to adult surgery on the battlefields of the South Pacific, to plastic surgery and then head and neck cancer and burn/trauma work at West Penn. Now he is in research.

"This has been an unbelievable experience," he said. "I have obvi-ously been a practicing doctor where decisions were made quickly, and action was taken quickly. That's the heart of being a surgeon. To be immersed in research now is a real change of pace. It calls for great patience."

"Everybody can be great, because everybody can serve."
— Dr. Martin Luther King, Jr.

"Harry Greb died in my uncle's office."

Dr. Gaisford is full of good stories. Somehow Harry Greb, who grew up in Garfield, a neighboring community cf Bloomfield, came up in the conversation. He may have been the greatest boxer ever to come out of Pittsburgh.

"I had a copy of his death certificate," said Dr. Gaisford. "Harry Greb died in my uncle's office. That was in 1926. My uncle's name was Dr. Charles McGivern. My mother was a McGivern. He was a native of Kittanning, but his offices were in Atlantic City. My uncle had taken out one of Greb's eyes and put in an artificial eye.

"He died during surgery. I remember as a kid that I went up to Conneaut Lake and saw Greb box. My mother had a New York newspaper that had the story about Greb dying. The headline read: GREB KILLED BY SURGEON. I wish I still had that paper (so did I). It's long gone. That surgeon was my uncle. Greb had some defect between his eyebrows. My uncle was to remove it. He administered novocaine and Greb had a reaction to it. He died in the chair. It was at 805 Pacific Avenue. I worked in that office with my uncle and remember it well. I'd see patients with him, between 1934 and 1938. That story was big stuff in New York because Greb had been such a great fighter. He beat Gene Tunney there once. Greb's mother died in this hospital, at age 96. That's just a little bit of family history."

There aren't many doctors who can tell you stories like that.

From Dr. Gaisford collection.

Franny and Dr. John Gaisford, at left, dine with Penny and Gen. Matthew B. Ridgway to celebrate his recognition as a distinguished military leader.

Ross Miller
A real soldier

"He doesn't like to talk about it."
— Belle Ross

Memorial Day parade is meant to remind us of wars that were fought to preserve this country, and men and women who served in our armed forces or support efforts. Memorial Day parades always remind me of other Memorial Day parades.

I remember as a child of seven or eight, standing on the sidewalk in downtown Pittsburgh with my brother, Dan, and our dad, watching the soldiers marching by, marveling at tanks and other heavy war equipment.

A Memorial Day parade that has stayed with me, in step all the way, is one I witnessed in 1982 or 1983 in Bedford, Pennsylvania. It was a parade where I learned a lot about my wife's Uncle Ross, her great uncle, really.

I was reminded of Uncle Ross, or Ross Miller Sr., when I attended a sports smoker in Jeannette in the winter of 1998. I met a man from McKeesport named John Kulik who hunted deer for 25 years with Ross's son in Bedford. Kulik attended the funerals of Ross and his wife, Belle.

They are both missed by anyone who ever met them. They were special in their simple, humble and grateful approach to life. My wife has a lot of nice relatives, and they were among the perks that came with the marriage.

Bedford was a great getaway place for us in the early years of our marriage. My wife's brother and sister-in-law, Harvey and Diane Churchman, and their two children, Jason and Emily, lived in Bedford back then, and it was a quiet, laid-back retreat.

Bedford is about a two-hour drive from Pittsburgh, east on the Pennsylvania Turnpike, and it's a trip into another age, when people passed on the sidewalk and smiled and said hello to strangers.

I miss going to Bedford and I miss its Memorial Day parade. As I recall, there were only two marching bands, one from the high school and one from the middle school, a few Cub Scouts and Boy Scouts, and about 20 military service veterans.

The parade passed quickly, but a local citizen cautioned us not to leave. "You've never been to a small town parade, I guess," the woman said. "They always come back."

Not once, but twice. Why not? It was a chance to see friends and neighbors once more, and the kids looked great in their band uniforms and majorette costumes. It was like a scene from "The Music Man."

Young WWI soldier Ross Miller
One of the boys from Bedford

"History teaches us to hope."
— Robert E. Lee,
American general

What really caught me off-guard — more so than the crackling fire from the bolt-action rifles — was to see my wife's great uncle, Ross Miller, riding in a car with some military brass in the middle of the parade. He was the lone surviving World War I veteran in the community. Only the day before, he and his wife, Belle, stopped by to say hello at the home of my wife's brother and sister-in-law, where we were staying.

Ross Miller was 81 at the time and I had known him about 13 years, and seen him at annual reunion picnics, but never heard him mention his military days. He never told one war story. I never left the U.S.A., going as far as Alaska, and I tell war stories.

"He went to France and was in battles over there, but he doesn't like to talk about it," said his wife as he passed in the parade. "He was 17 when he went over. There's a monument over in our town square, and he knew most of the fellows whose names are on it. He saw some of them get killed. His regiment was made up of all boys from Bedford County."

Later, I learned that Ross Miller had been gassed in one of the battles, and that he still was challenged by after-effects of the experience. There were reminders in the town square and nearby cemetery of veterans from the Civil War, Spanish-American War and even the Revolutionary War. There's a lot of history in Bedford. Ross Miller was a real veteran of a foreign war. Yet he never told any war stories.

Veteran Ross Miller prepares to ride in Memorial Day parade in native Bedford in May, 1977. Ross and wife Belle were a good couple.

227

Johnny Majors
On his Army days

"My parents didn't teach me to quit."

Johnny Majors remained a wonderful storyteller. He was in the midst of moving his office in the Department of Athletics at the University of Pittsburgh. He was moving from an office that adjoined the office of Steve Pederson, beginning his third year as the director of athletics, to a smaller office on the level below at Pitt Stadium. He was telling stories on the run.

From his office window, he could see Salk Hall directly across Sutherland Drive. Dr. Salk and Dr. Sutherland were reminders of past greatness on the campus. So was Majors. To his left, he could also see Scaife Hall, the home base of the University's nationally-respected School of Medicine.

All of the Majors memorabilia, framed awards and photographs paying tribute to a mostly marvelous college coaching career, were piled around the floor of his new quarters. He had truly been one of the great players and coaches in the college game. There was nowhere to stand or sit — it was a small office — so we sat down at someone else's desk in a central area nearby.

At my request, Majors had brought some photos from his early childhood, and his high school and college days as a storied player back home in Tennessee, and as he identified who was in the different photos, he started telling stories. Like most good storytellers, Majors couldn't restrain himself.

He had once been hailed as one of the elite college football coaches in the land, at Iowa State University for starters, and then even more so at the University of Pittsburgh and at his alma mater, the University of Tennessee. He and Tony Dorsett had quite a four-year run, culminating in a national championship for Pitt in 1976. Majors was Coach of the Year twice, in 1973 and 1976, during his initial Pitt tour. There was great excitement in Pittsburgh in those years, what with Pitt, the Pirates and Steelers all doing so well.

Things declined for him toward the end of his stay at Tennessee and it just didn't work out when he came back to Pitt in 1993. In his second four-year run at Pitt, the Panthers never posted more than four wins in a season. He had stayed on as a special assistant to Pederson. His duties were never really defined. He appeared at Pitt functions, that was about it. Majors had hired Pederson to work on his staff at Tennessee, and had recommended him as a successor to Oval Jaynes as the athletic director at Pitt, so he owed Majors a favor.

In truth, Majors was pushed out of his coaching post in both places, and the previous five years had been a period of frustration and feeling betrayed by friends and coaching associates. He felt

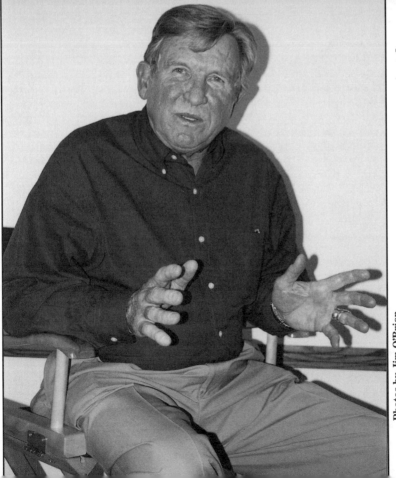

John
Majors

Photos by Jim O'Brien

particularly bitter toward Tennessee. It had to be difficult to swallow for such a proud man. He may have deserved better, but in the end he had not been effective or able to produce a winner. He'd become his own worst enemy. The magic was gone. Early on, it looked as if he might pull it off once more, but it wasn't meant to be. His staff wasn't up to his previous staff. Not many were. His successor, Walt Harris, had gone 6-6 and 2-9 in his two seasons at Pitt. School was still out on Harris. Fortunately, Majors had not lost his sense of humor. He liked to tell stories about his grandson, Brandon, 12 years old, his daughter's son, whom he and his wife, Mary Lynn, were raising in their home on the Oakland campus. Brandon was playing Pop Warner football and offered his grandpap his honest thoughts about the game from time to time, much to his grandpap's amusement.

Johnny Majors' face was that of a man who had been plowing farm fields in Tennessee for much of his 63 years, lots of wrinkles, especially around his eyes, as if he were staring into the rising sun. It was difficult to find his blue eyes as he had a perpetual squint. The more he smiled the narrower his eyes became. He looked so much like the pictures of his father that were spread out on the table before us. Seeing photos of his father and his family put him in a good mood, and reminded him of better times. He was such fun. His parents were both deceased; his mother — his most faithful fan — had died two years earlier. The photos reminded him of better days. Once upon a time, coaches like Majors used to spin stories to sportswriters all the time, passing time at a hotel on the road, or in the locker room after practice, or at a bar or restaurant near the stadium.

It was a different era. Coaches were comfortable in the company of sportswriters back then. There was a trust, a mutual understanding of what could be printed in the next day's newspaper and what was confidential, or off the record. It seldom had to be spelled out. There was simply a gentleman's agreement or understanding. Sportswriters weren't looking for dirt under the carpet in the coach's office. The sports page was a relief from the rest of the newspaper.

Majors must have provided a lot of those southern gentlemen sports writers with delightful easy-to-write columns in his heyday. Nowadays most of the exchanges between coaches and the sports media took place at sterile press conferences, with tape recorders, and there were few easy and casual chats. To think that Grantland Rice once hung out routinely with the likes of Babe Ruth, Ty Cobb and Bobby Jones.

Now most interviews with coaches and players had to be arranged through public relations officials, and they were often limited to a few hurried minutes, enough for a quote or two, a radio or TV soundbite. All very formal. Not real insightful or informative.

Majors was a throwback to a different era. There were rumblings beginning that Pitt Stadium might be abandoned by the Pitt football team in favor of a new stadium on the North Side that was being built for the Steelers. Majors and Pitt Stadium, it seemed, had outlived their usefulness. They had become relics, as one sportswriter put it. It

Johnny and his wife, Mary Lynn, pose with their children, Mary Elizabeth and John, back in the '70s in his first go-round as the Pitt head football coach.

Johnny Major's parents, Elizabeth and Shirley, were in the stands at University of Tennessee in 1956 to root for their son's team.

Gandpap can't slip tackle by grandson Brandon Harrill when Major's Tennessee team took on Virginia in 1991 Sugar Bowl.

tore your heart out to consider that. Two months later, Chancellor Mark Nordenberg started talking about tearing down Pitt Stadium. That hurt even more. In a letter to the University community, Nordenberg said "the stadium was no longer an asset to the football program."

It was a Tuesday, January 10, 1999. Majors was talking about his family, a family they still talk about back home in Tennessee. They left their mark in football on every level throughout the state. They were a remarkable clan.

It began in Lynchburg, most famous as the community where they distill Jack Daniels whiskey. That's "smooth sippin' Tennessee whiskey." According to the famous distiller's 1999 magazine ads, the population of Lynchburg was 361.

"I used to go get coal for my grandmother every day," said Majors, off on another story. "I'd bring it to her home in a scuttle (a metal pail used for carrying coal). On Saturday, I'd get her two gallons of oil. She'd use it for her lights, lamps and heating. That was my Grandma Bobo; she was my mother's mother. Her home was one block from the market square. She'd give me 50 cents a week, which was a lot of money for a kid in those days. She'd pay me on Saturday.

"I'd go to a store nearby and I'd get an R.C. or double Coke, the biggest possible soft drinks. I'd get one of my favorite candy bars or a moon pie, maybe some Planter's peanuts. I'd sneak back to my grandmother's house so none of my brothers or my sister would see me. I didn't want to have to share my cache."

I was not familiar with moonpies. Majors explained that they were sort of a chocolate cake sandwich with white cream as filling. The white stuff was the moon part of the so-called pie.

"I'd lay out all my stuff in this one little room," said Majors, "and I'd turn on her radio, and I'd listen to the broadcast of the Army football game every Saturday in the fall. I loved Glenn Davis and Doc Blanchard. They were my two biggest heroes. Davis was No. 41. Blanchard was No. 35."

Majors remembered their numbers and accomplishments like a kid who was still collecting bubble gum cards. For the record, Davis and Blanchard were All-American running backs at Army from 1944 to 1946. Army was the national champion in 1944 and 1945, interrupting a run of national titles for Notre Dame. The Cadets were coached by Earl "Red" Blaik.

"When the game was over," continued Majors, "I'd get my brothers and we'd go out and play football in the yard.

"I was the oldest kid in our family. I had four younger brothers and a sister. My dad was a football coach, so we grew up loving to play games.

"I was always arranging the games. I was in charge. It was not easy to get six or eight kids our age to play a football game. Half the players in the games were me and my brothers. I was always Army, which had a great football team at the time. My brothers were always

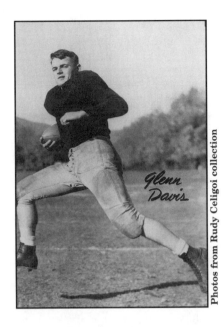

As a young man growing up in Pittsburgh, Steelers coach Bill Cowher admired Johnny Majors, the way Majors once looked up to Army's All-America heroes Felix "Doc" Blanchard and Glenn Davis in their heyday.

Notre Dame or Columbia, or somebody like that. I'd be Glenn Davis or Doc Blanchard. We used to play war games, too. This was during World War II, you have to remember. That's why Army had such a good football team. And there was lots of military training going on in southern states like Tennessee. So we were familiar with both. I was always the United States when we played war games. My brothers balked about this from time to time. They said they were tired of being Notre Dame and Columbia. My brothers would say they were tired of being Germany. Or Japan. And they said they wouldn't play unless they got to be Army or the United States. I would give up my title now and then just to have a game."

Majors would then laugh at his own story. He knew it was a good one.

He said he had many sports heroes in his youth, in addition to Davis and Blanchard. This was in the late '40s, and he was a fan of the Boston Red Sox and Ted Williams. He wasn't a New York Yankees fan, but he liked Joe DiMaggio. And he was a fan of Stan Musial of the St. Louis Cardinals.

Majors can rattle off sports names and dates and games with ease. "In basketball, I was a big fan of the University of Kentucky basketball team," said Majors. "Adolph Rupp had great teams at the time. They had Alex Groza, Ralph Beard and 'Wah Wah' Jones and Cliff Barker. Kenny Rollins came next."

Those were the great Kentucky clubs of the 1947-48 and 1948-49 campaigns, when the Wildcats claimed their fifth and sixth straight Southeastern Conference championships, and back-to-back NCAA titles. Majors was in grade school at the time. Sports are never bigger or better than they are for a 13-year-old or 14-year-old fan.

"I saw soldiers and tanks passing through our town, and nearby towns," said Majors. "That's how I got interested in Army in the first place. Fort Campbell, Kentucky, where the 101st Airborne Division trained, was two hours away from our home. I saw parachute drops.

"I used to tag along with dad for duck hunting in western Tennessee. He was an avid bird hunter. We always had good dogs. When we were out in the fields, I saw hundreds of bombers on training missions. B17s and B24s. They were in training formations overhead. I saw simulated aerial dogfights, different kinds of maneuvers. It was all very exciting for a young kid.

"There are certain incidents I remember. I saw a guy with a machine gun in our town's market square. I was eight or nine at the time, and I talked to the soldier with the machine gun. I told him about our family. He said, 'Do you think you could get your grandmother to make me some breakfast?' I ran to my grandmother's and she made him some eggs, with white gravy, some bacon and sausage and bisquits. He gave me 35 cents for that breakfast.

"There were troopers everywhere. My grandma had spring water in her yard, and my brothers, three of us, were running back and forth, filling up canteens, and running a shuttle service. They'd give us a nickle or a dime — it was like a fortune to us — and we'd hustle to help the soldiers and make some money at the same time.

"We'd watch them digging foxholes, preparing them for the real thing. It made a real impression on me. I remember D-Day somewhat. We heard about what was happening in Normandy. We saw the newspaper headlines, the news reels at the movie theatre.

"I remember a traumatic day when my dad was called up for a physical exam to go into the military. It was in 1943 or 1944. He was gone for two days. Now there were five of us kids and we were all worried about our dad going off to war. He went to Fort Oglethorpe in Georgia, just across the line from Tennessee, for his exam. They turned him down because of high blood pressure. If he hadn't been rejected, I think it would have been a real hardship for our family.

"But a lot of people did suffer hardships one way or another in those days. It was difficult. Otherwise, we had a great time growing up. There were a lot of great people there. A lot of my friends are still living there. I go back twice a year, usually around Christmas, and I always go to Lynchburg and to Huntland. They treated me good at home before I became a star, before I was ever heard of at Tennessee.

"My dad was asked to start a team at Huntland, which was 22 miles from our home. He also coached boys and girls basketball, and the boys baseball team. He left Lynchburg just as I was to begin high school. I was disappointed I wouldn't be playing for him.

"I was 14 years old when I started my first game at Lynchburg in 1949. It was a small school and we played in the lowest division, Division 5. We played Manchester, a town of 8,000.

"When my dad went to Huntland, he wasn't sure it would work out. So we kept our home in Lynchburg, and he commuted back and forth each day. He managed to be there for my first game. I could always throw a spiral pass and I could kick a spiral. I was warming up for this game at Manchester, and I couldn't do anything right. I couldn't make the ball spiral no matter what I did. I was scared to death. I was in the end zone in tears. I'm panicking. My dad came to my rescue. He could get on you pretty good when it called for it, but he had a real calming effect, too. 'It'll be OK,' he told me. We lost by 58-0.

"We went 3-5 that year. We beat my dad's team, 19-13, and I scored two touchdowns. My dad was never a curser, just damn or dang, but he was hot after that game. He said afterward that would be 'the last dang time one of my boys will play against me.' We all moved to Huntland the next year.

"These were tough times for a lot of people in World War II. Nobody had much money in our town when I was growing up. There was gas rationing, shoe rationing, sugar rationing. We had limitations, but we had everything we needed. There was plenty of food, plenty of playtime. We had enough chores to let us know what that was all about without being overworked.

"We had gloves, bats and balls. We could still afford to play our games. Our Dad took us everywhere. We saw a lot of sports. We'd go 20 miles to watch a high school game."

"He didn't make much money."

Johnny Majors was a member of what may have been the most famous football family in Tennessee. His father, the late Shirley Majors, was a highly-successful high school football coach for 13 years. At Huntland High School, his teams went 70-1-1 in one stretch. In John's senior season, the team lost only one game, and it was to Lynchburg, his old school. "That hurt," recalled Johnny Majors. His dad later served as the head coach at Sewanee (University of the South), compiling a record of 93-74-5. He was selected by the Football Writers Association as the Small College Coach of the Year in 1973, the same year his son, Johnny, received the Division IA Coach of the Year honors at Pitt.

Two of Johnny's brothers, Bill and Bobby, were great stars at Tennessee. Another brother, Joe, starred at Florida State, while a fourth brother, Larry, played for his father at Sewanee. "We were all single-wing tailbacks on our high school team," said Johnny. "Joe took my place, and Bill took his place, and Larry took his place. Joe played in 41 games at Huntland and they never lost.

"In Huntland, I led the state in scoring my last three years. I scored 153 points as a sophomore, 165 as a junior, and 213 as a senior. I scored a few as a freshman at Lynchburg and I had over 500 (565 points) altogether for my high school career.

Johnny was the biggest football star in the Majors family. He was an All-American tailback playing in a single-wing system at Tennessee. He led the Volunteers to a 10-0 record in 1956, a No. 2 ranking and a trip to the Sugar Bowl. He was named UPI's Back of the Year and finished second to Notre Dame's Paul Hornung in the Heisman Trophy balloting.

Majors was twice named MVP in the SEC, and in 1975 he was named to the 25th year All-SEC team (1950-1974). He was a charter member of the Tennessee Hall of Fame.

"When my dad was a high school coach, he didn't make much money," said Majors. "On Saturday, my dad did some barbering. Us kids would go with him when he went to Tullahoma, which was 13 miles from our town. We saw lots of soliders on the way up to Tullahoma. There was a Camp Forrest in Tullahoma. I remember one day we listened to the Army-Navy game at the barber shop in Tullahoma. Those guys were bigger-than-life heroes to us. They also had a movie house in Tullahoma. We didn't have a television or even a movie house, so radio was our main connection to the outside world.

"I looked forward to going to the movies in Tullahoma. Man, I

School Days
1945-46

Johnny Majors escorts Homecoming
Queen Dot Daniel at Huntland
High School in 1951.
At age 21, Johnny joins the family,
including Bobby, 7, and (sitting on
the couch) left to right, Bill, 17;
Shirley Ann, 16; Shirley, 43,
Elizabeth Bobo, 42; Joe, 19, and
Larry, 15.

looked forward to that. It was a thrill to go up to Tullahoma. We'd see the Movietone News between the serial and the feature film. We'd see Army football highlights in the movie news, and that's when we got involved in World War II. I was six years old and in first grade. Going to the movies was a big deal.

"Lynchburg was a small town. I remember the day they put up a traffic light for the first time on our main street. I remember the first time it flashed. I was fascinated by it."

"Majors turned me into a Pitt guy."
— Joey Diven

Johnny Majors came to mind as Joey Diven was departing Montefiore Hospital at the University of Pittsburgh Medical Center in early November, 1995. As his son was driving him out of the parking garage, Diven caught sight of Pitt Stadium, where he had spent considerable time on the sidelines when he was younger and able to stand on his own two feet.

Diven was a legendary figure in Oakland. He was once chronicled in a national magazine as "America's Greatest Streetfighter." He was a sidekick to Billy Conn — "The Pittsburgh Kid" and the world's light-heavyweight boxing champion. They put fear into a lot of tough guys.

But Diven finally met an opponent he couldn't handle — diabetes. He lost his right leg to diabetes in 1991 and some toes on his left foot four years later. He had been in Montefiore Hospital after suffering a slight stroke.

He was 65 and he wasn't what he used to be. The arrogance had gone out of his talk and his walk. A softer, gentler side was emerging. He was dying. The date of his passing was January 29, 1997.

Diven often stood on the sideline with the Notre Dame football team — his favorite college football team. But then John Majors came to Pittsburgh and Majors and Danny Marino, a super quarterback out of nearby Central Catholic High School, turned Joey Diven into a Pitt football fan. "With Majors, I love Pitt," declared Diven.

"Those other guys — Sherrill, Gottfried, Hackett — they never reached me. But Majors turned me into a Pitt guy.

"When he came back to Pitt the second time, he called me in the first few days. When a guy calls a nobody like me, that shows me some class. He's a good guy.

"I hope people give him enough time. I have a lot of faith in him.

"He always reminded me of Frank Leahy, the great Notre Dame coach. You do it his way or you're gone. I think he can bring them back. He's a good man. I just hope they give him the chance."

Winter had officially arrived in Pittsburgh. The work day started and ended in darkness, especially for football coaches. And it can't be much fun when you can't win for losing.

Johnny Majors was on a lot of people's minds, especially Pitt football fans, a beleaguered lot in recent years. Majors had turned in identical 3-8 won-lost records his first two years back, but improvement was promised and expected in his third season.

Pitt looked good in its first three games of the 1995 campaign, beating Washington State and Eastern Michigan, and losing a tough one at Texas. They should have beaten Virginia Tech at home in the fourth game, but gave it away. They lost Billy West and other key players to injuries in that game. They lost more than a game that day. They lost a season. I went away from the Stadium that day with a bad feeling. I thought Virginia Tech was going to be a good team, but that Pitt had Tech's number that day. The Big East wasn't that good and there was an opportunity to sneak in and steal something big. But it was all gone, in a single afternoon.

Even so, they should've beaten Miami on Homecoming, and didn't. Then came losses at Temple and at Rutgers, by scores that were hard to swallow even for Majors' most loyal backers. It wouldn't get any better. They ended up losing their last nine games and finished with a 2-9 record.

People were starting to wonder if Majors still had the magic. There had been positive signs at the start of the season, an improved and promising lineup — but more precariously thin on talent than anyone realized then — and a good start to recruiting for the 1996 class. But Pitt's poor performance on the field had erased the significance of those signs in most people's minds.

He had a year to go on the four-year contract he signed his second go-round at Pitt. In his first, he went undefeated (12-0) in his fourth year and won a national championship in 1976. He had Tony Dorsett, the Heisman Trophy winner and perhaps the single player who had the biggest impact on any college football program ever, and he developed that program with a coaching staff that spawned a lot of very successful head coaches, and may have been as good a staff as was ever assembled.

That was then and this was now. Majors had turned 60 and some were wondering whether he still had the steam and the stamina for the challenge. Hey, Joe Paterno was 69 and still going strong at Penn State. He was 68 when he turned out the best football team in the country just a year earlier. Even Paterno had a hard time pleasing his constituency. Fans have short memories.

"Even I burned the biscuits once in a while."
— Elizabeth Bobo Majors,
John's mother

"You wondered whether you'll
ever come out of it."
— Johnny Majors

"I've done it before, and I've been through bad times before in my life, as a coach and as a man and, as far as who you are and what you're going to do, well, you make the best of it," Johnny Majors told me in late October of 1995, sitting in endzone seats just above the entrance at Gate 3.

"I've always been an optimistic person who has faith in being able to get things accomplished. I didn't think it would be easy, and I knew it would be harder than the first time I came here. Things have changed — the 85 scholarship limit, and no more than 25 scholarships a year — make it more difficult to turn things around.

"But I'm one of those people who can look back as a kid, and know that a lot more good things happened in my life than bad ones. I've been fortunate for the most part. There are other things you know that give you a good feeling about your ability to do it again."

Majors wasn't in the best of spirits — this is a very proud man — but he managed a smile now and then. He wasn't about to roll over and die.

"You go through parts of your life when you wondered whether you'll ever come out of it," the coach continued, speaking in a gravelly near-whisper. "At Iowa State, for instance. I was 3-7 the first two years that I was a head coach.

"I wondered then: Will I ever be a head coach after this? The first team in Tennessee was 4-7, then 5-5-1, then 7-5. In our fourth year I thought we had our best team and we went 5-6. But we came back and went 8-4 the next year.

"We went 9-1-2 in my ninth year, 10-2-1 in my eleventh year, and 11-1 in my thirteenth year. We won nine games in both of the next two seasons. So it takes awhile to get a program where you want it to be. I know that from experience.

"Wherever you go, you go there to get something done. We thought our fourth team at Tennessee was going to be a good one. We'd been 7-4 the previous season (not counting a bowl game loss) and we had a better team coming back. We got killed our first two games, 44-0 to Georgia, and 42-7 to Southern Cal.

"Other coaches who've been successful struggled for awhile; I don't want to get into names, but I'm not the only one to go through this sort of thing."

I asked Majors if the disastrous season would hurt the recruiting in regard to the ten players who had already given oral commitments? Would it make it more difficult for others to follow?

During his All-America days as a tailback at Tennessee, Johnny Majors met Otto Graham, the All-Pro quarterback of the NFL's Cleveland Browns.

Back in 1956, Johnny Majors, left, and Lou Michaels of Kentucky, later a star lineman and place-kicker with the Baltimore Colts and Pittsburgh Steelers, were honored by Norman Downey of the Birmingham Touchdown Club as the season's outstanding back and lineman in the SEC.

"It depends on the type of people you're recruiting," said Majors. "If you were right about them in the first place they'll stay with you. We've had some adversity here, but you can see that we still need help and that you might be able to play early at Pitt.

"I'm a dreamer, but I'm also a realist. I thought we had the makings of a team that could win six or seven games this year. We've had a lot of bad breaks and injuries."

I brought up the Virginia Tech game, which didn't exactly make his afternoon.

"One of the worst," Majors began. "It was one of the most disappointing defeats. I don't like to even think about it. We lost more than a game. We lost two linemen, our top receiver, and our top running backs. We lost half our offensive team.

"We had lost to them 63-21 and 45-7 the two previous years. We were leading 9-0 at halftime. Look how far we'd come. That's a definite turnaround even though they might not be quite as good as they were the previous two seasons.

"It was a devastating loss. I hate to use that word... I can't say I've never been discouraged. I'd be lying if I said that. I've been discouraged, but I've never been distraught or devastated. I've been concerned about whether we can build a program in Pittsburgh. I felt like that the first time around. It couldn't be much worse than it was before I got here the first time.

"We had a special staff. I brought eight coaches with me from Iowa State. I wasn't able to do anything like that this time, when I left Tennessee."

Majors was asked how he identified the best possible assistants when he was assembling a staff.

"I think I'm a good judge of people of character and a good judge of phonyism — I've been fooled a few times, but not often. I've been good at coaching coaches and teaching them how to teach football and how to recruit.

"I chose people who had been part of good programs. Like Florida State, Alabama, Arkansas and Houston. I had coaches like Larry Lacewell, Joe Aversanno, Jimmy Johnson, Pat Jones, Jackie Sherrill. It was a move up for all of them. I knew a lot of them were most confident individuals; I had to make sure they didn't get out of hand. We had a lot of excitement at some of our meetings."

Majors had to laugh at that line.

"You have to be a good salesman," the coach continued. "To recruit you have to be an excellent salesperson and sold on your own convictions and sold on the coach you work for and organization you're working with. You have enough confidence and pride and you're going to get the job done. That means knowing people, being honest with them...knowing who you can trust. That's another critical thing about building a good base.

"My father had a great knack for saying the right things and meaning what he said. That was important to me. I studied people.

"I've been taught to be a positive person; that's the environment I came from, the climate I've been raised in. That's the leadership from my father and my mother.

"I never had had anything traumatic happen to me until my brother was killed in a train accident."

His brother Bill was a young assistant at Tennessee when he and two other coaches were killed when their Volkswagen was struck by a train in 1965.

"That was the most traumatic thing that ever happened to our family in all of our lives. We had the normal loss of family and friends, but that really hit us hard.

(When John Majors was ousted at Tennessee, his mother remarked: "Now I've lost two sons to the state of Tennessee.")

"My mother and father never had unresolvable problems. I never saw them distraught. They survived some tough times. My parents didn't teach me to quit.

"It's been challenging. It's not easy to face your team and come up with answers for your staff and meet the media when things aren't going well. But you always have to show up. You can't tuck in your tail and run for cover. I can't be positive all the time, but I'm going to show up."

"I didn't know if I was going to win."

Majors disclosed some things about himself I hadn't heard before, nor did I remember reading them. I thought he was being particularly honest about what he's all about, and how he managed to mask his earliest fears and concerns. It's poignant stuff since he appeared to be such a confident, outgoing individual who could successfully rally others around him when he was winning at Tennessee and Pitt. It's a lesson for others.

"From the beginning, I never said I knew I was going to make it as a coach," he said. "I didn't know if I was going to win.

"I was shy. I never wanted to go anywhere I felt uncomfortable or that I didn't know what I was supposed to do. I didn't want to go to a party because I didn't have the right costume. I didn't want to go to first grade because I didn't know how to read. My folks told me that's why you go to school.

"My family had so much to do with my hanging in there. It was a great support system. I had a lot of attention and affection all my life, but I never felt I was spoiled."

Some suggested to me back then that Majors might just give up the ghost and walk away from it all. I mentioned this to Majors. He just wagged his head.

"That's not my history," he said. He often goes back to certain games in his high school life where he learned something about

243

himself. "My first game in high school, back in 1949, I was 14 and we played Manchester. They were a Triple A team and we were A. They beat us 58-0. I threw three interceptions. I was too young to know any better. I never thought about not coming back the next week. You never thought about quitting.

"The next week we got beat 75-6. I still didn't quit. We lost games by 33-0 and 65-7 and 39-7 — I can still remember those scores vividly. We only won one game. I went to play for my father's school the next year. I played for my dad, he was a builder, too."

His father, Shirley, was a great football coach in his own right, at several high schools and at the University of the South. He died of a heart attack in 1981.

His mother, Elizabeth, was always a big booster as well. At 81, she was rooting for her son and reminding people that her son was already in the College Football Hall of Fame. She was a frequent visitor in the Pitt Stadium press box when her son was the head coach, and she was fun to talk to. In her heyday, she was known for making great biscuits. "Even I burned the biscuits once in a while," she'd say after a losing effort by one of her son's teams. She knew John would bounce back.

"I got that from my mother; my mother's never given up in her life," said John, "Things didn't always go right when we were growing up, but I never saw her give in to despair. She never let us believe that things weren't going to turn out all right.

"I like to think I have her tenacity. I know she never minded a good fight. Even if it was something like playing a piano in a recital, she was going to do everything to beat you."

That outlook was reinforced by his coaches at Tennessee, General Robert Neyland and Bowden Wyatt. "My sophomore year was one of the worst," recalled Majors. "We were 4-6. Wyatt took over for Neyland after that. Wyatt was the College Coach of the Year in my senior year.

"I started my coaching career with Wyatt as a graduate assistant. Then I went to Mississippi State as an assistant coach. We hadn't won a conference game in two years; we went to a bowl game my fourth year there. Wade Walker was the head coach my first two years and then Paul Davis. We went to the Liberty Bowl the last year it was played in Philadelphia. But I remember thinking during those early difficult days there: Will I ever get out of Mississippi State? Then I went to Arkansas as an assistant.

"I got my first head coaching job at Iowa State. We were 3-7 my first two years at Iowa State. We started off the next season 3-0. We go to Colorado and we're ready. We got beat 61-10. It was just the fourth game of season. Gawd! Where are we going now? I was 35 and wondering what was to become of me. And it all worked out.

"It hasn't been easy to talk to our team lately. I tell them I don't have all the answers. I tell them, 'We probably all have a lot of questions. Let's practice as hard as we can today. Let's go out and make things happen.' They know I have not given up on them."

Like father, like son, Shirley Majors and son, John, talk shop in 1968 when John was a head coach at Iowa State.

Football family — The Majors' team in 1952, from left to right, are Bob, Larry, Bill, Joe, Johnny and father, Shirley.

I didn't expect Johnny Majors to duck his latest challenge, or resign before completing his contract. It simply was not in his make-up.

"That's something I couldn't do," he said. "I'm the least important part of this program. Whether it's for your own ego gratification, you've got to keep trying. The most important thing is not for self-gratification.

"My one desire is to win because of what this program means to the players and to the people who do love Pitt. That's the reason I couldn't quit. I'd never want to be a part of bringing this program down. Right now we're not winning like we thought we would. I thought we had a chance to win.

"I have respect for people who've done great things at this school, like Jock Sutherland and Pop Warner, but mine's more imbedded into me because of people I've coached here before and the people I've met. The people can't believe we're not doing better by now.

"But they haven't shown me anything but their support. They're just unbelievable. I went to a little league football game after we'd lost to Temple, and young people and old people were patting me on the back and cheering me up. 'You just keep working,' said an old guy. He reminded me of my dad and mother.

"Nothing would mean more to me in my entire athletic experience than to bring the school back to competitiveness, for us to play on a high competitive level again. Nothing means more to me.

"I was lucky to have grown up in a family like mine. I didn't pick my family. I picked my wife; she's been so supportive. My brothers and my sister have always been behind me. I have a good network of friends. I've never been above needing support. I've been lucky to have a great support system."

> *"I would have to look at my background and what my dad taught me. That is: you are just as good as anyone, but you're no better than anyone. Never forget it. And you're going to have highs and lows. But if you let either excessive criticism or excessive praise get to you, either one will affect you adversely. There are two things that are difficult to cope with: too much and too little."*
> — John Wooden,
> Former UCLA coach

Joe DiMaggio
Meeting an American hero

"Fame irritated DiMaggio."
— Jimmy Cannon

Imet a lot of important people named Joe in my life as a sportswriter, from Joe Louis to Joe Namath to Joe Greene. I've interviewed Muhammad Ali, Michael Jordan, Mario Lemieux, Roberto Clemente and can't remember being nervous.

I was nervous the first time I ever met Joe DiMaggio. It was April, 1969, and I was in my first month as a sportswriter for a daily newspaper, *The Miami News*, when I was dispatched to Fort Lauderdale, where the New York Yankees were in spring training. I was told I could do a one-on-one interview with the great Joe DiMaggio, a distinguished visitor to the camp.

He was a tall, slender man with a toothy smile, looking sharp in a gray glenplaid suit, white dress shirt and tie, and we sat on a couch together. One of our staff photographers took several pictures of me sitting next to DiMaggio, a notebook in my hand. That was 30 years ago. I still have them.

I looked at them on Monday, March 8, 1999, when I heard on the radio that Joe DiMaggio had died at age 84. We had known for some time that Joe D. was not doing well, that he was in bad shape, but it still hurt to hear the bad news. Lung cancer was the culprit.

Babe Ruth was bigger than Joe DiMaggio, in body and reputation and his impact on Americans, but few others could compare to "The Yankee Clipper" as sports celebrities go.

Ernest Hemingway mentioned him in his prize-winning book, "The Old Man And The Sea," and Simon & Garfunkel put his name to lyrics while singing about Mrs. Robinson. "Where have you gone, Joe DiMaggio?"

He was one of America's all-time favorite ballplayers.

He was never really comfortable with his celebrity stature, however, and shied away from the spotlight.

I remember asking him that day in Fort Lauderdale if he realized what it meant for people to meet him, to shake his hand, to get an autograph, to say they spoke to him.

He nodded. "Yes, it took me awhile," he said softly, "but I do now. I'm getting better about it."

A few years later, when I was covering the New York Mets at spring training in St. Petersburg for *The New York Post,* I kept company as much as I could with Jimmy Cannon, a curmudgeon of a man, a nationally-syndicated columnist, who befriended DiMaggio early in his career and stayed close.

At one time, Cannon was the best sports columnist in the country. I was eager to hear what he had to say, while older sportswriters were ducking him. They were tired of his crusty ways, his damnation of all who drank, his stories.

I loved listening to Cannon tell stories about the great ones like DiMaggio and Hemingway, with whom Cannon had spent time in Paris during the War.

"Fame irritated DiMaggio," Cannon once wrote. "He is one of the loneliest men I've ever met and usually he moved through crowds. The flattery most men enjoy embarrasses him. I've spent most of my life in the newspaper business. Joe DiMaggio is the shyest public man I met. I like to gab and he's an accomplished listener so we get along."

DiMaggio won two American League batting titles, had a lifetime average of .325, was named Most Valuable Player three times. Yet he was said to be so private he led the league in room service.

DiMaggio led the Yankees to nine World Series victories in 13 years, and hit safely for 56 consecutive games in 1941 — one of the few sports records that may never be broken. DiMaggio was disappointed he didn't reach 57 because the H.J. Heinz Co. in Pittsburgh was going to hire him to do promotional work for them. 57 varieties, remember? It cost him $10,000.

He was also famous for marrying movie star Marilyn Monroe, an unlikely match if there ever was one. They were married less than a year, yet when she died he regularly put a rose at her gravesite. He never talked about her on TV shows, or wrote a book about their relationship. He was above such shabby behavior, so prevalent among celebrities these days. Dignity is a word one associates with DiMaggio. Class is another.

He carried himself with a special grace on and off the field. When I was working in New York, I loved to go to the Oldtimers' Games, which originated at Yankee Stadium, to see him. I loved to keep company with famous ballplayers of my youth, to see Sal Maglie, Don Larsen, Duke Snider, Mickey Mantle, Jackie Robinson, Willie Mays and Roy Campanella up close. Many of the writers, who grew up in New York, avoided such get-togethers. Maury Allen was one baseball writer who liked to schmooze with the old stars. His love for baseball was genuine.

None of those old-timers moved me as much as DiMaggio, and none of them said less. DiMaggio offered little. He kept his thoughts to himself. That may have been a part of his magic.

I never asked him for an autograph. You just didn't do those things back then. I have the mental pictures of seeing him in the press room and clubhouse, however, where they will stay and be forever cherished. Most of us have a pretty good idea now of where Joe DiMaggio has gone.

Roberto Clemente and Joe DiMaggio meet at Yankee Stadium.

It was a real thrill for this author, as a young reporter for *The Miami News*, to meet and interview the great Joe DiMaggio back in April, 1969.

John Havlicek
From Bridgeport to Boston

"He was the guts of the team."
— Red Auerbach,
Celtics coach

John Havlicek has long been one of my favorite sports heroes. No one played harder, could help his team in so many different ways, and few played as many minutes or scored as many points as Havlicek. His name was right up there with Kareem Abdul-Jabbar, Wilt Chamberlain and Elvin Hayes at the conclusion of his outstanding career in the National Basketball Association.

Havlicek wasn't as tall as that trio, and perhaps not as naturally blessed with ability as another all-out competitor, Michael Jordan, who came along since then. If you were putting together an all-time team, however, you would want him on it, even if he was coming off the bench as the sixth man.

Havlicek had a reputation as being "the best sixth man" in NBA history. They called him "Hondo," and he was a legitimate sports hero in every respect.

I was fortunate to be present at Cleveland's Gund Arena in February of 1995 when Havlicek was introduced as one of the NBA's All-Time 50 greatest players on the league's 50th anniversary. It was nice that it happened in Havlicek's home state of Ohio.

His name has also appeared in lists of the league's 20 greatest players. In 1980, Havlicek was named to the NBA's 35th anniversary team.

Havlicek has always held his head up high, and has that thin smile, like someone who knows something you don't, yet he has always been one of the most affable, approachable and agreeable athletes you will ever meet. Just a good guy.

It's hard to believe that he will be 60 come April 8, 2000. It's hard to believe he has slowed down any. Judging from his manner on the telephone, he's still has his head on straight.

"Like everybody else, I would like to be remembered in a certain way," he said in a long-distance interview. "I'd like people to think of me in terms of a guy who came from an obscure and humble background into the limelight without changing his basic nature.

"I would like to be thought of as an athlete who enjoyed the sport, rather than the controversy he could create surrounding the sport. I would like people to feel I had done something to enhance not only myself, but the game itself."

His place is secure in basketball history, and he was inducted into the Basketball Hall of Fame in 1983. He retired in 1978 — it's hard to believe Havlicek has not played in the NBA for over 20 seasons — after 16 seasons with the Boston Celtics, eight in which the Celtics won the NBA championship.

His No. 17 was retired immediately upon his leaving the game. Celtics coach/GM Red Auerbach called Havlicek "the guts of the team."

When Tom Heinsohn took over as coach, he let Havlicek control the game on the floor. "All John's ever wanted to do since he came into this league is win," Heinsohn said. "So I let him run things for me on the floor, and I also urged him to go over the mistakes of our younger players during the plane trips or whenever he felt like it."

At 6-5, Havlicek could come in at guard or forward and fit in beautifully with any four players. In Havlicek's first seven seasons, the Celtics won six championships.

Then the team's key player, center Bill Russell, retired. Russell had led the Celtics to 11 championships in his 13 seasons in the NBA. When Russell retired, he told Havlicek, "It's your team now."

Havlicek led the Celtics to two championships (1974 and 1976) when Russell was no longer in the lineup.

Overall, Havlicek was a member of eight championship teams in Boston. He was named the MVP in the 1974 Finals. A 13-time All-Star, he remains the Celtics' all-time leading scorer with 26,395 points, ahead of Larry Bird's 21,791.

He was the first NBA player to score 1,000 points in 16 consecutive seasons.

His career averages — 20.8 points, 6.3 rebounds and 4.8 assists — were good enough, but he consistently upped those numbers in the playoffs.

On the other side of the ball, he was named 1st or 2nd team All-Defense from 1969, when such a post-season team was first chosen, until 1976.

Havlicek was always in great shape. He would often mention how legendary football coach Vince Lombardi would remind his players that "fatigue makes cowards of us all."

He was always hustling. He was a man in constant motion, which helped free him for shots. He never thought of himself as a great shooter, but rather as a scorer. Just as Arnold Palmer found a way to get the ball in the hole, so did Havlicek.

His most memorable moment came in Game 7 of the 1965 Eastern Conference final against Wilt Chamberlain and the Philadelphia 76ers. With Boston up by one point, Havlicek's steal of Hal Greer's inbounds pass with five seconds remaining sent the Celtics back to the NBA Finals.

One of the most famous calls in NBA history, Celtics announcer Johnny Most's "Havlicek stole the ball!" would have been enough to immortalize any player.

"Sometimes you have to be lucky," allows Havlicek when he reflects on his good fortune as a professional athlete and ambassador for his sport.

251

"I was fortunate to be around the right people at the right place throughout my basketball career. I've had my share of luck, being with the right team, making the right shots..."

He concedes that his competitive spirit and unrelenting style had something to do with his success.

"By never giving up you'll give yourself more chances to succeed," he said. "If you play lackadaisically, you won't get as many chances."

Bob Ryan of *The Boston Globe*, one of the best basketball writers in the business, was a big fan of Havlicek.

Writing about Havlicek's farewell after 16 seasons with the Celtics, a wet-eyed Ryan wrote on New Year's Eve, 1978. "Who, therefore, symbolized Celtic spirit more than Havlicek, the lunchpail-toting kid from Lansing, Ohio who lacked Oscar Robertson's grace and Julius Erving's high rise tendencies and Jerry West's scoring touch, but who parlayed a matchless combination of stamina, determination and intelligence into the formation of the consummate basketball player.

"Havlicek is gone, and we are all aware that his equal will never brighten our lives again. But is it too much to ask of the players we do have to use Havlicek as a model? Is that just too much work to ask of today's players?"

He had many admirers in the NBA ranks.

"His number one goal has always been team triumphs, not personal accomplishments," said Warriors coach Al Attles.

NBA Hall of Famer Rick Barry said, "Havlicek is one player everyone can learn something from. Every coach tells his players to watch and learn from Havlicek. It's not just his play; it's his desire."

"It comes from where I grew up."

As he approached his 60th birthday, Havlicek appeared to have it made. He has parlayed his pro basketball career into his life's work and that suits him just fine.

He owned several Wendy's restaurants, and did promotional work, mostly customer entertainment, for several companies. The Havliceks have a beautiful home in Weston, a suburb of Boston, where he is still a revered sports figure. "I'm still doing what I've been doing right along," he said over the telephone in early May, 1999.

He sounds like a man who has it made, and no one deserves it any more than he does. He always took care of business, and he always hustled. He summers at Cape Cod and Hyannis, and winters from January to the first of May at West Palm Beach. It doesn't get any better.

After he called back promptly, which is his style, to update me on his activities and the state of his family, he added, "And you know the rest of my story..."

John Havlicek was model Celtics competitor.

Companies pay him to mix with their customers, to play golf and dine with them and establish positive relations, and Havlicek has few peers in that respect. He is good company. It's second nature for him to be nice to people. It's the way he was brought up.

"I have been doing that since I've been an athlete," said Havlicek during our telephone conversation. "When I was with the Celtics, I was always involved a lot in the community and participated in a lot of charity-related, fund-raising golf and other celebrity-type events.

"I still follow the game, though I don't see as many games as I used to. The Celtics are down this year, but I'm hopeful that they'll rebuild for the future. I still care about the Celtics and want to see them be champions again."

After the biggest of victories, and the most difficult of defeats, when he was starring for the Celtics, Havlicek always had time to talk about the games with the media, and it didn't matter whether the writer was from *The Boston Globe*, one of the TV networks, or the student newspaper at Harvard.

"It comes from where I grew up," said Havlicek when I questioned him about his approach or his personal philosophy. "Everyone had respect for one another. Everyone always tried to help each other. Everyone has a job to do. It was just one of the things I did to make my contribution.

"I felt it was the right thing to do. I didn't want anyone to think I thought I was better than anyone else. That's the way the people were that I grew up with."

John was the youngest of three children of Frank and Amanda Havlicek, born April 8, 1940 in Martins Ferry, Ohio. John's father had come to this country from Czechoslovakia at age 11, and his mother was of Croatian descent. The family owned a grocery store in Lansing. John played high school ball at nearby Bridgeport, Ohio, where he was all-state in basketball, football and baseball.

That Ohio Valley also produced some of the most agreeable and popular athletes I've ever dealt with, such as Billy Mazeroski, Joe and Phil Niekro, Alex and Lou Groza and Bill Jobko.

My maternal grandmother lived in Lansing and my mother grew up in Bridgeport, and I have an older brother, Richard, who still lives in Bridgeport. I always mentioned this to Havlicek as a door-opener whenever I would approach him for an interview during his playing days, but it was unnecessary.

Havlicek only knew one way to treat people: the right way. He played and lived by the golden rule. It was second nature.

"Where I come from, people always felt that everyone was equal," he said. "No one should feel that they were above everybody else."

At the same time, Havlicek has always had a confident air about him. Where did that come from?

"As an athlete, all people have a fear of not doing well; it's one of the things that motivates you," he said. "So I don't know if it was confidence as much as fear of failure. You want to reach a certain level of excellence, and once you get there you want to stay there, and maintain it.

"You don't want to revert back to mediocrity. I think the ones who did well feared not doing well. I wanted to become consistent, so you never let your guard down. You had that fear of not excelling."

Yet Havlicek must hold to certain values, and he must have developed a personal philosophy along the way that has served him in good stead ever since.

"Sometimes you have to be lucky," he said. "I feel fortunate about what I did. I try to put more positive things on my side of the ledger. I knew the difference between right and wrong, and I tried to put more rights on my side, and I tried to keep it very simple.

"Sometimes it's almost like divine intervention. I think some of us are chosen to do certain things. Maybe it's the way we live, the work ethic we embrace.

"I've had more than my share of luck, being with the right team, being with the right people, making the right shots. Sometimes you shoot the ball and you can't believe it goes in the way it does. Why?

"By never giving up, you'll get more chances to be successful. If you play lackadaisically, you won't get as many chances."

"A family is forever."
— John Havlicek

Havlicek had so many highs in his pro basketball career. I asked him to list a few of them randomly.

"The championships are the great things," he said. "Stealing the ball to help us defeat Philadelphia in the 1965 playoffs was one. Doing what I was able to do in that triple overtime playoff game with Phoenix in 1976. They called that the greatest basketball game ever played. I thought it was one of the most exciting, but there were too many mistakes in it for it to be called the greatest game.

"Individual performances aren't always that satisfying. We lost the first two games of the playoffs to the Lakers in 1969, and I thought they were two of the best games I ever played.

"Being able to make the league all-stars both offensively and defensively was gratifying, being able to make first team in both places."

Havlicek has drawn even more satisfaction from his family. He and Beth have been married for 33 years. They have two children, Chris, 28, and Jill, 25, who are graduates of the University of Virginia. Chris played basketball and Jill was on the lacrosse team.

When Havlicek spoke to us in May of 1999, he said Chris was working for Hard Rock Cafe and the NBA, involved in an NBA City project. He said Jill was married to a professional baseball player,

Brian Buchanan. They met at Virginia and Brian was the No. 1 draft choice of the New York Yankees, but was traded to the Minnesota Twins, and was playing Triple A ball in their system in Salt Lake City.

"I married a wonderful person and we have two terrific kids," said Havlicek. "I have to feel good about that. I've had quite a career, and done some special things. I made good money, and I didn't blow it.

"I have provided my family with a comfort zone that I think they enjoy. I think the responsibility of making sure that things go well for your family is an important one. I think it's more important than any basketball game.

"A game is here today and gone tomorrow, and it leaves memories. But a family is forever."

Havlicek credits two of his coaches, Fred Taylor at Ohio State and Red Auerbach with the Boston Celtics, with much of the success he has enjoyed.

"Fred Taylor was an important part of my life," said Havlicek. "Without him, I wouldn't have made it to the NBA. I never thought of playing professional basketball until I was a junior in college. I never saw a pro game until I went to Boston as their No. 1 draft choice in 1962.

"In the summertime, I played against people who played in the NBA, and I held my own.

"I owe a lot of credit to Fred Taylor. I wasn't a great athlete, and I didn't have great skills as a shooter or rebounder or passer. I always prided myself on not making mistakes, and being very fundamental. I learned so much of that from Fred Taylor.

"In Boston, the attitude there and the way they ran things was important to my growth and development. I fit right in. The ability of that team was awesome. At one time, when I first got there, we had seven players who had been on NCAA championship teams."

He was alluding to Bill Russell and K.C. Jones of the University of San Francisco, Clyde Lovellette of Kansas, Frank Ramsey of Kentucky, Bob Cousy of Holy Cross, Larry Seigfried and Havlicek of Ohio State.

"Red always looked into the backgrounds of a player," said Havlicek. "He liked a background of winning."

Havlicek certainly had the credentials when he came to the Celtics after graduating from Ohio State in 1962. His team went to the NCAA Finals all three of his varsity seasons in Columbus, and won one NCAA championship. Jerry Lucas was the star on that Buckeyes ballclub.

Havlicek was also a seventh round draft choice of the Cleveland Browns, though he hadn't played football since he was in high school. He was the quarterback, of course, of his team. He was also the star shortstop on the school baseball team. He could excel at any sport. He was that kind of athlete and competitor.

Woody Hayes tried to recruit him to Ohio State to play football. Hayes often called Havlicek "the best Big Ten quarterback who didn't play." Tom Matte, later a terrific running back for the Baltimore Colts, was the quarterback of the Buckeyes during Havlicek's days on the Columbus campus.

With the Browns, Havlicek tried out as a receiver and showed promise, but Paul Brown cut him at the end of summer training camp in favor of seasoned receivers.

Brown liked what he saw of Havlicek. He told him he thought he could keep him on what was then called the "taxi squad," as a paid practice player or what would now be called the developmental squad. "In time, I think you could be a real good football player," Brown told him. "But your future is in basketball. You're going to be great there. I don't want to hold you back from that."

So Havlicek joined a Celtics team that had won four straight NBA championships, and had to settle for being a top reserve in his early days.

John averaged 14 points per game in his rookie season. He also used his running ability and endurance to establish a style of constant movement on offense and defense. On offense, his movement without the ball enabled him to be in position to take good shots and get rebounds. His defensive pressure wore down opponents. He was a man in perpetual motion.

"One thing I learned from Red Auerbach," said Havlicek, who humbly accepted his role off the bench, "was that it's not who starts the game, but who finishes it, and I generally was around at the finish."

He worked hard in the off-season to improve his shooting and his ball-handling. He was lucky to have Cousy around for a few years to help him with his ball-handling. He made him dribble up and down the court every day at practice, first using his right hand, then his left hand.

He worked at his weaknesses. He worked at conditioning, which allowed him to run, run, run, up the court on a fast break, around and around trying to get open for a shot. He became the ideal basketball player. His all-out effort on defense and offense and his versatility made him one of the finest players in the history of the NBA. His role as a team leader was critical to the Celtics' success. He won so many games with buzzer-beaters. He wasn't afraid to take the key shots.

John's exemplary personality and lifestyle provided an excellent role model for youth.

Havlicek has the ability, unlike some former NBA stars, to temper his competitive spirit when he is out playing a round of golf with his employers' customers. Some guys still compete like an NBA championship is at stake, which is often counter-productive.

"There's not as much at stake now," he said. "It's not important for me to be a great golfer. I enjoy playing golf. I don't mind putting; it's a matter of touch and feel and I don't three-putt too many greens.

"But hitting those 180 yarders up to the stick is something else. It's like shooting from half court in basketball. You don't know if you'll get steel, glass or air. I don't put as much emphasis on it. It's something I enjoy.

"But I do find that the juices flow more when I'm in a team golf match, like best-ball. I like that better; I try to help the team. If you let other people down it's more painful. If I let myself down, I don't feel that bad. I can forget about it. I still hate to let someone else down."

Jim O'Brien

John Havlicek has taken this road home to Bridgeport and Lansing.

"I have long known that the nurturing provided by Crystal City (Missouri), my hometown, gave me a solid foundation from which to launch many a journey."
— Bill Bradley,
  Former U.S. Senator
  and New York Knicks
  Hall of Fame Player

Mark May
His father knew Satchel Paige

*"Coming to Pittsburgh opened
up a whole new world to me."*

S atchel Paige was his boyhood hero. He praises Jackie Sherrill
and Bill Hillgrove for helping him get started, as a football
player and as a football analyst on radio and TV, respectively.

Mark May remembers his roots, and the people responsible for
his success, or at least those who helped him when he needed a boost.
He had just been hired by CBS-TV for the National Football League
telecasts when we talked in the summer of 1998. He had also just been
hired by KDKA-TV to work with their sportscasting team on three
Pittsburgh Steelers pre-season games.

Satchel Paige was famous for saying, "Don't look back, somebody
might be gaining on you." May has no such fears. He looks back with
pride on his days in Pittsburgh.

May remains the same soft-spoken but easily understood young
man who endeared himself to everyone close to the Pitt scene when he
first came to Pittsburgh from his hometown of Oneonta, New York
back in 1976. During his student days, May often represented Pitt at
press conferences and social gatherings because he was good at it. He
was handsome, bright, affable, approachable and he could stand on
his own two feet and speak to an audience without breaking into a
sweat. I recall working a sports banquet with him at St. Mary's in
Allison Park and how impressed I was with his appearance and
aplomb. Everybody liked and was impressed with Mark May, and no
one boosted his star more than Dean Billick, then the assistant athletic director for sports information. May won the Outland Trophy in
1980 as the outstanding offensive lineman in college football. He
played 13 seasons in the NFL, 11 with the Washington Redskins. He
played in three Super Bowls with the Redskins and was an original
member of the Redskins' famed "Hogs." May spent the last two years
of his career with the San Diego Chargers and Arizona Cardinals.

He knows a good story when he sees one and, best of all, he
knows how to tell a good story. This will serve him well with CBS or
anybody else he works for. He also owns a chain of automobile dealerships, working out of Montross, Virginia, and it's pretty obvious that
this is a man who could sell you a new or used car. Even if you weren't
in the market for one.

When May was being recruited to play football at the University
of Pittsburgh, he said he visited the school on the same weekend as
Hugh Green and Rickey Jackson. That's mind-blowing.

They were escorted around the campus and city by Tony Dorsett,
who has just won the Heisman Trophy as the outstanding college

259

football player while leading Pitt to a national championship in the 1976 season.

"I don't take recruits on tours," Dorsett snapped at the trio at the end of the weekend. "So you better come here so I wasn't wasting my time. You have to sign."

All three picked Pitt as their college choice. Who was going to turn down Tony Dorsett?

All three were sensational players — Green finished second to George Rogers of South Carolina in the Heisman voting, the highest finish ever by a purely defensive player — and all three Pitt products would later play in the Pro Bowl.

Imagine getting three players of that caliber on the same weekend. In the same season. Over a three-year period.

It points up the caliber of football at the University of Pittsburgh in those glory days, and how Johnny Majors was able to win a national title, and how Sherrill, his successor, posted three straight 11-1 records from 1979 through 1981.

In addition to Dorsett, Cecil Johnson and Don Parrish played host to May, Green and Jackson during their weekend recruiting visit, and all three of those veteran Pitt performers went on to play pro football. Dorsett, of course, has been inducted into the College Football Hall of Fame in South Bend, Indiana and the Pro Football Hall of Fame in Canton, Ohio. Green has since gained College Football Hall of Fame honors. As a senior at Pitt, Green won the 1980 Maxwell Award as college football's outstanding player and the Lombardi Award as the nation's outstanding lineman. Jackson was a second round draft choice, and actually turned out to be a better and more durable pro performer, and won a Super Bowl ring with the San Francisco 49ers at the finish of his pro career.

"I was lucky to have a gift for gab."

Mark May was among the many University of Pittsburgh representatives who showed up on many Pittsburgh area golf courses throughout the summer of 1998 to help raise money for good causes.

May made the scene at The Club at Nevillewood in May and June to try his luck on the links in the Andy Russell Celebrity Classic for Children and, in turn, the Toyota Mario Lemieux Celebrity Invitational.

He was all smiles, as might be expected. The former Pitt All-American lineman and Outland Trophy winner (1980) and member of the Washington Redskins two Super Bowl championship teams (1983 and 1988), continued to move up in the sports broadcasting business.

He had recently joined the CBS Television Network's NFL broadcast team, having been the studio analyst for TNT's Sunday and

Mark May and his mentor, Bill Hillgrove, get together in press box during Steelers' game at Three Rivers Stadium in summer of 1998.

Danny Marino and Mark May enjoy 1998 reunion at Mario Lemieux's Celebrity Invitational Golf Tournament at The Club at Nevillewood.

Thursday night NFL broadcasts and a part of the three-man booth for TNT's NFL coverage.

"I'm very excited about the way things are going," said May.

He had gotten his start, thanks to his agent and former Pitt and NFL player Ralph Cindrich, with WTAE Radio, working as an analyst on Pitt football broadcasts with Bill Hillgrove during the 1994 season.

"Billy taught me the business," said a thankful May. "I was lucky to have such a good teacher. He was always telling me I wasn't going to be there too long, and I wondered why they wanted to get rid of me. He was trying to tell me I was going to get opportunities on an even higher level. He thought I had potential.

"I was lucky to have a gift for gab. Coming to Pittsburgh opened up a whole new world to me."

Everyone who ever met May after he came to Pitt from Oneonta in upstate New York in 1977 knew he was special, both as a football player and as a young man who would always represent the school in a first-class manner.

May mentioned that when he and other former Pitt players get together, at social events and golf outings, they always exchange thoughts about what's going on at their alma mater. He said everyone was cheered by what Walt Harris was able to accomplish in his first season at their alma mater.

"They were really struggling when I was working with Billy in the broadcast booth," said May. "But they seem to be on the upswing now. We're all pulling for Pitt to return to the prominence we once enjoyed."

"This is your chance."
— Ralph Cindrich

May came in for praise at a dinner to honor veteran NFL coach Joe Bugel in mid-May in Bugel's hometown of Munhall.

Bugel, an offensive line coach of the San Diego Chargers after a short stint as head coach of the Oakland Raiders, had hands-on experience with May in Washington and Arizona.

"He's the greatest overachiever I ever coached," said Bugel.

When I met May at Nevillewood, I asked him why Bugel regarded him as an overachiever. After all, Mark had been an All-American and Outland Trophy winner at Pitt and was a first round draft pick of the Redskins in 1980.

"I think I stumbled over every blocking bag on the practice field when I first reported to the Redskins," said May, smiling at the memory. "I think our head coach, Joe Gibbs, grumbled a few times. Joe bugged Bugel with 'So that's our No. 1 draft choice.' Everything I did after that was a bonus. I guess that's why Bugel believes I became an overachiever."

Mark May (No. 73 in center of photo) and teammates, left to right, Russ Grimm and John Riggins listen intently as coach Joe Bugel reviews offensive scheme in dressing room session of Washington Redskins.

He started out his pro career under Bugel at Washington and finished it with Bugel at Arizona. "When Joe got fired, I got a call from Buddy Ryan. He said 'We're not going to be able to play you.' I said, 'Fine, I'm retiring and I'm going fishing.' I figured I was off for awhile," said May.

"Then I got a telephone call from Ralph Cindrich in Pittsburgh. 'I got you a job,' he said. I said, 'Ralph, I'm not working this year.' He said, 'I got you a job broadcasting Pitt football. You said you wanted to get into broadcasting. This is your chance. You can't pass it up."

Once again, May had been recruited to come to Pitt. After the third game, May received another telephone call — this time from the San Francisco 49ers. They wanted him to come back and play for them. "Ralph told me I couldn't leave Pittsburgh," recalled May. "I took his advice. I was flying back and forth out of D.C. and doing the games, and doing a pre-game and post-game show on Redskins football for WTEM in D.C. I stayed with them for three or four years.

"I replaced Lawrence Taylor for TNT. TNT had just hired Tim Kiely away from ESPN, and Tim had known me from when he was a producer at WTAE. He is the son of Ed Kiely, who'd been the Steelers' publicity director before Joe Gordon got the job. So I still had Pittsburgh connections going for me. I started doing in-studio work, at the game site broadcasting, cable TV, you name it.

"It was Billy Hillgrove who weaned me away from Pittsburgh. I told Billy, 'you're my other father who helped raise me.' I was signed to come back for a second season at Pitt, but had to back off when the networks were calling. Billy Osborn took my place at Pitt.

"Every week, they get 50 tapes at TNT from announcers looking to move up the ranks. It's a very competitive field, but Billy believed I had what it takes to work in the NFL. So far, I've made the transitions successfully from one level to the next. I've done college and pro games. Billy's best advice was 'be over-prepared' for each outing."

"I'll never forget that first view of the city."

May remembers his first look at Pittsburgh, and how impressed he was with the place and the people he met there. "I was from a little town in upstate New York," he related. "Bob Matey was the coach who recruited me for Pitt. We came through the Fort Pitt Tunnels and wow! This is really it! I'll never forget that first view of the city skyline. It just jumps out at you.

"It had everything I wanted. The people were great. One thing Jackie Sherrill told me, 'I'll give you an opportunity to start as a freshman.' The other schools told me 'you'll start as a freshman.'

"I liked what Sherrill was saying better. I didn't really believe the other people. All I've ever wanted was an opportunity to prove myself."

Even so, Pitt people who were close to the scene in those days remembered that May bristled when he didn't start as a freshman. There was a lot of talent at Pitt in those days, but May made his mark soon enough.

He'd gotten a lot of attention from Penn State, Boston College, Maryland and Syracuse. There were times when he thought he should have gone to Syracuse. He doesn't feel that way anymore.

"In life, or whatever," Mark added, "if you give me a fair shot, an opportunity, I can live with that. It's my fault if I come up short.

"I'll always give it my best shot. You know, do the best you can. I was the first person from my community to go to college; I was the first person in my family ever to go to school.

"There were a lot of genuine people here. From the day I stepped on the campus, I had people looking after me. That first day I met a dentist and his wife, and that was Dr. Joe and Joan Smith, and they invited me to come down to their home in Aliquippa for dinner. I felt that type of warmth from the start.

"I still keep in touch with the Smiths, and see them from time to time, and they are like family to me. I felt that type of affection from them. Pitt was the place I wanted to be. In my first month, I had already been to their home for dinner. They still have my picture on their refrigerator door."

The Smiths still speak about Mark May in the most laudatory terms. They're quite proud of him and his success.

I recalled seeing May in action during a spring session in 1980, before his senior season. He was going up against a young basketball player named Sam Clancy. Pitt was in between basketball coaches — Tim Grgurich was gone and Roy Chipman hadn't come on board yet — and Clancy took advantage of the situation to try out for the football team. He had been a star in two sports at Fifth Avenue High School in the Hill District. May was manhandling Clancy that hot afternoon at Pitt Stadium. It was a real mismatch.

Once Chipman hit the campus, he called Clancy to his office and that was the end of Clancy's college football days. "The next time I played against him, he was playing for the Indianapolis Colts," recalled May. "Sam didn't make it in the NBA, but he put in 11 seasons in the NFL. He could've helped us at Pitt, I'm sure.

"We had what might have been the best college football team of all time at Pitt that year."

Pitt finished No. 2 in the country that year, behind Georgia in the AP and UPI poll. They were No. 1 in *The New York Times* computer ratings.

Whereas Pitt had only five players drafted off its 1976 national championship team, it had 12 players drafted off its 1980 team. It had three No. 1 picks in Hugh Green, Randy McMillan and Mark May, a

No. 2 pick in Rickey Jackson, three No. 3 picks in Greg Meisner, Carlton Williamson and Russ Grimm, four No. 5 picks in Bill Neill, Benjie Pryor, Lynn "Pappy" Thomas and Jerry Boyarsky, and a No. 11 pick in Rick Trocano. Several of them picked up Super Bowl rings. All but Pryor played in the NFL.

"We had 17 players drafted altogether, if you count the USFL," said May. "We had 26 players off that team who played pro ball. It was incredible. They sure turned me around. They'd taken a young country kid with too much body fat and turned me into an NFL player and a man.

"I loved the campus. I loved Schenley Park. I just loved everything about the place. It was perfect for what I wanted.

Underclassmen on the roster at the same time were Dan Marino, Jimbo Covert, Tim Lewis, Bryan Thomas, Dave Puzzuoli, Ron Sams, Rich Kraynak, Rob Fada, Julius Dawkins, Emil Boures, Sal Sunseri, Bill Maas, Jim Sweeney, Joe McCall, Tom Flynn, Dwight Collins and Al Wenglikowski, who were all drafted.

"We had a 22-2 record my last two years," remembered May, "and the team had another 11-1 season right after us. Our only loss my senior year was at Florida State (36-22). Our offense never had good field position that day. Rohn Stark was sensational in punting for Florida State that day and kept us in our own end of the field. We beat South Carolina (37-9) in the Gator Bowl at the end of the season."

The success of the 1980 team enabled Pitt to recruit the likes that year of Bill Fralic, Chris Doleman, Troy Benson, Marlon McIntyre and Billy Wallace.

Fralic, Lewis and Marino were also playing in Mario Lemieux's golf outing at Nevillewood, and all stopped by to say hello to May.

"When I see Timmy Lewis, I feel young because he's lost his hair," said May. "When I see Bill Fralic, and how good he looks, I feel old.

"I saw Fralic for the first time when he was in ninth grade," added May, after getting a big bear hug from Fralic. "He's a freak of nature. He was already so physically and mentally developed. When he first got to Pitt, he was already a senior as far as football was concerned."

I mentioned to May that even though he was a good student at Pitt, he never graduated because of the demands on his time elsewhere during his senior season. The same thing happened to Jim Covert, also a conscientious student.

"We went to the Gator Bowl, and from there I went to Hawaii, and from there to Japan to play in all-star games. Then I went to the NFL combine. I was on campus about three days once the season was over. So I had three-and-a-half years of education at Pitt."

"You just keep plugging away.
If you don't work nothing happens."
— Gypsy Rose Lee
Exotic dancer

"Satchel Paige was someone to look up to as a kid."

When I asked Mark May to name his boyhood hero, he surprised me with Satchel Paige. "That's because my father knew him," explained May. "They used to pluck chickens together in Jackson, Mississippi. My dad's name is Clarence. When Satchel Paige was going to be inducted into the Baseball Hall of Fame, my father told me we were going to Cooperstown to see Satchel Paige. 'We'll have dinner with him,' my father told me. And I said, 'Sure, sure we will.' I was about eight or nine years old at the time, and I just didn't believe my dad really knew such a sports superstar.

"Cooperstown was only 17 miles from my house. I still have the ball he signed for me. I read a lot about him, and learned about all the obstacles he overcame to get to the big leagues. I remember he said, 'Don't look back, somebody might be gaining on you.' I saw documentaries about him on TV. Satchel Paige was someone to look up to as a kid, someone special, especially for a young black looking for a role model. When I was 9 years old, I was a pitcher. I was 5-11, 230 pounds, and I could intimidate a lot of young kids then. I thought I was the second coming of Satchel Paige."

Jim O'Brien

Steelers defensive backfield coach Tim Lewis talks to former Pitt teammate Mark May at charity golf outing.

Danny Marino
Still A Pittsburgh Guy

"My boyhood hero was Terry Bradshaw."

There are over a hundred sports celebrity golf tournaments in Pittsburgh and western Pennsylvania every year, but few have a star-studded field that can compare with the one hosted by Penguins great Mario Lemieux at The Club at Nevillewood in June of 1998. It was officially called the Toyota Mario Lemieux Celebrity Invitational — "Where The Stars Shine!" boasted promotional billboards about town. There were Hall of Famers, present and future, wherever one looked at the awesome green layout above Pesto, Pennsylvania, a roadstop abutting Bridgeville, about 12 miles south of Pittsburgh.

The two most popular players in the field, no doubt, had to be Lemieux, who had retired from the National Hockey League two years earlier, and Danny Marino, a hometown boy then looking to his 16th season with the Miami Dolphins in the National Football League. They were two of the tallest, handsomest sports heroes to participate in the Toyota and UPMC Health System-sponsored event. Marino, about 6-4, 225 pounds and slightly shorter than Lemieux, is a striking figure, especially when he's flashing his dimpled grin. When he moves across the course, he's like a magnet, pulling people along with him. A year later, Marino and Lemieux would be joined in this same event by the recently-retired trio of Michael Jordan, John Elway and Wayne Gretzky.

Daniel Constantine Marino, Jr. was 36 and would be 37 by the start of the 1998 NFL season, while Lemieux was fast approaching 33. Both looked terrific. Marino wore a black golf shirt, a beige ballcap, and cream-colored slacks. When he had arrived at the clubhouse earlier in the day, pulling up in a chauffeur-driven white limousine that brought the participants to the clubhouse, Marino was wearing a white shirt with a dark stripe on the sleeves.

Several young fans were wearing the aquatic blue and orange jerseys of the Dolphins, with MARINO and No. 13 on the back. Marino obliged most, signing autographs on the go, posing for pictures, doing his best to accommodate all. When the crowd got too close, pressing against him, and making it difficult to hold a pen to a program, his face tightened and flared, and he directed the overeager fans, sternly, to back off a bit, to give him some room.

It must be difficult to be Danny Marino, I thought at the time. Sure, he makes six or seven million dollars a year to play quarterback for the Dolphins, and he has a beautiful home and family in South Florida, and fans everywhere. But it's not easy to get around, to move casually without anyone stepping into your path, when you just want to be left alone, or to live a normal existence.

**DANNY
MARINO**
1998 NFL
Man of the Year

I remembered visiting his family's modest home in the South Oakland section of Pittsburgh in the fall of 1981, a few days after the conclusion of the regular season schedule during Dan's junior campaign at the University of Pittsburgh. His neighborhood, one house snug up against another, was not much different from my boyhood home about three-and-a-half miles away. So I knew where he came from and how far he'd come, and it was unreal the success he had enjoyed in the interim. What a success story. You had to be happy for him and his family.

What I saw and heard in the company of the Marinos that memorable day still provides all the insight one requires to understand why Dan has done as well as he has, while maintaining a proper perspective about what's important and how blessed he has been, right from the beginning. I have always rooted for hometown sports performers, and he was near the top of the totem pole.

Johnny Unitas — ol' No. 19 — was my boyhood hero, and he was just one of the many outstanding quarterbacks to come out of Pittsburgh and western Pennsylvania to make their mark in college and pro ball. None of them, neither Unitas nor Joe Montana, has the numbers next to his name that Danny Marino can boast.

Five years after his retirement, Marino will surely be riding in a parade in Canton, Ohio prior to his induction into the Pro Football Hall of Fame. I hope to be there.

Marino's caddy at the golf outing at Nevillewood was his brother-in-law, Larry Richert, a local celebrity himself as a flippant, light-hearted weatherman and personality at KDKA-TV. He's an engaging guy. He also signed a few autographs. Richert is married to Dan's older sister, Cindi.

"You know that fierce, fiery look you see when the TV cameras catch Danny up close when something's gone wrong?" asked Richert during one of his spiels as a master of ceremonies at dinners throughout Pittsburgh. "Well, I've seen that same look in his sister's eyes."

Richert makes Marino smile a lot with his constant banter. As Marino was warming up for the day's outing, hitting practice tee shots, he was greeted by the likes of Lynn Swann and Chuck Noll of Steelers fame, University of Florida football coach Steve Spurrier and Pierre Larouche, another former Penguins star, and Pittsburgh businessmen and patrons who were paying big bucks to be spending a day with the stars.

Marino mixed with some of his former teammates who advanced from playing at Pitt to the pro ranks. They included Mark May, Bill Fralic, John Congemi, Emil Boures and Jimbo Covert.

He also saw another Hall of Famer, Jack Ham, along with his Steelers teammate from the '70s, Mike Wagner. They were all reminders of Marino's earlier days in Pittsburgh, playing for the Panthers and rooting for the four-time Super Bowl champion Steelers of the '70s.

Danny Marino and his brother-in-law caddy, KDKA-TV's Larry Richert, team up at Mario Lemieux Celebrity Invitational. Marino signed many autographs for fans in attendance.

"My boyhood hero was Terry Bradshaw," Marino told me when I approached him during a break in his pre-tournament activity. "I grew up as a big Steelers fan, and I wanted to be a quarterback in the NFL. That was my dream. Bradshaw was the best back then. So he was my man. I got to meet him when I was at Pitt, and that was a big thrill."

Unfortunately, Bradshaw seldom comes back to Pittsburgh, so Marino was the man this particular day, a nettlesome mix of sun and rain, drawing the biggest following. Marino is a fine golfer, as sports celebrities go, playing to a five or six handicap at the Weston Hills Country Club in Fort Lauderdale, not far from his palatial home in South Florida. His best outing was a 2-under par score at Weston Hills.

That's also the site of the Dan Marino FirstPlus Financial Celebrity Invitational, a February stop on the Celebrity Players Tour. Marino, Congemi and Covert were all associated with FirstPlus Financial, and see each other frequently, in Florida and at Pittsburgh golf and social venues. Covert switched jobs in April, 1999, returning to a financial service firm he had worked for earlier in Chicago.

Other recognizable stars at The Club at Nevillewood were baseball Hall of Famers Johnny Bench, Mike Schmidt and Rollie Fingers, HOF candidate Carlton Fisk, former baseball standout Andy Van Slyke, Pirates owner Kevin McClatchy, Steelers coach Bill Cowher, former 49ers quarterback John Brodie, former Vikings running back and "Hill Street Blues" star Ed Marinaro.

It was Marino, however, not Marinaro, who commanded the most attention this afternoon.

The kids and their parents pursued Marino, one of the greatest quarterbacks of all time. Marino remained a kid himself, a kid with compelling crystal blue eyes and wavy brown hair and a winning smile. He blushes easily, especially if anyone fusses over him too much, or tells him what a great player he's been. Dan doesn't seem comfortable when crowded; he'd sooner be sacked.

When Dan and his family travel anywhere in public, according to his father, there's an adult, usually a relative or friend, responsible for each of the children to ensure their safety and well-being. "There's man-to-man coverage," kidded his dad.

Some sports stars have trouble staying out of trouble, but Marino has been free of any negative notes since joining the Miami Dolphins. No real controversy.

In hindsight, it's a shame the Steelers didn't select Marino when they had the chance in the 1983 draft.

Steeler insiders remember how Dick Haley, a former Pitt and pro performer who was responsible for the team's scouting department at the time, told reporters, "Marino's got small hands."

Art Rooney Sr. often said, "We've got to find a way to keep this kid in Pittsburgh," but the old man was no longer calling the shots for the Steelers. He had turned the operation of the team over to Dan, the

Jack A. Wolf

Jack A. Wolf

Danny Marino was a man of many emotions as he performed for fans of all ages at Mario Lemieux Celebrity Invitational Golf Tournament. Youngsters wore jerseys of their sports favorites. Dan Marino Sr. is his biggest and most loyal fan.

Jim O'Brien

Sharon Pociask

oldest of his five sons. The Steelers had seen more of Marino than anybody, and that might have contributed to their indecision. They started looking for what was wrong with him. They were interested, even worked him out, but decided to go in a different direction. They felt their needs were greater for an outstanding defensive lineman. Didn't they recognize he was so special? A once-in-a-lifetime talent?

The Steelers didn't think they needed a quarterback because they thought Terry Bradshaw was physically fine and in his prime, which he was not, and that they had fine young prospects in Cliff Stoudt and Mark Malone. Neither proved to be up to the task when their turn came. The summer of 1983 was the one in which the Steelers drafted the star-crossed Gabe Rivera of Texas Tech rather than Marino. The Steelers had the 21st pick, and Marino was still available. That's difficult to comprehend. As it turned out, Rivera was in a terrible automobile accident near Three Rivers Stadium that first season. He was driving while intoxicated, according to police reports, and crashed head-on into an oncoming car, driven ironically by a Steelers fan. Rivera was blown through the rear window by the impact. Rivera ended up in a wheelchair for life. The other driver came out of it OK.

Most of the teams in the NFL passed on Marino in the first round, so the Steelers weren't the only team that missed a good bet. They had a history of blowing opportunities to secure great quarterbacks, going back to the days of Sid Luckman and Bobby Layne, whose rights they pitched over to the Chicago Bears. They nearly did the same when they picked Terry Bradshaw with the first pick in 1970. I have a postcard from Art Rooney to prove they weren't sure whether they should hold onto that pick or take players in a trade.

"I'm always asked if I wished Danny had been selected by the Steelers," said his father, when we spoke on April 11, 1999. "Heck, no. It couldn't have worked out better. I loved traveling to Miami in the early days. If he played in Pittsburgh, was I going to vacation on the North Side?" I sat next to Dan Marino Sr. on the dais at the 13th annual awards dinner sponsored by the Pittsburgh chapter of the National Italian-American Sports Hall of Fame. The elder Marino, 62 at the time, was one of the men responsible for founding the Pittsburgh group. That helps explain why Larry Richert always volunteers to emcee the event, held each spring at the downtown Hilton.

When I asked Mr. Marino what made him proudest of his son, he said simply, "Just because he's a good person."

Marino had been a role model throughout his stay in Miami. No problems, no controversy. He was involved in much community activity where his presence could help draw funds for worthwhile causes. He had been the Dolphins nominee for the NFL's Man of the Year Award the previous two years because of his continued contributions to children's needs, and won the league-wide award in 1998. That was quite a tribute to acknowledge all his efforts in that respect.

In June, 1999, Marino signed a new two-year contract extension, calling for a $6.5 million signing bonus.

"Danny gets the big picture."
— Fudge Browne,
Dolphins Community Relations

In mid-March, 1999, Danny Marino and his family proudly participated in a ribbon-cutting ceremony for the Miami Children's Hospital Dan Marino Center in Weston, Florida, about 40 miles north of Miami.

Dan and his wife, Claire, and their four children, Alexandra, Michael, Joey and Dan, were all smiles at the public gathering. It was Michael who had the honor of wielding the scissors for the ribbon-cutting. This center might never have been built if it weren't for Michael, who was diagnosed with an autistic spectrum disorder when he was two years old.

Dan was devastated when he learned what was wrong with Michael, their second child. Strange behavior had begun to be all too routine. At his second birthday party, for example, Michael put his hands over his ears and screamed as the family sang "Happy Birthday." He didn't even try to blow out the candles on his cake. That was just one of the signs that something was wrong with Michael.

Symptoms of autism are: slow development or lack of physical, social and learning skills; immature rhythms of speech, limited understanding of ideas, and use of words without attaching the usual meaning to them; abnormal responses to sensations, abnormal ways of relating to people, objects or events.

"He was not verbal. He was not affectionate. He didn't like hugs and kisses," explained Michael's mother, Claire Marino. "Now, he speaks well, he is very affectionate and very sociable. He's the ringleader of our street."

Dan could afford to fly Michael to medical facilities around the country to get the best possible care, which enabled Michael to be mainstreamed when it came time for him to enter school. Michael made tremendous progress. His autism is now regarded as a mild case. Seeing how well his son fared with proper attention, Dan wanted the children of South Florida to have the best possible care right in their own backyard. He made a commitment of $500,000 to expand the second floor of the facility, and he's going to help in raising funds.

"It's going to make it less expensive," said Dan, "and people are going to know they're getting the best care, too. It's also a regular children's hospital. I wanted a place here where everything — diagnosis and treatment — would be under one roof."

Dan and Claire Marino worked with Michael's doctor, Roberto Tuchman, and Miami's Children's Hospital to create the center which offers comprehensive health care to children with autism, diabetes and other chronic medical needs. The Marinos established the Dan Marino Foundation in 1992 to raise money for children's charities throughout South Florida.

Danny and Claire Marino and their children are at home in Weston, Florida.

"I've achieved a lot in my career — winning an MVP award, going to Pro Bowls, setting a lot of records — but to be recognized for affecting people's lives in a positive way at a time when that doesn't happen as much as we'd like, it's something I'm very proud of," said Marino.

While Marino never seems comfortable at press conferences, or during interviews with the media, and resorts to cliches and short uninspired remarks, he is most available to any kids with serious health challenges, and engages in warm exchanges. Marino is in more demand than any other athlete this side of Michael Jordan, who has also devoted a lot of personal time and generous attention to ailing youngsters during his storied pro basketball career.

It's a side of sports stars' lives that doesn't get much attention, and most, like Marino, prefer it that way.

It's strange, but Marino is one of many high profile quarterbacks in the NFL who have had sons with serious physical challenges. They include Jim Kelly, Boomer Esiason, Mark Rypien, Doug Flutie and John Elway. All of them are very involved as spokesmen and with fund-raising activities for different health problems.

Nancy Strom, president of the Make-A-Wish Foundation of South Florida, says Danny Marino is the most sought-after celebrity wish she encounters, even ahead of pop singer Gloria Estefan.

Most Make-A-Wish kids, who are challenged with terminal illness, want to go to Disney World, but that's not as big a deal for kids who are from Florida. Danny Marino beats out Mickey Mouse near Miami.

"If I can help the children feel better about themselves and help the families feel better about themselves, I want to do that," said Marino.

"Sometimes it's mind-boggling that a child's biggest wish would be to come to a Dolphins game and meet me. Although it can be tough emotionally because of their situation, it's also satisfying for me to see them happy and smiling.

"It's touching to know they feel that way, but it's hard to deal with sometimes. It just makes you think about what's important."

Marino is usually seen with a child after games, and sometimes following a Dolphins' practice session.

"Football is extremely important to me," said Marino, "but I think people and families and the reasons they come to me overrides whatever the circumstances of the game might be.

"A couple of times, I would start crying afterward. I didn't do it in front of the kids, but after I went to the locker room."

Dolphins Community Relations Director Fudge Browne, also a native Pittsburgher and the daughter of the late Joe Browne, former nice-guy columnist for the Pittsburgh *Post-Gazette*, coordinates these visits with Marino.

"People seem so surprised," said Browne, "when I tell them I'm going to go ahead and take the kids to meet Danny if we lost the game.

'You're not going to take them in now are you? They lost!' But something like this puts the game in perspective.

"Danny gets the big picture. Probably no one on this team deals with terminal illness as much as Danny. Cancer, leukemia, AIDS. It's hard because in a way, there's a lot put on Danny's shoulders. Can you imagine being the wish of someone's lifetime? I think Danny handles it well. It's kind of humbling."

I have learned much about Marino from personal interviews, and from a Marino information file provided by Harvey Greene, an old friend from our respective New York days, who is the senior director of media relations for the Dolphins and one of the best in the business. A grand total of 44 pages are devoted to Danny Marino in the Miami Dolphins' media guide. When I covered the Dolphins for *The Miami News* in 1969 there weren't 44 pages in the team's entire media guide.

Consider this story about a Make-A-Wish Kid named Bucky Hellman from Marino's hometown of Pittsburgh. Hellman visited Dan Marino on Christmas Eve of 1994.

Hellman was a 17-year-old boy dying of a rare nerve disease who came to South Florida for a Christmas Day game against the Detroit Lions. This was the boy's Christmas gift.

On the sideline at a workout the day before the game, the boy started giving Marino gifts, first a souvenir cup, then a trinket and then another trinket

The boy's mother was videotaping the interaction and Marino looked into the camera and wished everyone a Merry Christmas. The camera then focused on the boy who became very serious and said, "I just want to say this is the nicest thing that has ever happened in my life."

Then he handed Marino a lapel pin...a pin with an angel on it. "This is for you when I'm not here," Hellman told Marino. "It's to watch over you."

Marino took off his practice shirt, gave it to the boy, and went into the locker room. To cry.

Reflecting later on what happened, Marino said, "He was unbelievable. To think he was thinking that way — at that time of year and everything. It was hard to handle."

Something strange happened to me a week after I wrote the above story about Marino receiving his angel pin. I was doing a signing session at Waldenbooks at Century III Mall in West Mifflin. A generous 75-year-old woman named Mavis Trasp, who had shown me much kindness the past year with gifts of cookies and pies and such when I show up at that mall, had another gift for me.

It's important to know that I call her my "Christmas angel." She told me to close my eyes. She then affixed a pin to my sport coat lapel. Before I opened my eyes, I said, "I'll bet it's an angel." She scolded me. "You peeked," she said. No, I hadn't. I just had a feeling that it was an angel, someone to watch over me when Mavis wasn't around.

"I looked up to my dad."
— Danny Marino

When Danny Marino played at Pitt, he had a few opportunities to meet some of the Steelers he looked up to, especially Bradshaw. His coaches at Pitt, Jackie Sherrill and Foge Fazio, liked to associate with some of the Steelers coaches, and Marino would occasionally stop by and watch the Steelers practice at Three Rivers Stadium, or at their summer training camp at St. Vincent College in Latrobe. Marino would tag along as Bill Fralic would do later on. They had their eyes on the NFL from the start.

Asked about his boyhood heroes, Marino said, "Quarterbacks like Namath, Bradshaw and Stabler. In baseball, it was Willie Stargell, who I played catch with as a kid.

"There's nothing wrong with a kid looking up to a certain athlete," Marino continued. "Myself, I looked up to my dad. He was number one. I respected him for the way he lived, the way he spent time with me. Kids have to look for direction. If there's no father, they need to look at someone like a father. I dreamed of being like Terry Bradshaw when I was growing up in Pittsburgh, and I dreamed of playing quarterback in the NFL. Now I'm doing it and getting paid.

"I see a lot of young kids, and it's nice to see, it's worthwhile for me, when young kids get excited about seeing you. That's really kind of nice."

Marino admires other quarterbacks who are more contemporary, such as Joe Montana and John Elway.

He gets enthusiastic when he talks about Montana, another western Pennsylvania-bred quarterback, from Monongahela and Ringgold High School.

"He's won four Super Bowls," said Marino. "That's what he's done better than I do. But it's hard to compare us. Everybody has their own style of playing. You'll never know what I would have done if I had played for the 49ers and what he might have done if he was in my situation.

"Every opportunity he's had to win, Joe's done what he had to do to win. That's what you have to admire about him. He's been in four Super Bowls and he could have won two and lost two, but he's won all four. He was a big-time player and he played great in big ballgames."

"In a way, I was jealous."
— Danny Marino

On the day of the 1998 Super Bowl, Danny Marino had family and friends gathered around a big-screen TV at his home in Weston, Florida. He served stone crabs, California cabernet and Cuban cigars.

279

When I had dinner at his home in South Oakland 17 years earlier, we were all happy with the fare which was fried chicken and spaghetti made by his mother, Veronica, a green salad and fresh Italian bread. Nothing could be better.

In the 1998 Super Bowl, following the 1997 campaign, Danny's friend and fellow quarterback, John Elway of the Denver Broncos, realized a dream that both he and Marino had longed to fulfill. Elway, in his fourth try, finally had been on the winning side in a Super Bowl. He'd be getting a Super Bowl ring. And then another a year later.

"I was pulling for John because he's my friend, but in a way I was jealous," said Marino, who lost in his only Super Bowl appearance, in January 1985. "When I saw him holding that trophy, I almost cried."

He and Elway have enjoyed each other's company at golf tournament parties, country club bars and casinos. Their friendship dates back to an ABC-TV-sponsored tour that whisked six top college football players around the country in the summer of 1982.

Marino and Elway had eerily similar lives. They were among the six quarterbacks taken in the NFL's 1983 draft. They were both 1979 draft picks of the Kansas City Royals and New York Yankees, respectively. Marino on the fourth round and Elway on the 18th round, and both were high school pitchers. They both had a son who had a lifelong health challenge.

In his only Super Bowl outing, Marino and the Dolphins came up short, 38-16, to Joe Montana and the San Francisco 49ers. That was in Super Bowl XIX, following the 1984 season. Marino has never won a championship — not at Pittsburgh's Central Catholic High School, not at Pitt, not in the pros. Unless you count the AFC championship in his second pro season. Marino never wears the ring the Dolphins gave their players that year. He calls it "a loser's ring."

What's the big deal about the ring? So many ballplayers have sold their rings, including some of the Steelers. Glen Edwards comes to mind. Mike Webster was reported to have sold his rings when he got into financial difficulties about the same time he was inducted into the Pro Football Hall of Fame in the summer of 1997. Webster since has insisted that wasn't so, and has displayed his rings to disprove the allegation.

"Just that feeling of what it's like to be with a team that's the best that season, that year. That's why it's worth playing," said Marino, explaining his desire to get a ring.

Terry Bradshaw, who won four Super Bowl rings, says a quarterback's greatness is determined by the number of rings he can call his own, which would mean Marino didn't rank that high in Bradshaw's book. Marino doesn't want to get into a dissing contest with Bradshaw. "Terry was my man growing up in Pittsburgh, but he got lucky to be on a team with great talent," said Marino. "I'm hoping to be on one, too, before I'm through. You only deserve it if you get there and win it.

Danny Marino directs Miami Dolphins and, as Pitt quarterback below, shares a light-hearted moment with teammate Emil Boures.

"Listen, yes, it means a lot. And that's your dream. You gotta have dreams. But I can look back at my career knowing I worked hard for that goal each and every year, and I don't think it'll take away from my career if I don't get one. I'm just going to have to try to be happy knowing I did the best I can.

"There was a guy who was my college roommate — Tommy Flynn. He was the high school quarterback for a team that went to the state championship when I was the big guy in western Pennsylvania. Then he plays defensive back for Green Bay. They cut him, and the Giants pick him up and go on to win the Super Bowl. He blocked a punt in the playoffs and he got a Super Bowl ring. He was in that unique situation, he had a special part in it." Marino shook his head. "And it might never happen for me."

"You know exactly where you stand with him."
— John Congemi

Danny Marino remains true to his boyhood friends and high school and college teammates. He likes old friends, simple things, pizza and popcorn, loyalty. He sends a great deal of Dolphins' equipment, artwork, posters, memorabilia that he has signed each year for a fundraising auction to benefit the athletic programs at his alma mater, Central Catholic High School.

I attended such a Vikings auction in 1998 at the David L. Lawrence Convention Center, and the Marino memorabilia had to be the biggest catalyst for raising money.

"One of Danny's great traits is he's never lost what he was or where he came from," said John Congemi, Marino's friend and former teammate at Pitt, and himself a wonderful young man who remains close to his family and friends in Youngstown. "You know exactly where you stand with him — good, bad or indifferent."

Marino has jetted home to Pittsburgh on occasion to see hockey games, especially if the Florida Panthers are playing the Penguins. His wife's family is also from Pittsburgh. When he's acknowledged in the crowd by the public address announcer, Marino always gets a positive response. He remains popular in Pittsburgh.

He came to Pittsburgh in the fall of 1998 when the Dolphins had a bye week, and ended up delivering a pre-game pep talk to Art Walker Jr.'s Central Catholic football team prior to a game with New Castle at Arthur J. Rooney Field on the campus of Duquesne University.

"The Dolphins weren't playing and there was a hurricane blowing through Florida, so Dan thought it would be a good time to come

Pitt football alumni gathering attracts, left to right, Randy Reutershan, Randy Holloway, Danny Marino and their academic advisor and MVP, Dave Pistolesi. Marino watches tee shot amid many former Panther teammates at Varsity Letter Club golf outing. They were, left to right, Roman Matusz, unidentified contestant, Dean Caliguire, Marino, Jim Covert and Bill Cherpak.

to Pittsburgh and see family and friends," said old school chum Pat Karabinos.

"He called Brad Totten, a former teammate of his at Central, and asked him if they could play some golf at the Field Club, which Danny likes to play. Brad called me and asked me to join them.

"I jumped at the chance. It was a great day, a beautiful day, and we had a great day of golf. While we were driving around the course, we started thinking about how nice it would be if Danny could surprise the kids at Central and talk to them before the game that night.

"Danny was hesitant, at first, but he said he'd do it. The police let our car through at Duquesne when they saw it was Danny Marino in the car. As we were walking into the locker room, I heard one of the kids say, 'Danny Marino is here,' and one of his teammates said, 'Oh yeah, right.' That kid's eyes were this big when he saw Danny. He gave a nice talk. Central played a good game, but New Castle was too good. They ended up winning the WPIAL Quad A title. We kidded Danny that he'd have to deliver a better pep talk the next time if Central was going to win."

Art Walker Jr., whose father was one of the most respected coaches and administrators at Mt. Lebanon High School and Shady Side Academy, was as appreciative as the kids despite an 18-14 loss to New Castle. "It was something big for me, too," said Walker. "He put our school on the national map. For ten minutes, all our kids' eyes were on him. He told them he once dressed in the same locker room as they did. He told them all the things you're supposed to say. He also told them they should always go out to win, not just to play the game, no matter what they might have heard to the contrary."

Marino likes to bond with old buddies from his Pittsburgh days. "I wish I could get back to Pittsburgh more often," he said, while attending a football alumni golf outing. "That's definitely one place I can go and just blend in."

Bill Fralic, who starred for the Penn Hills High School team that beat out Central Catholic for the 1978 WPIAL title, pokes fun at Marino's efforts to remain one of the boys. "We *schlep* in like everyone else," offered Fralic, having some fun at Dan's expense, "and Marino arrives on a private chartered jet. Other than that, we're all the same."

When he's traveling in South Florida, Marino also often has a driver who doubles as his bodyguard at the wheel of a limousine. The driver's name is also Dan.

Bob Czerniewski, an executive with Stevens Painton Corp., recalled when he played sandlot football for the Oakland Vikings. His coach was Dan Marino Sr. Young Dan was the team's waterboy. "I've been with them at some social functions in recent years," said Czerniewski, "and I admire them both. They're a great team."

Because of his status as one of the top sports stars, Marino gets invited to celebrity parties in South Florida. "I've been invited to some of them, but I don't go," he says, matter of factly. Why not? "I don't know," he says with a shrug.

"He's still a Pittsburgh guy."
— Edwin Pope, Columnist,
The Miami Herald

He grew up in the same neighborhood where a young Bruno Sammartino used to lift sewer lids over his head, or so the legend goes, while building himself up in the weight room at the YM&YHA across the street from Pitt's Cathedral of Learning.

Edwin Pope, columnist for *The Miami Herald*, says of Marino, "He's spent more than a third of his life in South Florida and he's still a Pittsburgh guy."

Billy Sabo, Joey Carcia, Pat Sciulli and Larry Lamonde show up with Marino from time to time. Back in their boyhood days in South Oakland, they hung out together, played street games together — they'd play football, basketball, street hockey, baseball — and had their first beers together.

"Danny used to say my son, Larry, was the one who was going to make the big money, when he was pitching for Pitt," recalled Abby Lamonde, a retired member of the groundskeeping staff at Pitt who still ushers at Three Rivers Stadium. "He got as far as Triple A, which isn't bad."

It's not easy to become a big league player in any sport. Danny Marino knows he's been fortunate, but misses the kind of things he did in his old neighborhood.

"In high school, Dominic DiPaulo's dad made red wine in the cellar," said Dan. "We used to fill up Pepsi bottles. He had two fifty-five gallon drums in the basement. His dad was in masonry. That was good stuff." Same thing went on in my neighborhood, where most of the people on my street were Italians. Grapes were growing on trellises in the backyard. My friends' grandparents also made pasta and cheese in their cellars.

Dan's boyhood buddies are always eager to talk about their early days with Dan Marino, when they used to wear their football uniforms to mass at St. Regis Catholic School, and then follow the cheerleaders down the aisle and up the hill to Frazier Field for a game in the City Catholic Grade School Football League.

I remember when I was playing for St. Stephen's Grade School's team in Hazelwood that we had a game at Frazier Field. We narrowly beat St. Regis, but their cheerleaders stoned our cheerleaders. So it was a draw, at best.

Dan's dad used to pitch baseballs to him, and play catch with a football with him on the street where they lived. When Dan's dad wasn't available, Dan could be seen throwing a football at a stop sign outside his parents' home.

South Oakland has changed over the last 30 years. There are still a lot of Italians and Irish in the neighborhood, but many left for the suburbs, giving way to students, especially Asian students and instructors associated with the local universities and colleges. Nowadays, South Oakland is often referred to as South Korea by the old guard.

During Dan's playing days at Frazier Field, you could see the Jones & Laughlin Steel mills along the Monongahela River below, and the downtown skyline was off to the right. Marino wouldn't recognize the view now. The mills have been leveled and there are new technology centers. Soon he would be able to see a practice and training facility on the South Side that would be shared by the Steelers and Pitt football teams. It would be on the site where a steel mill once stood.

Pittsburgh is no longer a steel city, or a city of blue collar workers, no matter that the teams still promote the city and their teams in that tough-guy, take-your-lunchbucket-to-work image. Technology, education, medicine and service companies are the modern strengths of the area, and everyone needs to get wise to that.

Dan's first job as a teen was working at Johnny Rosato's Landscaping, just around the corner from his home on Parkview Avenue, across a deep ravine from Schenley Park. His father had worked there before him.

Young Dan earned $20 for a 12-hour shift, pulling weeds and trimming shrubs. Marino remembers being left on a sun-blasted hill in the morning and being told to weed the whole thing. He vowed he'd never cut grass or do any weeding again.

He remembers unloading boxes for a truck company and shoveling concrete for a construction firm owned by Central Catholic and Pitt booster Joe Massaro that was involved in a refurbishing project at Three Rivers Stadium.

Dan Kanell, the Dolphins' orthopedic doctor, starred in track & field at South Hills High School and the University of Pittsburgh. He grew up in the same neighborhood and played on the same playgrounds as Johnny Unitas, and was an Eastern discus-throwing champion at Pitt.

He's a big believer that there's something about Pittsburgh and western Pennsylvania that produced great sports competitors in those days.

Kanell's son, also Dan, played quarterback at Florida State and with the New York Giants in the National Football League. He was signed to play with the Atlanta Falcons for the 1999 season.

Talking about Marino and the value of his roots, Kanell commented, "He's got that mentality. Blue collar. They give you

Danny Marino remembers
where he came from.
These signs remain
familiar to him from
his old neighborhood.
He has always lived
in a gated community.

Photos by Jim O'Brien

Danny Marino

everything they have. You can't take it out of him. I see it all the time. I use him as a role model. When my son was the quarterback at Florida State (in 1994) I'd tell him , 'You've got to be tough. You've got to play like Marino, you've got to play sometimes when you're hurt.' He didn't grow up in Pittsburgh, unfortunately."

"He always cared about other people's feelings."
— Veronica Marino

No one has to tell Danny Marino about the major role his family, and what he learned at an early age, has played in his career success.

"I come from a great family, but that doesn't automatically mature you in all the right ways," said Dan.

"My dad was the coach of my Little League team. When it came to uniform numbers, he always made me wait till last to get mine. No special favors. That's how I ended up with 13 the first time, and I liked it and kept it."

His mother Veronica remembers. "In some ways," she said, "he's still the same as when he was little. He used to watch Lassie, and every week he'd end up crying. He always cared about other people's feelings."

Dan adores his mother, and he speaks in similar tones about his wife, Claire, whom he met a year after his student days at Pitt. Her grandparents were among the founders of Eat'n Park Restaurants and her maternal grandfather was credited with discovering chipped chopped ham at Isaly's. So she's a Pittsburgh Girl, for sure.

Claire and Dan met when Dan returned to Pittsburgh after his rookie season. "I'd gone to some of his football games in high school," she said. "He was supposed to be a big deal, but I didn't even know who he was." Dan doesn't buy that last remark.

Dan said of Claire: "She's been a great wife and a great mother. Without her, I'd be out of the league by now."

They shared a 12,000 square-foot Mediterranean-style house, located on the eastern border of the Everglades in a gated community in south Florida. There was a gate at the top of the steps leading to his humble home on Parkview Avenue, too. There was also a sign that said BEWARE OF THE DOG. So Dan grew up in a gated community, so to speak.

"You could stand on your porch and touch the neighbor's house," is the way Dan describes the coziness of his boyhood home.

The Marinos had five children at the outset of 1999: Dan, 12; Michael, 10; Joey, 9; and Alexandra, 6, and Niki Lin, a two-year-old they had just adopted from China.

Like his parents did for him, Marino always puts his family ahead of everyone and everything else.

"It seemed like a dream."
— Veronica Marino

When I reflect on Danny Marino, I can't help but think of the day that he and I walked through his neighborhood in South Oakland. We visited Frazier Field, since renamed Dan Marino Field. It's just up the hill from his old home.

The way young Dan sees it, the ballfield is named for his dad as well as for him.

Marino wrote in a memoir for young fans: "I learned the fundamentals of sports and fatherhood on that field. A dad who spends time with his son also becomes a friend."

His dad had lived in that same neighborhood all his life, the first 58 years, anyway, until Dan finally convinced his parents to move to South Florida. He wanted to look after them and he wanted them to share in his good fortune, and remain close to his family. His grandmother — his dad's mother, Julia Marino — and his sister, Debbie, 33, live in Weston, too. Dan Sr. told me his home was two minutes from his son's home.

I can still picture his dad sitting in the stands at Pitt Stadium, half way up, a seat on the aisle at the 50 yard line, often the only one in the stands watching practice. He kept a close eye on his son.

His dad keeps score on what sports writers are writing about Danny Marino, especially back home in Pittsburgh. "My dad keeps me posted on what you guys are doing," young Marino told me with a smile and a wink when we spoke at Nevillewood in the summer of 1998.

If you want to stay on Dan's good side you better get a good review from his father.

I was at a party at Sal Sunseri's home the day Sal and Emil Boures were both drafted by the Steelers. It was hosted by Sal's parents, Anthony and Ann, two warm down-to-earth individuals. Veronica and Dan Marino were there, too, as was their son, Danny, and several members of the Pitt football team and administration. "I envy Sal and Emil," Danny said that day. "I wish the Steelers would select me. I'd love to play for them."

Sal, always a media-friendly fellow, had invited sportswriters and sportscasters to his draft day party. Myron Cope and Bill Hillgrove were both present. Cope, in fact, even danced with Dan's mother. Hillgrove clapped and tapped his toes on the floor while Cope was showing his stuff. As a kid, Cope had gone to dancing school, and could have been the next Gene Kelly if he hadn't gone astray, at least that's what Cope has told some of his colleagues.

I visited the Marinos at their home in December, 1982, three days after a devastating season-ending loss to Penn State at Pitt Stadium. The final score was 48-14. It was Pitt's first loss in 17 games. It cost them the national championship.

Pitt led by 14-0 at the outset of the game after Marino threw two of the best TD passes Penn State coach Joe Paterno said he had ever seen. I was sitting in the stands that day and I would have to agree. They were like laser beams from "Star Wars." He nearly threw a third, but the ball bounced off the chest of receiver Julius Dawkins and into the arms of a Penn State defender in the end zone. Penn State scored the next 48 points in one of the greatest turnarounds in sports I've ever witnessed.

It may not have been the best of times to meet the Marinos. Then again, they showed how resilient they were, and how they had things in their proper perspective. I learned a lot that day that's still meaningful to the Marino success story. They were still good company, though the pain had to linger from that upsetting loss.

When I had dinner that evening at the Marino home, I remember how cheerful and pleasant they were. I remember there were photos of all the kids everywhere one looked, as many of Cindi and Debbie as there were of Dan Jr. They had a dog named Watson who looked like a German Shepherd.

"In part," said Veronica, "but he's also collie and who knows what else. He's just a mongrel."

I remembered the sign at the gate to beware of the dog, but Dan Sr. assured me all was OK.

"Don't worry, the dog won't bite you," said Dan's father as I entered their home. "The sign works better than the dog does to keep people out. How about a coffee, a beer or some pop?"

Everyone was coming home from school at about the same time that day, and there were hugs and kisses, and inquiries about the day's events from mom and dad. Danny and Cindi had their mother's ice-blue eyes and Debbie had her dad's dark brown eyes. Cindi was talkative, Debbie a bit shy.

Dan Sr. wanted to make sure I understood where he was coming from. Pointing toward his son, he said, "Hey, he knows I'm not all wrapped up in what he's doing athletically, or that his athletic success is so important. I treat him the same way I do my daughters. No matter what he does on that football field, I'm not gonna love him any more or less.

"What I want from Danny is that when he comes out of Pitt after four years there...what matters to me...is that I want to see him the same person with the same feelings and the same compassion as when he went in there. My responsibility is to make sure that happens, and to have some input into building his character."

At the time, the Marinos were motoring about town in a seven-year-old Chevrolet Impala. "If that breaks down," Danny declared, "I'll be walking."

Cindi walked to and from Pitt each day because the family couldn't afford to have her live in the dormitories. "I'd have to hit the lottery," said her dad. In time it seemed like he did.

·

Pittsburgh Curbstone Coaches celebrity guest speakers at 1982 session include, from left to right, Steelers' quarterback Mark Malone, Penn State football coach Joe Paterno and Pitt quarterback Danny Marino.

Danny Marino is flanked by Bishop Leonard and Steelers owner Art Rooney at CYA Dinner where he was named the 1985 winner of the Art Rooney Award. Pitt center Jim Sweeney is at far left in first row, along with Mayor Sophie Masloff, attorney Richard Zappala, then a future District Attorney, and Register of Wills Rita Wilson Kane, among others.

Dan's mother liked where they lived. "Some people put down Oakland," she said, "but I wouldn't want to live anywhere else. We don't go door to door every day, but they're always there. If you needed them, they'd be there in a hurry."

Her parents were Polish and she grew up on Polish Hill. "My girlfriend and I used to get passes to the Pitt football games in the mid-50s and we went there to see the boys," she recalled.

The Marinos made me feel comfortable right away. No pretense. "Please, you can use your fingers to eat the chicken," said Mrs. Marino. And her husband added, "Yeah, you don't have to impress anybody here."

Dan Sr. drove a delivery truck for the *Post-Gazette*, working during the early hours of the day, the 2 a.m. to 10 a.m. shift, to get papers out to the newsboys who delivered them door to door before breakfast. As a pre-teen, I was a *Post-Gazette* newspaper boy.

Mr. Marino once was the newspaper boy on the street where the Marinos were living, just a block away from his parents' home, the only other house he had ever called home in all of his 45 years.

He managed a Little League team that played at Billy Mazeroski Field, out behind where Forbes Field once stood.

He frequented Forbes Field as a youngster, and knew all the Oakland sports characters. He played football at Schenley High and sandlot ball with the Greenfield Preps. Bruno Sammartino was a student at Schenley at the same time, and when I spoke to Bruno in April of 1999 he told me he remembered Marino.

"I knew how Danny felt after the Penn State game," said his dad. "Hey, when I was at Schenley, we lost one game to Connellsville by 61-0, and the next week to Westinghouse by 61-6. So I've been there. And it didn't ruin my life.

"Somewhere down the line it might help him," his dad said of the Penn State setback. "It might help him become a man."

The house on Parkview Avenue had been home to the Marinos for 17 years.

Willie Stargell and Donn Clendenon once lived next door to Dan's grandmother, when the Pirates were playing at Forbes Field. "I used to go over there and catch ball with them in the street," said young Danny.

Danny pointed to a spot near the front of his home. "I always played right there," he said. "We played touch-tag football and street hockey, and games like release-the-peddler. This was the home base."

Indeed, it was always the home base. Danny Marino could have gone anywhere he wanted after he completed his stay at Central Catholic. He was offered scholarships for both football and baseball. The K.C. Royals wanted him as a right-handed pitcher.

"Quite naturally, as a mother, I thought it would be nice for him to stay here," said Mrs. Marino. "I never really let him know I felt that way. I told him, 'Whatever you choose to do, I want you to be happy.' But I'm so glad he's here.

"When I first saw him play at Pitt, I had to pinch myself. I knew it was happening, but it was like a dream. It's exciting to know this is all happening to my son. I think what he has is something God gave to him. I just pray to God that he stays the same nice kid he is all his life."

"You're not better than anybody else."
— Dan Marino, Sr.

In addition to driving a delivery truck for the *Post-Gazette*, Dan Sr. worked at a second job, landscaping, for a brief period. He wasn't afraid of work. His father had come over from Italy speaking no English and got whatever work he could. His father worked in a steel mill until he was burned to death in an accident at the age of 27. Dan Sr. was three years old at the time.

When the newspaper had a strike and the company bought out jobs in 1995, Dan Marino Sr. took the offer and moved down to South Florida to be with his son and four grandchildren. He had worked long enough; it was time to go.

They seem to be as close as a father and a son can be. Clearly, Dan's father did something right.

"You need to teach your children to have respect for everyone, whether it's the president of a company or the guy picking up the garbage," said Dan's father. "You respect these people the same. They're human beings. You're not better than anybody else. You just are not better than anybody. You know what I'm saying? You don't let anything ever change you. Anything."

On the subject of his son failing to win a Super Bowl during his career, his dad doesn't mince words.

"I've never seen him devastated," he said. "That doesn't take away from his career. You know what I'm saying. What's the difference? The scoreboard can't make you a loser. If you walk off the field with your head up, you don't lose. You don't hang your head for nobody. People in the stands think you're the greatest or you're the worst — it doesn't make a difference, their opinion. The only opinion that makes any difference is your own opinion of yourself. Nobody can make you a loser.

"The satisfaction that I always told him to pursue when he was a kid was that it doesn't make any difference how far you go or what you accomplish as long as you know you're as good as you can possibly be. Reach your potential, know in your own mind you were the best you could be."

Nor should anyone question his son's lifestyle.

The father reminds one of former Pirates manager Jim Leyland when he gets riled up because someone has brought up the subject of how much money he makes.

"That doesn't mean nothing. What the hell does that mean? You know what I'm saying. Sometimes he travels in a limousine or a chartered jet. You have an opportunity to get it, it makes more sense than riding down here looking for a place to park. And if you can afford to do that, that's what you do. If you can't afford it you don't do it. You come down on the bus. Just like if you can afford to help people in need, why wouldn't you?"

"I can throw it as good as anyone who ever played."
— Danny Marino

Danny Marino limps through the locker room before and after games. His right calf is noticeably smaller than his left. There's a screw in his ankle, a special protective sneaker encasing a heel that was injured in a game against the Cleveland Browns.

At 38 at the start of the 1999 season, Marino can't stand on his toes. He's had nine surgeries on his legs, and knee surgeries are so common that he refers to them as "oil changes."

Marino's knee was first damaged during his sophomore season at Pitt. Before his senior season at Pitt, Marino would walk into the Pitt training room, the syringe would pop into his knee and Marino would fill paper cups with a grotesque blood-and-fluid cocktail.

Marino hasn't missed many games. He makes no excuses.

"Whether I'm making $5 million, $4 million or $3 million, I'm going to enjoy the game, be competitive and always want to win," said Danny. "Those are my values. My work ethic is not going to change.

"You go out and play the game, show your talents, put yourself on the line. And you go out and play hard in a team game where the players are working together to try to accomplish a goal. It's a great feeling to be out there in that situation. Am I a pure passer? I'd say I can throw it as good as anyone who ever played. So if that's a pure passer, fine.

"If you ask any great player or great quarterback, there's a certain inner confidence that you're as good as anybody. But you can't say who is the absolute best. To be considered is special in itself.

"I think I can still throw the football as well as anybody and my knowledge of the game is better.

"Every year, individually, and as a team, I expect to be at the top. I always have that dream."

Jimmy Johnson, his coach in Miami, likens Marino's heart-felt enthusiasm for the game to that of boxers he has enjoyed through the years. "A lot of times it's not the guy that's got the most talent, but the guy that's got the most heart," Johnson said. "And he's had it for 16 years."

Johnson announced his retirement at the end of the 1998 season, but Marino was among those who talked him into reversing his field. Even though Marino isn't especially fond of Johnson — a detached, dictatorial sort — he didn't want to have to work with a new coach at this stage of his career. He had a year or two left, at tops, and still was seeking the Holy Grail.

"If it doesn't happen for me, I really don't think it will detract from my accomplishments," he said. "But I want to know that feeling. Personally, selfishly, I want to know what it feels like. I really believe we're this close."

He held two fingers an inch apart to make his point.

When it's over, how does Marino want to be remembered? "I haven't really talked about myself in that respect, but I'd like to be looked at as a team player. Just a guy who went out every week and tried to help the team. I'll be happy with my career, though. I've done stuff no one's ever done."

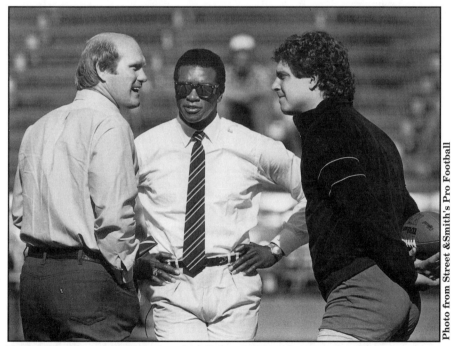

Photo from Street &Smith's Pro Football

Danny Marino, at right, enjoyed visit from network sports broadcasters, boyhood hero Terry Bradshaw and Ahmad Rashad, during his early years with the Dolphins.

Father Sam David
One of Doc Carlson's boys

"I never had the chance to say goodbye."
— Lou "Bimbo" Cecconi

A good man had left us. Father Sam David died peacefully in his sleep on a Saturday morning, May 8, 1999, at his home in the Pittsburgh suburb of Upper St. Clair.

That home is on the border of Bridgeville where, as a young man, he was a star high school basketball and baseball player. He went on to be the leading scorer for three seasons on the Pitt basketball team for Hall of Fame coach Doc Carlson in the late '40s.

"Doc Carlson was so demanding and difficult for me, at first," recalled Father Sam. "When I was on the team, I hated Doc Carlson. As I got older and matured, and realized what I had learned from the man, I grew to love him."

His teammates included two other good men, Lou "Bimbo" Cecconi, a former football coach at Pitt and later an athletic director and administrator at Steel Valley High School in Munhall, and Oland "Dodo" Canterna, also retired from his front office duties in the alumni office at St. Vincent College in Latrobe. Both all-around athletes, Cecconi came to Pitt from Donora and Canterna came from Freeport.

They were all kind, considerate individuals who shared a passion for people and sports. Their families were a reflection of their old-fashioned values.

They last played together in 1949 — 50 years earlier — at the Pavilion, a basketball court deep in the bowels of Pitt Stadium, and were among those Pitt alumni who were upset to hear about Pitt's plans to raze the stadium.

Canterna called Father Sam after I told him how ill his old teammate was, and he was planning on visiting him at his home within a week. I caught up with Canterna the evening of May 1 at the annual awards dinner of the Western Chapter of the Pennsylvania Sports Hall of Fame, held at the Sheraton at Warrendale.

Canterna, Cecconi and Father Sam were all enshrined at earlier dinners.

I tried to coordinate the visit to see Father Sam with Cecconi, but he was feeling poorly himself, facing surgery and a hospital stay the same week at Jefferson Medical Center. Cecconi talked to Canterna, but not to Father Sam.

"You just can't wait," said Cecconi, when I called to tell him about Father Sam's passing. "This makes you think. Oh, boy, I never had the chance to say goodbye."

Father Sam David, left, and wife, Janet, flank their daughter-in-law Sandy and their son, Joey, holding year-old grandson Jeremy.

"Whatever you send out to other people comes right back at you. They're called blessed boomerangs."
— Doc Carlson, Hall of Fame basketball coach University of Pittsburgh

Their college coach, Doc Carlson, often spoke about "blessed boomerangs," and how good things came back to you when you sent out good things to others. Dodo, Bimbo and Father Sam learned more than basketball at Doc Carlson's side.

Father Sam's son, Joey, followed in his footsteps, playing basketball at Pitt in the '80s. He was a starting guard, a high caliber performer on and off the court. His parents had taught him all the important things.

I visited Joey at his physical therapy clinic in Mt. Lebanon on a Friday morning at the end of April to have him check on some tendinitis in my left elbow. While there, I learned from Joey that his father, age 71, was in poor health. He was dying of congestive heart failure.

When I returned home that morning, I immediately called Father Sam. He and his family were long-time favorites of mine, and I wanted to talk to him. As Father Sam spoke, his words, as always, were profound. He has always had a calming effect on those he has touched with his kind manner and words.

He was a chemistry teacher and basketball coach at Chartiers Valley High School before he became an arch priest with the St. George Orthodox Church in Oakland, at Dawson and the Boulevard of the Allies, across the bridge from Schenley Park.

As Father Sam spoke to me on the telephone, I found myself grabbing some sheets of paper, almost instinctively, and writing down what he was saying. This may be the last time, I thought, I ever speak to him.

"I enjoyed good health most of my life," he said. "When I had my heart bypass surgery in 1988, that was the first time I was in the hospital.

"Things are rough for me right now, but I try to see each day as a bonus. I thank God for my life and the opportunity to do the things I wanted to do."

I asked him how his wife, Janet, was doing. She was a joyful woman who always complemented him so well. She was Janet Deep when they met, one of two girls and 13 boys in her family. "I thank my mother-in-law for having two girls and giving me one of them," said Father Sam, and you could see his smile in your mind's eye. "My bride keeps me going."

He was still seeing people from his church who called for him, to do a wedding, to do a funeral, to visit someone who was sick, to bless their home.

"They want to know if I can come out and do this or that," said Father Sam. "I don't feel up to it sometimes, but I hate to say 'no' to anyone."

He said he lost 35 to 40 pounds from his former 185 pounds, and felt poorly. "I have weak heart valves, and they're leaking," he said. "My doctors say there are no options remaining, not even a transplant. I'm told my heart's too weak. That hits you right between the eyes."

I could see those dark, liquid, always warm eyes, those dark brows, the dark tightly-curled hair. I remembered the time when my car went on the blink, and I was stranded on a road in Upper St. Clair several years ago, and Father Sam became my Good Samaritan. He picked me up and took me home.

I remembered when he called me to complain about something when I was doing publicity for the Pitt athletic department. He wanted to know why I couldn't get more publicity for Joey, who had just been named to the Big East All-Academic team.

I told him the media wasn't that interested in such items. "If Joey wants more publicity, he'll have to punch somebody in a bar in Oakland," I told Father Sam. Joey was just a good kid, no news there.

Joey had his own physical therapy clinic in Mt. Lebanon and was doing quite well. "I learned so much from my parents, and so did my three sons," said Joey David.

Father Sam talked about Joey, and his other son, Sam David of Bethel Park and his daughter, Daria Adams of McMurray, and his grandchildren. He said Daria was expecting another child. He was so proud of his family.

"I'll go on as long as God lets me," he said. "I can't be negative in my last days. This has been a beautiful month. I wake up and see the flowers in bloom, and I think I'm lucky. But unless you leave this earth, you can't go to heaven."

From the Mort Lerner photo collection

Pitt's top scorer for three seasons, Sam David, kneeling at far right first row in front of Coach Doc Carlson, in the Pavilion under Pitt Stadium where Panthers played their home games in late '30s. David's teammates included Dodo Canterna (8), Mort Lerner (16) and Bimbo Cecconi (13).

Curtis Martin
A class act

"Everything I do, God has given me the ability to do."

As a kid, Curtis Martin mistakenly thought he was a man. He was in a hurry to grow up and run with the fast crowd. He certainly had the inborn speed to keep up with them.

He had a thin beard at age 15 and looked older and he was able to get into Pittsburgh bars and clubs called Flirt's, the Strip's Edge and Forbes Studio. All hot spots at night. Curtis Martin was hot stuff, or at least he thought so. It took one frightful and fateful night to change his mind.

It was a night when he discovered he was running with the wrong crowd and in the wrong direction. All of a sudden, he was running scared. It led to a dramatic change in his lifestyle.

By reputation, this is one of the most solid citizens in the National Football League, a classy competitor in every respect. At age 25 in 1998, he was the star running back of the New York Jets and one of those responsible for putting them into the playoffs and creating the most excitement for the team since Joe Namath made good on his "guarantee" and beat the Baltimore Colts in the Super Bowl at the end of the 1969 season. It had been that long since the Jets had last won a divisional title.

Martin was dating Toni Braxton, a beautiful rhythm and blues singer who was performing on Broadway. He was seen with her on national TV in early 1998 when she won a Grammy Award at Madison Square Garden. They talked about that on the radio talk shows the next day back home in Pittsburgh. Was that our Curtis Martin with Toni Braxton? Nah. Yeah. Get out...

He was a handsome and rich young man in "The Big Apple," yet he remained humble. He continued to come back home to Pittsburgh during the off-season and spend time helping disadvantaged kids on the inner-city playgrounds find their way.

"That's what makes my heart sing, helping other people," said Martin, a happy guy who often seems too good to be true. "I want to know I served God like no other man."

If Curtis Martin sounds too good to be true let's just pray that he stays that way. He received national attention late in his rookie season when he attended the birthday party of a 9-year-old Patriots fan, Michael Plaschnik, simply because the kid stopped him in the parking lot outside Foxboro Stadium and invited him. You can only imagine how the kids reacted when Martin showed up at a popular sports bar/restaurant in Boston called the Charlie Horse for the birthday party.

Curtis Martin and his mother, Rochella, admire his new No. 28 jersey with New York Jets soon after he departed Patriots in favor of rejoining Coach Bill Parcells. Martin quickly became a fans' favorite in New York.

> *"There are so many dreams I've yet to find. But you're so far away. Doesn't anybody stay in one place anymore?"*
> — singer Carol King

Photos courtesy of Al Pereira/New York Jets

Martin wanted to be like Michael Jordan as far as being a positive influence on young people.

"Athletes have a great influence, and for him to be the best athlete, I believe he had the greatest influence on people, on kids," said Martin. "If someone, one of my sports heroes, would have come to me as a youngster and could have helped me and steered me, I could have saved myself a lot of heartache and my parents heartache, I could have lived a safer life and a more focused life. I may have done better in school or in a lot of different areas. When I go back to Homewood now, it's fulfilling to know that you can actually impact the future of a child. We have that power."

Curtis Martin was a good role model. He had been making all the right moves. His mother and biggest fan, Rochella Martin, had known great tragedy and disappointment in her life. She and her husband, Curtis Martin, had their only child May 1, 1973, and Curtis Sr. left soon after and Rochella and her family raised her son. Her mother and sister were killed — one in a robbery and the other in an auto accident — when Curtis was a kid. Rochella and her son remained close, and their love and concern for each other has paid rich dividends.

Anybody who grows up in Homewood is familiar with heartache. John Wideman, who used his talent as a basketball player to go from Peabody High School to the University of Pennsylvania in the late '50s, has written several books about growing up in Homewood which I have read. Wideman won national awards and honors for his writing — he made the most of all his opportunities — yet his own brother and son were imprisoned for killing people. Wideman writes out of anger.

Curtis Martin seems to be more of an optimist.

"I know what type of player Curtis is."
— Bill Parcells

Curtis Martin made another bold move in 1995. He could have stayed at Pitt and played one more year for Johnny Majors to strengthen his credentials and prove to the pros that he had the right stuff and the strength and durability to run with the big boys, but he chose not to come back to school.

A lot of people, including Majors, this author and Tom Donahoe, director of football operations for the Pittsburgh Steelers, thought Martin was making a mistake. We were wrong. We all knew he had ability, but we thought he needed to put a great season under his belt to be properly appreciated by the pros, and to be ready for that challenge.

Martin was drafted in the third round by the New England Patriots and turned out to be the steal of the year. He had a record-breaking season and was named the NFL's Offensive Rookie of the

Year. Had he stayed at Pitt, the Panthers might have fared better than their 2-9 record, and Majors might have bought himself another year as coach.

Martin might have made them more respectable, he might have been an All-American, the way Ruben Brown had been the year before on a 3-8 team. He might have been drafted higher, and signed to a much bigger contract. But Martin was happy with the way things turned out for him. The way he went from being a Dragon to a Panther to a Patriot and then a Jet was the stuff of wild boyhood dreams.

In his second pro season, he helped the Patriots defeat the Steelers in an AFC playoff game in the fog at Foxboro Stadium, and get to Super Bowl XXXI where the Patriots lost to the Green Bay Packers.

It may have taken Martin a little longer to make the big money, but he's not looking back. He was one of only eight running backs in the history of the NFL to gain over 1,000 yards in each of his first three seasons. Then he signed in April, 1998 as a restricted free agent with the New York Jets. And again he rushed for over 1,000 yards. He was only the sixth running back in NFL history to do that in his first four seasons.

Going to the Jets enabled him to be reunited with Bill Parcells, one of the top turnaround coaches in league history. Parcells had been his coach when the Patriots picked him and during his first two seasons in the league. Martin says Parcells has had a great influence on his life.

Martin and Parcells joined forces to help spark the Jets to a 12-4 record, the best in the team's history. Parcells had turned in a 9-7 report card his first year on the job. The Jets were 1-15 the year before that. What a turnaround in just two years. Parcells had won two Super Bowls with the New York Giants in 1986 and 1990. He was only the third coach in NFL history to take three different teams to the playoffs.

Parcells was putting his reputation on the line when he convinced the club leaders to offer Martin a contract when he was up for grabs.

To get Martin, the Jets sent the Patriots a first and third-round pick in the 1998 draft and signed Martin to a six-year $36 million contract. No one has to worry about how much money Martin is making anymore.

He had received $275,000 the previous season in New England. He played for the minimum salary for three seasons, and had failed at attempts to have his contract renegotiated. That's why it wasn't difficult for him to leave New England in favor of New York. Playing for Parcells again was also an attractive magnet to move.

"Bill, to me, is somewhat of a mentor-coach," Martin said. "I always tried to please him. He helps me get the most out of my talent."

At 5-11, 210 pounds, Martin was a runner of uncommon ability, in his own words, "a combination of explosiveness and elusiveness," and Parcells knew what the package promised.

"Every once in a while in my business," said Parcells, "you meet a young man who convinces you by his actions that he aspires to accomplish all the things his God-given talent will allow him to accomplish. When that happens to a coach, it ignites that flame in you to try to give all you can."

"It was easy to be in the wrong place at the wrong time."
— Curtis Martin

None of that might have been possible if Martin had not made a decision on that dark night when he nearly got killed by hanging around the wrong night spots, in dangerous places. It was a life-changing event for a young man who still had a lot of growing up to do, and had been lucky enough to escape with his life — finding an opening and running to it — which was the beginning of the development of a beautiful young man. Some of his boyhood friends were not so lucky.

Martin was hiding behind a car outside a bar in Pittsburgh. He never stayed closer to a blocking guard in his life as he did to that car that night. He didn't like the noise nearby. Bam. Bam. Bam. Somebody was shooting a gun; he had heard the sound before in his boyhood neighborhood in the Homewood section of Pittsburgh, a predominantly black lower income neighborhood in the city's east end. He had seen some of his best friends and kids he knew in the neighborhood with their chests ripped open by bullets, and he was certain he didn't want that happening to him. He didn't want his mother getting a telephone call that her son had been shot dead in the street. One of his best friends had been shot and killed that way.

"Just being from the neighborhood where I was from it was easy to be in the wrong place at the wrong time," he said.

Martin wished he was any place but behind that car outside that bar. Bam. Bam. Bam. Martin had walked out of the club moments earlier and into the middle of a dispute. That's when the music stopped and the shooting started. Martin was standing next to a man who was screaming at another man across the street. Suddenly both men drew guns, just like in the Old West. One of them fired a shot. The bullet glanced off the sidewalk and just missed Martin and that's when he ran behind a car. More shots were fired. Then there was a man at Martin's side, hiding behind that same car. Martin said something to him. "Why can't we come to a club without someone shooting?"

Then Martin sized up the man next to him. He recognized him as the man he had seen standing across the street with the gun at the start of the skirmish. The man was holding his gun; the gun was next to Martin's foot.

Martin decided it was time to be a running back. He came out of a crouch and took off. Full speed. Like a bullet. "I'm thinking, 'Don't let anyone think I'm the guy with the gun and shoot at me," Martin remembered.

That was the end of Martin being a frequent traveler on the night scene in Pittsburgh. Or in any city, for that matter. He had been doing it since he was 15. At that age, on an occasion when his mother was out of town, he borrowed her Cadillac Seville, and took his friends on a spin about the city's night spots. He was a good-looking dude who took pride in his appearance. He and his mother both wore good clothes, sometimes tailor-made; she worked at different jobs to get the money. She was a registered nurse, but did other tasks to make more money. She had moved them to a safer neighborhood in Point Breeze. Curtis said he spent 15 minutes brushing his teeth in those days, just to look his best.

Looking good was the most important thing in his life. Having fun was a close second. After escaping that shooting incident that night with his life intact, he had a life conversion. "I thought that there must be something more to life than this," said Martin.

"He's going to be one of the all-timers."
— Levon Kirkland

Martin was the subject of many run-to-success stories that were written and published during the 1995 football season. Many suggested he had played only one year of high school football before coming to Pitt in 1991. But he had played midget football for several years in his youth in Homewood, started to play his freshman year at Penn Hills High School and as a sophomore at Allderdice High School in the Squirrel Hill section of Pittsburgh, but injuries and lack of interest kept him out of the lineup. He came into his own as a senior at Allderdice and gained all-state honors for his efforts. That is when Pitt paid a call and offered a scholarship.

One of my proteges, Doug Miller, the assistant director of public relations for the New York Jets, hails from my neighborhood in Upper St. Clair and attended the University of Pittsburgh where he worked in the sports information office for two years. He was the third assistant I sent to the Jets' public relations office over a ten-year period.

"One's first book, kiss or home run is always the best."
— Clifton Fadiman, Essayist, anthologist

Miller was working in the Pitt sports information office when the Panthers offered Martin a scholarship. "What he was doing at Alllderdice was almost unheard of in this football hotbed," said Miller. "There was such an air about it. He was the next great player to come out of Pittsburgh after Tony Dorsett, Hugh Green, Dan Marino and Bill Fralic. He was an unassuming, polite kid from a very tough part of town. People were wondering if he was for real. Nobody had heard of him before that year."

Miller and Martin have a lot in common and get along well. "What a great guy and what a great player," Miller wrote in a letter he sent me in February, 1999.

"He certainly has the respect of all his teammates, coaches and office staff for his abilities and his high character. You've picked a real winner to write about."

Martin showed signs at Pitt of being a pretty special young man, on and off the field, barometers in looking back that hinted that he had the kind of talent and soul to do some of the wonderful things he would do in the pro ranks.

At the start of his senior season in 1994, Martin rambled for 251 yards against Texas in the opening game of the season at Pitt Stadium. Pitt lost an exciting contest, 30-28, but Martin left quite an impression on people in the press box, which included some Steelers scouts and this reporter. He hurt his ankle in the next game at Pitt Stadium against Ohio University, and never played again that year. Martin said he was ready to resume playing with four games left in the season, but Billy West was running wild as a sophomore in his place, and Majors wanted to keep Martin on the back burner so he would be eligible for a medical red-shirt from the NCAA. Majors was hopeful that Martin would return to play another season at Pitt.

Majors was desperately trying to rebuild a Pitt football program which had fallen on hard times. Majors had worked magic and won a national championship in 1976 with a great running back named Tony Dorsett. Now, on his second attempt at putting Pitt back into the national forefront, he wanted Martin to remain at Pitt and help him turn things around. Who could blame him? He thought it best for Martin, too, because Martin had missed so many games and many pro scouts were skeptical about his durability. They had not seen enough of him, even though he also had some great games as a sophomore and junior — he missed only one game that year — to be sure in their judgments. Though some say you only need to see a gifted back once to know he's something special, and some scouts always want to see the player at least one more time before they certify their scouting report.

I remember sitting at a dining table across from Majors at a party at WTAE studios to celebrate the 25th anniversary of sportscaster Myron Cope's association with the radio station, and talking about Martin before the NFL draft in 1995.

306

I suggested to Majors that somebody ought to tell Martin about what had happened to most of the running backs in recent years who had dropped out of Pitt with eligibility remaining to take an early fling at pro football.

They included Craig Heyward, Charles Gladman, Brian Davis and Curvin Richards. They were among the most gifted running backs in the school's history and all had pro potential. Davis flunked out; the others left on their own. Only Heyward made it, and he had more than his share of personal difficulties before he found himself. Majors took note of that, thinking it might give him some ammunition to make Martin realize he might be making a mistake in turning pro earlier than he had to, and perhaps before he was ready.

I offered another thought to Majors. "When I read all the reasons he should stay," I said, "I have never seen anything about how it might enable him to get his college degree. That should mean something, too."

Majors wagged his head. "He hates school," he said. "He doesn't want to go to class. That's been a problem."

What did we know? As it turned out, Martin was more than ready. It hurt Pitt's chances that he didn't stay, but it certainly worked out well for Martin. And, in many ways, he had a maturity and sense of perspective about him that many college graduates never acquire.

And Steelers scouts can only wonder whether once again — Danny Marino comes to mind — they had blown an opportunity to pick up a truly once-in-a-lifetime player right in their own backyard. Like Marino, Martin was a homegrown product, a Pittsburgh Kid in the truest sense. It was difficult to fault the Steelers' first three selections: tight end Mark Bruener, quarterback/receiver Kordell Stewart, offensive guard Brendan Stai. Bruener and Stai became starters at mid-season. Stewart slashed his way to national attention with his versatile triple-threat, make that quadruple-threat, talents (passing, catching, running and punting). But time might show that Martin would have been a better choice, even if a risky one because of an incomplete grade owing to his limited play at Pitt. Martin was more productive and consistent than any of those Steelers selections in his first four years in the NFL.

If there was any doubt about Martin's ability, he certainly erased it as a rookie with his performance in the next-to-the-last game of the regular season on a Saturday afternoon, December 16, 1995, against the Steelers at Three Rivers Stadium.

Martin resembled Dorsett as he darted here, there and everywhere, slipping away from this Steelers' defender and that Steelers' defender, showing the kind of speed and elusiveness of the special running backs. He carried the ball 20 times for 120 yards and he caught six passes for 62 more yards and a touchdown. Those of us who thought he should have stayed at Pitt felt pretty foolish.

The Steelers won, 41-27, so most Pittsburgh fans were pleased that Martin had such a tremendous day playing for the opposing

Patriots. Most Pittsburghers root for Marino in a similar manner, as long as the Steelers defeat the Miami Dolphins. Marino had a great game the year before at Three Rivers, but the Steelers won, which is a win-win parlay.

Many in the Steelers' locker room conceded that Martin was a most impressive rookie.

"I can't speak for the rest of the defense," said Steelers' lineman Ray Seals, "but in my opinion, he played the best against us. We had some other backs who were good, but he had the best overall game against us."

Levon Kirkland commented, "He's very slippery. If he continues doing what he's doing, stays humble and keeps working, he's going to be one of the all-timers."

Steelers' coach Bill Cowher, a Pittsburgh Kid himself, could appreciate Martin's performance, since his club had escaped with a victory. "He's a good back and he's good people," said Cowher. "I'm happy for him and I'm happy we don't have to play him again."

Martin was not satisfied. He had found over 100 tickets to take care of family and friends, and he wanted to come away a winner in every respect. Except for the score, he did. "We didn't win the game so it's nothing," said Martin of his performance. "What good is it?"

At season's end, Martin had convinced all the skeptics that he was the genuine article. He had been the 10th running back selected in the NFL draft, but he outdid them all. Top draft choice KiJana Carter of Penn State missed the entire season with the Cincinnati Bengals because of a knee injury. And Martin outran Heisman Trophy winner Rashaan Salaam of the Chicago Bears, most of the veterans in the NFL, and everyone else in the AFC.

Martin ended up being named the NFL's Offensive Rookie of the Year by The Associated Press. "My role when I came in was just to make the team," said Martin. "I felt that if I didn't hold anything back and stayed healthy, everything would take care of itself."

Martin scored 14 touchdowns and gained 1,487 yards to lead the AFC in rushing. It was the most rushing yards by a first-year back since Eric Dickerson had 1,808 with the Los Angeles Rams in 1983.

"I don't even know what records I set," said Martin. "After the games, if they tell me what records I set, then that's fine. But right now, I'm just trying to give my all to the team. I'm not worried about stats, I just want to win.

"And money is no issue to me. Not that I have an overabundance of money, but I can live comfortable or however. It doesn't matter to me how many hundreds of thousands or millions or whatever in terms of money I make. That's not an issue in my life anymore. I feel it used to be, but now it's not."

"He's a phenomenal back."
— Johnny Majors

Johnny Majors knew a great running back when he saw one. When he became the head coach at the University of Pittsburgh in 1973, the first prospect he visited was Tony Dorsett at his home in Hopewell Township, out by Aliquippa. Foge Fazio took him there.

Together, Majors and Dorsett did something that had never been done before. They brought about the biggest turnaround in any major college football program, and Dorsett was the single biggest factor in Pitt's success. Pitt was 1-10 the year before Majors and Dorsett showed up on the campus. They went 6-5-1 the first year, including a Fiesta Bowl appearance. Majors was named the College Coach of the Year.

Then they went 7-4, 8-4 and, in Dorsett's senior season, they went undefeated, 12-0, and won the national championship. Dorsett won the Heisman Trophy as the nation's outstanding football player. To appreciate his impact on the program, consider this: Gil Brandt, the draft guru of the Dallas Cowboys in those days, pointed out that Dorsett was the only Pitt player taken that year in the first six rounds of the NFL draft.

Majors returned to his alma mater, the University of Tennessee, the following season, which he now admits was a mistake. Pitt had great success the next five seasons under Jackie Sherrill, and for two seasons under Foge Fazio, then things fell apart. Mike Gottfried and Paul Hackett weren't the answer, so Pitt called upon Majors to come back and return Pitt to its once-proud national prominence. Had Majors remained in the first place, Pitt might have maintained the kind of excellence over a long period as Joe Paterno accomplished at Penn State.

In Majors' first outing in his second go-round at Pitt, the Panthers upset Southern Mississippi, 14-10, in a nationally-televised 1993 opener. Martin accounted for both touchdowns while rushing for 68 yards on 21 carries. "He did a great job tonight," said Majors. "Whatever it takes to win, Martin did it."

Martin also had seven receptions for 84 yards, including the game-winning touchdown. Martin had hobbled through the 1992 season with an Achilles' tendon problem, and had worked hard during the summer to get ready for his junior season. He had always hated weight training, but he got into the spirit of things to properly prepare himself for the 1993 season.

Martin liked his new coach. "At first, I didn't know what to expect," said Martin. "Now that he's been here for awhile I really like him. He has really motivated us. The discipline he commands is good for us."

Before that season even started, Martin had demonstrated that he was a special young man. He had not forgotten where he came from, and he often returned to Homewood — as often as two or three times a week while he was at Pitt — to work with the kids who played in the same midget football league where he had gotten his start.

Martin spoke to Shelly Anderson, the beat reporter for the *Pittsburgh Post-Gazette*, about his ties to his hometown. During a break at Pitt's training camp at Johnstown before the 1994 season, Martin talked about his thoughts when watching the kids at play in the midget football league.

"It's amazing to see how small I used to be and how I used to run around there," he said. "I take them under my wing sometimes, show them some techniques. A lot of them look up to people from the community who are doing something positive. They see me as a positive role model.

"I like to encourage them and follow them because there's a lot of people who have the talent to do it, but never do it. That's just about the situation I was in."

Martin told Anderson he had played for midget football league teams in Duquesne, McKeesport and Wilkinsburg. But after three years, he walked away from football. Nobody was pushing him to stay with it.

He played a little basketball and flirted with football at Allderdice High School, but was bugged by physical hurts of one kind or another, and simply had no real direction. Mark Wittgartner, the football coach, recruited him in the school hallways. It was a long process to convince Curtis Martin that he had the makings of a good high school athlete.

Allderdice is my alma mater, and I had played for several midget football teams in my hometown of Hazelwood, so this was all familiar territory. One year, in the mid-'50s, our Hazelwood Steelers team tied for the city midget football championship with the Homewood Scorpions, a team that was a feeder to Pete Dimperio's string of City League championships at Westinghouse High School. So I have always been a fan of Martin, being so familiar with where he came from, having similar roots.

Martin was grateful for Wittgartner's persistence and for the opportunity he provided a senior who seemed to be going nowhere with his athletic or academic life. "He just kept asking me and asking me," Martin remembered. "Finally, I said I would play for my 12th grade year. I got out there, and it must have been meant for me to play because I had a lot of success that year. I'm very happy I played."

Martin often made references to a greater power determining his actions, opening doors for him. He truly believed that God was his pulling guard, leading the way to daylight.

In that single season, Martin rushed for 1,705 yards on 229 carries, scored 20 touchdowns in 11 games and made the All-State football team. His coaches preached some things that would serve him in good stead in his career. "My high school coaches always told me a good back performs best when he's under pressure."

310

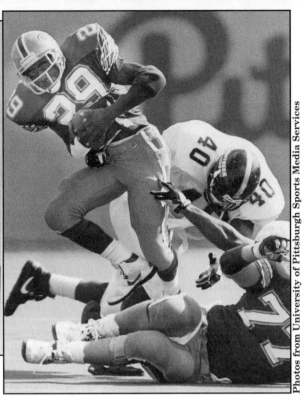

Photos from University of Pittsburgh Sports Media Services

Curtis Martin

During his Pitt days, Curtis Martin enjoyed sideline visits with NFLers such as his boyhood hero, Tony Dorsett, and (shown below) Mike Ditka, two of the Panthers' many All-America alumni.

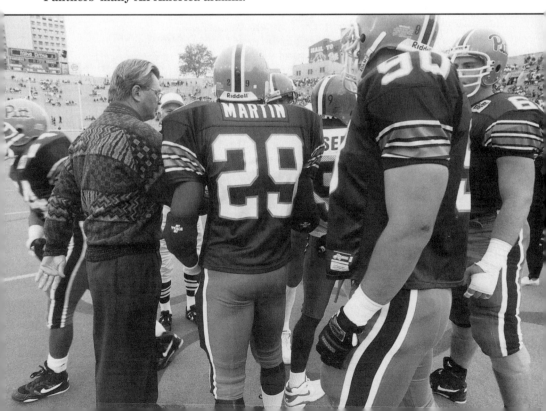

"I'd pull my socks all the way up like Tony Dorsett did."
— Curtis Martin

Martin was a toddler when his hometown pro team, the Pittsburgh Steelers, was the best in pro football. Yet, strangely enough, he looked elsewhere for models in his midget football league days. Franco Harris and Rocky Bleier were running the ball for the Steelers, but they were not the men Martin emulated.

"The guys I tried to pattern myself after," said Martin, "were Tony Dorsett, Eric Dickerson and Walter Payton. I tried to run like them and I even tried to wear my equipment like them.

"Tony's son (Anthony Dorsett Jr.) went to Pitt with me, and Tony was always one of my all-time heroes. I met him a few times and I always tried to talk to him and he'd give me tips about running. He came to a lot of our games to watch his son, but I got a lot of his attention, too. He'd tell me to do this and do that and it was great.

"When I was playing midget football, I made sure I had Eric Dickerson's number (29), and I even tried to wear my face mask like him and I'd wear my elbow pads like him and I'd pull my socks all the way up like Tony Dorsett did. That's what I was trying to do...be like Eric Dickerson and Tony Dorsett."

Pitt paid tribute to Tony Dorsett at its home opener in the 1994 season. He was honored at halftime. He had been honored that summer by induction into both the College Football of Fame and the Pro Football Hall of Fame. He was the only running back to lead his college team to a national championship and his pro team, the Dallas Cowboys, to an NFL title in consecutive seasons.

Martin maintained that he drew special spirit that day from Dorsett, who spoke to him at different intervals during the game. That was the day Martin gained 251 yards rushing in an exciting loss to Texas, 30-28. "He said to me at one time, 'Keep it up,' and I broke one on the next play," Martin said. "He's my idol. He's always been my idol, and it helped to have him at my side."

Majors pronounced Martin "a phenomenal back" following that game, which would be Martin's last complete game of the season. "Every great back is different," said Majors. "What sets Curtis apart is the way he goes into a pile and comes out of the pile." That was usually on the other side of the pile. The following week, he injured his ankle in a pileup during the Ohio University game. Scar tissue from an earlier injury complicated the recovery process. By mid-season, most people thought Martin would be shelved and red-shirted. Pitt was getting some good recruits and it was thought Martin could come back to be the cornerstone for the 1995 Pitt football team.

Martin wanted to resume playing in the 1994 season. He wanted to help Pitt finish on a strong note, he wanted to show the pros he was sound, and that he had the right stuff to merit their attention. He had made up his mind he wanted to turn pro. He grew impatient. A rift developed. Before one practice, strangely, Martin found his dressing room stall at Pitt Stadium had been cleaned out. His mother still seethes and rants about that. He gradually pieced his things back together again, and went on to the practice field. He did not complain.

He still doesn't. He doesn't like to discuss his situation at Pitt. "I don't like to bad-mouth anybody, I'd just rather not talk about it," he insisted.

His mother, Rochella Martin, is not as diplomatic as her son. I met Ms. Martin the first time during the Christmas-shopping season of 1995 at the Ross Park Shopping Mall. She was wearing a handsome New England Patriots leather jacket. Several Steelers were doing some shopping at the same mall that night. It was a few nights after her son had starred in a Patriots' loss to the Steelers at Three Rivers Stadium. She said some of the Steelers had spooked her before the game, telling her what they were going to do to her son in the ballgame. Ms. Martin wasn't sure they were kidding. I remembered seeing Ms. Martin in the stands at Pitt Stadium when her son was playing there. She cheered and carried on a lot, and stood out from the crowd in the section just behind Pitt's bench. There was nothing shy about Rochella Martin.

I mentioned Pitt and Majors to her, and she went into a tirade. "Don't mention that man to me," she said, knitting her eyebrows. She went into a long litany of complaints about Pitt's treatment of her son. "A lot of men could not have gone through what my son did," she said. "My son is 22. But he is far beyond some people twice his age."

Back in 1982, when Curtis was just nine years old, Rochella found her mother sprawled on a bed, a knife stuck so deeply in her chest that it penetrated the mattress beneath her body. It's a scene that still comes to mind, haunting her. No one ever solved the robbery/murder.

Rochella and her mother had been raising Curtis. Rochella had been a single parent since Curtis was three years old. "If you get sick," Curtis asked his mother at the time, "who's going to raise me?"

Seated on a plastic chair in Rochella's New and Used Clothing Store on Penn Avenue in Wilkinsburg, Rochella remembered how she felt at the time of that family nightmare. "I never wanted anybody to raise my child but me," she said. "By him saying that, it actually pulled me together. It was the only thing in the world that kept me from losing my sanity."

Earlier on, she had lost a sister in an auto accident. Rochella did whatever she had to do to make ends meet, and to make sure she raised Curtis in a proper environment.

She worked as many as four jobs at the same time and always made sure her son looked good when he went off to school each day. "I wanted him to be perfect when he left the house," she recalled, "because that reflects on you."

Still, she worried. She didn't want to lose her son to the streets, she didn't want to lose him the way she lost her sister and mother to the madness. "You hope, you hope, and you hope," she said. "It seems like there was never a minute of relaxing. Never." In truth, every day she feared for her son's life.

"I thought that the life I was living, in my mind, death was inevitable," said Curtis Martin, "just because you see it so much. You can be the most innocent person, and it can grab you."

That point was brought home once again in February of 1999 when Ebony Patterson, a 17-year-old senior student at Westinghouse High School, was shot in the head and killed as she was coming home from school, an innocent bystander, by a teen from Penn Hills who was shooting from a passing automobile at someone nearby.

Curtis bought his mother a nice home in the North Hills of Pittsburgh, and urged her to close her store, sandwiched between a dreary-looking bar and a print shop on Penn Avenue, and stay out of the inner-city for her own safety.

Rochella, 52 at the time her son signed with the Jets, was pleased that her son took such an interest in her, calling her on the telephone frequently from New York. They wrote to each other, and often exchanged Biblical messages.

"My mother had given Curt a $2 bill, and had written on it, 'To Curt, from Grandma — God bless you.'" she said. "He kept it with him forever, wherever he went he used to have it in his sock. I have it now in my drawer. When something happens like that (her mother's tragic death), it's so easy to just slip away. I tell people that maybe God sent him to me because down the line, this was going to happen.

"We were blessed, we know we're blessed and I thank God my son and my life turned out the way it has."

"I live by what I say."
— Curtis Martin

Martin was his own man, which is not always easy if you want to be one of the boys on the pro football scene. But Martin didn't run with the pack anymore. His mother helped him learn how to go his own way, the right way.

"I think that's where I'm different from a lot of people," said Martin. "I live by what I say. I don't have a desire to be in those places anymore. I'm into being committed to God and obeying His law and His rules. I see how much better my life is now.

"A few guys on the team have asked me to go out, but I really don't go out much. I don't drink. I've never been a heavy drinker. I might have had a cooler or something before, but I don't have that now. I don't choose to follow that type of crowd anymore."

He used to like rap music, but was more into gospel these days. He said he read his Bible daily.

"I just do what I like to do. I don't need that much, but that doesn't mean I'm not having fun."

Much of Martin's mental approach to being a pro athlete was fostered by his mother, who did her best to steer him clear of trouble in his youth, and still liked to run interference for him.

Rochella Martin was a proud mother. She always wore something that boasted that she was the mother of Curtis Martin, that the New England Patriots and then the New York Jets were her favorite pro football team.

In his youth, Martin was expected to be at home at night. His mother might call at any time from her different jobs. There were some household rules. One was that dirty dishes were to be cleaned, even one dirty dish, and put away.

His buddies thought his mother was a monster, she was so demanding. Even Rochella Martin has told her son in recent years that she might have been too tough on him, but she did what she did because she didn't want anything bad to happen to him.

Her son was always a sweetheart. She remembered him bugging her for $25 and then turning around and giving it to a man living under a bridge in Pittsburgh.

"Curt does some things, giving-wise, that I don't think I could do," said his mother. "I'm serious. There is nothing too valuable to him that he couldn't give to someone else."

One of Martin's boyhood buddies was Lawrence Jackson, who was a running back at Edinboro University, about a two-and-a-half hour drive north of Pittsburgh. Jackson often said something under his breath when he caught the wrath of Ms. Martin. But, as he grew older, he learned to appreciate her positive impact on her son's life.

"Curt learned how to be responsible from Ms. Martin," Jackson said. "She had to be the mother and the father. She had to show him not to be a punk. This generation needs more people like her because no one is raised that way anymore. If you hit a child now, everyone is like, 'She's a bad mother.' But now Ms. Martin is laidback because her job is done. She raised a man."

Mark Wittgartner was not the only person responsible for getting Curtis to come out for the Allderdice football team in his senior season. He had a little help from Ms. Martin.

"You're getting to be a senior," she told her son. "You can't go to school, come home and do nothing. You've got to get out of here. By tomorrow, I want you to be part of somebody's club, team or band." And that was how Allderdice got an all-state football player.

Allderdice doesn't have much of a football tradition, by the way, not like Westinghouse. Allderdice usually turned out good teams in tennis, golf, chess and sometimes baseball and basketball, but seldom had success in football.

Martin also became a born-again Christian at that time, and he believed it was a saving grace.

"I got to see a lot of buddies killed," he said of his days in Homewood. "I saw so many of my friends get their chests blown open or get sent away or bad things happen to them. I kept seeing this and I kept seeing it again and again and I'd be thinking, 'This could be me.'"

"He's so honest."
— Bill Parcells

Bill Parcells, the head coach of the New York Jets, said, "You meet very few kids like this kid nowadays. He's so honest, sometimes you get a little suspicious. It's kind of a refreshing thing.

"There are some guys out there these days who think they're better than they are. He's just all business. He worked hard in camp, he didn't miss any time, he's attentive, he studies.

"When we drafted him, I told him he would have the opportunity to play if he took advantage of it. He's done everything he's been asked to do. As a result, I feel like he's not only capable of playing, he's mentally geared and wants to play."

Parcells came out with a book in 1995 called *Finding A Way To Win*. Parcells offered some suggestions for getting the most out of an employee, from a pat on the back to a kick in the backside. You just had to know which button to push.

Midway through the season, after Martin had picked up 127 yards against the Buffalo Bills on October 23 in leading the Patriots to a 27-14 victory, Parcells approached him in the locker room.

"Well, you looked good for the first three quarters, but the fourth quarter it looked like you were running out of gas," Parcells told Martin.

That hit home with Martin. Martin started working even harder during the week, especially in the weight room, trying to build up his stamina. "It's almost like he challenges me with some little comment that he makes," said Martin. "I'm the type of person who never takes anything negatively. I let that motivate me. So I said to him, 'Well, I'll make sure the next time it doesn't look that way.'"

Two games later, Martin rushed for 166 yards, 22 of those yards came in the fourth quarter, including a 14-yard touchdown burst, in a 20-7 victory over the New York Jets. "That's become a goal for me, to show him and to just be ready and have the stamina and the endurance to do well, even in the fourth quarter, with a lot of carries in the ballgame," said Martin. "I love to carry the ball. I'd rather get it 40 times a game. I feel I get stronger and stronger and better and better the more I carry the ball."

Martin found all the inspiration he needed from a different book — The Bible — than the one Parcells put out. While he did not practice any particular religion, Martin said "I just follow The Bible. I focus on God. My mind doesn't even think about getting big-headed. I'm just grateful that I'm in this position. I feel truly blessed.

"I know a lot of people didn't believe what I believed. A lot of people might think I'm even crazy for saying the things I say. But it's just what I believe. I have faith in God that I can accomplish anything with Him."

When Martin felt tired in the late going, he got on himself. "When I get tired, and I'm feeling weak, I'm just out there saying, 'God, give me the strength to make this run.' Then I know I'll get a little rest and I'll be ready for the next one. I'll say, 'Give me the strength to get the first down or make a nice run.'"

Parcells was pleased to see that Martin had gotten his message, subtle or not so subtle. "You cannot help but be pleased with him," said Parcells in mid-December of 1995. "I think he's finding his way. He's really done a terrific job. And, as I've said, he seems to be strong."

Another bit of Parcell's philosophy to be found in his book is that if you're not improving then you're standing still. Martin spent a lot of time reviewing game tapes.

"I believe that helps me," said Martin. "When I get to watch the film, it will make me see the little things I could have done. I'll try to do those little things the next game. It definitely helps me not just to watch myself, but to watch other runners as well. It's not that I'm never satisfied, but it's just that I'm always trying to get better. I never like to stay at a standstill."

Martin demonstrated his strong resolve in a late-season 31-28 victory over the Jets when he was playing for the Patriots. On second and goal from the Jets' 1-yard line, Martin was stuffed on a quick hit into the line. Jets' linebacker Marvin Jones delivered a shot that stunned Martin. His mask was bent and he ended up with turf in his mouth.

"It may have been the hardest hit I took all year," said Martin, with more than a hint of pride. "We hit and my helmet exploded. It took all of the air out of my helmet. I just wanted to come back and make up for that. I don't like to take a hard hit and lose. Jones said something to me after the hit but I wasn't going to give him the satisfaction of answering. He had been growling at me all afternoon."

Martin was whoozy, but he was reluctant to leave the game. "And I had to get the ball on the next play, so I tried to shake it off. To me, that's a challenge and I don't like to lose one-on-one in the hole like that. He got the best of it the first time and I just said there's no way I'm not going to score the second time."

And Martin did just that. He took the handoff from quarterback Drew Bledsoe, took two steps and then leaped toward the end zone. He was hit by one Jet tackler, spun, was hit by another tackler, twisted and turned and knifed his way into the end zone.

That stretched the Patriots' lead to 10 points (31-21) and it gave them the insurance to hold on to a 31-28 victory.

"When I got back to the sideline they tried to put some air back in the helmet," recalled Martin. "They couldn't do it. It had been flattened."

"You can't play with those big dudes."
— A friend of Curtis Martin

Curtis Martin used to make his friends smile when he spoke about his desire to someday play pro football. Even his step-father told him he shouldn't waste his time on such dreams. "I remember," said Martin during his rookie season, "we went to a Steeler game two years ago. I said, 'I can do that.' We were watching Barry Foster. The hole opened and he didn't take it. He should have hit that hole."

When Martin said he would have hit the hole, his pals cautioned him on his know-how. "That's a whole different thing, you can't play with those big dudes," Martin remembered one of them saying.

After he ran for 170 yards on 34 carries against the Jets, Martin reminded his step-father, Robert Gibson, during a telephone conversation about some of the doubting things he had said that day when they were in the stands at Three Rivers Stadium watching Barry Foster and the Steelers in action.

"He just said, 'That's good, you're blessed.'"

The remark was something Martin could accept. "I prayed for this and it happened," he often said.

Curtis Martin (No. 29) lines up at tailback against Ohio State in early 1993 home contest at Pitt Stadium.

Roy Rogers
Riding those happy trails

A hero on the silver screen

A radio announcer informs you that Roy Rogers has died, and bam-bam, there goes another chunk of your childhood. Roy Rogers was a real star, a good guy. He carried two shiny six-shooters, but he never shot anybody.

He just shot the guns out of their hands and he did it, miraculously, without even drawing a drop of blood. This was definitely a more innocent era in our lives. He rode his horse, the beautiful golden palomino, Trigger, into the sunset. And he and his wife, Dale Evans, sang "Happy Trails To You." Now, at 86, he was gone for good, another movie star who left us in 1998.

When he got really upset, Roy Rogers, would say "Shucks," or something even milder. We didn't learn anything bad from Roy Rogers.

I remember riding home from the Hazelwood Theater with my buddies after seeing a movie with Roy Rogers. We rode our horses home. We sought out dirt alleys, empty lots and hillsides, which seemed more appropriate for riding our horses. You put your hands out in front of your chest like you were holding the reins of a horse, and that's all you had to do.

You also imagined you were wearing the kind of rhinestone cowboy clothes that Rogers favored. We also had Hopalong Cassady and the Lone Ranger and Randolph Scott. I even liked pretending I was Cochise and Geronimo. They were all different kinds of western stars than Clint Eastwood.

So I was excited when I had a chance to meet Roy Rogers in the flesh back in 1986 when he came to Pittsburgh.

I was working as the assistant athletic director for sports information at the University of Pittsburgh. The school was marking its 200th anniversary, and school officials brought Roy Rogers to the campus for Homecoming. He was to receive a Bicentennial Medallion for his meritorious career.

He spent most of the football game in the press box, where I was one of his hosts. He still looked like Roy Rogers. He was 74 at the time. He looked terrific. Best of all, he was still a good guy, so easy to talk to, so easy to be around. He was kind and generous, signing game programs for anyone who asked, posing for pictures. When my secretary, Bea Schwartz, suggested I get my picture taken with him, I was only too eager to oblige.

I must confess that I have always been a star-gazer, eager to meet and greet and interview and take pictures of famous people, especially stars of the theater and sports.

I checked out the list of the 100 greatest movies of all time that was released in 1998, and I had seen 94 of them.

Any time I have had a chance to say hello to somebody I admired in my youth I have taken advantage of the opportunity.

Around the same time I met Roy Rogers, I was in a press room at The Great Western Forum in suburban Los Angeles, and I saw Jack Nicholson snacking in the press room. Some of the sportswriters wondered what he was doing there; he didn't have a press pass. Some sportswriters worry about stuff like that.

Nicholson is a big fan of the Los Angeles Lakers, and I'm a big fan of Jack Nicholson. I introduced myself and told him I liked his movies. He shook my hand, gave me that Nicholson smile and said, "Hey, big guy, glad to meet you."

I've introduced myself at other sports settings to Robert Redford, Dustin Hoffman and Billy Crystal and did feel like a "big guy" because, much to my surprise, at 5-8½, I was bigger than all three of them.

When they're on the silver screen, however, they're bigger than all of us. Hey, Roy Rogers, happy trails to you. And thanks for the memories.

Roy Rogers is the good guy in the white hat, an Oct. 25, 1986 visitor in Pitt Stadium press box, flanked by Bob O'Connor of Pittsburgh City Council, and author Jim O'Brien, then assistant athletic director for sports information at Pitt.

Dr. Thomas E. Starzl
Hero in the hospitals

*"To do it right requires
an enormous commitment."*

D r. Thomas Starzl started talking as soon as he entered the room where I was waiting for him at his offices on the University of Pittsburgh campus. I always appreciated that about Dr. Starzl. I loved to listen to him. No matter the subject, Dr. Starzl has something significant and poignant to offer. Then there are times when you wonder where he's going and when he's going to come back to what you were talking about. He had a dog with him I'd seen once before, different from the ones I had seen at his side on prior visits. He introduced the dog to me. Her name was Ophelia and she was a mixed breed, mostly border collie, he thought.

There was a story behind this dog he had named after a Shakespearian character. "She had a harrowing experience when she was a child," said Dr. Starzl in the way of introductions. Yes, that's exactly what he said. Who have you ever heard refer to a dog as a child? A dog-lover, that's who.

"Some bad boys, we think, crucified her on the iron fence in front of our home," said Dr. Starzl, who lived at the north end of the Pitt campus. "Some bad things were done to her. Someone had put out a cigarette on her nose, too. I don't know how some people can be so cruel, or regard life as so unimportant.

"We took her down, patched her up a bit, and my wife, Joy, took her to a vet. We decided no one would ever menace this dog again. I've had her with me ever since. She doesn't like me to be out of her sight. She's been a good companion."

Ophelia had sad eyes, a mournful look that could seize your heart. No wonder, after her experience. She was a pretty dog. Dr. Starzl stroked her back as he spoke to me, the two of them sitting on a couch just across from me.

My older daughter, Sarah, and her husband, Matthew Zirwas, both third-year medical school students at Pitt, sat in on the session on May 12, 1999. I wanted them to hear Dr. Starzl talk about his inspirational life story.

My younger daughter, Rebecca, had brought a dog into our life for the first time in our adult years only the year before. The dog's name was Bailey, also a mixed breed, mostly Chow-Chow, we were told. Rebecca's boyfriend, Jason Cate, had saved it from being put to sleep at an animal shelter in Cleveland, and gave it to Rebecca. We all loved Bailey.

Because of Bailey's impact on our lives, and how she had seized the hearts of everyone in our family, I could better appreciate Dr.

Starzl's relationship with Ophelia. I could not have known how he felt just a year earlier. Dr. Starzl stroked the dog's back and ears the entire conversation. Ophelia licked his hands, rose up to his face a few times. Ophelia left his lap occasionally, but quickly returned.

Asked why she was named Ophelia, Dr. Starzl smiled and said, "She's named after the character in Hamlet, as you know. When we first had her, she behaved somewhat strangely. She walked in circles, and did some skittish things. Ophelia committed suicide, as you know, and we were hoping she wouldn't do that."

Dr. Starzl, as you know, likes to make his visitors feel smarter than they really are. He's a sensitive man.

Dr. Starzl cared about all life, it was that simple. After I read his book, *The Puzzle People*, it also struck me that he had done much of his early transplantation experiments on dogs. That had to be difficult for him, or it may account for his protectiveness toward dogs these days.

"I don't know about that," he said. "It was always difficult to experiment with dogs. It still is. It's a matter of priorities; there's no other way to work at anything."

Seeing Dr. Starzl and Ophelia on my birthday — August 20, 1998 — for an earlier interview session was quite a present.

Since my earlier visit, Dr. Starzl has received much national and local attention for his work. Seeing what has happened since I had been with him only heightened how I felt about the experience and our friendship.

The surgeon who performed the world's first successful liver transplant and was responsible for so many other breakthroughs in transplantation surgery and research was finally getting his due.

He was being hailed as a medical genius, as a man who had fought the good fight and championed anti-rejection drugs like cyclosporine and later FK-506 that made organ transplants routine. If Pittsburgh was known as "The City of Champions" in the 1970s for all its sports successes, it became known as "Transplant Town" for all its advances in transplantation surgery and research in the 1980s.

Since 1990, Dr. Starzl, now 73, had served as director of the Thomas E. Starzl Transplantation Institute at the University of Pittsburgh Medical Center. He had stopped practicing in 1990 at age 65.

"For one thing, I was pathologically fatigued, because the pace was enormous. We were doing 650 livers a year at the time — two a day. And I was in the operating room or the clinics all the time. I was fatigued, it seemed like, almost to death.

"The thing, of course, is age. I think you lose strength and I always thought you lose skill, just in the same way that quarterbacks have to get old, or running backs."

In April, 1999, *GQ* magazine carried a profile of Dr. Starzl in which he was hailed as "the greatest surgeon of the 20th Century." Earlier, his name appeared in a book *1000 Years, 1000 People:*

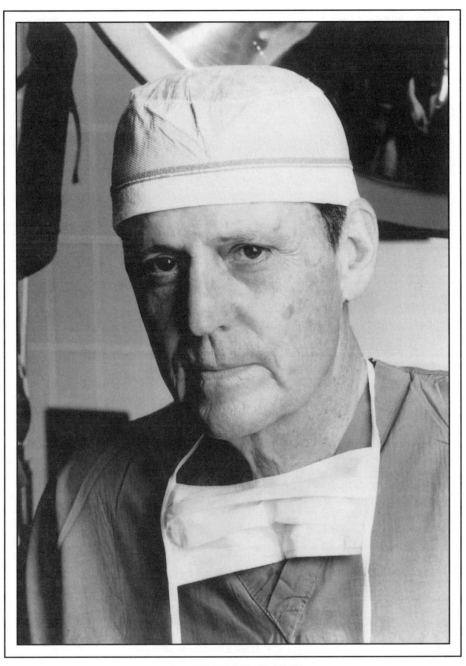

DR. THOMAS E. STARZL
Internationally-recognized transplantation pioneer

Ranking The Men And Women Who Shaped The Millennium. Dr. Starzl was listed No. 213 in the rankings, one place ahead of President John Adams.

At the outset of May, 1999, Dr. Starzl was the keynote speaker before 10,000 in attendance at the Civic Arena for commencement ceremonies of the University of Pittsburgh.

A few days later, he traveled to Chicago where he received the Global Conference Institute's Healthcare Humanitarian Award. I spoke to him upon his return, and congratulated him on all his recent honors.

"It's nice to be honored," he said, "but it's also a waste of time. I had to be away for two days, and I wasn't able to attend to my work. But it was a learning experience."

Dr. Starzl is supposed to be retired, but he can't stop. There's much work to be done. He remains committed.

I happened to get my annual physical at rival Allegheny General Hospital the same day that Dr. Starzl was getting his honor in Chicago. The doctor who examined me, Dr. Bernard Andrews, was a graduate of the University of Pittsburgh School of Medicine. He remembered when he used to see Dr. Starzl when he was a med school student at Pitt. "We'd be studying and Dr. Starzl would stop and get a cup of coffee," recalled Dr. Andrews. "He'd come back a half hour later. He drank a lot of coffee, it seemed. Some doctors were talking about him here today, and they were questioning whether he deserved to get all these honors. To me, he's a very special doctor and he deserves all this attention."

Dr. Starzl is well aware that he has his critics in the medical community.

"I think that if you're going to get something done that is counter-current, that is new, you have to do that (be so determined that nobody can stand in your way)," he said in answer to a question about his style posed by *Post-Gazette* writer Bill Steigerwald.

"On the other hand, I think I would have preferred — and probably planned — to live a more conventional life. But I think if you separate yourself from the normal or from the group, you're going to end up in the cross-hairs, and the snipers are out there. I wanted to work in an area where I could make a difference, where I could do something to advance medicine. It's pretty hard to get through a lifetime in one piece. At least I got that done."

As far as being rated the best in the business, Dr. Starzl said, "I was just as surprised as anyone else to see that. I wouldn't make a claim like that. A surgeon operates on people, and I'll bet you there are a thousand around the world and a couple dozen right here who can do that as well or better than I could."

I doubt that, in his own heart, he truly believes that. He was being kind and trying to keep the wolves at bay.

"It's always been interesting."
— Terry Mangan,
Dr. Starzl's secretary

Whenever Dr. Thomas E. Starzl steps onto an elevator at any of the hospitals of the University of Pittsburgh Medical Center it's said that everyone on board becomes silent. "Everyone just stares," said a woman physician. "Everyone is so much in awe of him."

That will happen when you have a building and an entire floor named after you at the UPMC complex.

Apparently it's not silent enough, however, to suit Dr. Starzl because he has sought a retreat across the street from the hospital complex, in a small, spartan room more befitting a med school student than the Director of Transplantation Surgery at the University of Pittsburgh Medical Center.

The windows are dirty, soot-stained enough to make you think Pittsburgh was still the Smoky City. There are no drapes. There is more space vertically in the high-ceilinged room than there is horizontally.

It is a third floor walkup above the Campus Book Store on Fifth Avenue, a strange setting, indeed, to find one of the world's foremost authorities on the transplantation of life-sustaining organs. When I first visited him there, back in 1992, there was a Pizza Hut directly under his offices. There's still a neighborhood pizza shop two doors away. There was a hint of pepperoni and cheese in the air.

"You can still smell the pizza," said his secretary, Terry Mangan, when I last visited him. "I think we'll always be able to smell the pizza."

Dr. Starzl doesn't mind the smell. If it keeps some away, that's all right, too.

"Nobody can get me here without a passkey," said Dr. Starzl with a demure smile. "I couldn't get any work done over there. Everybody wanted a piece of me. I had a big office on the fifth floor at Falk Clinic, but I wanted some peace and quiet. They can't get at me here."

But they do. Seconds after my appointed arrival, Dr. Starzl begs off to talk to a friend on the telephone for a few minutes. "He's an old friend, and he's having marital difficulties," Dr. Starzl would say later in explanation. "His wife has left him. It's hard; he's having a difficult time. He's devastated by it. I'm just trying to help the guy."

There's an honesty about Dr. Starzl I find so appealing. I think Dr. Starzl has to share what he knows. We're both like that. That's why we both like to write so much. He would instruct me when he didn't want something used in this chapter.

His life-long simple mission has been to help people. But there's much more to this man, one of the most admired and controversial figures in his field, certainly one of the big men on campus at Pitt. He has been held in high esteem, and rebuked because of the controversies that arise from fooling around in God's domain with life and death issues, ever since he first came to Pitt in 1981.

He provided even more insights into his life's story when the University of Pittsburgh Press published his moving and heart-wrenching autobiography, *The Puzzle People: Memoirs of a Transplant Surgeon* in 1992.

It had been nine years since Dr. Starzl stepped away from the operating table, retiring from active surgery following two operations on his own heart. His health was good again, his hours more reasonable and predictable, and now he was concentrating on research. "What's your goal?" I asked. "To make things better," he said.

He would be going to the lab after our interview, crossing Fifth Avenue as he did each day when he was ready to resume his research efforts.

"I'm devoting myself to a different kind of thing now," he said. "I want to know more about what happens after the transplant: why it succeeds, why it fails. By knowing that, if we can do that, we're pretty certain we can transplant animal organs into humans."

Dr. Starzl says mind-blowing things like that, without the roll of drums, as if he were passing along the score of a Pirates' ballgame.

While he was on the telephone with his old friend, I studied Dr. Starzl's surroundings, searching for clues about this fascinating figure, one I became familiar with during my five years in public relations at the athletic department and with the admissions office at Pitt from 1983 to 1987. He was someone I had become fascinated with, because of the hugeness of his achievements in the medical field.

To me, he was one of the school's most monumental figures, in the mold of Dr. Jonas Salk, who had discovered the anti-polio vaccine while doing research at the University back in the mid-50s, or Dr. Jock Sutherland, a dental school grad who had won a string of national championships while serving as the school's football coach in the '30s.

There are many pieces to the Dr. Starzl puzzle, and some could be found in that seemingly confining space he calls his office.

There were a few white lab coats hanging from hooks on the whitewashed walls. Yet Dr. Starzl was wearing his usual eclectic collection of clothes. He wore a dark blue windbreaker over a red turtleneck sweater. He had on light blue casual slacks, with a large cowboy buckle — he's been called a cowboy in his field by some of his colleagues, somewhat derisively — eye-catching red socks to match his sweater, and white sneakers.

It was the sort of garb I am accustomed to seeing him wear when he comes to the Pitt Field House to watch the Pitt basketball team, or to Pitt Stadium to see the Panthers play football. He is a big sports fan. It is another escape from the demands and pressures of transplantation work. He is also famous for late-night strolls about the streets of Oakland to release the tension.

He wore a jacket and turtleneck sweater, yet he had a window air-conditioning unit turned up high. He was curled up in his chair; he always looks chilled to the bone. The drone made it difficult to hear him, or the music he had on a compact disc player atop a nearby bookshelf. It was hardly quiet in this cell. His CD collection included much Mozart and Schubert, and, interestingly enough, lullabies and dances by Julianne Baird and Bill Croft.

His briefcase and desk were both littered with color-coded pens and Magic Markers. There were several Skrip ink bottles about the room. Who writes with real ink these days? The son of a newspaper publisher and editor, who moonlighted as a science fiction writer, that's who. There were boxes of generic dog biscuits. Where were the dogs? Tag along with us and you'll see.

Dr. Starzl's mother, by the way, was a nurse back home in Le Mars, Iowa, a "Music Man" kind of midwestern city, and her son says he knew when he was 10 years old that he wanted to be a doctor someday. His mother admired doctors. "When my time came," offered Dr. Starzl, "I wanted to escape." His mother's family came from Ireland, his father's from Germany.

There were a few books tossed randomly around the room. The titles included: *We Have A Donor* and *The Gift of Life*, and *So Your Doctor Recommended Surgery*.

Through those soot-stained windows I could see Children's Hospital, where Dr. Starzl can still see, in his marvelous mind's eye, the children such as Stormie Jones who were his patients, with whom he worked "the very large miracle" of organ transplantation.

Dr. Starzl can speak about Stormie Jones in the same breath as Danny Marino, and Chuck Noll and Charles Kuralt, Pittsburgh and the University of Pittsburgh and the University of Pittsburgh Medical Center, Dr. Frankenstein, Dr. Starzl's wife, Joy, and their dogs, Thor, Bevo and Ophelia, and is equally excited about each and every one of them.

"I can look back with wonder at being able to come to work with enthusiasm every day for nearly fifty years without ever having an absolutely clear idea of what the day might hold," he has said. "It would be easy to lose that kind of energy by trying to figure out far in advance what the future holds. If I have any good advice it would be: 'Do nothing for career development.'"

When Dr. Starzl finished his telephone call, I asked him if we could move to another room on the floor, perhaps to the rooftop area where I had waited earlier. I wanted to hear what he had to say, and it was hard to hear because of that droning sound from the air conditioning unit. There are other rooms on the third floor of the red brick building. His secretary of 16 years, Terry Mangan, is in one of them. "It's always been interesting working with Dr. Starzl," she said. Dr. Andy Tazakis, the head of pediatric surgery at Children's Hospital, was in an adjoining office when I first visited in 1992, but he had since retired to Florida. Other members of the transplantation team were in offices on the floor below. Another room on the third floor was a casual wide-open reception area where Dr. Starzl displayed many framed photographs of former patients, such as Stormie Jones. On Valentine's Day, 1984, the 6-year-old Texas girl became the first person to receive simultaneous heart and liver transplants. When she died in 1990, seven years after her first transplant, Dr. Starzl was heartbroken.

Stormie had a magic name and a magic smile and she captivated a nation with her heroic courage.

Dr. Starzl has slides of some of his former patients, showing them as they looked when they first came to him, and how they look now, little kids who've become college students. He keeps grateful letters he often receives from them.

Dr. Starzl recalled Stormie, and his other young patients, in remarks he made when he was appointed head of the University of Pittsburgh Transplant Institute in 1990:

"Without the sense of personal loss that goes with a dear name and face, there is little progress and no incentive for striving except personal or professional ambition," he said in a paper he prepared for the occasion.

"The field of transplantation is a young one, and almost all those who contributed to this new clinical specialty are still alive. They remember...their patients' names, not numbers of statistics. This is the power of the connection between the doctor and his patient."

Dr. Starzl is prolific when it comes to papers. According to the Institute for Scientific Information, in his prime he averaged one paper every 7.3 days, making him one of the most published scientists in the world. He would stop in mid-sentence during our conversation, and call Terry to his side. He would dictate a letter, or ideas he wanted her to put into a letter. "I don't want to forget," he'd say in the way of an apology for the interruption.

"They're publishing translations of my book in Italian, Spanish and Japanese," he told Terry. "They had to change the title in Japanese. Ours didn't make any sense there. It will be called 'Starting at Zero.' How about that?"

When I talked over the telephone with Terry on April 29, 1999, she said that Dr. Starzl was as busy as ever writing and publishing papers. She said he had 2,091 papers to his credit, at her latest count.

Dr. Starzl's hazel-green eyes always seem to be elsewhere. They seldom seem focused on your own eyes. And when they are, it's as if he is looking right through you. There is a mind at work; a mind working overtime. He has a wonderful memory, which is evident in his memoirs. He has an eye for detail, for dissertations. He is famous for being focused, yet his mind does wander. You have to pay attention closely to keep up with him and his mind.

There is a spareness about Dr. Starzl. His hair is close-cropped, the skin is dark about his eyes — he seems to be looking at you through a tunnel at times — and he is slender, almost bony. He wears interesting looking outfits.

He gave the background on other photos displayed about the reception area, one of Nancy Reagan, the former First Lady; of world dignitaries, or of his grandson, Ravi, wearing a tuxedo at a formal dinner.

We went up a few steps and out onto the black tar paper roof. It was walled in, and there was an old picnic table and benches. I expected to find Marlon Brando and his pigeons up there, as in the movie *On the Waterfront*. I sat on one of the benches. Dr. Starzl planted one of those white-sneakered shoes on the bench in front of me, and rested an elbow on his knee, and continued our conversation. He looked like a coach.

The sun was shining brightly behind him, so he was a dark outlined figure before me. He pointed to Schenley Park in the distance, a hilly green stretch across the street from Phipps Conservatory. I told him it was called Flagstaff Hill. High school and college cross-country teams run there. He appreciated being able to see such a large park from his viewpoint. "I like to come out here to eat, or to write," he said. "It's peaceful."

We simultaneously spotted a young woman in a red bikini sunbathing on the rooftop next door. Dr. Starzl's eyes shot up to acknowledge what we witnessed. The young woman probably had no idea of the identity of her next-door neighbor.

His hands caught my eye. They are long and slender, a surgeon's hands. A piano player's hands. They also have age spots on them. I mentioned to him that every time I have shaken his hand in greeting at the Field House or Pitt Stadium it always gave me pause for thought. Like I shouldn't be shaking his hands, or squeezing too hard, not the hands of a surgeon involved in such delicate work. Not someone's hands who are so precious. He smiled.

"I never worried about them," he said. "Maybe there's something symbolic about a surgeon's hands. But your hands are a mere extension of you. I never gave it a thought. I was always out playing baseball or basketball, and doing all kinds of dangerous things. Skiing or something like that. I didn't baby my hands, that's for sure. It's all a part of life."

I mentioned to him how I'd always enjoyed seeing him and speaking to him in the media room at the Pitt basketball games. "I love to watch people do skillful things, so I like sports, generally speaking," he said. "I think basketball is one of the supreme skill sports. Baseball has the same athleticism, except it's all in slow motion. It's a much more relaxed pace. Hockey is something else. It goes so quickly, I can hardly keep up. Maybe my eyes aren't as good as they used to be."

His hands, his eyes...more concessions to age.

I recalled that during the winter of 1991, I had talked to him in the media room during a Pitt basketball game at Fitzgerald Field House. I introduced him to my daughter, Sarah, who was 17 at the time, and a student friend of hers from Upper St. Clair High School.

The young man, a Korean-American named Brian Kang who aspired to be a doctor, was planning on attending Johns Hopkins University, one of the schools where Dr. Starzl did some of his medical studies. I thought meeting Dr. Starzl would be a big deal, possibly inspirational stuff.

In the same media room, the young man also met Dr. J. Dennis O'Connor, then the new Pitt chancellor, and Paul Hackett, the Pitt football coach. He came away most excited about meeting Hackett. Dr. Starzl came in tied for second.

When I related this story, Dr. Starzl smiled once more. "I'd be more excited about meeting the football coach, too," he said.

"I am intrigued by meeting people who have succeeded in whatever field they're in. To do it right requires an enormous commitment," said Dr. Starzl. "It's not just all natural talent. I have the same reaction to anyone who has done anything beyond the normal or average. I suppose the really good athlete is like the really good violin player.

"I met Chuck Noll about a month ago at an awards dinner sponsored by the Historical Society, and I was taken with him. I was surprised he was so small (about six feet even), so soft-spoken, not intimidating at all. He was easy to talk to. He seemed genuinely pleasant."

Some might be just as surprised in a similar manner if they met Dr. Starzl on the roof of his office. One hears reports that he can be a bully, most intimidating, and hostile in arguing his case in a hospital setting. Dr. Starzl has a stare that is icy; it can freeze the most formidable dissenter.

In so many ways, Dr. Starzl is a lot like Chuck Noll, who had retired (December 26, 1991) after 23 years as the head coach of the Steelers. Noll was no longer on the sidelines, but represented the Steelers on occasion as a goodwill ambassador of sorts. As Dr. Starzl goes to more and more awards and honors banquets to celebrate past contributions he likens his schedule to the tour of aging baseball players, appearing at old timers' games, or farewell games in one's last season of play.

Dr. Starzl and Noll both have a Germanic bearing about them. Both see themselves as teachers. They like an academic atmosphere. Up close and personal, they are softer and easy to speak to, whereas in the arena they can be steely-eyed, doggedly determined, downright obstinate, and difficult. Obviously, there are two sides to both men. They have both been to the mountain, yet they want to remain in Pittsburgh.

"It's always interesting to me that these people are famous and quite normal when you meet them," said Dr. Starzl.

I mentioned to Dr. Starzl that I had just read a book by Charles Kuralt called *Life On The Road*, in which the network TV story-teller and commentator wrote, "Many celebrated people are just folks when you get to know them."

Dr. Thomas E. Starzl has been cited as "Pittsburgher of the Year," but he shuns the spotlight, content to keep company with one of his dogs, Ophelia, who is constantly at his side.

Photos by Jim O'Brien

Dr. Starzl is flanked by two students at the School of Medicine of the University of Pittsburgh, Sarah O'Brien and her husband Matthew Zirwas, with whom he shared stories about his celebrated career on a rooftop area just off his Fifth Avenue offices.

Dr. Starzl stunned me momentarily by saying, "I met Charles Kuralt. My wife and I met him at a modest restaurant in Vienna."

Dr. Starzl doesn't like to travel these days. "There aren't too many airports in the world I haven't been in," he said. He spoke of looking for his mother's home in Ireland, near Limerick. She was a Mangan —no relation to his secretary — and there were Fitzgeralds in the family tree. My own heritage is Irish-German, so I could relate to some of Dr. Starzl's sentiments, and his story-telling style.

I also mentioned to Dr. Starzl how much my former secretary, Bea Schwartz, thought of him. Bea Schwartz was a super lady, a different sort of secretary and a different sort of person, with a vaudevillian heart, and a strong personal interest in people. How many have secretaries who not only shoot pool, but assemble their own personal cue stick before shooting a game? She used to make sure Dr. Starzl had tickets and game programs to Pitt sports events, and she gave him lots of special attention. She used to dote on Dr. Starzl when he would come to a basketball game, making sure he had something to eat and drink. He appreciated the attention.

When Bea Schwartz was dying of cancer at Presbyterian-University Hospital in 1987, Dr. Starzl stopped in her room to see her every day during the several weeks she was there. "When he leaves, the nurses and doctors all are amazed that I know him, and that he's a friend of mine," Mrs. Schwartz said to me in her final days. "'How do you know him?' They ask me." She was proud. She had a son who was a doctor.

"She was a unique person," recalled Dr. Starzl. "She was a knowledgeable person. I saw her the day before she died. She was in great pain, and she was not concerned that she was about to die. You have to make yourself available to make a friend like that. She made herself available."

I asked him about his dad and his newspaper background. During his student days at Northwestern, Dr. Starzl worked on the copy desk of *The Chicago Tribune*. "Read my book," he urged. "There's a lot in there about my dad. I was with my dad when he died. My dad's brother became a big-time newspaperman. He headed the Associated Press in New York. My dad had big-time ability, too, but he never got away.

"Maybe that's part of what drives me. Maybe it's the fear of failing. I think I had a perspective taught to me by my father's experience. I think my dad was in a world too small, not really fitting his talents. Maybe I was determined not to let that happen to me. There was always a symbolic detachment between my dad and his brother. My uncle spelled his name differently, S-t-a-r-z-e-l. My dad hated that. It pissed off my dad. Everyone always misspelled our name as a result of that.

"What I've done might even reflect a low self esteem. I wanted to make a difference on some level of performance. I was fully aware early on that I was doing something different. I think I still have a determined juvenile perspective, or youthfulness about me. I think that if you lose that you lose a cleanliness of mind. It makes it difficult to identify with new things.

"I think that's what happens when you get old. Sometimes it happens when you're 18 and sometimes it happens when you're 80. You don't want to lose that early enthusiasm. I've never been good at loafing. It makes me very nervous not having anything fruitful to do. Work can't hurt you."

I think I stunned Dr. Starzl when I asked him if he had ever seen the movie, *Frankenstein*. And did he ever see himself in the same light as Dr. Frankenstein, who took the body parts of dead people and assembled a giant and gave it life.

"It's a great movie," said Dr. Starzl with a wicked gleam in his eyes. "I saw it last when we were in Aspen. No, I never had any thoughts like that, about creating life. When I saw it again, I realized that he was originally presented in sort of a sympathetic light."

I mentioned that Dr. Frankenstein had a lot of critics who thought he was crazy. "I can relate to that part of it," he said. "There were lots of critics like that along the way. I didn't pay any attention to them. I had shown such transplants were feasible, so I knew where we were going early on. It would be foolish listening to people telling you what couldn't be done. We first showed with kidneys that we could successfully transplant them as early as 1962, that you could make kidneys work.

"I was one of about 25 doctors in the world who were working on it in 1963 and coming up with similar results. What we did in Denver certified it. As late as 1967, however, there was lots of discussion about the ethics of it.

"A kidney transplant wasn't completed successfully until the late '60s. Early on, it was thought to be impossible."

Dr. Starzl performed the world's first human liver transplant in 1963 and the first successful liver transplant at the University of Colorado in 1967. Dr. Starzl and his clinical organ transplant and research team went on to perform more than 1,000 kidney transplants at Colorado General and Denver Veterans Administration hospitals.

"When we started out we were working on the dark side of the moon, but now it's commonplace."

Nowadays, at the University of Pittsburgh, a transplant is performed every 12 hours. To date, more than 5,000 liver transplants have been performed at Pitt.

Dr. Starzl was brought to Pitt in the first place by Dr. Henry Bahnson, then chairman of the department of surgery, who started the cardiac transplant program at Pitt in 1968 when he performed the first heart transplant in Pennsylvania. In 1982, the University initiated a heart/lung transplant program.

The University of Pittsburgh's Transplantation Program (now named after Dr. Starzl) is one of the world's largest and busiest, where surgeons perform more types of organ transplants than any other institution, according to statistics provided by Pitt's Health Sciences News Bureau.

"In 1963, when President Kennedy was shot, I was working in a laboratory at a feverish pace at Colorado," recalled Dr. Starzl during our visit. "We were really laying the groundwork for liver transplants. We were right in the middle of a transplant with a dog when we heard that Kennedy had been shot. It was not yet known he was dead. One of the people in the lab was a Kennedy critic. He said, 'I hope the sunuvabitch dies.' It nearly created a fight before cooler heads prevailed. We were trying to create our own memorial to Kennedy. We called that dog JFK. He lived for a few weeks. When the dog died that's when the finality of it sank in with me that Kennedy had, indeed, died. Kennedy was a litmus in the transplant program. Your memory of that moment will remain with you forever.

"*The New England Journal of Medicine* carried an article about two weeks before his inauguration that said transplants were not possible. It was a biological barrier. A Dr. Burnett wrote that. Within a short time after that, we had a kidney transplant."

Just as Pittsburghers know where they were when Kennedy was killed, they also remember where they were when Bill Mazeroski hit the home run that beat the Yankees in the 9th inning of the 7th game of the 1960 World Series, when I was a freshman student at Pitt, working on the campus newspaper in the Student Union just across the street from Forbes Field.

"I was in San Francisco the day he hit the home run," Dr. Starzl said. "Everyone was going crazy. What the hell happened? It was three hours off Pittsburgh time. The game had just ended as we entered a barroom at the hotel at lunchtime. I was at the convention of the American College of Surgery. The Yankees were supposed to win."

There was commotion in the reception room, and suddenly two dogs shot up the stairs and out onto the roof where Dr. Starzl was standing. He identified the dogs as Thor, a French poodle, and Bevo, a Welsh corgi. They had been brought to the office by Dr. Starzl's wife, Joy. "She is the star of my book," said Dr. Starzl, as he greeted his wife. We had met before, and Dr. Starzl reminded his wife of that.

He showed me a picture of one of the dogs. "This is Thor as a young child," said Dr. Starzl. See, he said it again. He said he had to move into his present home, on Centre Avenue between Schenley High School and Pitt Stadium, because one of his former patients had presented him with a big dog, which he doesn't have anymore. "We were living somewhere that refused to permit us to have more than one dog," he said. "That was the most expensive dog I ever owned. I had to buy a new house because of it."

Looking at Joy, a beautiful petite woman who is his second wife, Dr. Starzl said, "She helps me a great deal. My great attribute in life was to be able to find great people to work with. It's not so much my own talent. I never lost anyone from anger or disagreement. It gave me a continuity over a period of years."

Dr. Starzl has been honored on an international basis, and I asked him what some of the members of the European medical community might think of his office digs. "Some of those people from Europe think this is like a John LeCarre novel. I'm the spymaster. We have a spiral staircase, and a secret exit. You can easily escape without being detected. You don't know what people expect. It doesn't get you very far.

"I had a son who said 'nobody wants to be average, but nobody wants to be abnormal.'"

There's never been anything average about Dr. Starzl, and he wants to be able to say the same about the University of Pittsburgh, and its Medical Center.

"The University of Pittsburgh has achieved special stature, given only to a few places, like the Ivy League schools," he said. "I hope they can cling to it, and take that last step. It's one of the last of the inner-city universities that supports a good lifestyle. Oakland resembles Cambridge at Harvard, if people could only appreciate the place.

"The city itself has a terrible inferiority complex. Like if this school's here it can't be very good. Or, if they come to Pitt they can't be very good students. It's harmful; it's an image fed by the newspapers."

He was referring specifically to all the controversy stirred up by the departure of Dr. Wesley W. Posvar as chancellor of the University, and the early efforts and installation (coronation?) ceremonies of his successor, Dr. J. Dennis O'Connor. "It's really surprising," said Dr. Starzl. "It's appalling. Maybe it will all wash away.

"No one escapes scrutiny and criticism around here. We knock off all our heroes. I really liked Dan Marino, for instance, but he, too, had mudballs thrown at him. I was sorry to see them re-emerge again (in an interview with Chuck Noll by Myron Cope on his WTAE Radio sports talk show a month earlier). I don't think that they (stories of fooling around with drugs in his early student days) are true. I think it's a big mistake. Marino comes from a strong family structure. The Steelers simply made a big mistake not drafting him."

I asked him about the Pittsburgh hospitals at large. "We have a very powerful hospital community," he said. "It's a big industry for the city. We've moved away from the steel mills into health care, high tech and support services that are seldom rivaled anywhere else in the world. The city is fortunate to have that. I believe in the blue and white collar elements of this community, but it hasn't been a blue collar town for quite a while. People who play to that image aren't paying attention. But we still have good workers here. I've said before that it took a town like Pittsburgh to make our transplant program succeed. This is a very work-oriented city. I don't think we could have gotten the job done (elsewhere).

"Now we have a great medical school associated with Pittsburgh hospitals. And by and large a very decent group of doctors, health care experts and staff people. The University is a tremendous resource.

The Medical Center, just like the whole university, has skirted with immortality from time to time, only to fall back, mostly because of political conflict within its own walls.

"We have had some great doctors here. The momentum is stronger, and has a deeper base than ever before. Its hard to see how this school can fail. I give a lot of credit to Dr. (Thomas) Detre, (who headed up the health sciences and medical/health care division at Pitt). Dr. Art Levine, his successor, looks like he will carry on the great tradition.

"There has been a lot of controversy and bitterness toward the leadership group, and how things are run, but they did some essential groundwork to turn things around. They have taken a diverse group of hospitals and pulled them together, consolidating hospitals into a University Medical Center, instead of a loose configuration of autonomous hospitals. Getting Eye & Ear hooked in, for instance, made us that much stronger. I am not sure how it happened. I am amazed at the transformation. It has all happened since I've been here."

For the record, the University of Pittsburgh Transplantation Institute which Dr. Starzl supervised, is a cooperative effort between Pitt's schools of medicine and science, with ties to Presbyterian-University and Montefiore University hospitals and the Western Psychiatric Institute and Clinic. Two additional facilities, Magee-Womens Hospital and Children's Hospital of Pittsburgh, are also affiliated with the program.

"It's now a citadel of learning. There's tremendous tradition," said Dr. Starzl. "They have made the pieces fit. It's payoff time now. I am certain they won't allow that to crumble."

Asked what's ahead for him, Dr. Starzl smiled warmly once more, and offered, "I never had a long-term game plan; I just come to work every day. I never thought of a career in a conventional way."

"I had dinner with Billy Conn."

As I said earlier, there is no subject one can introduce that Dr. Starzl can't offer interesting insights about. When I told him who else was being profiled in this book, during a conversation of May 7, 1999, the name of Billy Conn came up.

"I'm in good company," Dr. Starzl said. "I had dinner with Billy Conn at Tony O'Reilly's place in 1983. O'Reilly had a big lawn party at his estate out near the Fox Chapel Country Club. It was a magnificent evening. There were lots of Heinz people there, of course, but an interesting array of Pittsburgh civic leaders.

"Billy was there with his wife. They were a charming couple. You could tell he was a fighter. He was marked up. But he was not punch-drunk. You just knew he had been involved in fights."

Ever the sports fan, Dr. Starzl spoke knowledgeably about Conn's two title fights with Joe Louis. He knew all the details, especially of the first fight. When I mentioned Dr. Starzl's story to Mary Louise Conn, she recalled that night at the O'Reilly estate.

"Billy always said that there were lots of doctors who were big fight fans," she said. "For some reason they seemed to like boxers. They went to all the fights. We knew a bunch of doctors at Mercy Hospital who went to Billy's fights, no matter where he fought."

Dr. Starzl still knew the dates and the details about Billy Conn's fighting career.

"I was rooting for Billy Conn when he fought Joe Louis," Dr. Starzl said. "He was a pathologically handsome individual. He had it won until the 13th round, but he wanted to knock out Louis. Louis looked tired at the time, or maybe he was just playing rope-a-dope, as they would later call it. He was driven mad by this gadfly and he ended it with a fury."

He remembered seeing Louis many times when he was doing research and surgery at the Denver Veterans Administration Hospital. "I saw Joe Louis nearly every day for awhile," he said. "He was punch drunk and extremely paranoid. I'd see him shuffling along in the hallway. He was a pathetic creature by that time. It was sad to see him that way."

He also recalled meeting prize fighter Jake Lamotta (portrayed by Robert DeNiro in "Raging Bull" movie) in a hospital setting. "I've always been intrigued by fighters," he said.

He had also spent time with John Henry Johnson, a fighter who played fullback for the Steelers and several other teams in the National Football League. Johnson had short-term memory loss, but was fine when he talked about his glory days. Dr. Starzl smiled about that observation.

"I find myself grasping for a word now and then," said Dr. Starzl. "I used to take great pride in having a photographic memory. I remembered the page numbers where I had read some things in a book. I knew names and dates, but I'm not as sharp about things like that anymore. Age takes its toll on all of us. None of us escape that."

"Seek always to do some good, somewhere. Every man has to seek in his own way to make his own self more noble and to realize his own true worth."
— Albert Schweitzer, Doctor, clergyman and medical missionary

337

Michael Jordan
Local fan meets idol

"I'm a good luck charm for him."
— Adam Ference

A young man named Adam Ference will never forget Michael Jordan. Adam was among the many who watched the televised tributes to Jordan following Jordan's announcement that he was retiring from playing pro basketball. He can appreciate more than most why Jordan is just such an appealing personality.

They shared some special experiences when Adam was a teenager struggling with a life-threatening incident, asking a lot of "why me?" questions and needing a boost.

One day, just before Christmas in 1989, Adam was riding a school bus from his home in Clairton to Serra Catholic High School. Adam was a 16-year-old junior at the McKeesport school.

A troubled classmate, for no apparent reason, aimed a pistol at the back of Adam's head and fired off a bullet. Then the young man shot and killed himself. Adam slumped in his seat, bleeding from the back of his head. Students screamed hysterically on the bus.

Adam was lucky. The bullet lodged in his skull and did not penetrate to his brain. He was rushed to a nearby hospital and, from there, he was airlifted by helicopter to Presbyterian-University Hospital in Oakland.

While he was recuperating, his story was called to my attention. I was told that he was a big fan of Michael Jordan and I was asked if there was any way I could get Jordan to drop him a "get well" message or something. The man who made the request was Pat Hanlon, then the assistant public relations director of the Pittsburgh Steelers. He had previously been my MVP assistant in the sports information office at the University of Pittsburgh. More recently, he was the vice-president for public relations with the New York Football Giants. Hanlon had arranged for several Steelers to visit Ference in his hospital room, and now he was going the extra yard for the Ference family.

I was editor of *Street & Smith's Basketball* magazine, and had interviewed Jordan a few times. I had no idea if I could prevail upon him to do anything.

Jordan was contacted through the public relations office of the Chicago Bulls. Within a day, Adam received an autographed photo at the hospital. Then came a pair of Jordan's Chicago Bulls playing shorts, signed by Jordan. Later, Adam received an autographed poster from Chicago.

A few months later, through Nike, the manufacturer of the Air Jordan sneakers, I arranged for Adam to be awarded a scholarship to attend Michael Jordan's summer basketball camp in Chicago. The Ference family paid for his air fare.

Michael Jordan captured hearts of America as leader of Chicago Bulls.

"Today's success is often tomorrow's failure. A failure to maintain discipline causes it to evaporate immediately. It's that fragile. So never forget what you did right."
— Rick Pitino, Boston Celtics' coach
From his book, *Success Is A Choice*

The following NBA season, Adam and his father, Mike Ference, invited me to accompany them as their guest to an NBA game at Richfield Coliseum near Cleveland. Michael Jordan and the Bulls were coming to play the Cavaliers.

Without telling Adam, I arranged through the Bulls p.r. offices for Adam to meet his hero outside the visitors clubhouse before the game. Adam's father was trying to take pictures of the occasion with his camera, but was too nervous.

In a Kodak moment, Michael Jordan approached Adam's father and showed him how to use the camera. It didn't help. The pictures didn't turn out very good. One of Adam with the Bulls' coach, Phil Jackson, turned out OK and he still has it, as well as the blurred photos of him and Michael.

We sat in on history that night at the Richfield Coliseum. The Bulls beat the Cavaliers in overtime, and MJ scored 69 points, the most he ever scored in a regular season game. Only three players ever scored more points in an NBA game. Michael also had a career-high 18 rebounds and seven assists. It was a performance for the ages.

"He should take me with him wherever he plays," said Adam. "I'm a good luck charm for him."

Adam Ference turned 27 in March, 1999. He was married to the former Renee Lex, and they lived in West Mifflin. They had one child and another one was on the way. He was a salesman with C. Harper Chevrolet on Rt. 51 in Belle Vernon.

He was catching all the TV tributes in the gameroom of his home where all his Michael Jordan mementos are displayed.

"I had a different level of appreciation than most people watching," said Adam. "I saw someone I knew. I spent that week with him at his camp in Chicago, and became at ease with him. I remember when I was leaving he was on a pay telephone. He smiled at me and I just waved to him."

> *"I've always said our youth need models more than critics. But at the same time I'm well aware of the fact that we all learn through criticism; but for the most part youth are best served by the examples we leave them."*
> — John Wooden, UCLA basketball legend, from his book, *They Call Me Coach*

Joe Bugel
Best line coach in pro football

"I always told him to work hard
and make something of himself."
— His father, Joe Bugel, Sr.

Joe Bugel was back home in Munhall. He traveled there from his latest outpost, San Diego, to be honored at a testimonial dinner in his hometown on May 16, 1998.

The dinner was held at St. John's Social Center, about two miles from his boyhood home on Marietta Street, and it was attended by 450 fans and friends of the popular and respected pro football coach. It was both an entertaining and emotional evening for everyone.

Bugel was a 1958 graduate of Munhall High School. He was a mischievous kid back then and during his brief stay at the University of Miami. He ended up at Western Kentucky.

His testimonial was the best sports dinner this side of the Dapper Dan Sports Dinner to ever be staged in Greater Pittsburgh. Bugel's beaming eyes were a tip-off to how he felt about all the attention. He was hugging everyone in sight. Bugel, age 58 at the time, had been coaching on a college and pro level for 32 years. He was the head coach of the Oakland Raiders during the 1997 season, his second stint as a head coach in the National Football League, but that didn't work out and now he was the offensive line coach of the San Diego Chargers.

Bugel, whose dark brown hair was glistening with gel and made him look years younger, is one of those guys who will always have a job in the NFL. His wife, Brenda, was with him.

Marty Schottenheimer, the head coach of the Kansas City Chiefs who once tried unsuccessfully to hire Bugel, labeled him "the finest offensive line coach in pro football."

Schottenheimer said that even though Russ Grimm, the former Pitt standout who is now the offensive line coach of the Washington Redskins, was seated nearby. And Grimm is a lot bigger than Bugel. Grimm was a lot bigger than just about everybody in the hall. And funnier than everyone else on the program.

"It's hard to express in words what this means to me, as emotional as I am," said Bugel before the dinner got underway. "To be honored in your hometown is very special. There are a lot of people in this room who helped me early on, when I was trying to find my way.

"I thought I wanted to be a football coach, and I was lucky in my lifetime to work and learn under Woody Hayes, Bum Phillips, Joe Gibbs and Bobby Beathard. They don't come any bigger in football."

Dan Reeves, the head coach of the Atlanta Falcons, wrote a congratulatory letter in which he expressed this thought, "Nothing feels as good as being a hometown boy honored, does it?"

There were lots of big people and special people who turned out to pay tribute to Bugel, a hometown boy who never forgets where he came from.

His 90-year-old father, Joe Sr., was the one with the biggest smile in the room. "I always told him to work hard and make something of himself," said Bugel's dad. "I told him he didn't want to work in the steel mills all his life."

The steel mills are no more along the Monongahela River, but the area was still acknowledged as a place that produced people with a strong work ethic, committed individuals who will do whatever it takes to be successful, especially in the sports world.

Schottenheimer and his buddy and protege, Bill Cowher of the Pittsburgh Steelers, were the featured speakers who boosted Bugel as a good guy, liked and respected around the NFL and certainly in the Mon Valley.

Darrell J. Hess outdid himself in organizing and coordinating this dinner for Bugel, whom he had known since Joe's Little League days. Hess was a school guidance counselor whom Bugel has credited with pushing him and guiding him during his youth.

Hess had attempted to get all the NFL head coaches with western Pennsylvania roots to attend this dinner to honor Bugel and to raise funds for the Carnegie Library of Homestead. They raised over $15,000 for the library.

Mike Ditka of the New Orleans Saints, a Pro Football Hall of Famer with a Pitt and Aliquippa connection, had agreed to attend, but had to beg off the week before the event because of a conflict in his schedule, owing to family obligations. Dave Wannstedt of Baldwin, the head coach of the Chicago Bears at the time, had a team function to attend.

Schottenheimer and Cowher were big hits with the crowd, signing autographs and posing for photos for anyone who asked.

Foge Fazio, the defensive coordinator of the Minnesota Vikings from Coraopolis, Walt Harris, the head coach of the University of Pittsburgh, and Dan Radakovich, an assistant coach to Joe Walton at Robert Morris and a former pro aide from Duquesne, also spoke on Bugel's behalf. Nolan Harrison, a defensive end for the Steelers, had played for the Raiders when Bugel was the head coach, and gave a glowing report.

One thing players always appreciated about Bugel was he never swore at them and he was a great teacher and motivator who treated them with respect.

Sportscaster Myron Cope and yours truly were media representatives on the dais, along with sports impressionist Rick Gugliano. Ray Bodnar, the mayor of Munhall, presented Bugel with a special citation.

Jack Butler, the former Steelers defensive back and Blesto scouting executive who resided in Munhall, labeled Bugel "one of the good guys in our game."

342

Among those football personalities who paid tribute to Joe Bugel at his hometown dinner were, left to right, former Pitt and Redskins lineman Russ Grimm, Kansas City Chiefs' coach Marty Schottenheimer, Pitt's Walt Harris and Minnesota Vikings' defensive coordinator Foge Fazio.

Homestead sports luminaries Jim and Bill Campbell enjoy homecoming.

Ken Herock, a player personnel official with the Oakland Raiders, couldn't make it, but sent a personal message. "It would have been great to rehash some of our old Munhall High School memories: the long, hard football practices at West Field with Coach Nick Kliskey and the many basketball practices in the old gym at Munhall High with Hube Shiring. Even better was the Friday Night Dance after the game at the Park Arena, the Junction Pizza, Dell's Dairy Delite and Jim's Hot Dogs."

Bugel was the offensive line coach for the Redskins when they played three times in the Super Bowl, and won it twice. He lists Mark May, a former Pitt lineman who along with Grimm was one of his "Hogs" in D.C. as the greatest overachiever he ever coached.

Bill Campbell, chairman of the board of Intuit, one of the real high-tech success stories in California's Silicon Valley, offered personal remarks on behalf of a long-time friend. Bill had been the CEO at Intuit the past 4½ years.

Bill and his brother, Jim, former Naval officer, jet fighter pilot and one-time assistant athletic director at the U.S. Naval Academy, were two of the most impressive people present for the dinner.

I'll always remember Bill for captaining the last Columbia University football team to win the Ivy League title, and later for coaching at Columbia when I was working in New York. Sportswriters in New York really liked Bill Campbell.

Jim comes to mind because he caught eight passes from Roger Staubach when Navy dealt Pitt its only loss in a 9-1 season back in 1963, at the start of my senior year at Pitt.

Both remarked that they get emotional when they return home, especially when they pass the William V. Campbell Field, used by Steel Valley High School, which is named for their father, the former superintendent of the school district.

"Joe has heart," said Jim Campbell. "That's what Homestead and Munhall are all about. We drove down 8th Avenue and where we grew up last night. We drove by Homestead High. It's heart-breaking in some ways to see what's happened to some places that were so important to you."

Bill brought some business colleagues from Palo Alto along with him, and because of airplane mechanical problems, he had to charter an airplane out of Chicago to keep his appointment in his hometown.

The Campbells joined old friends the night before the banquet at Chiodo's in Homestead. They were disappointed that old friend Joe Chiodo was vacationing in Italy.

"I get choked up when I come back here," said brother Bill. "It's important to remember where you grew up. That's the measure of Joe Bugel. I know him as a son, a brother, a parent, a buddy, and he's an amazing guy."

Bugel was bleary-eyed, too, when he saw the joy in his father's proud eyes. His dad was a partner in a family-owned chrome plating and electroplating company, but retired 27 years ago. Joe Sr. served as a director of Great American Federal, and was chairman of the board for 12 years.

Great American Federal, Allegheny University Hospitals and the Campbell Brothers were sponsors who helped underwrite the dinner. It was, indeed, an NFL Spectacular.

Joe Bugel Sr. was seated in front of his son, Joe, and his daughter-in-law, Brenda, at recognition dinner in Munhall.

Jim O'Brien

"These are America's citizen heroes and heroines who came of age during the Great Depression and the Second World War and went on to build modern America. This generation was united not only by a common purpose, but also by common values — duty, honor, economy, courage, service, love of family and country and, above all, responsibility for oneself. Their everyday lives gave us the world we have today."
— Tom Brokaw in his book
The Greatest Generation

Tony Dorsett
He made a difference

George Gojkovich

*"He was just what
the Cowboys needed."*
— Gil Brandt,
former Dallas superscout

I can. I can. I can. Tony Dorsett said those two little words three times in succession as he delivered his acceptance speech on the front steps of the Pro Football Hall of Fame.

I can. I can. I can.

He urged us to repeat those words whenever we felt challenged or overwhelmed, whenever we thought something was too much, more than we could do, when perhaps someone told us we weren't equal to a task.

It helps, it really does.

When those damn deadlines are pressing, and you feel like you've just squeezed your head into an undersized football helmet, it helps.

I can. I can. I can.

Tony Dorsett showed us the way. His success story has always been an inspirational one. He was too small when he first showed up for practice at Hopewell High School near his home in Aliquippa. He wasn't tall enough, he didn't weigh enough. No one, not even back then, ever questioned his speed. He was always fast enough.

Even though he had a sensational high school career, some thought he'd be too small to play big-time football at Pitt. Even though he had a sensational college career at Pitt, some thought he'd be too small to be successful in the National Football League.

Dorsett fooled them all. He took the ball, feinted this way and that, left everyone else stumbling in his path, and zigged here and zagged there, and put up numbers like no other runner ever had before — on every level.

That's why he was saying those two little words over and over again at the Pro Football Hall of Fame induction ceremonies at Canton, Ohio back on July 30, 1994.

I can. I can. I can.

Tony Dorsett was a living example of "The Little Engine That Could" bedtime story for kids.

Dorsett never doubted himself, that's why.

"There's no place like home."
— Dorothy, in
The Wizard of Oz

"This is so exciting."
— Anthony Dorsett, Jr.

I'm prejudiced, I know, but I thought Tony Dorsett stole the show at the Pro Football Hall of Fame. The Class of '94 was a considerable one, including Minnesota Vikings coach Bud Grant, Cleveland Browns running back Leroy Kelly, St. Louis Cardinals tight end Jackie Smith, San Francisco 49ers defensive back Jimmy Johnson and Dallas Cowboys defensive lineman Randy White.

Several of them tugged at your heart-strings with some of the things they said, but none of them was quite as prepared and as effective as Dorsett, who turned the podium into a pulpit and delivered an old-fashioned Baptist sermon. He was 40 years old — hard to believe — and he had aged well.

Many of the former football stars walk awkwardly, or wobble, wherever they go these days, but Dorsett looked as sure-footed and nimble as ever. He appeared strong, proud, clear-eyed and erect.

Anybody who wears a Pitt ring, cares about the Blue and Gold, is employed by the University, or hails from western Pennsylvania had to feel proud if they were present for all the weekend's activities at Canton.

At a dinner the night before, for instance, when they introduced all the inductees and past Hall of Famers who were present, I felt a rush when a U.S. Air Force band played "Hail to Pitt" as Dorsett was ushered across a stage by a local pageant queen.

I was sitting alongside my pal, Bill Priatko, who played football at Pitt in the '50s. Priatko looked proud as a peacock when they were playing the school fight song. "This is great," he said.

The school fight song never sounded better, but it may have been the setting. There were laser lights and all sorts of special effects accompanying the visuals at the Civic Center in Canton. Multi-screened images of Dorsett in action for the Dallas Cowboys came at you from every direction. Super stuff.

Then, too, I had images of my own. I was working in New York when Dorsett was doing his stuff at Pitt, but I remembered a game when I accompanied old Pitt classmates from Manhattan to the U. S. Military Academy at West Point, and saw Dorsett personally destroy the once-proud Army football team with a 200 yards-plus rushing effort. I remembered sitting a few rows behind his parents at Michie Stadium, and how proud they were. I remembered a dank night at Three Rivers Stadium, the night after Thanksgiving, 1976, when Dorsett led the Panthers to a big victory over Penn State in the regular season finale. Pitt would go on to beat Georgia in the Sugar Bowl to complete a 12-0 season and win the national championship.

What sweet memories!

Dorsett was keeping good company in Canton. It's become an annual pilgrimage for me because I feel like a kid again, meeting and socializing with the stars of my youth.

In addition to the inductees, the different events were attended by the likes of Dick "Night Train" Lane, Marion Motley, Pete Pihos, Dante Lavelli, Arnie Weinmeister, Ray Nitschke, Bob St. Clair, Lou Groza and Doug Atkins. Nitschke and Motley have since died.

There were also some I covered, such as Earl Campbell, John Henry Johnson, Tom Landry, Ernie Stautner and Willie Brown. It's worth the 110-mile easy-motoring trip from Pittsburgh to see all these great players and coaches up close.

Dorsett seemed somewhat ill at ease at a social on the eve of the induction. Maybe the room was crowded, maybe he was uncomfortable because he couldn't run to daylight. He spoke to his son, Anthony Jr., who is a good two inches taller than him, and was then a defensive back on the Pitt team. He would later make it in the NFL as a defensive back with the Houston and then Tennessee Oilers, now the Titans.

"This is so exciting," Anthony Jr. told me. "People were mistaking me for my dad, asking me for autographs. I had to tell them, 'I'm not that Tony Dorsett!' But I'm so happy for my dad, and glad I'm here."

In his heart, so was his dad.

When Tony Dorsett spoke the next day in front of the Pro Football Hall of Fame, so clearly, with a well-thought-out message, a heartfelt offering, I remembered seeing a tape of him being interviewed when he was a student at Pitt. I thought about the progress he had made, the polish he had picked up along the way while playing professional football, and being exposed to situations that demanded he keep sharpening his skills and his speaking methods.

Among those who looked on with pride were former Pitt football coach Jackie Sherrill. I spotted one of Dorsett's former Panther teammates, Chuck "The Kamikaze Kid" Bonasorte, wearing one of those outsized Pitt sweatshirts he sells on the sidewalks on the Pitt campus. He, too, was waving wildly when Dorsett was introduced.

Tony Dorsett never forgot where he came from, and paid tribute to his parents and relatives and friends from his early days, but it was quite evident that he had, indeed, come a long way from Aliquippa.

"It's been a long journey for me to get back here," Dorsett said in his talk. "From Aliquippa to Pittsburgh to Dallas and now Canton. It's been a journey that's been filled with hope and been filled with heart."

"Past lives live in us, through us. Each of us harbors the spirits of people who walked the earth before we did, and those spirits depend on us for continuing existence, just as we depend on their presence to live our lives to the fullest."
— John Edgar Wideman,
Author from Homewood,
Sent For You Yesterday

University of Pittsburgh Sports Media Service

Jim O'Brien

Tony Dorsett, left, as he appeared in 1974 in his Pitt days and, at right, as he looked 20 years later at induction ceremonies at the Pro Football Hall of Fame. Dorsett was part of a great All-America and national championship tradition at Pitt, which included Marshall "Biggie" Goldberg of "Dream Backfield" fame.

University of Pittsburgh Sports Media Service

"Tony was one of the greatest ever."
— Johnny Majors

No other single player ever had the impact on a college football program as Dorsett did at Pitt. The team was 1-10 the year before he and Majors took over the program. They won six games and went to a bowl game the first time out of the blocks. They would, in time, win a national championship.

Pitt was paying tribute to Tony Dorsett at special ceremonies at its opening game of the 1994 football season, a September 3 date with the University of Texas. This was doubly appropriate, because the people of Texas could appreciate what he did for the Dallas Cowboys.

"Tony was one of the greatest pro and college football players ever," said Majors in early August, when asked about Dorsett's contribution to his success during his first stay at Pitt. "He's the only player ever to win a college championship, a pro championship, the Heisman Trophy and be inducted into the Hall of Fame for both pro and college football."

Dorsett joined Joe Schmidt and Mike Ditka as former Pitt players honored as inductees at the Pro Football Hall of Fame. His name can be mentioned along with other legendary figures at Pitt such as Pop Warner, Dr. Jock Sutherland, Marshall Goldberg, Hugh Green, Danny Marino, Bill Fralic. Dorsett may have been the most spectacular of them all during his days on the Oakland campus.

The only Pitt man to have had a greater impact was Dr. Jonas Salk, who discovered the anti-polio vaccine in a lab across the street from Pitt Stadium back in the mid-50s. Pitt should erect statues to Dr. Salk and Tony Dorsett on the campus.

I spoke to several people in Canton who knew Dorsett well, and they only reinforced my feelings about Dorsett's specialness to both the Pitt and Cowboys' program.

Gil Brandt sat in the row in front of me during the induction ceremonies. Brandt was wearing a Cowboys ballcap, even though he, like Tom Landry, who introduced Dorsett for induction, were no longer associated with the Cowboys. Brandt had been in charge of college scouting and player personnel during the Cowboys' championship seasons.

Brandt was a frequent visitor to Pitt Stadium during Dorsett's heydays there.

I asked him when he first fell in love with Dorsett.

"I helped *Playboy* magazine pick its college football All-America team every year," said Brandt, "and I met Tony before his second season at a *Playboy* get-together in Chicago. We were there to get pictures for the college football preview issue, and to have some parties and have some fun.

"Tony was just such a poised guy. I became enamored with him. Before his senior year at Pitt, Johnny Majors called me and said, 'I

Pitt officials welcomed Tony Dorsett of Dallas Cowboys back on campus in late '70s at Pitt Stadium. They were, from left to right, distinguished alumni Herb McCracken and Dick Swanson, head coach Jackie Sherrill and Chancellor Wes Posvar.

Tony Dorsett gained great support from his parents, Myrtle and Wes Dorsett.

need you here. I need you because this guy is thinking of leaving school early and going to Canada.' So I went up and talked to Tony, and told him why it would be in his best interest to remain in school, and wait for the NFL draft.

"To give you an idea of what he meant to Pitt's program," offered Brandt, "consider this. He was the first player picked in the draft in 1976, and the draft went seven rounds before another Pitt player — a punter named Larry Swider — was selected. Southern Cal had three guys in the first round, for instance.

"I think he's the only guy to win a college championship and a Super Bowl in back-to-back seasons, and he won them both in the same building (the Superdome in New Orleans). He was just what the Cowboys needed to go all the way."

That's why the Cowboys dealt several draft picks that year, including their first and three second-round picks, to the Seattle Seahawks in exchange for the top pick in the draft.

"They'll probably show him running 99 yards for a touchdown in the highlight film tonight," said Brandt, "but I saw the guy make a run for two yards, and a touchdown, against the Cardinals, that was one of the greatest runs I've ever seen."

Did Brandt know when he drafted Dorsett that he'd be so successful?

"I wish I could say I knew he'd play all those years, and be so spectacularly effective for so long, but that wouldn't be true. But, to me, there was no question he'd be a great player."

Preston Pearson had played alongside Franco Harris in the Steelers' backfield before he was traded to the Dallas Cowboys. "Tony has some very innate talents," Pearson said. "Where that comes from, who knows?

"I thought Tony would have been an even greater performer if he had been more willing to catch passes. He hated to catch passes. He told Tom Landry he didn't come to Dallas to do anything but run the ball. I think he realizes now that he'd have been even more spectacular if he'd been part of the passing game. If there was one thing Tony would do differently if he had to do it all over again I think it would be to catch more passes. Tony didn't want to catch the football back then, but I think he would now."

"I can smile about what I've done."
— Tony Dorsett

Dorsett went into the Pro Football Hall of Fame, by coincidence, on the same day that the Big 33 Classic was being played at Hershey.

It was in the Big 33 game that Majors first saw Dorsett in action. Before that, he had seen him only on film.

Majors remembers it well, especially one run.

"On that particular play, Tony took a pitch and started to his right and got boxed in," said Majors. "He reversed his field, kept giving ground and came back around the other end for a rather substantial gain.

"I don't remember whether he scored or how long the run was, but it was outstanding. Friends sitting next to me were standing, yelling and I told them to sit down and be calm.

"When the game was over, I went back to my motel room. I went in and closed the door and shouted, 'Hallelujah, we've got ourselves a tailback.' And that's the honest truth."

That run, in truth, was for 25 yards.

When Majors became the head coach at Pitt in 1973, the first recruit he visited was Dorsett. At that time, Dorsett was about 5-10 and 160 pounds, and some thought him too small for big-time college football. Woody Hayes already had Archie Griffin at Ohio State and was interested in Dorsett as a defensive back.

Dorsett came from an area in western Pennsylvania that had produced tough players: Hall of Famers Mike Ditka and Joe Namath, and players like Vito "Babe" Parilli, Jim Mutscheller and Joe Walton.

Dorsett was special. He would add an inch and about 25 pounds somewhere along the way, and he rewrote the college record book with his hard-slashing running. He became the first college back to rush for at least 1,000 yards in each of his four seasons and the first to gain more than 1,500 in three of them. As a senior, he ran for 1,948 yards (raising his career total to an NCAA-record 6,082 yards) and 21 touchdowns and won the Heisman Trophy. His rushing record remained on the books until 1998 when Ricky Williams of Texas broke it.

In the NFL, Dorsett became the first player ever to gain more than 1,000 yards in each of his first five seasons. He had 1,000-yard efforts eight times in nine years, his only miss coming in the strike-shortened 1982 season. Overall, he played 11 seasons with the Cowboys and a final one with the Denver Broncos, finishing with 12,739 yards rushing and 16,326 total yards. He passed Jim Brown in both categories and ranked second only to Walter Payton at the time of his retirement.

"When I leaf through the pages of my scrapbook someday," declared Dorsett, "I can smile about what I have done."

"Self-trust is the essence of heroism."
— Ralph Waldo Emerson

Chuck Klausing
The Wizard of Wilmerding

*"I enjoyed every place,
but Braddock was different."*

The year 1998 was the best of times and the worst of times for Chuck Klausing. On May 19, he received notification that he was being inducted into the College Football Hall of Fame, the pinnacle of his profession. On June 25, he received a telephone call from his son-in-law, Scott Marshall, informing Klausing that his 41-year-old daughter, Nancy, had died of a heart ailment.

The news, understandably, crushed Klausing. I had worked with Klausing one year at Pitt, in 1986, when he made the mistake of leaving Carnegie Mellon where he was a highly-successful head coach to serve as an under-appreciated assistant coach to Mike Gottfried. I knew Klausing as a conscientious man, a sincere and decent man, who was always concerned about his wife and kids — we shared stories about our kids — and I knew what a blow this had to be for him and his family. This was the worst loss he had ever suffered.

"Nancy was planning on being there when I received my honor," recalled Klausing. "She was going to travel from Morgantown to South Bend for my big day. Of course, she came to my mind during the ceremony. When I saw my family and friends in the audience, she was missing. It hurt."

It stole the steam from what should have been a thrilling triumphant weekend — August 14-15 — for him and his family. He broke down in tears when he mentioned Nancy during his acceptance speech.

He and his wife, Joann, who celebrated their 50th wedding anniversary, ironically enough, in the spring of 1998, had five children, Patti, Mary Lou, Tommy, Nancy and Kathy, 12 grandchildren and one great-grandchild.

"Nancy had so much charisma and was so popular," continued Klausing. "If I had her charisma, I'd have been a coach at Notre Dame or with the Dallas Cowboys."

That remark points up something curious about Klausing. Despite all his tremendous accomplishments as a coach, Klausing keeps tormenting himself by what might have been. He says, "I never look back at things of the past," but he does, indeed. He believed, understandably, that he could have been a successful football coach on a higher level.

He promoted himself behind the scenes for the Pitt position whenever it came open, he nearly succeeded in creating a player personnel position for himself with the Steelers, he might have been the head coach at West Virginia had he stayed there a little longer, rather than accepting the head coaching job at Carnegie Mellon.

354

Klausing left West Virginia two weeks before Bobby Bowden resigned to take the Florida State job. Had Klausing stayed in Morgantown another month, he thought he would have gotten the WVU job. "Certainly it would have been interesting," said Klausing.

Klausing kept reaching for the brass ring. He often spoke of a need to make more money. No matter where he coached, he never made the big bucks. He seemed obsessed by the idea, somewhat intriguing, that he wanted to leave his children a hefty inheritance. By his own example, he had already done that and more.

In 1972, he had talked to the Pittsburgh Steelers about a position to scout professional players. They liked his idea. "The Steelers were going to give me a good increase over what I was making at WVU, plus a budget of $200,000," recalled Klausing. "But I wanted to coach, so I didn't take that job.

"If I had, I might be doing what Tom Donahoe does now and be making a million bucks. I have no regrets, though."

It reminds one of lines by Marlon Brando in an Oscar-winning performance (1954) as a dock worker and club fighter, Terry Malloy, in one of my favorite movies and books, *On The Waterfront*: "I coulda been something," Malloy cried out to his brother. "I coulda been a contender."

Klausing must keep in mind that he was, indeed, something special, a champion in every respect, successful as a coach and, more importantly, as a husband and father and friend. He remains one of the most respected coaches in the tri-state area, a good man in every respect.

"I have been so fortunate to have coached so many years and made so many friends," he said.

Mickey Furfari, the venerable sports writer from Morgantown who has seen so many wonderful folks come and go at West Virginia, offered a good story about Klausing.

It goes back to when Bobby Bowden called Klausing at IUP on Christmas Day, 1969, to offer him a job as an assistant coach. Klausing was the athletic director as well as the head football coach at IUP at the time.

"I told Bowden I couldn't afford to come," Klausing related to Furfari. "But Bobby said they were willing to pay me one dollar less than his salary."

A couple of years ago, Bowden signed a contract for more than $1 million a year at Florida State. Klausing telephoned him to joke, "Hey, Bobby, I'll come for one dollar less."

Klausing met a lot of famous people in sports through the years and collected a lot of great stories. I helped him get his thoughts organized and to get started on a book he wrote and published in 1997 about his experiences, *Never Lost A Game, Time Just Ran Out*. He borrowed that line from Bobby Layne, the Hall of Fame quarterback of the Detroit Lions and Pittsburgh Steelers.

We took a trip down memory lane in 1997, touring towns where Klausing grew up and first made his mark as an athlete and coach, in Wilmerding, Pitcairn and Braddock. We even made a side trip to North Versailles where he found and recruited some of his most outstanding players for Braddock High. Every familiar face and place prompted a story.

Whatever main streets we walked, Klausing kept waving and calling out to old friends and fans. He once contributed to civic pride in those milltowns. When they were at their best, when the men were all busy and the main street shops were bustling, so was Klausing. He made the men and women and children feel like winners. And they were.

He would point to storefronts that were boarded up and tell me what once thrived there.

Klausing can't stop from seeking the Holy Grail in his profession. Like another western Pennsylvanian, Arnold Palmer, he has been possessed by the need to compete, to show his stuff, to keep working at his game, to keep learning, to keep yearning, reminding us of his philosophies, his accomplishments, his track record.

His wiry hair, his high wrinkled brow, the lop-sided grin, the blue eyes he keeps fixed on yours when he talks to you, the way he walks, the way he talks — out of the side of his mouth like former Bucs' broadcaster Bob Prince — come to mind when one considers Chuck Klausing. So does the way he folds his arms when he surveys a field, like a general, his Teutonic manner, similar at times to that of another famous coach of German heritage who left his mark in Pittsburgh, namely Chuck Noll, someone Klausing greatly admired and envied.

As impressive as Klausing's accomplishments were as a college coach, as the head man at Indiana University of Pennsylvania and Carnegie-Mellon University, and as a respected assistant at Rutgers, Army, West Virginia and Pitt, he is perhaps best remembered for what he accomplished earlier in his coaching career at Braddock High School.

Klausing's career spanned six decades, three high schools and six colleges. He was a winner wherever he worked, but nothing compared with his 54-0-1 record in six undefeated seasons at Braddock.

There was a victory before and after Klausing came to Braddock that framed a fantastic 56-game unbeaten string, the longest in the country at the time. A national hero, the Yankees' Joe DiMaggio, died the same month I wrote this chapter and, of course, he was best known for his 56-game hitting streak. So 56 was a number that defined DiMaggio and Klausing. "I never thought about that," said Klausing. Throughout his career, though, Klausing drew inspiration from magical men like DiMaggio.

Chuck Klausing (photo on facing page) gained national recognition at Braddock High in winter of 1961 in latter stages of 54 consecutive games without a defeat. He was photographed at plaque marking British General Braddock's defeat to the French and Indians.

BRADDOCKS DEFEAT

On this site Braddock's Provincial and Colonial Army met a disastrous defeat on July 9, 1755 at the hands of the French and Indians. This engagement is known as the "Battle of the Monongahela" or "Braddock's Defeat." Four hundred and fifty-six British soldiers are buried here in unmarked graves. George Washington, aide-de-camp to Braddock's was Braddock's

Klausing remained a student of the game. Less than a month away from his 74th birthday (April 19, 1925 birthdate) on March 24, 1999, I called him on the telephone at his home in Indiana, Pa. to check on some names and dates. I asked him if he was taking it easy, which was stupid of me.

"Not really," he said, and I knew he was smiling as he said it. "I got up at 6 this morning and got my swim in. Then I got in some real good reading for a few hours, a book relating to parents coaching youth football. I read for a few hours, something I really enjoy being able to do these days.

"I'm going to be hosting the first-ever all-youth football coaching clinic on April 10th at North Allegheny High School. I have a passion for youth football; I have three grandsons playing. These parents need help. They may not have any coaching background and sometimes they do things that aren't in the best interest of the kids. I've got a sponsor, Adams U.S.A., which manufactures football helmets and pads and athletic equipment in Cookeville, Tennessee. They may have me do this kind of clinic across the country under their banner. We've got over 300 signed up so far."

He also had some legendary prep coaches as consultants, such as Art Bernardi of Butler, Lindy Lauro of New Castle and Pete Antimarino of Gateway High School in Monroeville.

Klausing had conducted football clinics in Europe as well since he was supposed to have retired. He just keeps ticking...

Even though he had experienced some heart problems, Klausing claimed to be "a young 73," at least for a few more weeks.

I told him I'd be seeing him on April 11, when we would be joining one of my former Pitt classmates, Dr. Ernie Borghetti, in being honored by the Pittsburgh chapter of the National Italian-American Sports Hall of Fame. By coincidence, Klausing and I had both spent much of our youth in neighborhoods made up mostly of people of Italian heritage. Maybe that's why we were being honored now. We ended up sitting next to each other at the dais. Former Pirates scout Elmer Gray sat on Klausing's other side.

This was old hat for Klausing, who had been inducted into nine different halls of fame.

"He thinks he's Amos Alonzo Stagg."
— Mike Gottfried,
Former Pitt coach

Chuck Klausing can't quit the game. He's still studying it, trying to get better at it. Most young coaches don't devote the time and effort this man still brings to the task. They think they know it all. Klausing is a coach who has studied military leaders and their tactics, as well

Chuck Klausing, Joe Gasparella and Rich Lackner, left to right, have all served as the head football coach at Carnegie Mellon University. They were among honorees at 1999 awards dinner at downtown Hilton sponsored by Pittsburgh chapter of the National Italian-American Sports Hall of Fame.

Three legendary high school football coaches Chuck Klausing calls upon when he's conducting all-star clinics are, left to right, Lindy Lauro of New Castle, Pete Antimarino of Gateway in Monroeville, and Art Bernardi of Butler. They share an Italian heritage.

as Paul Brown, the Hall of Fame football coach from Ohio, and so many others. Whenever I catch Klausing at some function, he always recommends some book, usually historical in nature, he just read and enjoyed.

Klausing was a student of Field Marshall Erwin Rommell, Germany's "Desert Fox" of World War II fame. Klausing read his letters. Rommell believed in doing what the enemy least expected him to do. So on a fourth-and-one, Klausing might pass rather than smash the ball up the middle.

Klausing can tell stories about the Canton Bulldogs and Massillon Tigers as well as the Pottsville Maroons and Pitcairn Mohawks, going back to the pioneer days of pro football. He successfully used plays at Pitcairn and Braddock that his dad told him he'd seen those teams employ — like the "swinging gate" play which had everyone lined up on one side of the ball before the snap — and Klausing used to drive Gottfried crazy with such epic stories.

"He thinks he's Amos Alonzo Stagg," Gottfried once growled at me, something he was fond of doing. "To hear Klausing, you'd think he was the coach who invented the huddle and the forward pass."

Klausing is an irrepressible story-teller. He can't help himself. And he was a pretty good coach on every level. If Gottfried had listened more carefully, he might have learned something. Klausing advised him not to offer scholarships to prospects he didn't believe were academically up to snuff for Pitt — quarterback Darnell Dickerson from Detroit comes to mind — and Gottfried began to treat Klausing like a pariah, or grad assistant, in appreciation for his advice. Gottfried felt Klausing thought he was still coaching at academically-tough Carnegie Mellon.

Klausing was correct in his assessment of Dickerson. He was a talented athlete, but he was overwhelmed by the academic demands at Pitt, light as they are for most jocks. He was always in one difficulty or another, and departed Pitt prematurely.

Gottfried would give his eyeteeth to have a career record to compare with Klausing. He had a distinguished 46-year coaching career, including 19 seasons at the high school level. Then again, Klausing would love to be making the money and getting the national exposure (via ESPN) Gottfried has enjoyed the past decade.

At the time of his induction into the College Football Hall of Fame in South Bend, Indiana, Klausing ranked 14th all-time among all NCAA coaches with at least 10 years at four-year colleges with an .800 or better winning percentage.

He was honored along with the likes of Eddie Robinson of Grambling State, Don James of Washington, Wally Butts of Georgia, Bowden Wyatt of Tennessee, Donnie Shell, the former Steelers safety from South Carolina State, Danny White of Arizona State and the Dallas Cowboys, Charlie Flowers of Mississippi, Dave Robinson of Penn State, Dave Rimington of Nebraska.

Leon Hart of Turtle Creek and Notre Dame fame was one of the standout prep players Klausing caught in action early in his career.

Chuck Klausing

Klausing was ABC-TV's Small College Coach of the Year in 1979 after he direct-ed Carnegie Mellon University to championship of Presidents Athletic Conference (PAC) and advanced far in national playoffs. He was surrounded, left to right, by Bob Gasior, Gusty Sunseri, Joe Goldcamp, Gary Matz and Don Kaminski.

After Klausing left Braddock for Rutgers, he coached at West Point for three years (two of those under Paul Dietzel) and was the head coach at Indiana University of Pennsylvania for six years (1964-1969), posting a 47-10 record. Following IUP, he was an assistant for six years (1970-1975) at West Virginia, then ten years (1976-1985) as head coach at Carnegie Mellon, posting a 77-15-2 mark.

Klausing's combined record in his 16 years as a head coach at IUP and CMU was 124-26-2. He was ABC Coach of the Year in his division in 1979 and 1983. He had put in an unsuccessful bid to become the head coach at Pitt during his stay at CMU, and settled for an assistant's position several years later when Gottfried got the job. He wanted back in the big time so badly that he jumped at the opportunity to move across Oakland to Pitt Stadium. "I knew within a week that I had made a mistake," he says now, "but I thought it would look bad if I left then. I decided to stick it out for a year and then leave."

He tries to put a positive spin on it, but I know how hurt he was at the time. He admits he was too old to recruit the way one has to in Division I football, that it was difficult to go from being a head coach to an underutilized assistant, and to go along with Gottfried's wishes in some areas.

After one year as a Pitt assistant, Klausing concluded his wondrous coaching career as head coach at Kiski School in Saltsburg, where he had a seven-year record of 28-22-4 before retiring. He and Joann enjoyed living in a house on Kiski's beautiful campus during his stay there. After he retired, they returned to Indiana, Pa.

"I studied what Paul Brown did at Massillon."

"I enjoyed every place," said Klausing, looking back on his storied career, "but Braddock was completely different. It was the first time I coached blacks and whites. In my first year there, I had eight whites and three blacks in my starting lineup. By the time I left, I had eight blacks and three whites in the lineup. I studied what Paul Brown had done at Massillon and that helped me. Braddock gave me everything Brown had at Massillon. I guess it was the crowning of my career. "

Klausing also told me he had attended a funeral of one of his former players at a Baptist church in Braddock just the day before.

Jerome Mans, 60, was one of "the most agile and shiftiest runners," according to Klausing. Mans went to North Carolina A&T, the first in his family to go to college. "Now 20 some members of his family have gone to college," continued Klausing. "That's quite an achievement.

"Jerome had been in a wheelchair for 30 to 35 years. He was injured by a landmine explosion while in Vietnam. I saw some of my other players at the church. The preacher gave an emotional sermon. Jerome's brother gave the eulogy and it was quite moving. His brother is a high school coach in Florida. He told me he was going to a clinic of Bobby Bowden's at Florida State. I was on Bobby's staff at West Virginia. So I gave him my card and told him to show it to Coach Bowden as an ice-breaker."

I had accompanied Klausing to a funeral in Wilmerding when I interviewed him at length two years earlier. Now he was telling me on the telephone that he'd been going to too many funerals.

"Too much, too often," as he put it. "My dad told me to make sure you go to every baptism and wedding you're invited to, and that you should go to the funerals of family and friends. That's stayed with me."

Chuck Klausing could go home again because he could find old friends on the street corners and at the funeral homes in Wilmerding, where he lived the first 18 years of his life, with the exception of one year in his mother's hometown of Irwin.

One of the friends, a former schoolmate, was, at age 73, still running numbers, taking bets from people stopping in their cars in broad daylight on the main street of Wilmerding. The friend was a one-time football player with the nickname of "Rack," short for "Racketeer." As a youngster, when the teacher asked the students to write down what they wanted to be when they grew up, Klausing recalled that this character wrote "Racketeer."

In Wilmerding and in Pitcairn, where he had his first job as a football coach at age 23, Klausing was welcomed by folks who recognized or knew him when he took me on a whirlwind tour of towns that shaped his life. A woman who was working as a receptionist at the funeral home said, "It's always nice to see you, Mr. Klausing." He had a little bit of Art Rooney in him when it came to attending so many funerals.

We walked across football fields where Leon Hart of Turtle Creek and Fran Rogel of North Braddock and Kenny Reaves of Braddock had once played. Klausing pointed out homes and buildings, landmarks from earlier days, and had a story for all he saw.

Klausing played ball at Westinghouse Memorial High School in Wilmerding. When he was playing ball on Saturdays at Slippery Rock, he'd come home and play for the Wilmerding Alumni in sandlot games on Sunday. He recalled a game they played against the highly-regarded Pitcairn Mohawks, who were quarterbacked by Walter "Pete" Antimarino, later a great coach at Gateway High School. The game ended in a 7-7 tie. Klausing remembers details like that.

"Wilmerding had a lot of athletic pride when I was growing up there," recalled Klausing. "But we had only one player who ever made it to the major leagues in baseball. His name was John 'Shine' Cortazzo. He was reputed to have been the best player ever to perform in the Middle Atlantic League, and Stan Musial, Joe Cronin and Eddie Stanky had played in that league. Cortazzo flirted with a .400 batting average in the minors, but he only had a cup of coffee in the majors. But us kids in Wilmerding thought he was the greatest."

A check of *The Baseball Encyclopedia* points up that "Shine" Cortazzo was born September 26, 1904 in Wilmerding, Pa., and died March 4, 1963 in Pittsburgh. He was a little fellow, just 5 foot 3 inches, 142 pounds. He was up for a cup of coffee, all right, playing in one American League game in 1923 with the Chicago White Sox. He came to bat once as a pinch-hitter and failed to get on base. He got "up there," though, as they liked to say in the old neighborhood.

Klausing was one of the kids Cortazzo would later take to Pirates' games at Forbes Field, sometimes stopping at the Schenley Hotel to talk to opposing players and managers he knew from his days in the minor leagues. "That's when Ralph Kiner was hitting home runs all the time," said Klausing. "It was great to go to the games with someone who knew someone."

I remembered as a kid in Hazelwood that we had one big league ballplayer we could call our own. His name was Julius "Moose" Solters, and he went blind at the end of his ballplaying days. I don't know why he lost his sight. He was a fixture at all our community sports banquets. He was 6 feet, 190 pounds in his playing days, a giant compared to Cortazzo, and performed for nine years in the major leagues, from 1934 to 1943, with the Red Sox, Browns, Indians and White Sox. Solters played in 938 games and had a career .289 batting average and 83 home runs. As a kid, I was not aware that Solters had such a solid record in the big leagues.

He wore dark eyeglasses, combed his silver-gray hair straight back, was always well-tanned, dapper in a gray suit — he looked like Juan Peron, the Argentine dictator. But Solters seemed like a pleasant man. In Hazelwood, he was forever a hometown hero.

"I remember where I come from."
— Chuck Klausing

When we were in Wilmerding, we ran into Pete Cortazzo, 73 at the time, who was "Shine" Cortazzo's brother. There are Cortazzos and churches on every corner in this neck of the woods. Several of them are coaches, they have a heritage in that respect at East Allegheny High School, and they've made their mark in surrounding communities.

Klausing could point out a spot where he said he had the best newspaper sales spot a kid could have. "It was right at the gate of the Air Brake Company, and I'd catch the guys coming out of work. I'd have all my papers folded and they'd take a paper out of one hand, the change out of the other hand. I'd sell 100 papers in 15 minutes. Papers costs a nickel then."

He pointed out where Father Jack O'Malley served as a pastor at St. Jude The Apostle Church on Westinghouse Avenue. The former St. Aloysius Church on Caldwell Avenue was now the parish center for the merged churches. Father O'Malley was a bit of a rebel priest, a strong liberal who was always making his superiors nervous. He came out of St. Raphael's in Morningside and starred as a basketball player at St. Francis College of Loretto, right after Maurice Stokes, and was good enough to get drafted by the Detroit Pistons.

The abandoned football stadium at North Braddock Scott High had graystone seats, like Druid ruins. Weeds and moss covered the stone, and the place was crumbling. Not in Klausing's eyes, however. Klausing could see it the way it was when thousands of fans overflowed the stadium during Friday night football games. Our mutual friends, Fran Rogel, Bill Priatko and Rudy Celigoi, who went to school and played sports at North Braddock Scott, still saw it the same glorious way. The huge gray stones were landmarks in their lives. To me, it looked like a cemetery. Irrepressible optimists, these guys lived forever in Pleasantville.

He pointed out the Elks Club where his ballteam used to have its pre-game meals for home games.

Klausing and I had met at the Forest Hills Gourmet Deli, since closed down, and drove to Braddock, near where Chuck's wife, Joann, grew up. His Braddock High School football team played their home games at North Braddock Scott Field and practiced on a field just across the street, also in North Braddock. It's no wonder that was such a great rivalry.

"I remember where I come from because I frequently come back for funerals," commented Klausing. "I check the obit page every day to see if anyone I know has died."

Braddock was a different matter. Like surrounding Mon Valley communities such as Duquesne, McKeesport, Clairton and Glassport it had gone to pot when the steel mills shut down or cut back on activity. This is where he made his mark and gained national attention, including a four-page feature story in a November, 1959 issue of *Sports Illustrated*, so it still had appeal for him.

The schools were missing. North Braddock Scott had been leveled only a few months earlier, and Braddock High's practice field had been replaced long ago by the Benjamin F. Fairless Elementary School on Library Avenue. Benjamin Fairless was president of U.S. Steel in the '50s. A plant near Philadelphia is named for him as well, the Fairless Works.

Bob Prince, the "Voice of the Pirates," used to routinely call attention to Ben Fairless arriving at Forbes Field for a Bucs' ballgame. "My ol' friend, Ben Fairless, has just arrived," cried Prince, an irrepressible name-dropper. "Hi, Ben!"

The high school itself was an empty lot. "This looks more like our football field looked," he said, surveying the crushed gray stones.

Even Sacred Heart Church, the Polish Catholic Church where he and Joann were married, was missing. It had burned down. There were abandoned churches, where babies had been baptized and men and women were married, across the landscape, some had been merged with others.

We visited the mansion where the superintendent of the steel mill once lived. It's still impressive, and has extensive gardens in the backyard.

He pointed out an old school building where local legend Billy Knight once played basketball before he went to Pitt and played in the NBA.

We drove by the Edgar Thomson Works in the U.S. Steel division of USX Corporation along the Monongahela, just across the way from Kennywood Park. It was the first steel mill of Andrew Carnegie and had great historical significance. Three years earlier, USX invested $250 million in a state-of-the-art continuous caster as a "commitment to keeping steel making in the Steel City," as they announced. (By the way, Carnegie's first public library is also located in Braddock.)

We were at what is called "the hot end" of the Mon Valley Works. They take coke, iron ore and limestone and raw materials that go into making steel. A continuous caster produces solid slabs of steel, which are shipped across the river to a sister USX plant, the Irvin Works in West Mifflin, where it is finished in sheets.

About 1,000 work at the Braddock plant. As many as 5,000 worked there during World War II. The industry was more labor intensive in those days. It's more dependent on technology these days to enable them to remain competitive on a global basis.

It's a robust reminder of Braddock at its best.

Klausing recalled that Harry Stuhldreher was the superintendent of the U.S. Steel Edgar Thomson Works and frequently attended Braddock's football games when Klausing was the coach there. Stuhldreher was a member of the famed "Four Horsemen" of Notre Dame, along with Don Miller, Elmer Layden and Jim Crowley. Stuhldreher wrote letters of recommendation on behalf of Klausing to several schools, including Pottstown and Massillon. One learns a lot of history in the company of Klausing.

"There was great teamwork."

Chuck Klausing was born in a home just two homes removed from a football field in Wilmerding, now Memorial Field for the YMCA Southeast Area Program Center.

The Klausings moved two houses down the row when his parents got their own home. Originally, they had been living with his father's parents, which many young couples did in those days.

"We lived at 541 Westinghouse Avenue originally, until I was seven or so," recalled Klausing. "My dad played a penny on 541 on 'the numbers' one day, and he hit and collected $6.30. He bought my sister a baby doll and me a football with that money. Imagine doing that today."

Klausing's father, Charles Klausing, was the son of immigrants from Hanover, Germany, and was the burgess and mayor for 24 years, and a lay minister and missionary in the Lutheran Church. His wife of over 50 years was named Alma. Chuck converted to Catholicism before marrying Joann.

Chuck Klausing had coached Pitcairn to a 30-22-2 record in six years before going to Braddock. "I was watching one of our future opponents, East Pittsburgh, against Braddock when I catalogued the fact that Braddock had two great running backs coming back the next season of 1954," recalled Klausing.

So he knew something about the Braddock football team when he learned of and applied for the job opening. He was the only applicant for the Tigers' coaching position. "Some coaches were reluctant because there were some problems at Braddock," he said. Mostly political in nature, he remembered. Nothing ever changes in that respect.

The Tigers had won their final game in 1953 under Henry Furrie and went unbeaten through 54 games under Klausing. His record at Braddock was 53-0-1.

The six straight championships is the longest streak in the WPIAL. After the tie with Midland in the 1954 title game, Braddock won the next five titles outright. No other WPIAL team has won more than three in a row without a tie.

After Klausing left for Rutgers to take an assistant's position, Bob Teitt took over and his 1960 team won the first game, but lost the second to Hopewell, coached by Klausing's former aide, Bill McDonald. The Tigers won the rest of their games that season. So the unbeaten streak was over at 56 games over eight seasons.

"The teams which kept the streak alive had great chemistry," Klausing told Mike White, the outstanding scholastic sports writer for the *Pittsburgh Post-Gazette*. Klausing also cited his great coaching staff of Teitt, McDonald, George Hays and John Zuger.

Klausing still has a ballcap he wore during his days at Braddock High. Some fan gave him a Notre Dame ballcap. Klausing told his team that ND stood for "No Defeats," and he wore it for a *Sports Illustrated* picture in 1959.

Klausing recalled the great games against arch-rival North Braddock in 1958 and 1959. Both teams entered the 1958 season-ending game with unbeaten records. Braddock won both in the last minute of the game.

In the 1958 regular season finale against North Braddock before more than 9,000 fans, Braddock won 9-6 on Roland Mudd's 37-yard field goal, which hit the top of the cross bar and fell over.

In the 1959 finale, before 10,000 fans at Scott Stadium, quarterback John Jacobs led an 83-yard drive for a touchdown late in the game. He hit Ray Henderson with a 26-yard touchdown pass with 37 seconds left in a 15-12 victory for Braddock.

"We had two outstanding quarterbacks during that time," said Klausing. "Both were All-American scholastic players. Mark Rutkowski, who tore up his knee in the Big 33 game, and John Jacobs, who played for Arizona State, the Dallas Cowboys and Washington Redskins."

Three Reaves brothers made notable contributions to the Tigers' streak. Joe Reaves, the eldest, was the top back in the WPIAL, scoring 15 touchdowns in his junior season and 20 as a senior. He went on to play at the University of Cincinnati.

Larry Reaves played at Arizona State and with the New York Jets.

Kenny, the youngest, played in 10 NFL seasons with the Atlanta Falcons and St. Louis Cardinals. "He was my quarterback in my last year at Braddock," recalled Klausing.

Roland Mudd was one of the stars. He played at Minnesota and in the Rose Bowl and became a coach in North Carolina. Another outstanding player was Curtis Vick, the MVP of the Big 33 game against Texas and in the Rose Bowl while at Purdue.

Braddock defeated Waynesburg, 25-7, in the 1959 WPIAL playoff championship, and Klausing accepted an assistant coach's position at Rutgers the following season.

Klausing checked the record books and discovered that it took Braddock 18 years to win 56 games prior to his stay there. Braddock's national mark has since been surpassed by a high school in Kansas.

"I had six years of great academics and great athletics at Braddock," Klausing told Huddie Kaufman, a scholastic sports writer and historian at the *Tribune-Review*. "Our teams were not fast, but quick. There was great teamwork, and though we had a 50-50 racial balance, I never heard any racist remarks in my time there.

"Braddock was a great shopping district at the time; the mills were all working. There was lots of community pride and a great educational system, led by the late Joe Stukus, the principal of the high school."

How did Klausing convert a so-so program into such a juggernaut? The school was 12-20-1 in four previous seasons. "He was a perfectionist," said Cody Mudd, who became the police chief in Rankin, but was a defensive tackle and kicker on the 1955 team. "He wanted things done his way and done right."

John Smonski of White Oak was a reporter for the *Braddock Free Press* and wrote a book on the Braddock High School football history. "You'd have to say the coaching is what did it," said Smonski, who once provided high school football ratings for *Pittsburgh Weekly Sports*. "Those kids listened to him. They did everything he said. Those guys had nothing but respect for him."

Klausing was 29 when he took the job at Braddock, following six years at Pitcairn.

He recruited some kids from neighboring school districts who didn't have their own high schools and could choose from among several neighboring schools. There was one section of North Versailles called Crestas Terrace, overlooking the Parkway East near the George Westinghouse Bridge.

Klausing not only sold some outstanding young athletes to attend Braddock, but he picked them up in the morning and drove them to school, and took them home at night. Running back Curtis Vick, whom Klausing calls the best player he ever had at Braddock, came from Crestas Terrace.

"I was a real gym rat."

When we were in East Pittsburgh, he said he used to go to the East Pittsburgh Boosters Club, and that's where he met his wife, Joann, who grew up in Braddock and worked at the Westinghouse plant in East Pittsburgh.

He said Baron Elliot, Lee Kelton and Jack Purcell and their bands used to play at dances there. He pointed out where East Pittsburgh High School was located at the top of the hill. "I was a math teacher there in 1948," he said proudly.

We visited the Wolvarena, the stadium in Turtle Creek that is used by Woodland Hills High School. George Novak was the coach and athletic director at Woodland Hills. We saw the weight room under the stadium seats, a chalkboard with x's and o's left there by Coach Novak and his staff. There were slogans about the locker room. Blue was the dominant color. There were over 12,000 seats. "This is as good a high school stadium as there is in Western Pennsylvania," said Klausing.

Woodland Hills draws students from Braddock, Rankin, North Braddock, Swissvale, Wilkins Township, Turtle Creek, East Pittsburgh, Edgewood and Churchill.

"This is where Fran Rogel led North Braddock to a big victory over Leon Hart and the Turtle Creek team," said Klausing.

"As Rogel walked around the field after the game, the millworkers filled his helmet with money. He picked up $200 to $300 that day, the fans were so appreciative of his great game.

"Yes, this is where Leon Hart played. I was at Penn State at the time, and came home on weekends when I could. I saw him play against Braddock and North Braddock. They were Monday games, I remember. If it rained, they simply postponed it to a later date when it was dry enough to play.

"North Braddock had a great team in that era. Hart was 6-4, 220, and he was a pretty danged good basketball player, too. You could tell he was a dominant high school player, as a tight end and defensive end.

"I coached in an All-Star Game here. Neil Brown and I coached the Allegheny County team and Dave Hart coached the Western Pennsylvania team."

He pointed out the YMCA on a nearby hillside. It's where he learned swimming, basketball, boxing and gymnastics. "My dad signed me up at the Y when I was 9 years old," recalled Klausing. "It cost $3 a year. I was a real gym rat.

"I see so many things around here that bring back memories. I was a boxer when I went to Penn State, and boxed intercollegiately as a 155 pounder. I learned to box at the Wilmerding YMCA. My coach was a guy named Jack Rovesta. He fought Art Rooney three times. He won once, lost once, and they had a draw. I was always lucky to have good coaches."

Klausing explained that he joined the Marines right out of high school. He was invited to be in the V-12 program, and he was sent to Penn State. He attended Penn State for 16 months on an accelerated academic program. He was there for two football seasons and one boxing season, as he put it. Then he went to training camp with the Marines and trained at Parris Island and Quantico. He was still 20 when he was assigned to the Pacific Theater. "The War had ended by the time I got there, in August of 1945," he said. "I came out of the service and enrolled at Slippery Rock State College, and graduated from there in 1948."

We drove from East Pittsburgh to Trafford. Klausing pointed out that Westinghouse once employed 25,000 workers in the Turtle Creek Valley, and now its biggest mill was simply an empty shell.

He pointed out the Pennsylvania Rail Road line and related how some kids used to ride it to school.

"I never missed a day's work," said Klausing. "I had twelve years of perfect attendance in grade school and high school. I enjoyed going to work every day. You learned a good work ethic growing up around here."

We drove by Westinghouse Air Brake Company (WABCO) and the Westinghouse museum in Wilmerding. "They once had 5,000 workers here," said Klausing. "Now they have 200.

"Every house in the community was built by Westinghouse." he said. "Then the government forced the company to sell them, and (Pirates owner and real estate mogul) John Galbreath bought all of them in 1942 and resold them to the people here."

He stopped in front of the house on Air Brake Avenue — address 432 across from the mill — where he lived from 7th grade on, until going off to college. It was a duplex, pink and red brick, with an aluminum awning. "I'm thinking about things I haven't thought about in a long time," he said.

Chuck Klausing can go home again and see old friends in Pitcairn, his first head coaching assignment, and at his boyhood home on Air Brake Avenue in Wilmerding. Pitcairn was once one of the largest railroad yards in country and Wilmerding was where George Westinghouse was headquartered.

He pointed out one of the WABCO buildings. "Josh Gibson used to be a janitor there. They had a shop baseball league, and there was an all-black team that included Gibson and some of the guys from the Homestead Grays and Pittsburgh Crawfords. The team was called the Black Sox."

He mentioned a basketball player named Fred Crum, who worked there and played for the Wilmerding Y team. I'd heard of Crum when I was growing up because he was living in Greenfield at the time.

"I've been told he was better than Paul Birch or Charley Hyatt," said Klausing. "That Y team won a national AAU tournament."

He talked about Tom Casey and his punting feats on the football field near his home. Casey could kick the ball out of the park. Klausing snapped for him. Casey went on to play in Canada and was all-CFL five times. He ended up becoming a neurosurgeon at the Cleveland Clinic, and was a storied character in Wilmerding.

He pointed out the Westinghouse Castle, where George Westinghouse once had his office, and which now serves as a museum housing all sorts of Westinghouse memorabilia. It's worth visiting to see all the old Westinghouse products — irons, TVs, fans, toasters, mixers, ranges, radios, all sorts of home appliances — and to appreciate the genius of George Westinghouse. He invented many wonderful things in addition to the air brake.

Seeing the building brought back another painful memory for Klausing. "My sister, Dorothy, and I were sled-riding down that hill in front of the Castle," he recalled. "I was five at the time, and she was ten. She rode a sled right into that building down there, and she broke her hip. She limped the rest of her life.

"My mother worked there in World War I, back around 1916-1917, and that's how she met my dad. All my family worked in that plant. Everybody used to walk over the bridge to go to work. I never have forgotten where I came from. I still have a lot of friends here. They're always glad to see you."

We stopped in Pitcairn and walked around the field where he first coached. "I was 23, just out of Slippery Rock, and I was a head coach my first year," said Klausing. "I can't believe there's grass here now. It was a hard clay field when I coached here. There was not a speck of grass. The railroad took care of the field. We'd have loved it if there'd been some grass."

He showed me how the goal posts were positioned right up against a fence on a field that flanks the main street in Pitcairn. That was once the Home of the Mohawks.

"I was paid $2,000 for teaching back then, and $300 for coaching the football team," said Klausing, "and I was married at the time. We lived with her father, then my folks. My oldest daughter was born when I was working there."

He pointed to a spot where he had once pulled off a so-called "sleeper play" during his days at Pitcairn. "In the '40s and early '50s, everyone had a sleeper play," said Klausing. "We pulled it off right here. It was the trick play of the era.

"When I took the job at Braddock, I heard about this kid in North Versailles named Ben Powell. North Versailles didn't have a high school of its own. They could go to East Pittsburgh or McKeesport or just about any nearby school. Powell was a WPIAL junior high school champion in the 100 and 220 yard dash.

"My friends told me about him. I went to see him play junior high basketball. I started to recruit him to go to Braddock. McKeesport was recruiting him, too. They had a booster club and they said they would provide a cab every day.

"I told him, 'I'll pick you up and take you to and from school.' I got Ben Powell to go to Braddock. When I came to pick him up, there were three other kids waiting with him. I'd drive four of them to school. Three of them were great football players. Powell scored 15 to 20 touchdowns a year. He went to junior college; he wasn't much of a student. Johnny Jacobs played four years in the NFL with the Cowboys and Redskins. Curtis Vick might have been the best of the three; he eventually played for Purdue. He's dead now. Bill King was on the team from that bunch, but was not a star player. I really lucked out when I recruited Ben Powell."

P.S. When writing a book like this, you have to call back several times to the people you interview to make sure you have the names and facts right. The fourth and last time I called Klausing, on March 31, 1999, he answered all my questions, and then offered a thought of his own.

"Today would be Nancy's birthday," he said of his late daughter. "She'd be 42 today. So Joann and I went to Mass this morning in her honor. I get real emotional just thinking about her."

Joann and Chuck Klausing's clan included, left to right, Kathy Kilkeeney, Tom Klausing, Pattie Simmons, Marylou Billings and Nancy Marshall. Nancy died in 1998, the same year the Klausings celebrated their 50th wedding anniversary and Chuck's induction into the College Football Hall of Fame.

Josh Gibson and the Homestead Grays
Willie Pope played with those guys

"Those were good days."

The summer and fall of 1998 was the best of baseball seasons. The home run derby between Mark McGwire and Sammy Sosa rekindled interest in the game for many of us.

McGwire finished with a record 70 home runs, Sosa was second with 66, both breaking the Roger Maris mark of 61. Their feats reminded us of Babe Ruth and Mickey Mantle, Ralph Kiner and Hank Greenberg, Roberto Clemente and Willie Stargell, and famous home runs by Bobby Thomson and Bill Mazeroski.

One great baseball player who should have come to mind more often was Josh Gibson, one of the greats from the days of the Negro Baseball Leagues. Gibson was known as "the Babe Ruth of the Negro Leagues." Next to Satchel Paige, he was the biggest attraction in black baseball.

Gibson hit either 71 or 75 home runs for the Homestead Grays in 1931. Record-keeping was sketchy, to say the least, the difference between exhibitions and legitimate league games blurred by the passing of time, the caliber of competition was sometimes sandlot at best.

Gibson hit 68 home runs in another season.

I asked Bill Nunn Jr. about the credibility of Gibson's home run numbers. Nunn, a respected scout for the Steelers for nearly 30 years, was previously the sports editor of the *Pittsburgh Courier*, once a national daily that served the black community.

"Some of those games were against local sandlot teams," noted Nunn. "But Gibson was regarded as a better hitter than Roy Campanella, who got his start in the black leagues. Campanella hit his share of home runs in the major leagues."

Indeed, Campanella was the National League's MVP three times, 1951, 1953 and 1955, while catching for the Brooklyn Dodgers. He hit 41 home runs and had 142 RBI in 1953.

Gibson and Satchel Paige were the two best known stars in the Negro Baseball Leagues in the '30s and '40s. They played for the Homestead Grays, who divided their home schedule between Pittsburgh and Washington D.C., and for the Pittsburgh Crawfords. It's another, often overlooked, part of Pittsburgh's glorious sports history. Gibson began as a pro with the Grays at 18, and he also played for the Crawfords as Paige's battery mate.

Gibson died at age 35 in 1947 of a brain tumor, three months before Jackie Robinson broke the color barrier in Major League Baseball. Robinson was one of 58 players who came out of the Negro Leagues to make it in the majors. Robinson's signing with the Dodgers was the beginning of the end for the Negro Baseball Leagues.

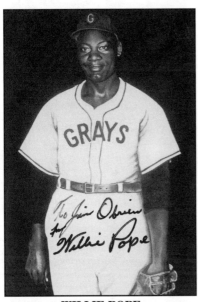

WILLIE POPE

JOSH GIBSON

Willie Pope leans into picture with KDKA-TV's Dave Crawley and former Pirates pitcher Bob Purkey of Bethel Park at '98 Seniorfest at PPG Plaza.

Willie Pope pitched for the Homestead Grays toward the end, from 1946 to 1948. One of 12 children of a coal miner's family in Library, Pope now lives in Homewood. His kid brother, outfielder Dave Pope, was one of four blacks who played for the Cleveland Indians when they won the American League pennant with a 111-43 record in 1954.

I shared an autograph signing booth with Pope in September at Seniorfest '98 at PPG Plaza. For the second September in a row, we were joined by Bob Purkey, the former Pirates pitcher who continues to own and operate an insurance agency in Bethel Park, and Dave Crawley, the KDKA-TV feature reporter who's had a life-long love affair with baseball. He grew up in Virginia, yet credits the late Bob Prince for inspiring him to get into the media business.

Pope wore a Grays ballcap and the blouse from a modern version of a Grays uniform, and attracted much attention.

One can learn a lot talking to oldtimers like Pope and Purkey, big favorites among the sponsoring Allegheny County for Aging Department, or by visiting the local library and getting out some books about the Negro Baseball Leagues.

Pope, a 6-3, 215-pound right-hander, once pitched a no-hitter against Minnie Minoso's Cuban All-Stars in Washington, D.C. That was the highlight of his career.

"Those were good times," said Pope. "We just wanted to play ball. We weren't concerned about politics. It was great for Jackie Robinson that he broke the color barrier, but it was bad for the rest of us. We were all out of jobs."

Pope enjoyed the summer of '98 as much as any baseball fan. We were playing to an older crowd, of course, at the 25th edition of the Seniorfest. Many of the seniors were aware of the Grays and the Crawfords, and recalled those days while Pope was signing autographs for them.

They identified themselves as being from Homestead or Munhall or West Mifflin, Lawrenceville and Lincoln Place, Ambridge and Aliquippa and other outlying communities or city neighborhoods. Some recalled seeing the Grays, playing at Forbes Field, or at West Field or on Third Avenue in Homestead, or McKeesport, or against the Crawfords at Greenlee Field on Bedford Avenue in the Hill District.

John Doloughtey Sr., 80, of Lawrenceville, said his father sold life insurance on the Hill. As a boy, Doloughtey recalled going up to Bedford Avenue to see the black ballplayers in action.

"Gibson wasn't exactly an idol of mine, but he was someone you could appreciate," declared Doloughtey.

Charley Rogy, 79, remembered selling newspapers as a kid in Homestead, and meeting some of the ballplayers. "What's the number? They always wanted to know what the number was. I'd see them in a pool room."

He talked about Cum Posey, who played ball at Homestead High and later played baseball and basketball at both Penn State and Duquesne University, and bankrolled the Homestead Grays. He

376

talked about Gus Greenlee, "the numbers king of Pittsburgh," who sponsored the Pittsburgh Crawfords. Rogy wore a Pitt baseball cap. He got a degree in industrial engineering there in the late '30s and worked at U.S. Steel. Rogy really enjoyed talking sports with Pope.

Herman Thomas, 67, of Homestead, excitedly recalled seeing the Grays play at West Field. "My father used to take me around to see them play. When they played the Crawfords, it was like a holiday. I saw Buck Leonard, 'Cool Papa' Bell, Satchel Paige and 'Smoky' Joe Williams. Williams lived across the street from us when I was a kid. He was right behind Paige as pitchers went in those days. I played with his kid."

Street & Smith's Baseball Yearbook

Satchel Paige chatted with Roy Campanella, the paralyzed Dodgers catcher, at Brooklyn's Ebbets Field in August of 1959, before taking the mound against the Havana Stars. They had both starred in the Negro Baseball Leagues.

Kurt Angle
He came home with Olympic gold

*"My family taught me how
to wrestle and how to win."*

A relaxed, well-tanned Kurt Angle was comfortable in a corner
table on the first level at Atria's Restaurant & Tavern. "It's
great to be in your hometown," said Angle. "People always treat
you so nice."

Atria's is a landmark establishment at a bend in the road where
Dormont gives way to Mt. Lebanon while traveling on Rt. 19 South,
about three miles from downtown Pittsburgh. Angle grew up in
Dormont, swam in that huge community swimming pool South Hills
commuters can see on Banksville Road traveling to and from the city.
Then the Angles moved to Mt. Lebanon, where Kurt first gained
attention as a wrestler and football player. His mother had since
moved just up the road to the neighboring community of Scott
Township.

When he became an Olympic gold medal-winning hero at
Atlanta in the summer of 1996, Kurt was claimed as one of their own
by all three communities.

People there can still picture Kurt on his knees, his hands folded
in grateful prayer, crying unabashedly after officials awarded the
decision to him following eight minutes of agonizingly tough wrestling
in which the first mistake could cost the gold medal. The picture was
reprinted in newspapers throughout the world.

Some of his biggest boosters were in Atlanta rooting for him.
Most were watching the Olympic Games on TV and will never forget
how they felt when Angle's arm was hoisted in victory. He captured
the hearts of sports fans throughout the world with his joyous
celebration.

Kurt could see his mother and family and friends in the stands.
He thought about a wrestler friend from Pennsylvania who had been
shot dead in a bizarre murder earlier in the year. He was thinking
about his late father who had been his inspiration. The American flag
went up, the national anthem was playing, and Kurt couldn't hold
back the floodgates.

Tears streamed down his cheeks on the victory stand. We loved
him.

He came down off the victory stand, approached his mother and
hung the gold medal around her neck. People who never knew Kurt
Angle before suddenly loved this guy from Pittsburgh.

This tribute was offered to him in the next month's *Mt. Lebanon
Magazine*: "You're what a champion should be — a good son and
brother, a good citizen and a good role model for the kids."

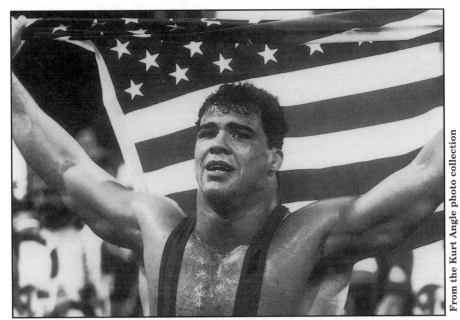

Weeping for joy, Kurt Angle captured the nation's heart with his gold-medal winning effort in the Olympic Games in Atlanta in August of 1996. At bottom, he's shown in action in one of his preliminary round matches.

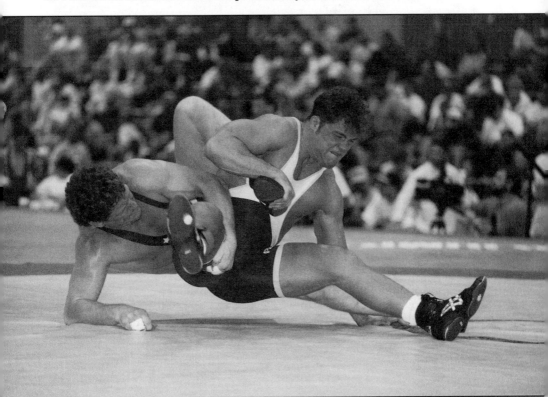

People in Mt. Lebanon could remember when they used to see Angle running the streets of their community as he pushed himself to get in shape for such competition. He'd run four miles, and then sprint up steep hills. And do it again and again.

"It's amazing what your body can do," Angle said at the time. "It's just that your mental part takes over, and you think you can't do it. If you get the physical and mental parts moving toward each other, you can do it. It's amazing what God has given us. But we set our own limits and we end up failing."

He worked out every day, between five and seven hours a day, running, lifting, jumping rope and wrestling. "I live with him," said his mother, "and I never see him."

His mother, Marie Angle, sometimes called Jackie, and family and friends are frequent diners at Atria's. After all, two color photographs of her son Kurt, wearing the gold medal he won in freestyle wrestling in the 1996 Olympic Games in Atlanta, are framed on the wall. He autographed both photos with gold signatures.

They are in the midst of many photographs, school pennants and sports memorabilia calling attention to achievement in the area, mostly by Mt. Lebanon High School athletes, that were collected by Nick Atria, the previous owner of the restaurant.

"In a way, it's as important to be pictured here," claimed Kurt, "as it is to be in any Hall of Fame."

This was at a luncheon meeting on Tuesday, February 16, 1999 and two of Atria's principal owners — Pat McDonnell and Allison Hoffman — and regular patrons stopped by the table to introduce themselves and shake hands when they recognized Angle, a real celebrity, in their midst. The sun had come out and was shining brightly to welcome Angle.

"I don't usually do this," began Roy Nickell, a sales engineer who stopped in for lunch, "but I just wanted to shake your hand. I come from Cleveland, and I'm a Browns' fan and we haven't won much lately, so I wanted to shake your hand. You're a winner. It's nice to meet a winner."

Angle smiled back and thanked him for his kind comments. Who wouldn't want to be acknowledged as a winner?

"That had to be so exciting," put in McDonnell, "being the best in the world!"

Angle agreed it was exciting.

"You had to beat some good guys here just to get to Atlanta," continued McDonnell.

Angle agreed they were good. "Yeah, some guys who had been beating me," added Angle, always the humble one.

"What turned it around?" asked McDonnell.

"I had never tried to figure out how to beat them," said Angle. "This time, instead of just competing, I thought about how I could win."

"There must have been so much pressure on you in the Olympic final," McDonnell continued.

"Oh, there was," Angle agreed. "I couldn't sleep the night before. My eyes were wide open."

"What was the name of the guy you beat to win the gold medal?" asked McDonnell.

"It was Abbas Jadidi of Iran," Angle came back. "In the 220-pound division."

That's when Tommy Nee, a Pittsburgh club fighter in his youth, came into Atria's. Nee helped Rich Lackner as an assistant football coach at Carnegie Mellon University, looking after the linemen.

"He'd be a good heavyweight boxer," noted Nee in the background, pointing toward Angle.

Another more famous sports face appeared, almost on cue. That was sportscaster Myron Cope, a first-time caller at Atria's. He'd done some boxing himself in his youth, but is best known for his excited yoi-yoi commentary on the Steelers radio broadcasts for nearly 30 years.

What a coincidence, as Angle and I had been talking about Cope and some other Pittsburgh sportscasters only minutes before. For a difficult year, Angle was one of them. I had been complimenting Cope to Angle on his ability to sustain his enthusiasm and for always doing his homework in preparation for his radio shows. He sounded as excited on his last show as he had on his first show.

Cope sat at a table by himself, just outside the rear room of Atria's where some of Pittsburgh's finest boxers are pictured in something of a local shrine to the sport. I first met Myron Cope, coincidentally enough, at a boxing tournament when I was 14 years old. He was covering the Golden Gloves at the Pitt Field House for the sponsoring *Post-Gazette*. I was the sports editor of *The Hazelwood Envoy*, and our local team, the Glen-Hazel Boys' Club had dominated the Pittsburgh Golden Gloves, winning 11 of 12 team titles in one stretch.

I asked Cope that day what I had to do to become a writer, and he said, "You have to sit down and start writing."

As I sit at my word processor, working on this book, Cope's advice still rings in my ears. He was right.

I still can't believe Cope came out of the woodwork like he did that day, the first time he'd ever been at Atria's. Art Rooney always said it was better to be lucky than good.

As Cope and Angle posed for a photo in front of a picture of the Garfield great, Harry Greb, Cope cried out, "The last wrestler I had my picture taken with was Carlton Haselrig."

That would prompt an exchange between Cope and Angle, and later spark some inside stories about Haselrig from Angle. Haselrig won six NCAA wrestling titles at Pitt-Johnstown and was a 12th and last round draft choice of the Steelers in 1989 who went on to become a starting offensive lineman for the Steelers and a Pro Bowl guard in 1992.

Cope had campaigned unabashedly on his sports talk show and draft weekend shows for the Steelers to take a chance on Haselrig, who had not played football in college, but showed great strength and agility while winning three Division I and three Division II heavy-weight wrestling titles. Cope can't help but boast of his brainy idea during the day-long broadcast of the NFL draft proceedings each year.

Angle had some first-hand experience with Haselrig that helped shed light on his strange, downright disturbing, sports story. Haselrig's stay with the Steelers was shortened considerably, and abruptly, by his off-the-field problems.

Haselrig ran into all kinds of problems and run-ins with the law because of drinking and chemical substance abuse, wild behavior, and was in and out of pro football. He'd had two or three NFL comebacks, but was still regarded as a ticking time bomb.

Haselrig had been one of the real success stories in sports, then one of the biggest disappointments. Cope took credit for his early success with the Steelers, but not his fall from glory. I had spoken to Haselrig over the telephone when he was with the New York Jets, holding down a starting lineman's job. He told me the sort of things I wanted to hear, as addicts do, and then his name was in the newspapers for another misdeed. And he was no longer with the Jets. They, too, had thrown up their hands in disgust.

Cope, who had cut back on his work schedule considerably, was between visits to his ear doctor and his physical therapist, Joey David, the former Pitt basketball player. He stopped at Atria's for lunch and was reading the daily newspaper.

Every so often, Cope would direct a comment or observation at our table. Angle got a kick out of Cope, as so many do in Pittsburgh.

"Haselrig had tremendous strength, agility and moves," added Angle. "He could have played tailback for the Steelers. I knew how physically gifted he was. I also knew he had a dark side to him.

"He came to Clarion to train with me for the nationals. He was out every night at house parties until 4 in the morning. He was throwing it (booze) down every night. Here we were getting ready for the nationals and his idea of training was to get wasted every night. He'd sleep for three hours and work out with me at eight o'clock.

"He was head and shoulders above everybody, but his late nights showed up in the way he wrestled. You could tell he wasn't in the best condition. He won the finals, 1-0, and all his matches throughout were close. He should have won, 20-0. He didn't work on anything. It all came so easily to him. I rooted and cheered for him. There was no one better. Then he had that early success with the Steelers. The drinking caught up with him, though. It was frustrating to see someone throw his life away. It looks like he's back on track. I hope so.

"You want these stories to have a happy ending."

> **"The reward of a thing well done
> is to have done it."**
> — Ralph Waldo Emerson

Kurt Angle enjoys social scene at Atria's Restaurant & Tavern in his old neighborhood along Mt. Lebanon-Dormont border, where he is honored on the Wall of Fame. He also met and swapped stories during lunch with sportscaster Myron Cope. Boxer Harry Greb is pictured behind them.

"I gave it my best effort."
— Kurt Angle

A rerun of the Espy Awards on ESPN the night before was showing on two TV screens at Atria's. These are annual awards for the top athletes in all sports given by the most-renowned and respected sports cable network. As Angle talked about his career, and the powerful influence of his family in shaping his stardom and his personality, images of home run hero Mark McGwire, tennis great Billie Jean King, and NHL star Wayne Gretzky flashed in the background. It was a virtual kaleidoscope of sports stars.

Angle would offer compliments about those he admired. He plain gushed about Gretzky. He was a big fan, and still didn't see himself in the same light. Probably because his time in the spotlight was so short by comparison.

It was going on three years since that magic day in Atlanta, and Angle was anxious about his future. He had gotten married on December 9, 1998 and was about to embark on a professional wrestling career. He wanted to be successful in both ventures.

He and his wife, the former Karen Smedley of Greensburg, were living in Ben Avon, near Bellevue just north of the city. She operated a tanning salon in Scott they had bought from his brother Eric. That's how Kurt kept such an even tan in the winter in Pittsburgh. It's tough to get a tan in Pittsburgh in the summer.

There was so much uncertainty, however. He had brought his gold medals for winning the Olympics and NCAA championships, as I asked him to, and displayed them for me and those who approached the table. All the compliments and handshakes from people who still regarded him as a hero in his hometown had to be reassuring.

Angle was all smiles, but he was asking as many questions as I was. He confessed to being a little scared, but that's how he always felt before any of his major wrestling challenges. I reassured him by telling him that I thought Muhammad Ali was always scared before his big fights, that it wasn't an unnatural feeling.

Friends had told him that he had been criticized the previous week on a Pittsburgh sports talk show for "selling out to his sport" by signing a contract to become a professional wrestler. Worse yet, his feat of winning the Olympic gold was put down as no big deal. If that wasn't enough, he was also criticized for being a second-rate sportscaster.

Those are more putdowns or takedowns than even a strong wrestler is willing to endure.

"I worked so hard for that gold," said Angle, screwing up his face in an agonized look. "No one has the right to belittle that accomplishment. Whatever I did, I gave it my best effort."

Angle was also taken to task in a column by Tony Norman in the *Post-Gazette*. Norman was a pro wrestling fan while growing up in Philadelphia, but felt that wrestling had taken a few wrong turns in what it promoted these days, ala obscene gestures, sexual innuendos, violence, racism, you name it.

"He'll make a lot of money tarnishing his squeaky clean reputation," wrote Norman. "He will become far more interesting than his Olympic persona.

"Angle is about to find out that when he enters pro wrestling, he'll leave as corrupted as any two-bit jobber hauled off the loading dock to benefit (World Wrestling Federation promoter Vince) McMahon's little circus. That's what fans want. That's what sells.

"Too bad Bruno (Sammartino) couldn't get to the former Olympian before he went to the dark side."

The father instincts in me wanted to advise Angle not to go there, that it wasn't what he was really all about, not what he had worked so hard to accomplish. And when he gets his fill of pro wrestling, his image will no longer be that of a former Olympic wrestling champion, but rather of whatever role he assumes as a pro wrestler. I felt he was ill-advised, and not looking at the long-term picture. Why did he turn down the opportunity to become a pro wrestler when the offer was first on the table, and for a lot more money? What were the misgivings then? Had they been diminished simply by a desire to make some quick cash? The look in Kurt's hazel eyes switched at times from joy to puzzlement to wounded. From this international champion one can learn that it's okay to have fears, to have self-doubts, to hurt and cry. It's how one responds to life's challenges that determines a real champion.

Another lesson is that sibling rivalry can be a driving force in one's formative years. It should also make one think twice, however, about putting all of your eggs in one basket.

I spoke to Kurt briefly over the telephone a few months after our luncheon meeting, in mid-May, 1999. He was talking to me from his automobile as he drove to Memphis for his next wrestling match.

I asked him how things were going.

"Same old, same old," he replied.

Already, I thought.

I advised him to make sure he got out of the hotel and toured towns like Memphis, and to keep a journal.

"What am I going to do now?"
— Kurt Angle,
morning after Olympic victory

Kurt Angle made quick work of a salad, baked salmon, baked potato, steamed vegetables, coffee and ice water while reflecting on his fantastic story, going from being a wrestler everyone could wipe the mat with as a youngster to winning world-wide recognition.

I mentioned to Angle that only the week before I had interviewed Roger Kingdom, a gold medal winning hurdler in the Olympic Games in 1984 and 1988.

"I got to meet and know Roger in 1995, about a year before the Olympic Games," recalled Kurt. "I started going to UPMC to rehabilitate an injury, and Roger seemed to be there a lot. He was working out across the street at Pitt Stadium, and he was having some physical problems, too.

"He didn't know me from a hole in the ground, but I was excited about meeting a two-time Olympic champion. We were both getting ready for the 1996 Olympics. He was really something. I thought, wow, this guy is never going to stop running."

After finishing second at the nationals in 1994, Angle decided to re-evaluate himself. He stopped wrestling for nine weeks — his longest break from the sport — and asked himself, "Do I want to end up as the No. 2 guy on Team USA, one of the guys who could have been there, but just fell short?

"I was taking a back seat to wrestlers who weren't as good as I was. They would beat me, make the team, and then lose to all the international guys I knew I could beat. So I figured the problem had to be mental."

He decided he didn't want to be second best, worked even harder than before, and gained a berth on Team USA.

"After I made the Olympic team, Roger Kingdom called me to offer his congratulations," remembered Angle. "That meant a lot to me. I saw him a few times after that, and he was always great with me. Just a regular guy.

"As one of the legendary Olympic champions of all time, Roger was selected to stand with President Clinton at one of the ceremonies preceding the Olympic Games in Atlanta. There was Roger up on the stage, standing next to the President, and I was proud to know him. As I saw it, he was from my hometown. And he was representing the United States Olympic team."

I mentioned that Kingdom was concerned about his future as well, wondering if he had made a mistake in not pursuing a coaching opportunity at the University of Miami the previous year because he wanted to continue to compete in the international track & field circuit.

Angle nodded when I mentioned that it's important to seize opportunities while the flame is still burning from the Olympic Games. The flame and the attending fame can be fleeting. A Pittsburgh-born artist named Andy Warhol warned us about the brevity of fame.

"I remember the way I felt the next morning after I'd won the gold medal in Atlanta," Angle said.

"Before that, all my life was about the Olympics. I realized that day that it was all over. I asked myself, 'What the heck am I going to do now?'

"I knew I didn't have the desire to go another four years of torture to compete in the next Olympics. It's hard on your body. It's hard on your mind. I didn't want to do it all over again.

"I was with my family at a house where we were hosted during the Games. I went to bed about five in the morning. I got up at 6 a.m. because I had to report to the Olympic Village to make an appearance on the Today Show.

"I got up feeling like I had accomplished this great thing. Then I thought, 'What the heck am I going to do now?'

"I didn't know I was going to get a job as a sportscaster here in Pittsburgh. I had no idea what would happen next."

That brought up a chapter in Angle's young life that left him feeling frustrated and unhappy. WPGH-TV (Fox Channel 53) was just beginning a news show after Angle's Atlanta accomplishment, and felt that hiring a hot popular hero like Angle would attract viewers. Alby Oxenreiter, who was also from Mt. Lebanon, had left WTAE-TV in favor of a better position on the sports reporting team with the new show in town.

Angle remains a friend of Oxenreiter, and believes that Oxenreiter was too busy with a start-up situation to provide the mentoring Angle badly needed to learn the business. Angle was obviously uncomfortable under the bright lights, and came off poorly. He didn't read his own scripts well and he often appeared stiff before the camera. If something went wrong, as it frequently did in the WPGH-TV studios in those early days of developing a news show, Angle didn't adapt well. He was ripped by local TV critics and in columns by sports writers for his self-admitted amateurish efforts.

"I was doing a job I wasn't qualified to do," said Angle. "I received no coaching. There was no teaching. Just do it. I never had a chance to enjoy it. I was offered a five-year contract, but I signed a one-year contract because I wasn't sure I'd like it.

"It was always a job I didn't enjoy. I was computer illiterate. I had to learn to edit on the job. I was writing my script on my own, something I'd never done in my life. I was promised a talent coach, but it never happened."

One of the highlights of his year as a sportscaster was meeting Mario Lemieux. "I was in the Penguins' locker room after a practice to do some interviews," recalled Angle, "and he went out of his way to come over and greet me.

"He said, 'I'm Mario Lemieux,' like I didn't know who he was. 'Kurt, I just wanted to say congratulations, and I wish you the very best in your sportscasting. If you ever want to go golfing someday, let me know.' Mario Lemieux was my favorite athlete of all time, so it meant a great deal to me."

The smile left Angle's face as he reflected on how it never really worked out for him.

"I did the best I could do, and it wasn't good enough," he said. "They wanted me to become a sports reporter instead of an anchorman, which they should have had me doing in the first place, but I just wanted out. I left on my own.

"I had some things going for me that kept me busy. But I wanted to be competing again, in some form. I couldn't see wrestling. Then the World Wrestling Federation approached me again, and they offered me a five-year contract. There it was and I took it.

"I will make my debut in six weeks. I've been going to training camps to learn a certain system. It's sports entertainment; they don't call it wrestling anymore. The idea appeals to me on three levels:

"One, there's the athletic side. Two, there's a character side, playing a part. It's almost like a soap opera. There are certain things they do that I need to learn how to do. Three, there's the business side.

"It's not even wrestling, really. It's like a circus act. You come to town and you leave. You try to put on a great show. I always wanted to be an athlete. I wanted to be an actor. I wanted to be a business man.

"Is it a step up? Hell, no. This isn't even wrestling. It's another career. It's a way for me to provide for my wife and myself. There's only a handful of millionaires in the WWF. I've got to make a name for myself before I can make any real money at it.

"In 1996, after I'd won the Olympics, they offered me a multi-million deal and I turned it down. It's not what I wanted to do at the time. Now I'm getting the lowest amount of money they give to a starter. I'm not bitter about it; I have to prove myself. It's the story of my life."

I asked Angle what role he would play in the wrestling matches. Good guy? Bad guy? Masked marvel? Any costume?

"I don't know," he said. "We haven't worked that out yet. But I've told them I won't do anything racist or sexist. I've been told my debut match will be a big match, and will attract a lot of attention. They consider it one of their biggest moves.

Angle's agent was sports attorney Ralph Cindrich, a former pro football player from Pitt and Avella, who was living in Mt. Lebanon. Cindrich lined up appearances for Angle.

"I'm already booked to do a lot of important TV shows," said Angle. "The Today Show is doing a documentary about an amateur wrestling champion entering the professional ranks. They have taped me at a training camp in Stamford, Connecticut, about 40 minutes outside New York."

I suggested to Angle that, considering how former pro wrestler Jesse "The Body" Ventura had become the governor of Minnesota, that he, too, might have a political future.

"I won't say I won't," answered Angle. "I'm starting to care about a lot more things. I see things that are right, and things that are wrong. Now I care more.

"I used to watch TV every day. All I wanted to watch were sitcoms. Now I'm more interested in CNN and the other cable news and roundtable discussion shows. I guess I just grew up."

When Angle was growing up, I wonder if he ever dreamed about running away and joining the circus. He was smiling, however, and I didn't want to spoil his day by posing a difficult question.

"Anything's possible if you put your mind to it."
— Kurt Angle

I had heard Kurt Angle speak at an awards dinner at the Westin William Penn ballroom the previous April, and been impressed with his presentation, and his story of hard work and persistence.

He talked about how he discovered midway through his career at Clarion (Pa.) University how to get the best out of himself as both a wrestler and a student. He improved dramatically in both directions in his last year-and-a-half.

He went back to the beginning to explain just how far he'd come as a wrestler.

"My message is how anything's possible if you put your mind to it," Angle said. "My record was 2-16 my first year in wrestling and one of the wins was by forfeit. So I only really won one of my matches. I was pinned 13 times. When that happens, you figure this isn't your sport.

"Coming from my family, however, a tough and physical family, if you don't follow through on something like that then you're considered a sissy.

"I took a lot of lumps from the age of 8 to 16. I was constantly getting my butt kicked. I refused to give up on that. I see kids today that if they're not good right off the bat they just quit. My coach at Clarion — Bob Bubb — told me he had 70 kids on his wrestling team in the early '70s. Now they have a tough time having a full team. I hate to see kids give up too early on themselves."

Bubb had since retired as coach at Clarion. He had finished fourth in the NCAA wrestling tournament during his days at the University of Pittsburgh, and built a wrestling program at Clarion that could compete with anyone.

Angle explained that the NCAA permits its Division I wrestling programs to offer 9.9 scholarships at any given time, and there are ten weight categories. "There are 22 starters on a football team, and they get 90 scholarships," said Angle. "It doesn't make any sense."

So wrestling coaches like Bubb have to offer partial scholarships to field a full squad. "Only blue-chippers get a full scholarship," said Angle. Bubb gave Angle a full scholarship to get him to come to Clarion.

After all, Angle had won two WPIAL titles and one PIAA title in his senior year at Mt. Lebanon High School. "I was seen as a heavyweight who moved well," he recalled, "and I had a lot of offers."

"I won the gold, but I was just part of a family."
— Kurt Angle

I asked Angle to go back to his days in Dormont, where it all began. "I was the youngest and most fortunate in our family," he said. "I was protected by all my brothers. I didn't make the same mistakes they made in many areas, and they kept me pointed in the right direction. Those guys made me who I am.

"The oldest could have been a champion if he'd come along when I did, and had the same opportunities, and the same is true with all my brothers. My family has kept me pretty humble. I went out and won the gold, but I was just part of a family.

"I still don't think I've accomplished all I wanted to do. My family instilled that in me, to never be satisfied or to rest on your laurels.

"My father, Dave Angle, died in 1985 when I was a junior in high school. He was a mean roughneck, everybody was afraid of him. People looked at him and said, 'I don't want to mess with this guy.' He was a hard worker. I never saw him much. When he died, our family actually became closer.

"My brothers were all big, and all rough and very competitive, especially my oldest brother, Mark. Mark is considered the toughest S.O.B. Pittsburgh ever created. He never asked for a fight or looked for a fight, but he had a reputation for beating up people. One time, when he was in eighth grade, he beat up two police officers — they were undercover cops — and he didn't know who he was messing with.

"He was 5-10, 185 pounds in eighth grade — a man — and he spent some time in a reform school in New Castle. He was there for over a year.

"He took up wrestling when he was a junior at Keystone Oaks High School, and in his first year in wrestling he went to the state tournament. That summer he took fifth place in the Greco-Roman wrestling nationals. That was unreal, amazing.

"Mark never told me how good he was. Neither did his coach at Keystone Oaks, Dave Kling. I found out from my coach at Mt. Lebanon High School, George Lampranakos. My coach told me how tough he was. Then it really hit home. After all, my coach had over 400 wins as a high school wrestling coach. He'd seen a lot of good wrestlers in his day.

"They were amazed at Mark's talent. He ended up going to a junior college in Arizona. He got married and had a child while he was in junior college. Then he had another child, two children in two years. He was ready to go to Arizona State University, where they have a great program. But he was trying to balance a family, school, finances and wrestling, and it wasn't working out.

"He left the junior college and got a job. He had to provide for his family. He felt greedy about trying to be a college wrestler when his family needed his support and involvement. So he let his dreams go.

Kurt with mother, Marie, his biggest booster.

Kurt with wife, Karen, his main squeeze.

Kurt Angle

Kurt's toughest competition has always come from within his family, from left to right, John, Eric, Le'Anne in his arms, David and Mark.

"His son, Mark Jr., is doing extremely well as a wrestler now. He's a junior at Clarion, and he's the top-rated college wrestler in the country. He was a four-time national champion in high school at Canon-McMillan. Bob Bubb retired last year, and Ken Nellis, from Shaler, is the head coach there now.

"My brother Mark lives out his dreams through me and his son. Mark had a big impact on my career. David was my oldest brother and he taught me how to hit a baseball and stuff like that. He was very technical in his approach to all sports. John taught me how to play sports, too. He made me wrestle on the living room floor. Mark started the wrestling in our family. John followed and then Eric, who was a year older than me.

"Eric and I used to battle every day in practice. He'd barely beat me all the time. I wanted to be better than him. It was such a battle. He never wanted me to be better than him.

"I wanted to quit. I was embarrassed, and I felt disgusted. I'd pretend I was injured. My brothers figured this kid wasn't going to make it. In one match, I got pinned and I hurt my neck. I'm walking off the mat, and I'm holding my neck and making a face. Mark said to Johnny, 'He's not cut out for this.' I hated that. I wasn't an Angle.

"They wouldn't let me quit. 'No, you're wrestling,' they told me. They'd make sure Eric and I kept wrestling each other. We were getting into fights with each other. They were trying to teach me not to be afraid to be physical. They wanted me to be tough. They thought I was scared and they wanted to take the fear out of me.

"In wrestling, I was emotional and I cried before I went out for the gold medal match in the Olympic Games. It was always like that...being so scared.

"As a kid, my brothers always orchestrated my activity. I was pretty much the sissie of the family. They didn't like that about me. They wouldn't let me be like that."

I had a question. "Who's the real Kurt Angle?" I asked him. He repeated my question.

"I'm not real complicated," he said. "I'm a very simple person. I can only focus on one thing. That's why I had problems after I won the gold medal at the Olympic Games. I was pulled in different directions. All of a sudden I was a sportscaster, a public speaker, delivering motivational speeches at banquets and business luncheons, doing this or that. I didn't like that. I didn't do anything really well. I needed to be focused.

"I'm not blessed with a lot of brains. I'm not a genius. I'm not the smartest individual. But I like to push myself. I recognize my shortcomings, and try to work off my strengths."

> *"Hitch your wagon to a star."*
> — Ralph Waldo Emerson

"I knew he had a dark side to him."
— Kurt Angle on Carlton Haselrig

I asked Kurt Angle if he were scared about finding satisfaction in his life after the Olympic Games. "Yeah, I'm a little scared now," he said, looking up to see how I'd react to that confession.

"I was in such a shell when I was working toward the Olympic Games. I never went outside that shell. I was going to train until I won that gold. I retired at the prime of my career. Now I've got to keep plugging in other ways."

I asked Kurt why he hadn't considered coaching for a career, a natural step for an outstanding athlete in an Olympic sport.

"The responsibility factor is a concern," he said. "It would have to be in college, I think. You're not only coaching the kids, but you're a parent. You're responsible for them, for their behavior, for what they're doing, for how they're doing in their classes.

"I used to look at Coach Bubb and wonder how he did it. He'd tell me, 'I wish all my kids were like you, but they're not.' I knew it was hard on him. They went down from having 70 wrestlers to having 16 on the team. If somebody gets out of line now, you can't kick them off the team because you've got a numbers problem, and you need them. That's the point we've gotten to in our society.

"Kids say to me, 'How'd you get so good in wrestling?' I never really thought I got that good. I look back and I said I sucked. I still had so much to learn. I had no defense, and little offense, not enough moves."

Penn State football coach Joe Paterno had been honored as the Dapper Dan Sportsman of the Year the week before at the biggest sports banquet in the city, held at the Hilton.

In 1997, Angle was similarly honored. It was a big night in his life. "I sat between Michael Moorer, the boxer from Monessen, and Troy Loney of the Penguins," recalled Angle. "It was great to be up there on the dais.

"The four finalists for the award were all up there. So I was with Mario Lemieux of the Penguins, Jeff King of the Pirates and Jerome Bettis of the Steelers. I thought Lemieux was going to get it because it was his last year with the Penguins."

Seeing Cope across the room reminded him of Carlton Haselrig. "I was a big fan of Haselrig," said Angle. "I wrestled him in college. We had some great battles, but we became good friends. In fact, my first match as a college wrestler was against Haselrig. I was a freshman and he was a senior. I'll bet you know who won.

"I lost by one point, 4-3. It was my introduction to college wrestling. He hit a double-leg on me and took me off my feet. He really hit me. He taught me how far I had to go to be the best. My fourth bout was against Dean Hall of Edinboro University. He was Bruce Baumgartner's protege. I beat Hall. He had beaten Haselrig twice, so I knew I could be good. I was an 18-year-old freshman and I was scared to death before that match. Then I beat him. That was my turnaround match. Bruce was in his corner, and it made me realize I could go up against the best wrestlers and win."

"I hope I helped him."
— Bruce Baumgartner

By coincidence, I had been with Bruce Baumgartner two weeks earlier at a sports banquet in Meadville, sponsored by the Crawford County Chamber of Commerce. Baumgartner is a legendary figure in the world of wrestling, the greatest freestyle heavyweight wrestler in American history.

Baumgartner, the wrestling coach and athletic director at Edinboro, was one of the speakers at the sports awards dinner and signed autographs for many young admirers.

He was introduced by broadcaster Lanny Frattare, who represented the Pirates along with young pitcher Chris Peters.

Baumgartner had won medals in four different Olympic Games, from 1984 to 1996, twice winning gold medals, and had been chosen captain of the USA Olympic team for the Atlanta Games. He carried the American flag for the Games opening ceremonies, leading the parade of 600-plus U.S. athletes before an estimated world-wide TV audience of more than 3.5 billion people. He was easily the biggest man at the banquet.

He was one of only eight U.S. athletes to medal in four different Olympiads.

Baumgartner and Angle had worked out together in preparation for the 1996 Olympic Games. "I'd like to think that we made each other better," said Baumgartner, who is one of Angle's biggest admirers, during an interview before the banquet program got underway.

"Kurt worked hard for just about everything he's got. You can ask anybody about Kurt, and they'll all tell you what a hard worker he is. When he was at Clarion, he came up to train with me. He stayed at my house. He helped me to be a better wrestler, I hope I helped him.

"He had an innocence about him. He's a good person. He has real ability. He was given a huge of amount of ability and he learned how to use it. He committed himself. There are a lot of people with more talent. It's what you do with your talent that's important. I have respect for all the Olympians. I never watched it until I was in it, in 1980 and 1984. I tried to emulate Dan Gable, one of the greatest wrestlers who ever came out of this country."

He said he was close to David Schultz, the wrestler who was shot and killed before the 1996 Olympic Games, shot in his driveway by multimillionaire John E. duPont, a wrestling devotee, in January before the Olympic Games. "And I am close to Jeff Blatnik, the wrestler who has been challenged with cancer. He inspires everybody with his attitude, and how he has handled this challenge. Those situations make you realize how lucky you've been."

Baumgartner had a reunion at the Meadville banquet with Tunch Ilkin, a former Steelers lineman who'd been a classmate of Baumgartner during their days at Indiana State University. Baumgartner captured the NCAA Division I title as a senior at Indiana State in 1982. Ilkin and sportscaster Bill Hillgrove both told lots of funny stories about what it was like to work with Myron Cope.

"I used to get asked what Terry Bradshaw and Jack Lambert were really like," said Ilkin, a Pro Bowl tackle late in his career. "Now everyone wants to know what it's like to work in the same booth as Myron Cope."

Jim O'Brien

Four-time Olympic wrestling medalist Bruce Baumgartner of Edinboro University is flanked at 1999 Meadville sports banquet by, left to right, Pirates broadcaster Lanny Frattare, Steelers' analyst Tunch Ilkin, Pirates pitcher Chris Peters and Pitt and Steelers broadcaster Bill Hillgrove.

"Go confidently in the direction of your dreams. Live the life you've imagined."
— Henry David Thoreau

Connie Hawkins
Hawk still flying in Phoenix

"You should see my tan."

March is the time of the year when the legendary Connie Hawkins would be showing up at high school basketball play-off games in Pittsburgh and its surrounding communities.

He would usually be accompanied by another local legend, Kenny Durrett, the operator of a sporting goods store in the city's east end. Durrett first gained fame at Schenley High School, leading the Spartans to a PIAA title as a junior, and later starring at LaSalle University and in the NBA.

That was before "The Hawk" finally flew the coop in 1992 and departed Pittsburgh, his adopted city, in favor of Phoenix, where he had gained NBA All-Star status with the Suns in the early '70s. Pittsburgh produced some Hall of Fame basketball players in Maurice Stokes and Jack Twyman in the mid-'50s, and some pro stars in the '70s in Kenny Durrett and Maurice Lucas, but no greater player than Hawkins ever called Pittsburgh his home.

Hawkins was a hero and inspiration to both Durrett and Lucas, who came out of Schenley High School to gain fame.

"The Hawk," as he was known for his high-flying style, was not born and bred in Pittsburgh, but he certainly grew up in Pittsburgh, and chose to remain there after he was finished with his professional playing career.

"I miss all my friends like Kenny in Pittsburgh," said Hawkins, 56 at the time of our telephone interview and, I was told by mutual friends, looking better than ever since the Suns financed some extensive cosmetic dental work. "But I sure like all the sunshine in Phoenix," said Hawkins. "You should see my tan. I don't have to shovel the snow to get my car going in the morning. I like to play tennis more than basketball these days, and I can play it all the time out here.

"At least I'm working. I couldn't get a job there. I couldn't get arrested there."

Hawkins returned to the Suns in 1992 as a community relations representative. Jerry Colangelo, the president and CEO of the Suns, always had a special place in his heart for Hawkins and hired him to represent the Suns.

"I enjoyed my time in Pittsburgh," said Hawkins. "I'm very happy now. I'm happy with myself, I'm happy with my life. I'm happy that Jerry offered me this job. This has been the best part of my life so far."

In addition to making community appearances, Hawkins worked with the City of Phoenix conducting summer basketball camps and

Connie Hawkins conducts clinics for young fans in Phoenix area on behalf of the Suns. Connie is credited with making the Suns a bonafide NBA team in their second season, and remains a popular figure in Phoenix.

clinics at America West Arena, the home court of the Suns. He joined several other former Suns stars, Neal Walk, Tom Chambers and Dennis "Moe" Layton, in promoting the team through interaction with area youth.

I had last seen him on August 23, 1997 at a 30th year reunion of the ABA at the Hoosier Dome in Indianapolis. It was great to see all the guys who played and worked in that upstart league. The Hawk was one of the most popular players at the reunion. Gabe Rubin and Jason Shapiro, who owned the Pipers, were among those who hugged Hawkins. They came in from Florida to see some of their favorites. Julius Erving and Billy Knight were among those eager to see The Hawk.

His professional career began in 1961 with the Pittsburgh Rens of Abe Saperstein's American Basketball League. From the first day, he was the star of the team.

He had been booted out of the University of Iowa in his freshman year of 1960 when he was implicated with basketball-fixer Jack Molinas in his native New York. He was later cleared of any wrongdoing during his days in the American Basketball Association and permitted to play in the NBA which had originally banned him.

After the ABL folded in its second season, Hawkins played four seasons with the Harlem Globetrotters, dazzling fans with his remarkable basketball wizardry.

I remember seeing him play for the Porky Chedwick All-Stars, who included Walt Mangham of New Castle and Jim McCoy of Farrell, in a sandlot league at the YM&YWHA in Oakland after the ABL folded.

The Pittsburgh Pipers came into being in 1967 and Hawkins led that team to the ABA's first championship and was once again named his league's most valuable player. The Pipers moved to Minnesota for the ABA's second season. When they returned to Pittsburgh the following year they did so without having Hawkins in their lineup, which meant they had no chance of being successful the second time around. It was hard to believe that more than 30 years had passed since the Pipers' championship season in Pittsburgh.

He had left the ABA — having successfully sued the NBA with the help of Pittsburgh attorneys Roz and David Litman — to join the Suns in 1969-70 after Phoenix won his rights by virtue of a coin flip with Seattle in 1969. Present NBA commissioner David Stern was the attorney who represented the league in that case.

"I never saw anyone who cared more about their client than the Litmans," Stern told me once.

Hawkins played four seasons in the Valley, and was an All-Star performer each of those seasons. He averaged 20.5 points and 9 rebounds. He played three more seasons, two for the Lakers and his final year with the Atlanta Hawks.

"He was one of the greatest players I ever went up against," said Hall of Famer Kareem Abdul-Jabbar.

398

Phoenix Suns

Jim O'Brien

Connie Hawkins wore No. 42 in honor of Brooklyn boyhood hero Jackie Robinson during his days with Phoenix Suns. Hawkins enjoyed seeing his former bosses with Pittsburgh Pipers, Gabe Rubin, left, and Jason Shapiro, at 30th anniversary season reunion of ABA in Indianapolis on Aug. 23, 1997.

Hawkins' No. 42 was retired by the Suns in 1976. Asked the significance of his number, Hawkins said, "It's very simple. There was a guy who played for the Brooklyn Dodgers named Jackie Robinson. I was one of his admirers. When I was a boy in Brooklyn, we used to go to Ebbets Field, sneak in the back and watch the games. We would talk about him back then. We knew everything about Jackie."

Hawkins was enshrined in the Basketball Hall of Fame on May 11, 1992. I take personal pride in having been responsible for putting together a personal history and recommendation package while nominating Hawkins for the Basketball Hall of Fame in 1991. During my years as the editor of *Street & Smith's Basketball Yearbook*, I had served a three-year term on the nominating committee for the Basketball Hall of Fame. I was familiar with the system. It's different from both the Baseball Hall of Fame and the Football Hall of Fame voting process, which are both done in a different way as well.

It was exciting, and an honor, to participate in a teleconference phone call session each year with the likes of John Wooden, Dean Smith, Eddie Donovan, John McClendon and Henry Iba, who also served on the Hall of Fame committee.

"I finally realized I had arrived," Hawkins said of the Hall of Fame ceremonies. "I was at the top of my profession. I was with the best of the best. You know you've made it then. Nobody can say you weren't one of the best basketball players of all time."

The Hawk and I had a history. I had seen him play with the Pittsburgh Rens, the Porky Chedwick All-Stars, the Pittsburgh Pipers and all those NBA teams. We had been friends for a long time. He said I was the first reporter he called to say he was leaving Pittsburgh for Phoenix back in his pro playing days. He made good on a promise when he did that. I was working for *The Miami News* at the time. When David Wolf wrote that wonderful biography of Hawkins called *Foul*, he called on me to provide some of Hawk's history.

Born July 17, 1942 in Brooklyn, Hawk attended Boys High — also the alma mater of two other basketball greats, Sihugo Green of Duquesne and Lenny Wilkins of Providence who went on to NBA stardom — and was a 1960 high school All-American. He also earned two letters in track.

In more recent years, Hawkins liked to boast about his tennis prowess. He liked to tell people he teamed with John McEnroe in the Nike Celebrity Doubles tennis exhibition in 1994, and insists he carried McEnroe. Hawk has always had a great sense of humor which helped him through his most difficult days early in his pro career.

> **"I was there (Bosnia) as sort of a black Bob Hope."**
> — Connie Hawkins

"It was scary at first."

Some of his best friends wondered whether Connie Hawkins had lost his mind when they heard that he traveled to the Balkins in mid-April, 1999 — just weeks after the NATO bombing began there — to entertain our soldiers. They were not in harm's way, but were stationed where they were on call in case ground troops were ever employed. He was shooting hoops with the troops and having a great time.

"That will be the reaction of my friends back home," said Hawkins when he was interviewed in Bosnia.

"They've already asked. 'Why do you want to go to Bosnia in the first place? Are you crazy?'" said Hawkins who went on a tour of U.S. bases in Bosnia along with former pro basketball players Charlie Scott and Dwayne Washington.

"I was there as sort of a black Bob Hope," he cracked, showing his sense of humor was still intact. "The guys were so appreciative we were there, that made it all worthwhile. We were on the Bosnian side, so we weren't in a war zone."

Hawkins played ball with the soldiers "so I could be one of them. The women and men over there are putting their lives on the line for me, so the least I can do is go over there and thank them for their efforts."

They played shoot-around with the soldiers, joined them for lunch, had a question and answer session, and signed autographs.

"It was scary, at first," confided Hawkins, "but they assured me that I'd be safe. I saw some stuff that made you think twice about being there, though. This was the first time I'd done anything quite like this. We're walking around in flak jackets and helmets. And it's a lot of weight. You have to give credit to the soldiers who have to wear this stuff every day."

Hawkins went to Europe the first time when he was about the same age as the soldiers. When the ABL folded, he toured the world with the Harlem Globetrotters for four years. NATO was not dropping bombs anywhere they were playing, however, as they were in the Balkans. After growing up in Brooklyn, though, Connie was always a cautious fellow.

Air Force Staff Sgt. Marcelious Lunsford was one of the soldiers enjoying the visit, and told a wire service writer, "This is really great. We shot around. They still got it. It was awesome to be playing with them. I hope my family believes it. I got a few pictures to prove it.

"Seeing these players do a layup here, right in front of me, just makes you forget about what's happening outside. We all needed something like this."

The former NBA stars also visited Taszar, Hungary. The NBA Legends Tour was sponsored by U.S. Army Europe. Hawkins was happy to get back to Phoenix following the tour. No one reported whether or not he received any hazardous duty pay from the Suns.

"I was Dr. J before Dr. J was."
— "The Hawk"

Connie Hawkins could hear the good-natured teasing in the background, as he sat in a booth being interviewed at the Edgewood Tennis and Fitness Club, just east of Pittsburgh, and he smiled that toothy smile, familiar to fans who followed him during his pro playing days.

Two waitresses and two other workers who were putting up photos of former and present Pirates and Steelers in a sports bar-restaurant in the club had just picked out a framed poster of Michael Jordan of the Chicago Bulls.

"Here's a real basketball player," hollered out the one fellow, hoping Hawkins would hear him. "How come we can't find any photos of Hawkins here? Didn't he used to play basketball, too?"

Hawkins had to laugh. It was that or cry. It's the story of his life.

Later, one of the fellows in the restaurant stopped by the booth where Hawkins was holding court, and said, "Why don't you bring us a photo of yourself so we can hang it up? I hear you were a pretty good basketball player in your day."

Pretty good?

Neither the waitresses nor their fellow workers had ever seen Hawkins play basketball, they admitted, but, indeed, they knew he was pretty good. Enough people they knew had said so.

How good? Well, Hawkins was doing some of the same things Michael Jordan was doing on a basketball court before Jordan was ever born. "The Hawk" was one of the first high-flyers in the world of professional basketball. When Jordan was young, he idolized Julius Erving. When Julius Erving was young, he idolized Connie Hawkins. That's how Julius Erving came to be known as Dr. J — because of the unique way and high-flying flair with which he operated on a basketball court.

"I was Dr. J before Dr. J was," he liked to say. Hawkins said Elgin Baylor had been an inspiration to him in that regard. Dr. J followed him, and Michael Jordan followed Dr. J in the category of high-flyers.

Hawkins was a hero, a schoolyard legend, for lots of young athletes in his native New York area. He was wrongly implicated in a basketball-related gambling scandal when he was a freshman at the University of Iowa in 1960, banned from NCAA and NBA play for a long period, and forced to perform on the fringe for too many years.

The Phoenix Suns won a coin flip with the Seattle Supersonics for the right to sign Hawkins for the 1969-70 season, the franchise's second year in the NBA. Hawkins promptly led the Suns to their first playoff berth, topping the Suns in scoring with a 24.6 points per game average, and was a first-team All-Star performer. He made the NBA All-Star Game each of his four full seasons and was voted the team's

George Kalinsky/New York Knicks

"The Hawk" soars above New York Knicks' 1970 NBA championship team, including Cazzie Russell, Walt Frazier and Willis Reed, at Madison Square Garden in his hometown.

Street & Smith's Basketball Yearbook

Pittsburgh Pipers ABA championship team of 1967-68 included, left to right front row, Jim Jarvis, Tom "Trooper" Washington, Charles "Chico" Vaughn, captain Connie "The Hawk" Hawkins, Art Heyman, Charlie "The Rifle" Williams and Craig Dill. Back row, left to right, trainer Alex Medich, Steve Vacendak, Tom Kerwin, Leroy Wright, Willie Porter, Richie Parks, Arvesta Kelly and Coach Vince Cazzetta.

MVP by the Phoenix fans after the 1970-71 season. He averaged 20.6 points per game during his career with the Suns. He also ranked among the team's all-time top rebounders.

At 6-8, 215 pounds, he wore No. 42 with great pride, and gave the Suns almost instant credibility because not too many expansion franchises — except for the Milwaukee Bucks with Kareem Abdul-Jabbar — ever had players of his superstar caliber.

Hawkins had won All-City and All-America honors as a high school player in Brooklyn, but had to play in basketball's underground after he was bounced out of Iowa for the crime of accepting a $10 or $20 bill here and there from a former NBA ballplayer named Jack Molinas who had been kicked out of the league years before for gambling. A Columbia grad, Molinas would hang around schoolyard basketball games in the New York area, and give some of the kids money from time to time so they'd have spending money. It cost Hawkins and a few of his friends dearly in the long run.

At 19, Hawkins won the MVP award in the ABL. At 26, he was the MVP in the ABA. Both times he led pro teams in Pittsburgh and averaged between 27 and 28 points per game.

After he was finished playing in the NBA, he returned to Pittsburgh. The Litmans were still looking after him. He stayed at a two bedroom apartment near the Edgewood Tennis & Fitness Club, an apartment complex owned by Eugene Litman, a Pittsburgh entrepreneur. Litman, one of the owners of the Rens, would later own a piece of the Pirates in the investment group put together to save the Pirates and stayed on with the team assembled by Kevin McClatchy.

Asked why he chose to live in Pittsburgh back then, Hawkins said, "I knew Pittsburgh was one of the most livable cities in the world before Rand-McNally did. I knew that long ago. I've been around the world with the Harlem Globetrotters, but there's no place like Pittsburgh.

"I liked New York and I loved Phoenix — the fans were so great to me there — but it's cheaper and easier to live in Pittsburgh and everybody has always treated me well here. I'm happy here. All my friends like it here. When my brothers came here, they never wanted to go back to Brooklyn."

As you can see, The Hawk is happy wherever he's appreciated.

"The Hawk" has always moved to the beat of his own drummer — a slow, funeral-like beat at that. He only played one year of pro ball in LA with the Lakers, after the Suns sent him there in a trade for Keith Erickson, eight games into the 1973-74 season, but he's always been "California laidback" in his lifestyle.

When Hawkins played for the Pittsburgh Pipers, it was the responsibility of trainer and team equipment manager Alex Medich of Duquesne to make sure Hawkins got up and got to practice on time.

He had all the money he needed, thanks to his NBA retirement checks, plus a stipend he had received over a 20-year period as a settlement for the money and proper acknowledgement he missed during his eight-year ban from the NBA.

At ABA's 30th year reunion in Indianapolis in August of 1997, Connie Hawkins was reunited above with former ABA foe and Phoenix Suns teammate (1971-72) Charlie Scott. Below, left to right, former ABA stars, left to right, are James Jones, Scott, Spencer Haywood, Dave Robisch and Hawkins.

Before he went back to Phoenix, Hawkins didn't really have a job. He helped Durrett out at his sporting goods store on occasion, but that was about it. Hawkins was never overly ambitious. Like Bill Mazeroski, he never demanded much from life.

Kenny Durrett talked about how he and Hawkins got to know each other.

"He's always been like a brother to me," said Durrett, 50 years old and still standing tall. "When he first came here to Pittsburgh with the Rens, I was trying to learn how to play ball at Herron Hill Junior High. I was horrible. He took me aside and showed me some things. I figured if he could take time out of his valuable schedule to show me some things, then I should work harder. My team won a state championship when I was a junior in high school. I always wanted to be like 'Hawk' was.

"I could talk forever about what a great person he is. He's my best friend. And if things hadn't happened to him that prevented him from playing college and pro basketball with the best, he'd have been doing the same sort of things as Michael Jordan."

"I had to run to the store."

Hawkins was asked to talk about his early days in Brooklyn. Talking about the greatest influence in his life, Hawkins said, "My mother, Dorothy Mae Hawkins. When I was young, if I did anything wrong, she would beat me with the ironing board, whatever she could get her hands on. Now I thank her for it because it kept me on the straight and narrow. She was the one that turned my life around. She laid down the law with me. She didn't want me to get into any trouble, or get hurt.

"Back in the '60s, the biggest problems were almost the same as what's going on today: gangs, drugs, violence. But back then, it wasn't about guns, it was mostly about baseball bats and knives. You could get beat up pretty good back then. I remember I had to run to the store and run back home and hope nobody saw me because they would rob you and take your money before you got to the store.

"The area we played at on Saturdays and Sundays, guys would get up in the morning, go to the schoolyard and play ball. If you got there too late, you'd be out there all day because we played if you won, you played again and if you lose, you sit down. You may not get on the court again. It made guys go out there and play hard. There were a lot of great players out there, schoolyard players, but still good players. Playing ball was a good way to stay out of trouble."

> *"It's like Connie Hawkins once said, 'The older you get the better you used to be.' But that's just with sports."*
> — John McEnroe
> Tennis champion

Bob Friend Jr.
Really lives up to his name

"My father is the best man I ever met."

A day in the sun with Bob Friend Jr. was a refreshing experience. Here was a young man making a name for himself in the professional golf ranks who began life with a name familiar to baseball and political fans in Pittsburgh.

His dad pitched for the Pirates from 1951-1965 before finishing with the Mets and Yankees in 1966 with a 197-230 career record, and was Allegheny County controller for two terms. At age 67 in the summer of 1998, Bob Friend was still working for Babb, Inc., a leading insurance broker on the North Side. He had cut back on his schedule, but he was still servicing his established accounts.

"Bob's been great for us right along," said his boss, Ron Livingston Sr. "And he's able to enjoy his son's success in golf at this stage of his career, which is great for both of them. It's been fun for all of us to watch this develop."

A mainstay on the 1960 World Series-winning Pirates, one of the most popular teams in the city's rich sports history, Friend remained a familiar face. He regularly participated in Andy Russell's Celebrity Golf Classic for Children at The Club at Nevillewood, for instance, was a mainstay at Pirates Alumni activity, and often appeared at local fund-raising golf events.

His son, Bob Jr., made an appearance in late May, 1998, at a fund-raising golf outing at St. Clair Country Club. Bob hit a tee shot with the field at the 195-yard No. 7 hole, and posed for pictures with all the participating foursomes. He was 5-8, 180 pounds, and wasn't nearly as big as the former football players and hockey players who participated in the outing, but he had a solid and athletic look about him.

This was for the benefit of The Second Mile ("Providing Children With Hope & Help"), founded and directed by Jerry Sandusky, the defensive coordinator on Joe Paterno's Penn State football coaching staff.

So there were lots of former Penn State football players in the field, such as Matt Bahr and his brother, Chris, both former pros more at home with kicking tees, Shane Conlan, Mark Battaglia, Bill Koontz and Todd Blackledge.

There were Hall of Famers, too, in Mario Lemieux of the Penguins, and Bill Fralic, the former Pitt All-American who was a Pro Bowler for the Atlanta Falcons and Detroit Lions.

Young Friend drew most of the attention, however. His was an interesting success story, in so many ways, and everyone wanted to know about his recent successes on the pro tour.

At age 34, he had cracked the pro tour for a second time, and had earned over $170,000 in 13 PGA events to that point in the schedule. By year's end, he placed 57th on the money list and kept exempt status for the first time with total official tour earnings of $492,189. That's almost as much as his father made in 16 major league baseball seasons. All things considered, appearances, exhibitions and non-tour events, Bob Jr. made about $575,000 for the year.

Just a week or so prior to his exhibition appearance at St. Clair Country Club, young Friend finished sixth in the GTE Byron Nelson Classic at Irving, Tex., winning $65,000. He fired a seven-under par 63 for the first-round lead to gain the national spotlight.

In March of 1998, he finished in the top ten at the Honda Classic near Fort Lauderdale and won $55,000.

Friend was fun to talk to, as good at gabbing as his father had always been. Writers on the PGA Tour liked his story, his bloodlines. His dad had been a top-notch pitcher and a popular fellow for a long period. Twice he was the winning pitcher in the All-Star Game and he won 22 games in 1958. Plus, the son had refused to go away, working hard after a four-year absence from the PGA Tour, to qualify again. He was a good story in his own right.

He was born in Pittsburgh on December 5, 1963 — shortly after the city and the world were shocked by the assassination of President John F. Kennedy.

He won the 1985 Pennsylvania State Amateur Golf Championship while he was a student at Louisiana State University.

He turned pro in 1987 after his LSU days and competed on the South African Tour, the Canadian Tour and the Nike Tour. He cracked the PGA Tour in 1992. He stayed long enough to ask the former Leslie Minard to marry him on a network golf telecast, before slipping down and returning to the Nike Tour in 1994. Two years later, he was working as a teaching pro at Inverness Country Club outside of Toledo. He hadn't played on the PGA tour since 1993. He had four years to think about whether he had the game and guts to compete at the top level. He dared to dream that he could do it, and he got all the encouragement he needed from his wife and parents.

He persevered and got his playing card back in 1998. This was a young man who needed a final round 63 — imagine that, a 63! — to earn his PGA Tour card at qualifying school the previous fall.

"The 63 at qualifying school was very gratifying," Friend said. "It's not like a 63 the last day of a tournament to have a fifth place or higher finish. Anything lower than fifth and I was gone. I wouldn't have qualified."

When you hear Bob Friend Jr. speak, he sounds so much like his father. He sounds more like a Hoosier than a kid from Fox Chapel.

At the time of our meeting at St. Clair Country Club, he had been married for five-and-a-half years to Leslie, and they had two children, Charlie, 2½ and Elizabeth, just six months old. So there was pressure to bring home the bacon.

Bob Friend Jr. was joined in May, 1998 by Mario Lemieux of Pittsburgh Penguins at golf outing at St. Clair Country Club to raise funds for The Second Mile, a program aimed at helping children that was founded by Penn State football coach Jerry Sandusky.

In his insightful book, *A Good Walk Spoiled*, writer John Feinstein captured what someone like Friend faced in finding his way on the PGA Tour:

"There's no sport as melodramatic as golf, where a single missed putt can cost a player thousands of dollars in lost prize money, or can even cost him his spot on the tour," offered Feinstein.

"Pressure is a relentless thing in golf. It follows you up the ladder, nipping at your heels no matter how high up you go. Players start out saying that if they can get their card they'll be happy. But just making money isn't enough for a competitor. He wants to win."

Feinstein detailed the astounding tension at the top, the do-or-die pressure on non-star players fighting for a spot on the tour at the annual qualifying school.

"It's harder than playing on the tour," offered Friend.

He also spoke about all the attractive automobiles, like Cadillac DeVilles, Mercedes-Benz and Lincoln Continentals, that are provided for the pros at the various tour stops. "I don't know how anybody can bitch about it," said Friend. "We are always treated in a first-class manner. You ought to be having some fun. And you're getting paid for it, too!"

Later that same year, in mid-September, he would be the second-round leader at the Canadian Open with a 8-under par 136 after two days at the Glen Abbey Golf Club in Oakville, Ontario. He finished second, losing in a playoff to Billy Andrade, and took home $237,000, his best payday to date. He had missed making the cut in nine of his previous 12 tournaments, which points up how tough it is to get to the Saturday-Sunday segment of the weekly competition.

"My goal all year was to keep my card and not go back to that torture test," said Friend, referring to the qualifying school. "For me, the best way I could do it was to be very process-oriented — work on how to be relaxed, have fun, pick out a target and not worry about the results."

"When you make a commitment, you should keep it."

Bob Friend Jr. was too young to remember his dad in the majors — "I think I was three or four years old when he stopped playing," said Bob Jr. — but he had tagged along to a few Old Timers' Games, and always enjoyed the fuss the Friends drew from fans at such events.

Young Friend had a confident air as he mixed with all the participants at St. Clair Country Club. Only the day before, at Muirfield Village in Dublin, Ohio, Friend had played nine holes in a foursome headed by host Jack Nicklaus in preparation for The Memorial that

From the Friend family album

Bob Friend Jr. and wife, Leslie, have their laps full with Elizabeth and Charlie.

Jim O'Brien

Two of the most popular Pirates of all time, Billy Mazeroski, left, and Bob Friend, teammates in the '50s and '60s, get together at 1998 golf outing at Bob Murphy's Quicksilver Golf Club in Midway.

same weekend. When Friend signed on to make a guest appearance at St. Clair, he didn't know he'd be playing in The Memorial.

"From a competitive standpoint, I'd be better off getting in another day at the course at Muirfield," offered Friend, "but, hey, I'm with great guys on a great course on a great day in my hometown. My father told me a long time ago that when you make a commitment you keep it."

His father, for example, had a commitment to play in Andy Russell's tournament, as well as signing autographs at a card show in Philadelphia the following day. He was going to keep those commitments even though he would have preferred following his son at Muirfield.

As it turned out, young Friend missed the cut by two shots with a 2-over 147 after two days at Muirfield.

What impressed me most about young Friend was when he told me, "My father is the best man I've ever met. He's the most loyal, honest guy I've been around. He's been nothing but a positive influence in my whole life. I've been blessed my whole life. My mother is super; I've got two great parents.

"My wife, Leslie, is beautiful and we've got two great kids. She's been so supportive of my determination to make it on the tour. My father went through it. He knew what it took to be a professional. As long as you do your best, he taught me, you have nothing to look back on with regret."

I was struck by some of the comments Friend made about his family as we talked at St. Clair that day, and how grateful he was to have their support.

"My mother Pat has put her stamp on me as well," he said. "I'm more outgoing, like she is. There was always a positive atmosphere. No one was allowed to be negative in my house, or you'd get a kick in the rear."

He also knows that today's athletes, whether it's golf or baseball, make a lot more money than they did when his dad was coming out of Purdue to pitch for the Pirates. "My dad was born 25 to 30 years too early in that regard, but he was rich in other ways, and we never wanted for anything," said Bob Jr. "My dad has never complained about anything in that regard. He never felt cheated in any respect, just the other way around.

"I'm not sure I'd be doing what I'm doing if I hadn't grown up the way I did. When I was playing at Oakmont as a kid, my dad often reminded me of my good fortune to have that kind of opportunity. I was a member of the club at the age of 13.

"My father told me when I was 15, 'You grew up at the Oakmont Country Club. Not too many have that advantage. I don't want to ever read about you complaining about a course or conditions.' My dad is from the same school as one of his contemporaries, Arnold Palmer. I take my lead from them, and the way they treated and respected other people.

"Golf is a very difficult game."
— Fred Couples

"I've learned a lot from my dad. He also said it takes as much effort to lead a lousy life as a good life, and the choice is yours. He also said, 'We sleep in the bed that we make.' He's got lots of those sayings. My dad was a great ballplayer and he's a greater person. He instilled in me a very strong work ethic and taught me that even though it was a game, I'd have to work very hard to get to where I wanted to go and work harder to stay there."

The Friends knew their son was dedicated. He would caddy in the morning, hit balls and take lessons in the afternoon, and then come back in the evening on his own for more practice.

"I love doing what I'm doing," he said. "I realize how tenuous it is, and how it can be gone before you blink. But I'm going to enjoy it while I can. Since I got a later start than most pros on the tour, I'm glad the Senior Tour is so successful these days. I have that to look forward to as well. If I work hard, and keep my head on straight, which I believe I can do, I can have a nice life as a touring pro golfer for many years to come.

"I get to play the finest golf courses in North America, and I get paid to do it. There are hundreds of thousands who would like to be out there.

"My dad talks all the time about the importance of character. He'll say, 'Don't sell yourself short. Don't look up to those name brands.' Every time I talk to him I get some kind of message. We talk a lot. He asks a lot of questions.

"I loved playing football when I was young. My idol was Dick Butkus, the fearsome linebacker for the Chicago Bears. But I realized soon enough that I wasn't big enough to play football. And golf appealed to me more than baseball."

At age 13, Friend had an opportunity to caddy when the 1978 U.S. Open came to his home club in Oakmont. His player was paired with Tom Watson on one round and that provided the spark.

"Being right down inside the ropes with Watson," recalled Friend, "I decided then and there that's what I wanted to do. There wasn't any doubt about it. I didn't want to be a lawyer, accountant, doctor or anything else."

One of his big thrills in 1998 was playing in tournaments where he was in the same field as Watson, and, at the GTE Byron Nelson Classic, where he was on the same scoreboard as Watson.

He made the cut eight times in his first 13 tournaments in 1999, but he wasn't satisfied, feeling he could do better. "It took him awhile to get back on track," said his father, "but that's not unusual." His best finish on the PGA Tour, as of June, was in the top 30 at the Bob Hope Classic. Even so, he wasn't complaining. "I'm not going to panic," said Bob Jr. "I'm more patient now and I just have to grind away at it." He did qualify that same month to play in the 1999 U.S. Open.

He had picked up a $30,000 first prize in the Panama Open, a non-tour event, back in January, which put him in the Gene Sarazen World Cup in suburban Atlanta, where he finished in the top ten and came away with $40,000.

Because of his success in 1998, Friend was getting better pairings. He teed off with David Duval in Phoenix and with Nick Faldo in Atlanta. At the Bay Hill Classic, he played with tournament host Arnold Palmer and Seve Balasteros, two of the game's legendary figures.

Strolling the same fairways with the likes of Nicklaus, Watson, Palmer, Balasteros and some of today's top players has to be a thrill for young Friend. As a child, shadowing his dad, he got to mix with Roberto Clemente, Willie Stargell, Ted Williams and Mickey Mantle, so he's aware that he's led a charmed life in many ways.

His dad was present to see him get a hole-in-one on the 8th hole of the second round of the Tournament Players Championship in Jacksonville, one of the most prestigious tournaments. It was a 4-iron, 225-yard shot and was only the second hole-in-one ever carded on that hole, according to his father.

Friend had to pinch himself over his good fortune. "My wife, Leslie, is the greatest," he volunteered. "My father told me a long time ago how important it was to have a great wife when you were a professional athlete. He pointed out how some football players got picked up for fooling around with drugs. He said booze and drugs brought down a lot of athletes. But, he said, a bad woman will bring you down just as fast.

"Leslie and I went to O'Hara Junior High School together, then her family moved to Kentucky. But we stayed in touch. In October of 1991, we announced our engagement on national TV, and we were married January 9, 1993. She's my best friend. She's the best girl I've ever met in my life. She's also the prettiest girl I've ever met who didn't act like it.

"She's made a lot of sacrifices so I could chase my dream. She never uttered a peep when things were tough. She never complained. When I told her I thought I wanted to play again, that I wanted to go for it on the pro tour, she never wavered from encouraging me to do just that. When I left my job at Inverness, she backed my decision. She's the best, a true diamond, the Hope Diamond. I missed getting my PGA Tour Card in 1996 by two strokes, and played the Nike Tour instead. And she was still behind me. She's always been a hundred percent behind me. I'm blessed. I've been blessed with ability, but more important with great parents and a great wife. They deserve an awful lot of credit for my success."

"I have never met a father and mother who did not want their children to grow up to be uncommon men and women.
May it always be so."
— Herbert Hoover,
former President of U.S.A.

Jerry West
"Mr. Clutch" from Cabin Creek

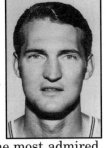

"Yes, I wanted the ball."

Jerry West wears well. He has long been one of the most admired and popular figures in professional sports, yet no one has a stronger will to win. He wants to beat you, but he smiles while doing it.

Somehow he manages to balance what would seem to be contradictory roles and demands, the way he once could do just about everything imaginable to handle a basketball and pressure in the toughest competition in the business.

In short, Jerry West has long been a class act, one of the best the National Basketball Association as well as the National Collegiate Athletic Association has ever been able to boast about. He is an enduring example of excellence. He has been a leader with the Lakers, on and off the court, for 40 years.

It is tough to capsulize his career, but he was a three-time All-America at West Virginia University, averaging 24.8 points for his career. He was named the outstanding player in the 1959 NCAA Finals when the Mountaineers reached the final game under Fred Schaus before bowing to Pete Newell's University of California club, 71-70. West was just a junior that year.

West was a schoolboy phenom at East Bank High School, leading his team as a senior to the state championship. He was the first West Virginia player to score more than 900 points in a season.

Over 60 colleges came calling at his humble home in Cabin Creek, West Virginia, but he decided to stay home and play at West Virginia. He starred for a freshman team that went 17-0.

In his next three varsity seasons, he averaged, in turn, 17.8 points, 26.6 points and 29.3 points per game.

After helping the U.S. to a gold medal in Olympic basketball competition, West was the top draft pick of the Minneapolis Lakers who moved to Los Angeles the same year. It was the beginning of a beautiful relationship. He had the right name to be a star on the West Coast. Some sports fans back East thought they named the area after him, the way they had named his home state and college after him.

He played much of his pro career with Elgin Baylor as well as Wilt Chamberlain. Jack Kent Cooke owned the Lakers back then and was responsible for making the financial commitment to get them.

West starred for 14 seasons with the Lakers, and was the third player in NBA history to score 25,000 points. He was named to the Naismith Basketball Hall of Fame in 1979. No one discusses all-time NBA teams without West in the lineup.

He led the NBA in scoring in 1970 and he led the NBA in assists in 1972. He could do it all. At the outset of the 1998-99 season, West was in fourth place on the career scoring average list at 27 points a game, behind Michael Jordan, Chamberlain and Baylor.

He averaged over 20 points every season except his rookie year, and averaged over 30 points on four occasions (1962, 1965, 1966, 1970). He was also a defensive force, being named to the NBA All-Defensive First Team four times. They didn't name such a team for much of his pro career.

During his illustrious NBA career, West was named All-NBA first team ten times. He was selected to 14 All-Star Games, capturing the MVP award in 1972. He was the MVP in the 1969 NBA Finals. His most remarkable ability was the way he lifted his game for the play-offs, averaging 29.1 points in 153 playoff games — second-best in league history — and 40.6 points in 11 playoff games in 1965.

West retired in 1974 because of injuries, and coached the Lakers for three seasons (1976-1979), compiling a 145-101 record, winning the Pacific Division title in 1977. He served as the Lakers general manager from 1982-1994 and then as executive vice president beginning in 1995.

There were disquieting rumors making the rounds at the start of the 1998-99 season regarding whether West would remain with the Lakers, but he signed a multi-year contract for $3.5 million per year to remain. Owner Jerry Buss didn't want to lose him. His No. 44 is among those retired jerseys hanging in the rafters at Lakers' home games.

In addition to bringing such marquee players as Magic Johnson, Kareem Abdul-Jabbar, James Worthy and recent stars like Shaquille O'Neal and Kobe Bryant to LA, West helped build five NBA championship teams in the '80s and establish a franchise that's always in the running.

He felt the Lakers of the '80s were better than the Michael Jordan-led Chicago Bulls of the '90s. "We had almost every component you'd need — great coaching, great offense, great defense and not a good bench, but a great bench," said West. "I'm prejudiced, but I think the '87 Lakers team would have won, for sure."

"He always had the touch."
— Cotton Fitzsimmons

Jerry West was the best at what he did as a player for the Los Angeles Lakers, as an All-America at West Virginia University in his native state, and in his continuing role as the general manager and front office leader of the Lakers.

There remains a trace of West Virginia twang in that easily recognizable voice, a humbleness of remembering where he came from — a stark coal-mining community called Cabin Creek — and yet he has picked up a lot of polish.

Jerry West excelled as front-office official for Lakers and as floor leader in his playing days. West was interviewed by Pittsburgh-born and bred Jack Twyman of ABC-TV Sports, himself a Hall of Fame basketball performer. West, below, is challenged by Oscar Robertson and Willis Reed in NBA All-Star Game.

He is affable and approachable. He signs an autograph for anyone who asks, and is gracious with those who seek his time and attention. If he bristles, he does his best to hide it. For the record, he was not responsible for bringing Dennis Rodman to the Lakers for a brief and disastrous stay during the 1998-99 season.

He is at ease with everyone, and can handle himself in Hollywood, or at courtside at the Great Western Forum where he could find movie stars such as Jack Nicholson and Dyan Cannon on a regular basis. He has come a long way from Cabin Creek.

He is no longer "The Zeke From Cabin Creek," which was the title of an article I remember reading in *Sport* magazine when West was a three-time All-America at WVU, and I was a wide-eyed teenager in Pittsburgh, about two hours away — the roads weren't as good back then — from WVU's Morgantown campus.

He was one of my boyhood heroes, and he has never done anything to tarnish that image.

The last time I was in The Forum, about ten years back, and visiting with West, he did something, a simple gesture, but to me it points up what West is really all about.

We were in his classy office, chatting about his career, and as we were leaving I asked where the men's room was located. Most people would point you in the general direction and say something like, "Go down the hallway and turn left, and it's somewhere there on the left side, maybe two doors down."

Not West. He approached it the same way he worked as a basketball player and the same way he worked as the Lakers' front-office leader. He left no room for error. He personally escorted me to the door of the men's room.

It was no big deal with West, even though, as it turned out, it was well out of his way.

I have several personal memories of West which I would like to share. These are special memories.

The first time I ever saw West in person was when I was a student at the University of Pittsburgh back in the fall of 1962. I was with the Pitt football team which was in New York to play Army at Yankee Stadium.

We were staying at the old Manhattan Hotel, which was about a block or so away from the old Madison Square Garden — the "real" Madison Square Garden to anybody 45 years or older in New York — and one day I saw the Lakers team coming through the lobby after a shoot-out session at the Garden, then located on 8th Avenue at 49th Street.

They were so tall and so sleek, and so handsome looking in their purple and gold warmups. I saw West and I saw Elgin Baylor. A check of the NBA record book shows that West was averaging just over 27 points per game that season, and Baylor was averaging 34 points a game. What a one-two offensive combination.

I just stared at them.

A year or so later, I came back to Manhattan, taking a 12 hour bus ride from Pittsburgh with my older brother, Dan. We caught the Rangers against Bobby Hull and the Chicago Black Hawks one night at the Garden, from way up in the rafters, and the next day we were back to see the Lakers against the Knicks.

West was so-so in the first half, and the Lakers trailed at halftime. But he went crazy in the second half, hitting one long outside jumper after another, splitting nothing but net on most of his shots, to lead the Lakers to a comeback victory. He had been absolutely brilliant.

I came back to New York for a longer stay in April of 1970 to work as a sports writer at *The New York Post*. One of my first assignments — I have to pinch myself even today at my good fortune — was to join three other writers from *The Post* to cover the Knicks in the playoffs.

Those writers included beat writer Leonard Lewin, and our two lead columnists, Milton Gross and Larry Merchant. I started off doing sidebar features about the Knicks during the semifinal series with the Baltimore Bullets, and then the NBA Finals against the Lakers.

I was at The Forum the night West hit a 65-foot shot to send the game into overtime, which the Knicks ended up winning. To this day, West will tell you that it was a "shot" — a legitimate shot he had taken in practice from time to time just to see how you had to push it to hit the shot — and not a heave.

West was always a good interview, even in defeat.

Years later, when I was working as the assistant athletic director for sports information at my alma mater, the University of Pittsburgh, I recall how cooperative West was when he would attend Pitt games, scouting for prospects.

Whatever you asked West to do he would do it. He would sit for interviews for pre-game shows or half-time shows, or post-game shows, radio or TV, stations for the home team or the visiting team, and talk to the sportswriters who were at courtside. He gave serious attention and thoughtful answers to anyone with a microphone or notebook who interviewed him. He would sign autographs for anyone who asked. I admired the way he continued to comport himself in a first-class manner.

Who could ask for a better boyhood hero?

Check out the NBA logo. The player pictured on it, or outlined anyhow, the one that appears on so many official basketball banking boards in my neighborhood and your neighborhood, is Jerry West. He has long been an NBA model.

When I was last with West in his office, I noticed a painting behind him on the wall. He was portrayed along with the likes of Wilt Chamberlain, Bill Russell, Elgin Baylor, Oscar Robertson. Not bad company.

What struck me as we spoke was the confidence he possessed. He wanted to take the big shots, he said. He knew he was special, even if he didn't act that way when he was off the court. He kept to a rigid schedule. He had strong self-discipline. He had a routine, especially on the road, which was like a religion to him.

He made sure he was always ready to play. He felt he had to pick up his game a notch on the road, because conditions were more difficult, and he had to assume more of a responsibility to lead his team. "Yes, I wanted the ball," he said in his soft-spoken manner.

Cotton Fitzsimmons was coaching the Phoenix Suns and they were the opponent at The Forum that night. Fitzsimmons sought out West to say hello before the game. I got the impression West is one of Fitzsimmons' heroes as well.

The Suns beat the Lakers that night, and Fitzsimmons raved about West before and after the game, and again the next day in the hotel lobby where the Suns were staying.

"He has the hands of a safecracker," offered Fitzsimmons. "He always had the touch. In basketball, in golf, you name the sport. He has always been one of my favorite people. What a competitor!"

A class competitor, for sure. That's why they called him "Mr. Clutch." No one has represented the NBA in a better manner for so many years.

"I haven't forgotten where I come from."

The 1998-99 NBA season was a difficult one for the Lakers and Jerry West in the team's final campaign in the Great Western Forum. Everyone's status was in question. Del Harris gave way as coach at mid-season to ex-Laker Kurt Rambis. Dennis Rodman came and went in a two-month nightmare. I remember thinking that I couldn't believe that West would want a Dennis Rodman on his ballclub, no matter his rebounding and defensive ability. West had to retch at the sight of Rodman.

There were stories about whether West would remain with the team, but they were temporarily assuaged when he signed a new three-year contract. When I last spoke to West on the telephone, on May 19, 1999, I had the impression he might not come back. He sounded fed up with the whole scene. In June the Lakers signed Phil Jackson to a four year $20 million contract to coach the team.

The Lakers had two of the most talented players in the NBA in Shaquille O'Neal and Kobe Bryant, but they didn't jell. They were underachievers and disappointments during the lockout-shortened season, and flops once again in the playoffs. West was always at his best in the playoffs, and this had to be hard to swallow.

He couldn't deal with the large egos. "The coaches are worse than the players anymore," said West. "I don't know where they're coming from. The coaches' egos are bigger than the players' egos. They all want power, control. It's tough to build a team thing."

Jerome Alan West would turn 61 the following week (May 28, 1938 birthdate). He had two families, so to speak, in California. He had three children from his first marriage, David, 39; Michael, 36; Mark, 35; and two from his second marriage to Karen, namely Ryan, 20, and Jonnie, 11.

"I'm trying to make it here for a few more years," he said, "but I don't know what's going to happen. I'm going to see how things go."

He said he had spoken only the day before to another former West Virginia All-America, Rod Thorn, who was now the senior vice president for basketball operations, and the right-hand man for Commissioner David Stern. Thorn was responsible for leveling fines and O'Neal had ripped into a referee during a playoff game the night before. West also enjoyed talking to Thorn, the pride of Princeton, West Virginia. They spoke the same language.

I told West I had seen him on a TV interview a few nights earlier, and that my wife, Kathie, called attention to the fact that he still had a West Virginia twang in his voice after all these years.

"I'll never lose that," said West. "I don't want to. I'm proud of being from West Virginia. I don't forget where I come from. When I retire, I hope to spend more time there. I really enjoy going back there. I sneak in and sneak out of there every year for about two weeks. I go to Greenbriar to relax and see old friends. I drive around Charleston and check out how things are going there. I like to take my younger kids there with me.

"I'm not Mr. West there. I'm just Jerry. I have no pretenses about who I am. It's no big deal. I haven't really changed. At least I don't think I have. In my present position, I have to talk more now at public functions and things like that, but I'm still fairly quiet. I'm a bit of a loner, which I like. I just don't understand some of these people anymore. They've forgotten what a great game this can be, and how fortunate we've all been just to be here."

"We want people who are adaptable, self-disciplined and who have an entrepreneurial outlook. Above all, we look for motivation. When I look at the most successful people I've worked with, I always see the same attributes: common sense, passion and dedication. Give me managers with those qualities, and I'll give you an unbeatable team."
— William R. Johnson,
Heinz President and COO
at Carnegie Mellon University

Curtis Aiken
From Buffalo with love

"I knew there was much more to life than basketball."

C urtis Aiken had come a long way from his hometown of Buffalo, New York. The former Pitt basketball standout made the most of the opportunity the University of Pittsburgh presented him when he was recruited by Roy Chipman and his staff to play for the Panthers in 1983.

He was a real success story, carving out quite a career in a community relations and promotional role with Cameron Coca-Cola out of Washington County for twelve years, and then in a construction venture with former Pitt basketball teammate Jason Matthews.

They were the principals in a minority entrepreneurial effort called SGS Group, a construction supply and real estate development company headquartered in Centre City Towers in downtown Pittsburgh.

"I was offered an opportunity to stay on with the new owners at Coca-Cola after the Cameron family sold the company," said Aiken, "but I saw this as an exciting opportunity, the sort of thing I wanted to get into long term."

I had an opportunity to speak to Aiken and Matthews when they attended a holiday season party in December, 1998, hosted by Joe Massaro Jr. at the Churchill Country Club.

Aiken was always a source of pride to Pitt fans and boosters like Massaro who have witnessed his growth.

Aiken was a sharp kid from Buffalo, an inner-city kid whose mother died when he was a child, whose father drifted away, and whose maternal grandmother raised him and his four brothers and sisters as best she could.

Aiken struggled at the start of his Pitt career, athletically and academically, but the people associated with the Pitt program helped him. He not only was a starting guard for four years (1984-87) but he came away with a bachelor's degree as well for his hard work.

Many kids ignore or walk away from such help, but Aiken was a street-smart kid who came to recognize the good guys from the bad guys and welcomed their assistance and support.

In 1984, the year after Aiken arrived, Chipman and his staff succeeded in bringing in one of the best recruiting classes in Pitt basketball history headed by Charles Smith and Demetreus Gore, then Jerome Lane a year later, and Pitt basketball gained and merited national attention.

Aiken helped attract these other top talents to Pitt.

Aiken wasn't always happy with what transpired at Pitt during his stay. There were highlights and lowlights. He complained to Chipman about his role and playing time.

Yet Aiken rallied round Chipman when their coach discovered in 1996 that he was seriously ill with cancer, and was one of the few players present at his funeral service when Chipman died in 1997.

Chipman had come to the Civic Arena and Field House on occasion to catch a game, to see old friends, to enjoy the atmosphere he once found so compelling, but one that would eventually become a torture chamber for him. He resigned when the pressure took the fun out of the job. He was replaced by Paul Evans in 1987.

"I saw Coach Chipman when he was sick," said Aiken. "It was during the last game of the 1995-96 season at the Arena. When I saw Coach Chipman, we hugged and talked to each other. I wished him well. I told him it was good to see him. Our differences were basketball differences. After I was gone from Pitt, I realized the experience had been a good one for me. I knew there was much more to life than basketball. I never had any problems with Chipman as a person. Our differences were just on the court.

"If it wasn't for basketball, and if Chipman hadn't brought me to Pittsburgh, in the first place, I wouldn't have had the opportunities I've had here. I didn't have any more opportunities than the other players, but I took full advantage of mine. I worked for Joe Massaro's construction company my freshman year at Pitt, and then I worked for Don Cameron from my second year on."

It was the beginning of a beautiful relationship with the Cameron family which owned the regional Coca-Cola Bottling Company in Washington County. "Curtis has been great for us, too," said Don Cameron, the firm's general manager.

Curtis represented the company in the youth and ethnic market. "The three best things that ever happened to me at Pitt," confided Curtis, "were meeting my wife, Adrianne, meeting Don Cameron and meeting Dr. Stan Marks. They have all helped me grow up and succeed."

Dr. Marks is a highly-respected oncologist at Allegheny General Hospital who has been a long-time booster of Pitt basketball, and befriended Aiken during his Pitt stay. When the Camerons sold out in 1999, however, Aiken opted to go into some private business projects rather than remain on in a similar capacity with the new owners.

As of June 1, 1999, Curtis Aiken was living in a new "dream home" in Franklin Park with his wife, Adrianne, and their daughter, Alexis, who was five years old. They were expecting a second child in July. The Aikens had been married for ten years. Adrianne Penn, who is from Pemberton, N.J., graduated from Pitt in 1988 with a degree in information science, and worked at Pitt while completing studies for an MBA at the Katz School of Business. The Aikens had resided the previous eight years in Squirrel Hill.

As point guard at Pitt

With wife Adrianne and their daughter, Alexis

Talking to Franco Harris, Steelers Hall of Famer, at Pitt Field House.

With former teammate Joey David at Pitt Field House in February, 1998.

Jason Matthews and Aiken attend Christmas party hosted by Panthers booster, construction magnate Joe Massaro Jr.

Curtis Aiken

"She's the best thing that ever happened to Curtis," offered former teammate Joey David.

Curtis Aiken's smiling face appeared on billboards and on the sides of buses in Greater Pittsburgh to promote the Boys & Girls Club, and he stayed in the public eye as an analyst for a few Fox Sports TV presentations of Pitt games.

From about the age of five, Curtis spent a great deal of time at the Boys Club in Buffalo. In 1997 he was named a regional spokesperson for what is now called the Boys & Girls Club. "We had girls at our club in Buffalo," recalled Curtis. "They needed to be off the streets, too, so the director let them in."

"It helped me stay out of trouble when I was young," attested Aiken of his early Boys Club experience, "and it continues to provide that kind of support for kids today. I'm hoping I can help some kids find their way, and benefit from some of the experiences I had. We all need help."

The NCAA keeps introducing legislation to push athletes away from alumni and boosters. They want to squelch the excesses, and that's understandable. At the same time, many alumni and boosters have been positive forces in the lives of young athletes, and helped them develop in positive ways.

The trick is in finding the middle ground.

When Roy Chipman succumbed to the ravages of cancer in 1997, Aiken and Joey David sat next to each other in a pew at the memorial service for Chipman at Beverly Heights Presbyterian Church in Mt. Lebanon. They were the only former players present that afternoon.

"I never had a role."
— Curtis Aiken

I remember one night at the Arena in 1998, when Aiken made a fast break before the game was over. "I want to get home before my daughter goes to bed," he explained. That had a nice ring to it.

"Shortly after I got my degree, I knew I was glad I went to Pitt," said Aiken. "After I got out in the real world, I realized how important a degree was.

"Originally, I was all set to go to Kansas. I had been recruited there by Jo Jo White, who played there before starring for the Boston Celtics. But his boss, Ted Owens, the head coach, was fired. I was interested in Syracuse, which was close to my home, but Pearl Washington went there. And he was a real rival of mine, from playing against him in high school and in the New York Empire Games over the summer. I didn't want to be on the same team. John Calipari and then Chipman came after me. I wanted to play in The Big East; I wanted to be able to play against guys like Pearl Washington.

"I didn't play enough early in my career, certainly not as much as I had been promised I would play when I was recruited. That was the source of some of my early unhappiness. I never had a role; one game I'd be the No. 1 guard, the next game I'd be the No. 2 guard. Had to adapt to something new at every practice.

"It was three years before I finally got comfortable, and that's when Chipman announced he was retiring. I never understood why he did that. I never asked him why; it's one thing I've wanted to ask him."

When I told Curtis I had visited Joey David at his home the night before, he said, "I just loved Joey as a person. He was real caring, a good guy. No hidden agendas. He tried to help me when I first came to Pitt. He knew I was under a lot of pressure; there were great expectations for me. I always knew I could go to Joey if I needed help."

Curtis was also grateful for his friendship with Charles Smith. He played in a golf tournament hosted by Charles Smith the previous season and had a chance to play with one of his boyhood heroes, Randy Smith, who played for the NBA's Buffalo Braves and set a record for playing in the most consecutive games.

I asked him why he thought Charles Smith stayed at school after he'd been drafted in the first round by the NBA to get his degree. "I'm sure he did it because his mother wanted him to get a degree," said Curtis. "Charles was always grateful to his mother for her love and guidance. His mother didn't have to tell him do it; he'd been brought up that way."

Curtis also credited the late Dr. Edward Bozik, Pitt's director of athletics at the time, for encouraging him and Smith to stay in school and get their degrees. "Dr. Bozik was OK with me," said Curtis. "He kept after me and Charles. It was important to him that we get our degrees. He did a lot to help me aside from basketball."

Curtis could only wonder what Smith's situation was like, growing up with a mother motivating him to do well. "My mother died when I was four," he said. "She died of a heart attack. My dad is still living in the Queens section of New York. We stay in touch. He was not doing well and he couldn't provide for us. There are no hard feelings. There were five of us children. I was the third. I have two younger brothers, and an older brother and sister."

His maternal grandmother, Mariam Aiken, who raised him, died at age 84 on July 23, 1996. "She died on my birthday," continued Curtis. I remembered that his paternal grandmother, with whom he was also close, had died during his student days at Pitt.

"When it is dark enough, men see the stars."
— Ralph Waldo Emerson

Boys of summer
Sandlot stars were early heroes

"These guys were good ballplayers."
— Dick Kraft

They get together on the first Wednesday of each month. They meet for breakfast at Falce's Restaurant on Main Street in Munhall. They bill themselves on their mailing list as "The Boys from Hazelwood" even though most of them, age-wise, are in their late 60s and early 70s.

Some of them were the best ballplayers in our hometown, an inner-city community located along the Monongahela River, between Greenfield and Homestead. They were giants in my youth.

Dick Kraft kept calling me for a year, urging me to join him and his buddies for breakfast. Kraft lives in Bethel Park, but his heart is still in Hazelwood. Elmer Tackes comes all the way from Canonsburg to be there.

"I heard they talked about the old days in Hazelwood," said Kraft. "And I enjoy that. These guys were good ballplayers."

There's no suitable place in Hazelwood where they'd want to meet, which tells you a lot about what's happened to Hazelwood since their heyday, and how much Munhall has spruced up its main business stretch.

There were about 20 of them filling up the back room at Falce's Restaurant on May 4, 1999 and it was good to see them. They looked a lot older than when I had last seen them, but they were saying the same thing about me, no doubt.

I was grayer than most of them, though they were ten to 15 years older than me. Bobby Geier, a third cousin of mine who was one of the toughest guys in town, had a hearing aid. It felt good to get a big hug from him. He still had a great sense of humor, and was fun company.

Bo Johnson, who's lived in West Mifflin the last three years, said, "I enjoy seeing the guys. I wouldn't want to do it every week, but it's a nice break. I don't know too many people where I live now."

John "Kutsie" Karafa, a home run hitter as a sandlot star, lives in West Homestead now. His older brother Joe was also a long-ball hitter who played minor league ball. His brother Jimmy was a respected football lineman. They were all big guys. They were the next best thing to Ralph Kiner for a kid who loved sports.

When I broke in as the sports editor of *The Hazelwood Envoy*, a bi-weekly in our community, I was 14 and they were in their mid to late 20s. Some of them still have clippings from stories I wrote about them. They were the first ballplayers I wrote about. Back then, few in our neighborhood had TVs, and there weren't many ballgames on TV in those days anyhow.

So sandlot sports were a big deal. We couldn't afford to go to too many games played by the Pirates and Steelers, or Pitt, so we were eager to attend games on our local fields.

Back then, youngsters used to bring their gloves and shag flies during batting practice when the big boys, or adults, were playing. Knowing them and talking to them was exciting. It made you feel like a big deal. I can still see them, at their best, playing ball at Burgwin Field, just two blocks up the hill from my home on Sunnyside Street.

Billy "Ace" Adams was my first legitimate sports hero. He had a name out of those sports book series by John Tunis and Clair Bee that young boys used to read. He excelled in all sports. He went to college late, but he ended up as the starting quarterback at Carnegie Tech.

Just a few years back, Ace Adams taught me how to hit a better backhand stroke in tennis. There isn't any game he doesn't know how to play. Then, too, he's a good guy and everyone likes him.

John Mamajek played football at Central Catholic and The Citadel, and went to training camp as a place-kicker with the Steelers, but failed to stick. He later coached the football team at Serra Catholic High School in White Oak.

Frannie Bonasorte was a good football and baseball player. He went off to Lenoir-Rhyne College in Hickory, N.C., where he was a receiver for a few seasons. He left in his junior year to sign as an infielder with the St. Louis Browns.

He played some minor league baseball. "But I couldn't hit the curve, and that's all they threw you down South," he says now. "So I came home."

It seemed like we had a lot of talented athletes in Hazelwood, but most of them didn't stay in school or with the major league teams that signed them.

"A lot of athletes in Hazelwood didn't go anywhere," Bonasorte said. "Maybe we lacked ambition or staying power."

Bonasorte ended up working at the Monongahela Connecting Rail Road, and moonlighted as a bartender for 26 years at the South Hills Country Club. His six sisters were all waitresses and hostesses there. They kept the club going.

Peggy was an assistant manager and hostess, Rose was a secretary, and the waitress staff included Annabelle, Irene, Katherine and Henrietta. Two of Frannie's sisters-in-law, Gerri and Mary Ann, worked there at times. The Bonasorte family was the backbone of the South Hills Country Club.

Sam Rende, whom I see at every golf outing or sports event in the area, attended the reunion. Rende and his brothers formed the band that played at my wedding reception in the summer of 1967.

Some brought old team photos and pictures from the past, hoping someone might be able to identify some of the ballplayers. Each picture sparked a memory or story.

Once more, they were the boys of summer.

Pittsburgh Proud
Sports Book Series

Here is information relating to the series of books about Pittsburgh sports subjects by Jim O'Brien that are available to you by mail order:

KEEP THE FAITH
The Steelers of Two Different Eras
Interviews with Steelers of the '70s and the '90s to show what they shared in common, and what was different about the challenges they faced. These are the Steelers of Chuck Noll and Bill Cowher, or Art Rooney and Dan Rooney. Going to Ireland in the summer of '97 brought this all home. 448 pages, 200 plus photos. Hardcover: $26.95, plus sales tax and shipping charges. (ISBN # 1-886348-02-2)

DARE TO DREAM
The Steelers of Two Special Seasons
Profiles of the Steelers and their families from the 1994 and 1995 seasons, when the Steelers had two of the best seasons in the team's history, and even got to the Super Bowl under Bill Cowher. Family photographs and stories, especially those offered by their mothers, offer special insights into the Steelers of the modern era. 480 pages, 270 photos. Limited number of books remain. Hardcover: $26.95 (ISBN # 1-886348-00-6). Perfect bound softcover: $16.95, plus charges. (ISBN # 1-886348-03-0).

WE HAD 'EM ALL THE WAY
Bob Prince and His Pittsburgh Pirates
Personal reflections on Bob Prince, who was "The Voice of the Pirates" for 28 seasons (1948-1975), and one of the most talked-about and controversial characters ever to grace the Pittsburgh sports scene. This book also catches you up on what's become of the Pirates of the same era who remained in the Pittsburgh area after they retired from playing the game. 432 pages, over 200 photos. Hardcover: $26.95, plus sales tax and shipping charges. (ISBN # 1-886348-03-0)

DOING IT RIGHT — The Steelers of Three Rivers and Four Super Bowls Share Their Secrets for Success
Tales of the glory days of the Pittsburgh Steelers. Interviews with the stars of the '70s, as well as players from the early days of the franchise, and those who followed the championship seasons. If you've wondered whatever became of some of your favorite Steelers, here are

the answers. 536 pages, with over 250 photos. Hardcover: $24.95, plus sales tax and shipping. (ISBN # 1-916114-09-0)

REMEMBER ROBERTO
Clemente Recalled By Teammates, Family, Friends and Fans

Pirates Hall of Famer recalled by those who knew him best. Interviews with his wife and sons, and his celebrated teammates during his 18 seasons as an All-Star rightfielder at Forbes Field and Three Rivers Stadium. This was the first adult book on Clemente to come out in over 20 years. 448 pages, over 220 photos, many borrowed from players' personal photo albums. Hardcover: $ 24.95, plus sales tax and shipping charges. (ISBN # 0-916114-14-7)

MAZ AND THE '60 BUCS
When Pittsburgh And Its Pirates Went All The Way

Interviews with all the living members of the World Series champion Pirates of the 1960 season, and five of the key members of the New York Yankees. Chapters on every one of the Pirates of that season. An intriguing reminiscence of what Pittsburgh, particularly Oakland, was like in the early '60s. Reproduced autographs of all the players. 512 pages, over 225 photos, many from players' personal family photo albums. Hardcover: $24.95, plus charges. (ISBN # 0-916114-12-0)

PENGUIN PROFILES
Pittsburgh's Boys of Winter

Stories reflecting on the history of hockey in Pittsburgh. Interviews with many of the recent stars, from Mario Lemieux to Jaromir Jagr, to early stars such as Jean Pronovost and Syl Apps. 448 pages, over 200 photos. Hardcover: $24.95, plus charges. (ISBN # 0-916114-12-0)

HOMETOWN HEROES
Profiles in Sports and Spirit

A variety of inspirational stories about men and women from the tri-state area who excelled in some way to become heroes in their hometowns. 432 pages, over 200 photos. Hardcover: $26.95. (ISBN # 1-886348-04-9)

For more information or to place an order please call Jim O'Brien at his home office (412-221-3580). Or write to: James P. O'Brien — Publishing, P.O. Box 12580, Pittsburgh PA 15241. Pennsylvania residents should add 6% sales tax to price of book, and Allegheny County residents should remit *additional* 1% sales tax on price of book, plus $3.50 for postage and handling. Please provide specific signing instructions. Books are mailed the same day the order arrives. You can also contact Mr. O'Brien by e-mail: jpobrien@stargate.net.

Ethel Collins

Doris Kearns Goodwin, a Pulitzer-prize winning author and sports enthusiast from the Boston area, offered her thoughts about writing history in an interview with Jim O'Brien at 1998 Town Hall South Meeting.

"I believe the real challenge in writing history is to resist the tendency so prevalent today — to label, stereotype, expose, denigrate — and instead to bring empathy and understanding to our subject so the past can really come alive in all its beauty, sorrow and glory."
— Doris Kearns Goodwin

Kurt Angle
Jean Pronovost
Harvey Haddix
Roger Kingdom
Connie Hawkins #42
Jimmy Majors
John Havlicek
Sam Huff
Kosie Hlede #25
Les Bradley